HOW SOCIAL MOVEMENTS MATTER

Social Movements, Protest, and Contention

Series Editor: Bert Klandermans, Free University, Amsterdam

Associate Editors: Sidney Tarrow, Cornell University
Verta A. Taylor, The Ohio State University
Ron Aminzade, University of Minnesota

HOW SOCIAL MOVEMENTS MATTER

Marco Giugni, Doug McAdam, and Charles Tilly, editors

Foreword by Sidney Tarrow

Social Movements, Protest, and Contention
Volume 10

University of Minnesota Press
Minneapolis • London

Published by the University of Minnesota Press
111 Third Avenue South, Suite 290
Minneapolis, MN 55401-2520
http://www.upress.umn.edu

Library of Congress Cataloging-in-Publication Data

How social movements matter / Marco Giugni, Doug McAdam, and Charles Tilly, editors ; foreword by Sidney Tarrow.
    p.   cm. — (Social movements, protest, and contention ; v. 10)
Includes bibliographical references and index.
ISBN 0-8166-2914-5 (hardcover). — ISBN 0-8166-2915-3 (paperback)
1. Social movements.   2. Protest movements.   I. Giugni, Marco. II. McAdam, Doug.   III. Tilly, Charles.   IV. Series.
HM131.H625   1999
303.48′4—dc21   99-17529

11 10 09 08 07 06 05 04 03 02 01   10 9 8 7 6 5 4 3 2

Contents

Part II: Comparative Perspectives

Foreword

Sidney Tarrow

Marco Giugni, Doug McAdam, and Charles Tilly have put together a subversive reader. Everyone who has worked on social movements knows how important it is to try to understand their outcomes. Almost everyone admits the extreme difficulty of doing so. Some of us make halfhearted attempts anyway; others retreat to the tried-and-true terrain of studying movement origins; a few take refuge in phenomenology.

Giugni, McAdam, and Tilly are braver souls. After obligatory curtsies in the direction of caution, they and their collaborators strike out boldly to detect, discriminate among, and define the outcomes of social movements. As if this were not subversive enough, they and their contributors refuse to limit themselves to the most direct, short-term effects of movements— national, institution-based policy outcomes. Though experts like Paul Burstein and Dieter Rucht contribute to the book lucid treatments of direct policy effects, even their contributions are unconventional: Burstein questions the distinctiveness of social movements altogether, and Rucht elaborates a complex model of movements' environmental impact—both through policy and beyond it.

But the most subversive message of the book is found in its authors' willingness to go beyond the range of national policy and political impacts of social movements and into such nonnational areas as the international peace movement (Meyer); such nongovernmental areas as movement effects on scientific institutions (Moore); such cultural areas as the changing discourse of protest policing (della Porta); and such noninstitutional areas as the effects of movements on the life course (McAdam).

The authors, it is true, touch base with familiar old friends in social movement debates: debates about whether disruption or moderation pays greater dividends; whether internal or external resources make more of a difference for movement success; whether purposive or unintended outcomes of movements are more important; and whether the changes initiated by movements are durable or ephemeral. But their true contributions are more subversive:

- questioning, on the one hand, whether movements are distinct from interest groups (Burstein) or whether they are best seen not as groups at all, but rather as structured contentious performances (Tilly)

- turning away from the search for invariant causal models toward a search for historically contingent combinations of factors (Giugni, Tilly), a shift that directs attention to the mechanisms responsible for translating structural determinants into action and outcomes (Moore, Meyer, Rucht)

- displacing the tried-and-true configurative case study with paired comparisons that tease important outcomes and their causes out of differences in similarly situated cases (Kriesi and Wisler, della Porta, Gelb and Hart, Meyer, Koopmans and Statham)

- taking social movement research out of its intellectual ghetto by linking movements to processes of democratization (Kriesi and Wisler, della Porta) and even embedding hypotheses about movement outcomes in a theory of democracy (Burstein)

The authors of these pieces do not have all the answers—nor do they pose all the questions. In focusing mainly on progressive movements (bar Koopmans and Statham), they have little to say about either the religious or the retrogressive movements that have surfaced in the 1990s. In focusing on the United States and Western Europe, they do not help us understand the rare but dramatic successes of movements in authoritarian systems. And, but for one chapter (Amenta and Young), they do not come to grips with how movements solve collective action problems.

The conclusion, by Tilly, dips a broad net of proposals for further research into the stream of research on movement outcomes, urging scholars simultaneously to work "upstream" by identifying instances of movement effects, then seeing whether the hypothesized causal chain is actually operating; to work "downstream" by identifying instances of the causal chain in operation, then seeing whether and how its hypothesized effects occurred; and to work "midstream" by examining whether the internal links of the causal chain operate as the theory requires. Movement fish beware: Tilly intends to hook you from several directions at once!

These are cavils. In *How Social Movements Matter*, Giugni, McAdam, and Tilly provide a road map of the current state of research on movement outcomes, open that map to unexplored provinces, and put high-test gasoline in the engine. If in the process, they threaten to broaden the field of social movements into a general approach to contentious politics, the field will be the richer for their efforts.

Preface

During the past decade or so, systematic literature on social movements has been growing at an impressively fast rate. Yet, in what has now become a real "growth industry," there are still some areas that have remained somewhat understudied. The outcomes and consequences of movements certainly constitute one of these relatively neglected areas of inquiry; investigators have generally given much more attention to origins and trajectories of social movements than to their impact on routine politics, on their social environments, on other social movements, or on the participants themselves. The principal aim of this book is to draw attention to this crucial aspect of movements by presenting a number of essays completely devoted to it.

To understand why and how public displays of protest by relatively powerless social actors may be effective, and what consequences they produce, is of utmost importance, for the history and present of human societies are studded with such public displays. In fact, it has become a common state of affairs to maintain that social movements are crucial actors in the processes of social and political change. However, much less common—though not totally lacking, as Marco Giugni will show in the introduction—are scholarly analyses of the processes and mechanisms by which they bring about their effects. Analysts of social movements need to examine both intended and unintended consequences of movement activity. This volume makes several steps in this direction.

The essays in this volume concentrate on concrete social movements rather than general theories and broad processes of social change. A companion volume assembled by the same editors (*From Contention to Democracy,* published in 1998) gives more attention to general issues. Although the introduction and conclusion to the present book sketch the practical and theoretical problems involved in tracing consequences of social movements, by and large the essays report concrete investigations.

The carrying out of this project has been facilitated by a number of persons and institutions to which we are sincerely grateful. Of course, a big thank-you goes to all the contributing authors, who have given the book its final shape. Bert Klandermans, editor of the Social Movements, Protest, and Contention Series at the University of Minnesota Press, helped us get our book into this still young but already important series. We also express our appreciation for the help of all those associated with the project at the Press. The initial steps of our manuscript there were handled by Micah Kleit, acquisitions editor. Although we sometimes disagreed on specific matters, the final product benefited greatly from his effort and advice. After he left the Press in January 1998, editorial assistant Jennifer Moore continued to work on the project. They both executed their responsibilities with skill and efficiency. Laura Westlund, managing editor, brought the manuscript through the production process and helped make it the book you have in your hands. Tammy Zambo skillfully copyedited the full manuscript. Marco Giugni's involvement in this project was made possible by a research fellowship granted by the Swiss National Science Foundation, which is warmly acknowledged. Doug McAdam and Charles Tilly are grateful to the Andrew W. Mellon Foundation and the Center for Advanced Study in the Behavioral Sciences at Stanford, whose combined sponsorship on a project on contentious politics brought them into close collaboration.

Introduction

How Social Movements Matter:
Past Research, Present Problems, Future Developments

Marco Giugni

On August 28, 1963, between 200,000 and 500,000 people (depending on who made the estimate of the crowd size) marched on Washington, D.C., to lobby for the civil rights bill that President John F. Kennedy had sent to Congress on June 19. It was the largest political demonstration in the United States to date. Although this massive protest was dubbed the "March on Washington for Jobs and Freedom"—thus combining civil rights and economic demands—the recent civil rights mobilizations in Birmingham gave demands for freedom much more emphasis than those for jobs. The march had been organized at a meeting held on July 2 at New York's Roosevelt Hotel, attended by the leaders of the six major civil rights organizations. After two months of intense preparation, everything was ready for the march. Tens of thousands of participants, most of whom came on buses charted by local branches of the movement, gathered at the Washington Monument and assisted at a morning entertainment featuring several singers sympathetic to the movement, among them Bob Dylan and Joan Baez. Then, before noon, demonstrators began to march, heading to the Lincoln Memorial, the stage of the main rally and a highly symbolic site for the organizers on the centennial of the Emancipation Proclamation. Despite the authorities' fear of a riot—among other precautions, 15,000 paratroopers were put on alert—the event went on peacefully through speeches and songs heard by the huge audience. Finally, Martin Luther King Jr., the leading figure of the movement at that time, stepped up to the podium to deliver his closing address. His speech began with the following words: "I am happy to join with you today in what will go down in history as the greatest demonstration for freedom in the history of our nation" (qtd. in Kasher 1996: 120). By the end, what should have been an

*ordinary closing speech had become one of the most salient moments in the his-
tory of the American civil rights movement when, in response to the crowd, King
began his final passage with "I have a dream."*[1]

The March on Washington is only one among a series of events that the civil
rights movement staged during the peak of its activities, between 1954 and
1968. Through bus boycotts, sit-ins, freedom rides, marches, demonstrations, and many other protests and acts of civil disobedience, thousands of
people attempted to reinstate a sense of justice in the country. Were all these
efforts successful in the end? The Civil Rights Act was passed by Congress
on July 2, 1964, exactly one year after the March on Washington was organized by the six major civil rights leaders. But was this act, which banned
racial discrimination in public facilities and in voting rights, a direct effect of
the march (or of the whole range of activities of the civil rights movement,
for that matter)? If so, which actions by the movement were most effective
in producing this outcome? Was the act a result of mass demonstrations like
the one in Washington, gathering peaceful and diverse masses, or of more
disruptive tactics such as sit-ins and civil disobedience? And what about
other actors at the time? Perhaps the movement was not responsible for the
elimination of (formal) racial discrimination; perhaps this was a result of the
open-mindedness, or of a strategic stance, of mainstream politicians within
Congress; or perhaps it was a combination of external pressures and internal
reformist orientation. Furthermore, the Civil Rights Act was only one step
forward, though a fundamental one, toward the broader goal of achieving
(informal) freedom and equality. Did the movement reach some gains in
this respect? Finally, what other, unintended effects did the mobilization of
the civil rights movement produce? For example, one could argue that, if the
passage of the Civil Rights Act of 1964 was a result of the movement's mobilization, then mobilization could have helped other minorities in their struggles for more freedom and equality. But the movement's mobilization also
provoked strong repression by the authorities and violence by segregationists
in the South, which in turn enhanced a positive image of the movement in
the public opinion (Garrow 1978).

These kinds of questions concerning the impact of the civil rights
movement have a series of conceptual, theoretical, and empirical implications for the study of social movements in general. Although the impact of
the civil rights movement has received greater attention than that of other
movements, much more work is needed on this topic.[2] As several scholars
have pointed out at different times (Berkowitz 1974; Gurr 1980; McAdam,
McCarthy, and Zald 1988; Tarrow 1993), the study of the consequences of

social movements is one of the most neglected topics in the literature. We need more systematic studies that can shed light on various aspects of movement impact, in particular on the potential consequences, on the conditions and circumstances that favor certain consequences as well as the processes leading movements to have an impact, and on the actual effects obtained by past as well as contemporary movements. The lack of scholarly work on this topic is all the more unfortunate if we consider that one of the raisons d'être of social movements is to bring about changes in some aspects of society, a fundamental goal of movements which is often acknowledged but only rarely addressed explicitly. Furthermore, a better understanding of the impact of social movements on different aspects of society concerns both specialists and nonspecialists, for movements are a basic component of contemporary societies and, in particular, a major vector for the articulation of underrepresented political interests.

In an attempt to contribute to filling this important gap, this volume brings the consequences of social movements to center stage. It does so by addressing two general questions: on the theoretical level, which aspects of society can social movements modify and how? And on the empirical level, what impact have contemporary social movements had in different countries? In the end, we hope, the essays presented here will inform us about how movements relate to more general processes of social change and will put us in a better position to see how social movements matter, the fundamental question that guides all the essays. Thus, the volume is divided into two parts, each one devoted to one of the aforementioned questions. In the remainder of this introduction, I will first provide a brief survey of what has been done so far on the nature, scope, and conditions of the consequences of social movements. Second, I will address the two main questions by discussing some problems and shortcomings that have made research difficult and that need to be met if we are to go any further in the study of this crucial aspect of movements. Finally, I will conclude with some general remarks about two important issues with which this volume deals only in part: the durability and the direction of the changes brought about by social movements.

What Has Been Done So Far

While the study of consequences is still underdeveloped within the social movement literature, the field is not as empty as many observers have claimed.[3] However, work on the outcomes of social movements has rarely been pulled together and systematically surveyed and theorized. Although it is difficult to classify all these works, most of them deal with one or both of two related but distinct issues: the disruption/moderation debate and the internal/external debate. Both issues are addressed by William Gamson's *Strategy of Social Protest* (1990), a book that, almost a quarter of a century after its first edition came out, can still be regarded as the most ambitious and most systematic effort yet to analyze the impact of social movements. The book is basically a critique of the pluralist perspective on American society.[4] Gamson, through an analysis of the careers of fifty-three American challenging groups active between 1800 and 1945, questions the permeability and openness of the American political system. Specifically, the author aims to answer several related questions: "How can we account for the different experiences of a representative collection of American challenging groups? What is the characteristic response to groups of different types and what determines this response? What strategies work under what circumstances? What organizational characteristics influence the success of the challenge?" (5). In fact, the latter question turns out to be the focus of the analysis, and the question of the circumstances under which specific strategies work is secondary.

Gamson's study prompted a number of critiques, most of them raising methodological issues (e.g., Goldstone 1980; Gurr 1980; Snyder and Kelly 1979; Webb et al. 1983; Zelditch 1978). However, apart from its intrinsic achievements and specific shortcomings, one of the book's contributions is that it set in motion a fruitful discussion among movement scholars. In particular, it provoked a sometimes harsh debate on the two issues that have dominated the literature on movement outcomes. Let me provide a brief overview of each of these issues.

Disruption versus Moderation

One of the prevailing themes in the research on the consequences of social movements is whether disruptive tactics are more likely to have an impact or, on the contrary, whether moderate actions are more effective. In its simplest form, this debate has been framed by the following question: Are disruptive (or even violent) movements more successful than moderate ones? Perhaps not surprisingly, the answers to this question are far from consensual.

Gamson's study directly provoked a series of reactions, particularly to his finding that the use of violence and, more generally, disruptive tactics are associated with success. Several reactions have come from reanalyses of Gamson's original data, which he included in the book's appendix. For example, Steedly and Foley (1979) repeated Gamson's analysis using more sophisticated statistical tools, such as factor analysis, multidimensional scaling, multiple regression, and discriminant functional analysis. Their results support Gamson's findings about the positive impact of challengers' willingness to use sanctions. Similarly, Mirowsky and Ross (1981), in an attempt to determine the locus of control over movement success (an issue I shall discuss in more detail), have also elaborated on Gamson's findings concerning the effect of violence, and have basically agreed with him.[5]

Other authors have found that, in contrast to the pluralists' claim that moderation in politics is more effective than disruption, the use of force or disruptive tactics by social movements improves their chances of reaching their goals (McAdam 1983; Tarrow 1998; Tilly, Tilly, and Tilly 1975). Much of the existing research on the effects of violence or other constraints used by challengers has dealt with strike activity. It is here, perhaps, that results are the most contradictory. Taft and Ross, for instance, on the basis of a study of violent labor conflicts in the United States through 1968, concluded that "the effect of labor violence was almost always harmful to the union" and that "there is little evidence that violence succeeded in gaining advantages for strikers" (1969: 361–62). Similar results have been obtained by Snyder and Kelly (1976) in their study of strikes in Italy between 1878 and 1903. They found that violent strikes were less successful than peaceful ones. These results were contradicted by, among others, Shorter and Tilly (1971) in their study of strikes in France. They suggested that there is a positive relationship between the use of violence and strike outcomes.[6]

The impact of disruption has been analyzed extensively through the example of the urban riots of the 1960s in the United States.[7] A great number of these studies are related to Piven and Cloward's influential thesis about the impact of disruptive protest on the welfare state (1993).[8] In fact, Piven and Cloward (1979, 1993) are among the scholars most firmly convinced of the effectiveness of disruptive tactics by social movements.[9] According to them, disruption is the most powerful resource that movements have at their disposal to reach their goals, since they lack the institutional resources possessed by other actors, such as political parties and interest groups. At the opposite end of the violence/moderation continuum, authors such as Schumaker (1975) have argued that militancy is generally not conducive to success. In a more nuanced attempt to specify the conditions and circumstances under which violence or, more generally, the use of constraints leads to success, the same author has stressed two conditions for the effective use of constraints: when there are direct confrontations between protesters and their targets; and when there are confrontations between protesters and a hostile public, a situation which is likely when challengers have zero-sum demands (Schumaker 1978). Yet he also found that the use of constraints and zero-sum demands triggers public hostility and, consequently, is less effective than moderation.

Thus, if considered in absolute terms, the disruption/moderation debate might be more apparent than real. The effectiveness of disruptive tactics and violence is likely to vary according to the circumstance under which they are adopted by social movements. In particular, the movements' political context plays a decisive role, as available political opportunities, various institutional features of the political system, and the propensity of rulers to repress protest activities either facilitate or constrain the movements' impact. It is likely that when regimes are vulnerable or receptive to challenges, disruption works, whereas when they are not, disruption invites repression. Furthermore, the cultural climate may make disruption either more or less effective. Finally, it has been shown that the capacity of movements to achieve their goals depends on their ability to create innovative and disruptive tactics (McAdam 1983), the use of which varies according to the moment in a protest wave (Koopmans 1993).

Internal versus External Explanations

Related to the disruption/moderation issue is the question of whether movement-controlled variables or some aspects of a movement's environment better account for its success. In other words, here we have a debate between internal and external explanations of social movement outcomes. This second debate is evident in Gamson's study (1990). By testing a series of organizational variables on the success or failure of a sample of challenging groups, he pointed to the crucial role of organizational, group-controlled variables. His conclusions were supported in reanalyses conducted by several authors (e.g., Frey, Dietz, and Kalof 1992; Mirowsky and Ross 1981; Steedly and Foley 1979). A similar stress on internal factors has been shown in the case of various movements and protests, such as rent strikes (Brill 1971), the women's movement (Clemens 1993), and the pro-choice movement (Staggenborg 1988) in the United States.

The internal/external debate has been framed within the broader pluralist/elitist controversy. While pluralists view protest groups as effective and the political system as responsive to external demands to the extent that these groups do not stray too far from proper channels (Dahl 1961), elitists see protest groups as seldom effective and the political system as unresponsive (Parenti 1970; Bellush and David 1971). Generally, the pluralist assumption of the permeability of the political system—especially the American political system—has been challenged theoretically as well as empirically (Bachrach and Baratz 1970; Edelman 1964, 1977; Gamson 1990; Lowi 1969, 1971; McAdam 1982; Schattschneider 1960; Shorter and Tilly 1974).

Within the narrower field of social movements and collective action, this controversy has been translated into a perspective that stresses the importance of bargaining for the success of challenging groups (Burstein, Einwohner, and Hollander 1995; Lipsky 1968, 1970; Wilson 1961). The most elaborated theoretical statement in this regard was probably made by Lipsky (1968), who concluded that the acquisition of stable political resources that do not rely upon third parties is an essential condition for challengers to be successful in the long run. Thus, on this level, the controversy is between authors who think of social movements as being capable of obtaining certain results independent of external support and those who see the latter as a necessary condition. These two viewpoints grossly reflect the different perspectives of resource mobilization theory and the political process model. The former conceives of social movements as being weak and lacking the indigenous resources to be successful on their own, while the latter suggests, on the contrary, that social movements have enough resources and disruptive potential to induce social change, when confronted with a favorable political opportunity structure.

In contrast to the works underscoring the importance of organizational variables necessary for social movements to have an impact, a series of studies stress the importance of the political environment and the context of social support (e.g., Barkan 1984; Goldstone 1980; Kitschelt 1986; Jenkins and Perrow 1977; Lipsky 1968, 1970; McAdam 1982; Schumaker 1975). Kitschelt, for example, in his comparison of the antinuclear movement in four Western democracies, has made a strong case for the structural determinants of social movement success, arguing that success strongly depends on political opportunity structures. Similarly, Tarrow (1998) makes a case for the crucial role of political opportunities in shaping the long-term effects of movements on the individual, institutional, and cultural levels. Albeit in a more provocative manner, the importance of movements' larger environment for their outcomes is also acknowledged by Piven and Cloward (1979). They show, through research on the unemployed workers' movement, the industrial workers' movement, the civil rights movement, and the welfare rights movement, that the impact of protest movements, as well as their emergence and the forms of their mobilization, is delimited by social structure, in particular by the features of institutional life that shape a movement's opportunities for action, model its forms, and limit its impact. According to these authors, social movements can succeed only insofar as they act disruptively and as political circumstances lead the rulers to make concessions.

In the end, however, even more than the disruption/moderation debate, the internal/external debate might be more apparent than real. Much as the effectiveness of disruptive tactics varies according to the situation in which they are adopted, the impact of movement-controlled variables may depend on the very context of protest. This, at least, is what works by Kowalewski and Schumaker (1981) and, more recently, Amenta, Carruthers, and Zylan (1992) suggest. Future research, as has been suggested, should therefore look for a synthesis that incorporates both strategy and structural constraints (Frey, Dietz, and Kalof 1992). Our volume builds on this search for a bridge between internal and external accounts of the consequences of social movements.

Defining and Determining the Consequences of Social Movements

Although this brief overview is a far cry from exhausting the extant literature on the consequences of social movements, it does point to some problems that have hindered research on this topic as well as to several shortcomings that call for further research. Three issues are worth mentioning in this context: the definition of movement outcomes (mostly in terms of success or failure); the focus on policy outcomes; and the problem of causality.

Looking at Success or Failure

A first limitation of existing studies on the consequences of social movements and collective action relates to the notion of success. Much previous work has attempted to determine to what extent and under what conditions protest succeeds or fails. From Gamson's *Strategy of Social Protest* to the plethora of studies concerned with the impact of the urban riots of the 1960s, the fundamental question guiding research was, when do movements succeed? The very subtitle of a book by two leading scholars testifies to this focus on the success or failure of movements: *Why They Succeed, How They Fail* (Piven and Cloward 1979). In other words, scholars have mostly been interested in relating observed changes to movement demands.

To be sure, to determine whether social movements succeed or fail with respect to their stated goals is certainly a legitimate way to approach the subject matter. Several contributions in this volume follow this avenue of research. Yet this perspective has its dangers. First, it assumes that social movements are homogeneous entities. Thus, success or failure tends to be attributed to an entire movement. This may hold true in some cases, but often there is little agreement within a movement as to what goals must be pursued. Social movements are complex sets of groups, organizations, and actions that may have different goals as well as different strategies for reaching their aims. Hence, a given change is not necessarily perceived as a success by all sectors of a movement. Second, to concentrate on success raises the problem of subjectivity. Briefly put, success is often not assessed in a single manner by everyone. While social movement success has an objective side, it is in large part subjectively assessed. Movement participants and external observers may have different perceptions of the success of a given action. Moreover, the same action may be perceived as successful by some participants but judged as a failure by others. Third, to talk about success is problematic because it overemphasizes the intention of movement participants in producing certain changes. While it is certainly true that social movements are rational efforts aiming at social change, their consequences are often unintended and are not always related to their demands.[10] Furthermore, such unintentional consequences may be positive as well as negative for a given movement.

The essays gathered in this volume, we hope, reflect the fundamental distinction between purposive and unintended consequences of social movements. If the former can be considered successes of at least a part of the movement, the latter are out of its reach and can even be counterproductive. Some unintended outcomes consist of only minor and short-term changes, but, more interestingly, sometimes movements modify certain fundamental features of social life. To identify the range of potential changes that movements can provoke unintentionally is a major task of research in this field. The contribution by Doug McAdam in this book, for instance, shows how social movements can produce changes in the demographic patterns of society independent of their stated, more contingent goals. Another illustration of unintended consequences of movement actions is provided by Donatella della Porta's essay. To some extent, the transformation of the public discourse about the right to protest and the related broadening of the space for political action in Germany and Italy were effects hardly anticipated by either movement participants or external observers. Social movements often produce consequences that are much broader than their contingent goals and that are often not foreseen. Charles Tilly's conclusion extends such discussion by examining the relations between explanations of social movement processes and analyses of their outcomes, arguing that students of the consequences of social movements need to take into account both aspects.

Focusing on Policy Outcomes

Related to the focus on success and failure is the prevailing attention scholars have paid to policy changes as a potential outcome of protest. The preceding review of the literature clearly shows to what extent research has focused on policy outcomes. This is partly a result of the dominant role played by resource mobilization and political process theories during the last few decades. These approaches conceive of social movements as *"collective challenges, based on common purposes and social solidarities, in sustained interaction with elites, opponents, and authorities"* (Tarrow 1998: 4; emphasis in original).[11] Thus, following this perspective, movements aim primarily at changing some aspects of their political environment. This prevailing definition of movements as political phenomena, together with the difficulty of empirically studying certain types of effects, has led scholars to focus on policy outcomes. In effect, policy changes are easier to measure than changes in social and cultural arenas. Therefore, much research has focused on the policy impact of movements by relating their action to changes in legislation or in some other indicator of policy change (e.g., Amenta, Carruthers, and Zylan 1992; Banaszak 1996; Burstein 1985, 1979; Burstein and Freudenburg 1978; Costain and Majstorovic 1994; Gelb and Palley 1987; Huberts 1989; Tarrow 1993). This is also the reason we have several empirical assessments of the impact of antinuclear movements, an impact which has been measured through a decrease in nuclear energy production or a delay in plant construction allegedly provoked by the movements, although results are quite discordant (e.g., Kitschelt 1986; Jasper 1990; Joppke 1993; Midttun and Rucht 1994; Nichols 1987).

Again, it should be clear that to study policy or, more broadly, political consequences of movements is a legitimate task in itself. Since we in this volume share the foregoing definition of social movements as sustained challenges to authorities, we shall devote much space to this type of consequence. The contribution by Paul Burstein, in particular, looks at policy outcomes of social movements. In addition, all the chapters in part 2 pay particular attention to this aspect of movements. However, if we restrict our analysis to political effects, we fall short of giving a complete picture of the consequences of social movements in at least three respects. First, for movements to be successful, it is not enough to produce policy change. What really matters, in this context, is that such change be translated into new collective benefits for beneficiary groups. Thus, several authors have looked at the extent to which movement mobilization brings about collective benefits (or fails to do so), such as improved economic conditions or more equal opportunities for minority groups (e.g., Amenta, Carruthers, and Zylan 1992; Burstein 1985; Piven and Cloward 1979, 1993). The contribution to this volume by Edwin Amenta and Michael Young addresses precisely this issue, making a case for the need for inquiry into this type of impact.

Second, even political outcomes of social movements are not limited to obtaining policy gains. Other types of effects are located in the realm of politics. Kitschelt (1986) has stressed three types of outcomes: procedural, substantial, and structural.[12] Policy outcomes correspond to what he called substantial impact. There seems to be a certain agreement about this threefold distinction (e.g., Gurr 1980; Kriesi 1995; Rochon and Mazmanian 1993). We also agree that protest can produce political changes in three ways: by altering the power relations between challengers and authorities; by forcing policy change; and by provoking broader and usually more durable systemic changes, both on the structural and cultural levels.[13] The chapters in part 1 are, to some extent, distributed according to this typology. Other researchers have offered more subtle typologies of possible outcomes. One of the best known is provided by Schumaker (1975), who defines social movement outcomes in terms of the responsiveness of the political system. Specifically, he distinguishes five criteria of responsiveness: access responsiveness, agenda responsiveness, policy responsiveness, output responsiveness, and impact responsiveness (see also Burstein, Einwohner, and Hollander 1995; Rüdig 1990). This typology avoids the problems deriving from a perspective that looks at movement success or failure. Nevertheless, the focus remains on the political effects of social movements.

Third, collective action is hardly limited to its political aspects. Social movements also have a cultural dimension, and scholars are increasingly acknowledging the need to study this aspect of movements more deeply (e.g., Morris and Mueller 1992; Johnston and Klandermans 1995). Accordingly, movements also have a range of potential effects in the social and cultural realm. As it has been recently pointed out, "Collective efforts for social change occur in the realms of culture, identity, and everyday life as well as in direct engagement with the state" (Taylor and Whittier 1995: 166). This is all the more true when we are dealing with new social movements, which, as students of these movements have pointed out on several occasions, have a strong cultural orientation (Brand 1982; Melucci 1982, 1989, 1996). Mobilization, for example, may result in a strengthening of internal solidarity and identities, the creation of countercultures, shifts in public attitudes toward a given issue, and so forth. While cultural effects of movements are more problematic to study empirically than their political effects insofar as it is more difficult to measure them, it is nevertheless possible to do empirical research on cultural outcomes of movements. Although the main focus of this volume is on the political impact of social movements, several contributions also pay attention to their cultural effects, attesting to the feasibility of studying them empirically. The most explicit attempts to address this aspect are perhaps made by Donatella della Porta, who shows how the transformation of public discourse on the right to protest in Italy and Germany can be seen as a result of a symbolic struggle between protesters and authorities; and by Doug McAdam, who deals with cultural changes brought about by social movements particularly on the individual, microsociological level.

The Problem of Causality

As several authors have acknowledged, scholars who have conducted empirical research on the consequences of social movements have frequently found themselves on shaky ground.[14] Several methodological difficulties have hindered research. I have already hinted at the difficulty of measuring the potential impact of movements. However, the problem of causality, that is, how to establish a causal link between a given movement and an observed change, is probably the main difficulty scholars have encountered. Simply put, how can we be sure that an observed change is the result of a social movement's mobilization? How can we eliminate the possibility that such change would not have taken place anyway, as a product of other social forces or as the result of a broader protest cycle involving several movements and actions? How can we determine whether the observed change is the product of movement activities or the result of a reformist move by political authorities?

This problem can be partly overcome by making certain methodological choices. First, we should aim to gather data not only about a given movement and its alleged outcomes but also about the actions of other actors. Five such actors seem to be particularly relevant in this respect: rulers, political parties, interest groups, the media, and countermovements when they exist. By gathering data widely, we can control for the role of other actors and, hence, make a better assessment of the movement's actual impact on the observed change. A second choice consists of looking not only at potential movement-related explanatory factors, such as levels of mobilization, strategies, or organizational strength, but also at other broad social-change variables, such as political opportunity structures or sociodemographic factors. Third, we need to set up a comparative research design. By comparing similar movements in different contexts or different movements in similar contexts, we can improve our chances of finding a relationship between movement activities and outcomes. Fourth, we have much to gain from a perspective that focuses on the processes through which outcomes are produced. In other words, by analyzing the link between a given movement and some of its alleged outcomes in a dynamic manner (i.e., over time), we will have a greater chance of singling out the mechanisms through which movements bring about change. A final methodological option that may improve our knowledge of the link between social movements and their consequences consists of looking not only at cases in which a given movement's action has led to a change, but also at situations in which no outcome can be observed. In terms of movement goals, this means studying failure as well as success.

However, these and related methodological options will at best only mitigate the problem of causality if research, as has frequently been the case in the past, seeks invariant models of collective action.[15] As Tilly has pointed out, "The employment of invariant models . . . assumes a political world in which whole structures and sequences repeat themselves time after time in essentially the same form. That would be a convenient world for theorists, but it does not exist" (1995: 1596). Tilly's caution applies to the specific sub-field of research on the consequences of social movements where researchers have often indulged in searching for general laws and universally valid propositions and models. They have looked for the determinants of successful movement action or for the factors that facilitate movement impact in general.

Looking for general causes and invariant models is doomed to failure, for there are no such invariant patterns in social life. In fact, this may be all the more true when we are dealing with the consequences of social movements, as we are confronted with variation in the characteristics of movements, in the contexts in which they operate, and in the outcomes of their activities. Instead of searching for general explanations, we would do a better job by taking into account the historically contingent combinations of factors that shape the possibilities for movements to contribute to social change. This would lead us to accomplish four tasks: to define the range of potential consequences of movements; to specify the types of impacts on which we want to focus; to search for the plausible relevant factors of such observed change; and to reconstruct the causal patterns or histories that have followed from the movement's action to the observed change. The latter point includes an explicit or implicit parallel with counterfactual accounts, that is, other possible explanations, on the basis of the relevant factors. The task becomes, then, to eliminate the other accounts on the basis of the available information. Figure 1 illustrates this approach. It is an approach that we have tried to adopt in this book, to the extent that following a common framework is possible in a collective volume. In spite of the difficulty arising from the assembling of authors who sometimes follow different perspectives, we think that the essays gathered here show how research on the consequences of social movements will provide better results by following this simple yet necessary methodological approach and by abandoning the search for invariant models.

The methodological agenda I have just sketched does not imply that we should abandon the search for broad correlations between certain variables and the particular movement effects on which we focus. However, this is only a first step, to be followed by a second step through which we

Figure 1. Methodological agenda for the study of the consequences of social movements

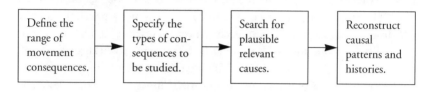

| Define the range of movement consequences. | Specify the types of consequences to be studied. | Search for plausible relevant causes. | Reconstruct causal patterns and histories. |

reconstruct meaningful causal explanations that link observed changes to movement action. In both steps, research has a lot to gain from a comparative perspective.

The Comparative Agenda

Much recent research on social movements is informed by a comparative perspective. An increasing number of works follow a comparative design to explain the emergence and development of movements (e.g., della Porta 1995; Kitschelt 1986; Kriesi et al. 1995; McAdam, McCarthy, and Zald 1996; Rucht 1994; Tilly, Tilly, and Tilly 1975). This is, in part, a result of the hegemonic place that the political process model has come to hold in the field. In particular, scholars have compared movements cross-nationally to explain variation in their mobilization, forms of action, and, more rarely, outcomes. By acknowledging the richness of comparative analyses for the understanding of collective action, this volume takes the comparative agenda seriously and tries to show its usefulness for the study of the consequences of social movements. It does so in two ways: first, in an implicit manner, by gathering essays that discuss different movements; second, by presenting a number of chapters that explicitly compare a given movement cross-nationally.

Taken as a whole, this book provides us with a way to compare the processes leading different movements in different places to bring about different types of effects. For example, we can see whether the factors that help movements obtain policy outcomes are the same ones responsible for changes in the public discourse or for bringing about institutional change. Similarly, we can determine whether the processes that lead to the impact of, say, the women's movement resemble those involved in the outcomes of the peace and ecology movements. As it appears, the impact of social movements depends more on historical and contingent combinations and sequences of events than on general, invariant sets of factors. This kind of implicit comparison, however, does little more than provide an impressionistic picture of the variation in movement outcomes. To fully take advantage of the richness of a comparative perspective, we need to set up a more systematic comparative agenda. To be sure, this is not possible to do here, but we have tried to come closer to a truly comparative design by asking each of our contributors in part 2 to write a chapter devoted to a particular movement and to compare its impact cross-nationally. Moreover, to render the comparison more plausible, we asked the contributors to pay special attention to a specific type of outcome, namely, political outcomes.

Thus, the four chapters in the second part of this volume attempt to assess the impact of several major contemporary movements in comparative perspective. Of course, the aim here is not to provide a definitive assessment of all types of effects of all the movements dealt with. The goal is, rather, to show how different conditions and historical circumstances are conducive to varying movement outcomes. Furthermore, since there are movements in all parts of the world, we had to make choices. Although the availability of scholars working or having worked on the four movements discussed posed some objective constraints on our choice, we deliberately commissioned essays so as to concentrate on movements that have strongly mobilized in the Western world during recent decades, particularly in Western Europe and the United States. By thus adopting an implicit "most similar systems design," we hope to highlight the characteristics of the political system that facilitate movements to produce, or prevent them from producing, certain outcomes. Three of the four chapters in this part are devoted to the new social movements, which, as some have pointed out (Kriesi et al. 1995), have been the protagonists of the last few decades. Joyce Gelb and Vivien Hart compare the role of women's movements in Great Britain, Sweden, and the United States and highlight their varying effects due to country-specific factors. David Meyer compares peace movements in Germany, the United States, and New Zealand, focusing on their impact on foreign policy matters and showing how the interplay of domestic and international factors conditions such impact. Dieter Rucht looks at the consequences of ecology movements in a cross-national as well as a cross-issue perspective, comparing France, Germany, and the United States. Finally, since new social movements are typically movements of the left, we thought it useful to include a chapter on a contemporary movement of the right. Ruud Koopmans and Paul Statham hence address the impact of mobilization by movements of the extreme right in relation to the politics of immigration in Germany and Italy. While the definition of the extreme right as a social movement is open to discussion, to study its impact comparatively appears nevertheless to be a crucial task in light of the recent rise of this kind of protest in several Western countries.

We are confident that this broad comparative perspective will yield many insightful findings about the political consequences of social movements and the role of national contexts in accounting for the varying impact of different movements. However, this partly purposive and partly constrained selection forced us to exclude several major contemporary movements from our discussion, such as labor, antinuclear energy, and student movements, as well as the civil rights movement. For the reason mentioned earlier, we also decided not to discuss movements outside the Western world. Notwithstanding these limitations, we think that the range of movements discussed in part 2 highlights the richness of a comparative perspective for the study of the consequences of social movements. To be sure, case studies also provide insightful results, especially in that they can advance our theoretical knowledge of how social movement outcomes occur. The value of case studies rests above all on their allowing us to examine in detail the processes through which social movements contribute to bringing about certain changes. This kind of approach is most useful when we are interested in showing the consequences of a particular movement more than in determining what characteristics of movements lead to certain outcomes and what factors ultimately account for such outcomes. However, a comparative approach is a more viable solution when we want to test an explanation about movement outcomes and to generalize the results obtained from case studies. A sound comparative design allows us to test specific hypotheses in different contexts and, hence, to assess the role of different variables. In the end, only comparisons can yield generalizable results about the consequences of social movements.

To adopt a comparative perspective means to shift from the study of the determinants and causes of social movement outcomes—a perspective that clashes against the problem of causality—to the conditions and circumstances of their occurrence, that is, the specific conditions under which a given type of impact is possible when protest arises. If social movements are conceived of as rational, political efforts aimed at social change, the political conditions of the occurrence of certain changes become central to the analysis of social movement outcomes. The crucial, yet not exclusive, role of political factors appears in many of the essays gathered in this volume. By comparing different movements in different countries, the volume as a whole attempts to single out the political conditions that facilitate movements in bringing about social change.

The Durability and Direction of Change

I will conclude this introductory chapter by spending some time on two issues that will only be grazed in this volume but that deserve much attention by analysts of social movements. If we are to understand how movements contribute to social change, we need to provide answers to questions of the durability and direction of change. How durable are the changes brought about by social movements? Are these effects mostly positive or mostly negative for both the society and the movements themselves? These two questions have often been framed in terms of the institutional impact of movements and in terms of the contributions of movements to democracy.

As far as the first question is concerned, several authors have underscored the indirect and long-term effects of social movements and protest, as opposed to their direct and short-term effects (e.g., Tarrow 1998). Generally speaking, we may draw a parallel between policy outcomes and short-term effects, on the one hand, and between institutional outcomes and long-term effects, on the other hand. After all, institutions change more slowly than policies. Therefore, if we want to inquire into the consequences of movements in the long run, we need to study how they can alter political institutions as well as those durable aspects of social organization that we may call social institutions.

In their aim of changing the status quo, social movements face a fundamental dilemma. If they ask for short-term policy changes, they have a greater chance that such changes will occur, but they will not alter, in a fundamental way, existing structures and practices. If, instead, movements demand long-term institutional changes, they will encounter more difficulties in realizing such changes, but when they do so, they have a more durable impact. Hanspeter Kriesi and Dominique Wisler, in their contribution to this volume, maintain precisely that social movements rarely alter political institutions and only under very restrictive conditions located on the economic, cultural, and political levels. The extreme version of this dilemma is that, while reformist movements may obtain numerous gains of minor scope, revolutionary movements are only rarely successful, but when they do succeed, the changes they bring about are fundamental and often longlasting reversals of the existing social and political structures. Seen from the point of view of the movements, this is a strategic dilemma. From a scholarly perspective, however, research on movement outcomes must first distinguish between the conditions that give rise to reformist social movements and those that provoke revolutionary situations, and then must analyze the ways by which policy change and revolutionary outcomes occur.

In addition to affecting state or political institutions—no matter how broadly defined—social movements may also produce institutional change on the social and cultural level. This means that research, following a more sociological perspective, should look at social and cultural institutions as well. Movements not only challenge state structures but also aim at redefining the sets of social relations that presuppose such structures and the symbolic elements that justify them. More importantly, movements can have an institutional impact both on the political level and on the social and cultural level. In this volume, the chapter by Kriesi and Wisler looks at the impact on political institutions, while Kelly Moore's contribution focuses on the broader effects on institutions on the societal level. Investigating the mechanisms that allow movements to bring about such long-term changes is a fundamental task of research if we want to understand better how collective action relates to social change. This impact, I should add, can occur regardless of whether change is a result of a purposive challenge or an unintended consequence of action. Similarly, Doug McAdam's study of the biographical impact of activism sensitizes us toward long-term transforming patterns brought about by participation in protest activities. This should make us aware of the potential impact of social movements on social and cultural institutions.

As for the question of the direction of the changes produced by social movements, various authors have maintained that movements are a source of democracy, that is, a vector for the democratization of society. While this is usually a rather implicit assumption, several authors have stated this relationship explicitly and show it empirically (e.g., della Porta 1995; Koopmans 1995; Tarrow 1989). Donatella della Porta, for example, accomplishes precisely this task in her essay. By analyzing in detail the interaction between protesters and the state around public discourse about the right to demonstrate, she points to a democratization of the Italian and German societies insofar as movements have contributed to enlarging the space for political action. However, nothing assures us that movements *always* make society more democratic, and this is true also for the so-called left-libertarian movements that have dominated the unconventional political arena during the last few decades. It would be wrong to proceed from a normative point of view that assumes that the contributions of social movements are "positive" in all circumstances. Such a point of view would mean mistaking reality for our desires and taking for granted something that must be demonstrated empirically.

Even assuming that social movements always go in the direction of a democratization of society, their impact in this regard depends very much on how we define democracy, for example, whether we adopt a legalistic or a participatory definition of democracy (Held 1987), following the American or the French tradition, respectively.[16] If, on the one hand, we conceive of democracy as a set of formal norms and rules that grant the aggregation of individual interests, then the democratizing role of social movements will consist of an enlargement of formal rights and freedoms. The introduction and expansion of channels of access due to movements' actions can thus be considered an impact on democracy. For example, the public hearing procedure in the United States expanded following, and very likely was caused by, continuing pressure from the social movement sector, in particular from peace and antinuclear movements. If, on the other hand, we follow the tradition started by Jacques Rousseau and, accordingly, think of democracy not as formal rules but, rather, as the actual participation of citizens in the public sphere, then social movements will have a democratizing impact simply by "showing up" in the public space. This holds regardless of whether we look only at the number of collective actors—that is, movements—that participate in the political game or, in a more sophisticated manner, at the quality of the relations between collective actors in the democratic process (Habermas 1984). In either case, such participatory politics will create the foundations for strong democracy (Barber 1984).

It should be clear, however, that if an assessment of the effects of social movements on democracy depends on our definition of the latter notion, such impacts are also likely to vary according to the context within which movements operate. For example, while I certainly do not want to say that all Western societies are more democratic than non-Western societies, the characteristics of democracy and the democratization process are certainly very different in these two contexts. In addition, the context within which movements can have an impact on democracy not only varies across space but has changed over time as well. The concept of democracy is not the same today as it was, say, in the 1930s. If we fail to acknowledge the shifting meaning of those aspects of society which social movements can affect, we will hardly be able to explain how such impact occurs.

What Is Next?

In this introduction I have tried to do two things. On the one hand, I have provided an overview of the extant literature on the consequences of social movements, which is the main focus of this volume. To be sure, I have provided not an exhaustive list of theoretical and empirical works on this topic but rather a selection of the aspects that researchers have tended to emphasize in their attempt to assess the impact of movements. Specifically, we have seen that previous work has revolved around two issues: the disruption/moderation debate and the internal/external debate. Existing studies present a number of problems and limitations. Here I have stressed three such shortcomings: the tendency to look at the determinants of success or failure of social movements, a narrower focus on policy outcomes, and the problem of causality. In the final analysis, these shortcomings stem largely from the tendency to look for convenient yet nonexistent invariant models of collective action.

On the other hand, I have prepared the terrain for the essays included in this volume by briefly discussing what I think are two major issue areas that research on the consequences of social movements should address. First, there is a need for theoretical and empirical work on different types of movement impact. On the basis of the shortcomings of previous work, I have suggested that, if we are to reach a better understanding of the consequences of social movements, we should go beyond the notion of the movements' success to include the unintended outcomes of their actions, to expand the range of potential consequences to include broader social and cultural effects, and, finally, to avoid the search for invariant models in favor of an approach aimed at reconstructing the causal paths that link observed changes to the role of social movements in producing such changes. The essays in part 1 of this volume reflect such a need to look at different types of outcomes. Second, I have stressed the need to adopt a comparative perspective in the study of movement outcomes. Specifically, research should take seriously the idea of making comparisons across countries, across movements, and across time in order to highlight the social and political conditions under which movements are more likely to have an impact. The contributions in part 2 are thus devoted to an assessment of several contemporary movements, focusing on their political outcomes but also hinting at other types of consequences.

The field of social movement outcomes, while full of valuable empirical work on various movements in different places at different times, still lacks a coherent theoretical framework that will set the pace for future research on the topic. While this volume does not provide such a framework, we hope it will at least encourage scholars to make the study of the consequences of social movements a central and durable concern in social movement research, an endeavor that should help us in reflecting on the complex connections between social movements and the durability and direction of the changes they produce on the political, social, and cultural levels.

Notes

I thank Doug McAdam, Salvador Sandoval, and Charles Tilly for their comments on a previous draft of this introduction.

1. The description of the March on Washington is based on information from Kasher (1996).

2. On the impact of the civil rights movement, see, in particular, the excellent work of Button (1989).

3. For a review of the literature on the outcomes of social movements and protests, see Amenta, Carruthers, and Zylan (1992), Burstein, Einwohner, and Hollander (1995), Gurr (1980), Jenkins (1981), McAdam, McCarthy, and Zald (1988), Mirowsky and Ross (1981), and Schumaker (1978). For a more recent overview, see Giugni (1998).

4. See, in particular, Dahl (1967), who particularly represents the pluralist perspective on American society.

5. Other reanalyses of Gamson's data or related works include Frey, Dietz, and Kalof (1992), Goldstone (1980), and Webb et al. (1983).

6. For recent work on the effectiveness of strikes, see Cohn (1993) and Franzosi (1994).

7. See, among others, Berkowitz (1974), Betz (1974), Button (1978), Colby (1982), Feagin and Hahn (1973), Hahn (1970), Hicks and Swank (1983, 1992), Isaac and Kelly (1981), Kelly and Snyder (1980), Jennings (1979, 1983), Mueller (1978), and Welch (1975). Useful reviews of the literature on the racial riots of the 1960s can be found in Gurr (1980) and Isaac and Kelly (1981).

8. See Piven and Cloward (1993) and Trattner (1983) for an overview of the works related to Piven and Cloward's thesis. See the authors listed in note 7 for the part of their thesis dealing with the urban riots during the 1960s. On the part concerned with relief expansion in the 1930s, see, among others, Jenkins and Brents (1989), Kerbo and Shaffer (1992), and Valocchi (1990).

9. Piven and Cloward have strongly emphasized disruption as a winner and organization as a loser, an approach which has provoked a debate in the literature (Gamson and Schmeidler 1984; Roach and Roach 1978, 1980; see also the rejoinders by Cloward and Piven 1984, as well as Piven and Cloward 1978, 1980; and see further Piven and Cloward 1992).

10. On the unintended consequences of social action, see Tilly (1996).

11. The most famous version of this state-oriented definition has been given by Charles Tilly (1984: 304).

12. The first two types of effects resemble the twofold typology in Gamson's study (1990).

13. Tarrow (1998) has proposed a slightly different typology by distinguishing effects of protest cycles on the political socialization of participants, on political institutions and practices, and on political culture. However, these types of outcomes point to changes at the individual, political, and institutional levels.

14. An overview of methodological problems and some suggestions for further research can be found in Gurr (1980) and Rucht (1992).

15. Several methodological suggestions for the study of social movement outcomes have been made by Gurr (1980) and Snyder and Kelly (1979), among others.

16. Gould (1988) has called these two definitions of democracy, respectively, pluralist and socialist.

Part I
Types of Consequences

1

Social Movements and Public Policy

Paul Burstein

Sociologists and political scientists are of two minds about the consequences of social movements. On the one hand, they believe that social movements have important consequences. As William A. Gamson noted in his path-breaking *Strategy of Social Protest* (1975; second edition, 1990), it makes sense to view social movement organizations (SMOs, which he called "challenging groups") as part of the normal democratic political process only if they often achieve their goals—and, he concluded, they do. "The interest of many scholars in social movements stems from their belief that movements represent an important force for social change," wrote McAdam, McCarthy, and Zald (1988: 727) in their much-cited review (see also Tarrow 1994: 1).

Yet, on the other hand, sociologists and political scientists also believe that social movements seldom have much impact. They have two basic reasons for this belief—reasons which are of special interest because they are contradictory. Some argue that SMOs seldom have much impact because democracy works so poorly, while others argue that they have little impact because democracy works so well.

Gamson takes the former view, contending that for challenging groups, the United States "is no well-functioning democracy. Rather, it is a members-only system with formidable ways of keeping the door shut. That some challengers have the pluck and perseverance to gain entry in spite of such obstacles is sorry evidence for permeability [to new influences]" (1990: 177–78).[1] SMOs do poorly because the government is unresponsive and, thus, not truly democratic.

Lohmann, in contrast, argues that SMOs often do poorly when governments *are* responsive and democratic. In a well-functioning democracy, elected officials know what the public wants and respond to its demands; they would be foolish to respond to SMOs rather than the majority, because doing so could cost them reelection. Indeed, Lohmann writes, "[i]t is puzzling that rational political leaders with majoritarian incentives would ever respond to political action" by SMOs or other organizations (1993: 319).

Thus, we are confronted with two sets of contradictory claims: that social movements strongly influence public policy, and that they do not; and, in the latter case, that they have little impact because democracy functions badly, and because it functions well. In this chapter, I argue that social movement organizations and interest groups can influence policy, but this influence is strongly constrained by two key aspects of democratic politics: electoral competition and limits on the ability of citizens and legislators to pay attention to many issues at the same time. Because elected officials must constantly strive for public support, they respond primarily to the wishes of the majority, especially when the majority feels strongly about an issue. SMOs therefore cannot directly influence policy when they disagree with the majority on issues it cares about. SMOs can influence policy directly, however, on issues the public cares little about; and they can influence policy indirectly by changing the public's policy preferences and its intensity of concern about particular issues.

Social Movements and Democratic Politics

My focus is the impact on public policy of what Tilly has called "national social movements" (1984: 304)—movements that challenge national governments. Such movements, Tilly writes, are an essential part of democratic politics, a product of the same forces that led to the development of electoral politics and modern political organizations (which he calls "created associations"). To understand the impact of such social movements, therefore, we must examine their role in the democratic political process; to do this, in turn, it is necessary to delineate some basic elements of a theory of democratic politics (a task often neglected by those who study social movements).

Simply put, democracy works. The struggle for representative democracy, which began 350 years ago during the English Revolution, was predicated upon the belief that if the people of a country win the right to vote and to freedom of speech and association, they can control what their government does. Modern scholarship is showing, ever more conclusively, that the struggle has not been in vain. Democratic governments respond to their citizens often enough and consistently enough, especially on issues important to those citizens, for us to conclude that democratic institutions really give citizens substantial power over government.

How do citizens exert such power? The best explanation, in my opinion, is provided by what I call the theory of democratic representation. In this theory, elected officials have three primary goals. First is reelection, which for most legislators takes precedence over all other goals. Legislators also want to win influence for themselves among their colleagues and to promote what they believe to be good public policy; these are important goals but secondary, seldom pursued when doing so would risk electoral defeat (Fenno 1973; Mayhew 1974).

Knowing elected officials' goals, we can see what will get them to support specific policies—the number of votes they think their actions will win or lose them at election time. Officials thus want and need information about what the public wants and how it is likely to respond to their actions; and, indeed, mechanisms for communicating information have become central to democratic politics (Ferejohn and Kuklinski 1990). Much political action intended to influence elected officials—protest demonstrations, lobbying, letter writing, contributing to campaigns, and so on—will be effective primarily to the extent that it provides them information about what citizens want from them.

The key mechanism for communicating information in democratic politics is elections; not only do the results inform elected officials about how well they have satisfied voters' demands, but the information is of a kind that cannot be ignored—it gives some officials the right to remain in office and requires others to seek employment elsewhere. As a means of communication, however, elections are extremely crude; they convey voters' global judgment about candidates but provide no information about the reasons for those judgments (Kelley 1983: chapter 9). Elections ensure that elected officials will try to satisfy the electorate's demands, but they provide little information about the demands themselves.

Needing more information than elections provide, politicians have created other means to ascertain what the public wants; and members of the public, wanting to convey more information than they can through voting alone, have developed ways to communicate with candidates. Much of the effort on both sides has gone into creating organizations: political parties, interest groups, and social movement organizations. Political parties were developed, in part, to improve communication between elected officials and the citizenry, and the party label itself has come to provide useful information, acting as a "brand name" that tells the public much about the likely policy stances of its candidates (Aldrich 1995; Arnold 1990).

Formally organized interest groups developed long after parties; in fact, many of the earliest ones were created in response to what some groups (particularly in business) saw as the failure of parties to represent their interests. They won a place in American politics when they convinced politicians that they provided better information about citizens' preferences than the parties could and, at less cost, and that they could mobilize voters who shared those preferences (Hansen 1991; Walker 1991).

From this perspective, legislatures may be viewed as devoting much of their effort to acquiring and processing information. Some political scientists argue that legislatures are organized in large measure to gather information about the likely consequences of legislation and the preferences of voters; efficient legislatures will do so as cheaply as possible. Legislators want the information so they can minimize the risk of being blamed at election time for outcomes they did not foresee. According to this view, special interests cannot dominate the legislature, at least not in the long run, because legislators risk defeat if they respond to special interests rather than to the majority (Krehbiel 1991).

Thus, many of the organizations we associate with democratic governments have been developed, at least in part, to make such governments responsive to the public. No one claims, however, that democratic governments always do what the public wants.[2] Sometimes the cause may be what most people suspect: some groups are especially powerful and can get what they want even when the public is opposed. Proponents of the theory of democratic representation contend, however, that there are also other reasons for nonresponsiveness, one of which is especially important to this essay: limits to the cognitive capacities of individuals and the carrying capacities of organizations, particularly legislatures.[3]

Neither individuals nor legislatures have the capacity to address many issues at once. Individuals deal with this problem by ignoring most issues most of the time, relying on friends, organizations, the mass media, and candidates for office to let them know when an issue demands attention. Legislatures deal with it by delegating power to committees and administrative agencies, relying on these and other organizations (including political parties, interest groups, and SMOs) to let them know when an issue requires the legislature's full attention (Jones 1994; Krehbiel 1991; cf. Hilgartner and Bosk 1988).

From this perspective, the public will strongly affect public policy on issues it is very concerned about; but when it turns its attention elsewhere (as it is almost always bound to do), those who remain intensely concerned—notably, interest groups and the relevant legislative committees and executive agencies—have the opportunity to exert greater influence. Public policy may move farther and farther from public opinion, until something brings the public's attention back to the issue. Then the public may reexert its influence and bring policy back into line with its preferences. Thus, the public arguably has the power to make policy reflect its preferences but often fails to do so. On the whole, the proponents of democratic representation conclude, elected officials often do what the public wants because the institutions of democratic politics provide the information that makes responsiveness possible and the incentives that make it likely.

Social Movement Organizations, Interest Groups, and Political Parties

Where do social movements fit in this picture? To answer this, we must first ask what a social movement is. No single definition is relied on by everyone, but it is helpful to look at those provided in two classic articles. McCarthy and Zald define a social movement as "a set of opinions and beliefs in a population which represents preferences for changing some elements of the social structure and/or reward distribution of a society" (1977: 1217–18). For Tilly, "the term *social movement* applies most usefully to a sustained *interaction* between a specific set of authorities and various spokespersons for a given challenge to those authorities" (1984: 305; Tilly's emphasis). Common to both definitions is a desire for change, with McCarthy and Zald emphasizing the desire itself—"opinions and beliefs . . . preferences"—and Tilly the interactions it leads to (cf. Tarrow 1994: 1). So far, so good—both definitions include what comes to mind when social scientists think of social movements. Unfortunately, however, they seem to include routine interest-group politics and party conflict in legislatures as well. For example, the National Association of Manufacturers expresses a desire for change when it seeks to weaken occupational health and safety laws and often interacts with members of Congress in pursuit of this goal. And what does the minority party do in its interactions with the majority if not represent preferences for changing the reward distribution?

McCarthy and Zald realize that they risk being overinclusive and even ask, "Is a SMO an interest group?" (1977: 1218). Their answer highlights what has come to be seen as the key distinction between social movements and SMOs, on the one hand, and other political phenomena and organizations, on the other: social movements are at the "margins of the political system," and SMOs are less institutionalized than interest groups and have fewer routine ties with government. Other scholars focus on different attributes of SMOs, but all emphasize that it is their marginality which distinguishes them from other political organizations; they represent constituencies not previously mobilized (Gamson 1990: 16), speak on behalf of constituencies lacking formal representation (Tilly 1984: 306), or employ unconventional, disruptive tactics (McAdam 1982: 25).

Unfortunately, all these attempts to distinguish between SMOs and other political organizations share the same flaw. Each focuses on a continuum— of institutionalization or unconventionality of tactics, for example—and in effect declares that it can be divided at an identifiable point, with SMOs on one side and other political organizations on the other. But none of the continua are defined precisely; how particular organizations could be placed on the continua is never spelled out; and the rationale for locating the dividing point in one place rather than another is never made clear. These are not, I believe, minor definitional problems; instead, the very attempt to distinguish between SMOs and other political organizations reflects what Stephen Jay Gould has called humanity's "deeply (perhaps innately) ingrained habit of thought" (1995: 39)—an inclination to categorize, which is so strong that we mistakenly find dividing points along what are truly indivisible continua (for an elaboration of this argument, see Burstein 1998b).

To understand the place of social movements in democratic politics, I would return to the "created associations" so central to Tilly's thinking. Convention has it that there are three types—three categories—of such associations that are central to democratic politics: political parties, interest groups, and SMOs. Ultimately, I think, it is impossible to distinguish among them in terms of the characteristics usually used to define them (marginality, etc.). Trying to finesse the problem by claiming, as Tilly does, that social movements are interactions rather than organizations is no help, because there is no better way to distinguish among kinds of interactions than there is among kinds of organizations. Thus, it is not useful to think of SMOs as something different from interest groups.[4] What's more, often it is not useful to think of either one as different from political parties. Parties, too, are associations created to help people achieve their goals in democratic politics; the real difference between them and other such associations is legal, not organizational—parties are political organizations that have a place on the ballot and a formal role in organizing legislatures. It is most useful to think of there being two types of nongovernmental political organizations—political parties, which have special legal status; and what we might call "interest organizations" (a combination of "interest groups" and "social movement organizations"), which do not—while remembering the many similarities between the two.

Thus, any hypothesis about the impact on public policy of organizations conventionally labeled SMOs will also apply to those that have been conventionally labeled interest groups, and most will apply to political parties as well. Accepting this fact will help us understand democratic politics, because it implies that we need just one theory about collective action in the context of democratic politics, not multiple theories about purportedly different types of organizations. It can only be to our benefit to realize, for example, how similar Gamson's concern about SMOs' winning "acceptance" is to Hansen's concern about interest groups' winning "access" (Gamson 1990; Hansen 1991; cf. McAdam, McCarthy, and Zald 1988: 720), or how seamless is the set of "protest" activities that includes both street demonstrations and arguments before the Supreme Court (Burstein 1991).

The Impact of Interest Organizations: Hypotheses and Evidence

The theory of democratic representation suggests hypotheses about the impact of interest organizations on legislative action—on the content of legislation and the timing of its enactment—and on the implementation of legislation. The hypotheses presented here are about the power of interest organizations collectively; they address neither the impact of particular organizations, resources, and strategies nor the role played by legislators' perceptions in the political process. The hypotheses are necessarily somewhat tentative, because relatively little work on interest organizations, particularly by sociologists, has been motivated by this theory.

The Direct Impact of Interest Organizations

The first and most critical hypothesis is one I have not seen in the literature on social movements, yet it is an immediate implication of the theory.[5] Many of those who write about SMOs emphasize how difficult it is for them to influence government. Why so difficult? The most common claim is that other groups, particularly economic elites, are more powerful than SMOs and get their own way instead. The theory of democratic representation suggests an alternative explanation, however: perhaps interest organizations (including SMOs) fail to get what they want because a majority of the *public* wants something else. That is, when elected officials want intensely to be reelected, when the public pays attention to only a few issues at a time, and when elected officials want and need accurate information about the public's preferences, we propose the *direct impact hypothesis*: The greater and more persistent the majority favoring a particular policy, and the more important the issue to that majority, as perceived by legislators, the smaller the direct impact of interest organizations on legislative action.

The size of the majority matters to legislators because they want to be sure their actions represent the majority; the bigger the majority, the less likely the officials are to be mistaken. Persistence matters because legislators want to be as certain as possible that the majority preference will remain the majority through the next election. Importance matters because it is on the relatively small number of issues very important to the public that electoral reward-or-punishment is most likely. Finally, perceptions matter because legislators can act only on the basis of their perceptions of the public's preferences. Legislators and those in the popular majority want the perceptions to be accurate, so that the former can respond to the desires of the latter. The popular minority, however, want something else—that legislators inaccurately see the minority view as more popular than it actually is (see Arnold 1990; Page and Shapiro 1983).

To test the direct impact hypothesis for any particular issue, we need data on legislative action, legislators' perceptions of the direction and intensity of the public's preferences, and the activities of interest organizations. To understand the political process and not just legislators' perceptions of it, we also want to know the public's actual preferences. Unfortunately, although this hypothesis and others I will present here follow fairly directly from the theory of democratic representation, they have not been presented in quite this way before. As a result, very few studies have been designed to test them; indeed, very few even incorporate the variables needed for such tests. Thus, the evidence available can be no more than suggestive.

We do know that changes in public policy in the United States are correlated quite strongly with changes in public opinion and that the relationship is especially strong when the majority is large and the issue important to the public (see, e.g., Page and Shapiro 1983; Stimson, MacKuen, and Erikson 1995; and the review in Burstein 1998a). When the relationship between public opinion and public policy is very strong, there is little room for direct influence by interest organizations; such an inference is not a substitute for data but should be kept in mind.

Studies that analyze how legislative action is affected by public opinion and interest organizations generally find the former to have far greater impact than the latter. For example, congressional action on equal employment opportunity, the Vietnam War, gender issues, and controversial Supreme Court decisions has been far more strongly affected by public opinion than by interest organizations (Burstein 1985: 85–87; Burstein and Freudenburg 1978: 114–16; Costain 1992: 150–55; Ignagni and Meernik 1994). Even indirect measures of public opinion (such as constituency demographic characteristics and general political attitudes) have proven to be far more important than the contributions of political action committees (PACs; Wright 1985).

Opportunities to test the direct impact hypothesis are often missed, because those who study interest organizations so often ignore the theory of democratic representation. A good case in point is the controversy between Skocpol and her collaborators on the one side (Skocpol et al. 1993; Skocpol 1995) and Sparks and Walniuk (1995) on the other, about why many American states enacted mothers' pensions early in the twentieth century. Skocpol et al. argue that state legislatures were strongly influenced by federations of women's groups—that is, that interest organizations had a direct impact on legislative action. Sparks and Walniuk disagree, claiming that even though women did not yet have the right to vote in many states, legislators believed that they would soon get it, and that women strongly favored mothers' pensions—in other words, it was the opinion of voters (or potential voters) that mattered, and the women's groups had no direct impact on legislative action.

This disagreement seems to provide a good opportunity to test the direct impact hypothesis: Sparks and Walniuk's argument is consistent with it, and that of Skocpol et al. is not. Unfortunately, however, the test never quite happens. Skocpol (1995) argues convincingly that Sparks and Walniuk didn't make their case, because their data analysis was flawed; but she does not respond to their theoretical argument. Skocpol et al. suggest that public opinion might be important—referring to "nationwide groundswells of public opinion" (1993: 691) and women's federations' exercise of a "surprising influence on . . . public opinion" (Skocpol 1995: 721)—but never actually examine its impact on legislative action. Skocpol rejects Sparks and Walniuk's assumption that legislators are motivated mainly by electoral concerns, writing that "I do not like to engage in pure theoretical deduction about what 'must have been' in the minds of state legislators when they voted for mothers' pensions" (1995: 728), but she provides no reasons of her own why legislators would do what women's federations wanted. Why did legislators enact mothers' pensions? In the end, all Skocpol does is conclude, rather lamely, that "mothers' pensions became 'an idea whose time had come'" (1995: 728). It would be more useful had she responded with either a better test of the direct impact hypothesis or a better theory, but she did neither.

Other scholars analyze public opinion and interest organizations in ways that make it difficult to assess their roles in the democratic process. The importance of incorporating all the relevant variables is made plain by the ambiguities associated with findings seemingly contrary to the direct impact hypothesis. O'Connor and Berkman (1995) find that public opinion has strongly correlated with abortion policy in American states, controlling for a variety of variables, including religious affiliation. When state membership in the National Abortion and Reproductive Rights Action League (NARAL) is added to the equation, however, the coefficient for public opinion declines to statistical insignificance; NARAL membership has had a far greater impact on policy. This might be taken to mean that interest organization activity is more important than public opinion, but this is not O'Connor and Berkman's conclusion; they interpret NARAL membership as indicating the "intensity of opinion" on the issue (1995: 450). Is this interpretation correct, or might NARAL have had an impact independent of public opinion? Without a direct measure of intensity, there is no way to tell. Rosenfeld and Ward take the opposite point of view: rather than considering organizational activity an indicator of public opinion, they consider public opinion a measure of the "extent" of a social movement (1991: 53)—an approach that makes it impossible to determine whether interest organizations can directly affect legislative action independent of public opinion.

What Does the Public Really Want?

I have argued that interest organizations have little *direct* impact on legislative action when they oppose the clearly and strongly expressed wishes of a popular majority. That does not mean, however, that interest organizations have *no* impact on legislative action. The theory of democratic representation and the logic of the first hypothesis suggest three ways for interest organizations to influence legislative action: by changing legislators' perceptions of the public's preferences or their intensity; by changing the preferences themselves; or by changing the importance of the issue to the public.

Legislators' perceptions play a key role in democratic politics, and all the participants know it. Legislators need information about what the public wants, but accurate information is often difficult to acquire—so difficult, in fact, that some political scientists describe legislatures as organized to a very substantial extent around the need for such acquisition (Krehbiel 1991). Interest organizations can influence legislative action by convincing legislators that they have significantly underestimated the strength of support for a policy proposal—that what the legislators thought was minority support is really majority support, that an issue of seemingly low salience is really of high salience, or that preferences that seemed fickle have become solid. Thus the following *information hypotheses*: The greater the amount of new information on the public's preferences provided to legislators by interest organizations, the greater their impact on legislative action; information provided by organizations with a reputation for credibility will have an especially great impact. When the information is verifiably accurate, interest organizations stimulate legislatures to act in accord with public opinion; when its accuracy cannot be verified, interest organizations may have an independent impact on legislative action.

The key point is that the information must be new, in the sense of unexpected (this argument owes much to Lohmann 1993). As legislators try to keep informed about what the public wants, they may look to letters from constituents, visits from lobbyists, public demonstrations, newspaper editorials, public opinion polls, and so on. Most of what they see will be routine, requiring just enough monitoring that they will promptly notice any change in the public's preferences or the intensity of its concerns. Information out of the ordinary will alert them to the possibility of change and cause them to begin monitoring their sources of information more carefully.[6] Because they need information that is accurate as well as novel, they will give added weight to information from organizations that have proved credible in the past and that have an interest in continuing a relationship with the officials in the future (Hansen 1991).

To test the information hypothesis adequately, we need over-time data on the information available to legislators and on their subsequent actions. Having data on the information over time would enable us to distinguish between routine "news"—basically, news that fits whatever pattern has been established—and real news that departs from the pattern. What we actually have are bits of suggestive evidence.

Lohmann (1995) contends that demonstrations in the San Francisco Bay Area against the 1991 Persian Gulf War were ignored by politicians and supporters of the war because they were so predictable; Bay Area residents demonstrate against all American military actions. Antiwar demonstrations in Kansas City, however, were seen as more likely to have an impact; supporters of the war there felt obliged to organize their own demonstrations to counter any impression that Middle America was opposed to the war. Following a similar logic, Lohmann (1994) argues that demonstrations against the East German regime in late 1989 were effective not so much because of the numbers of people involved but rather because the demonstrations grew in size so rapidly—from an estimated 6,500 participants on September 25 to 60,000 two weeks later and to 325,000 on November 6— that they astonished both government and populace with the breadth and depth of discontent they revealed. Focusing on lobbying rather than demonstrations, Hansen (1991) concludes that the farm lobby won influence in Congress between 1919 and 1932 by convincing members of Congress that it could provide reliable information about what farmers wanted. He concludes, more generally, that "interest groups *are* influential, but not because of their ability to bring 'pressures' to bear on members of Congress. Rather, interest groups are influential because they direct lawmakers' attention to some pressures rather than others" (1991: 227; Hansen's emphasis). Finally, Meyer and Marullo argue that the American peace movement influenced Congress and the president by showing, through referenda and public opinion polls it encouraged, that the American public was more favorable to a freeze in nuclear weapons than had been supposed (1992: 116–19).

Changing the Public's Preferences

The theory of democratic representation argues that the major determinants of legislative action are the public's preferences and the intensity of its concern; from this follows the direct impact hypothesis that interest organizations have little impact on legislative action when the public's preferences are clear and intense. For interest organizations finding themselves in such circumstances, a key—but indirect—way to influence legislative action will be to change the public's preferences. They can do so in two ways: by altering the distribution of preferences on an issue as currently framed, or by reframing the issue—changing what the preferences are about. Thus, the *public's preferences hypothesis*: The greater the impact of interest organizations on the public's preferences on an issue as currently framed or as reframed, the greater their (indirect) impact on legislative action. This hypothesis can be falsified by showing that changes in the public's preferences caused by interest organizations do *not* lead to the desired changes in legislative action. This could happen if the theory of democratic representation is incorrect, and, for example, business organizations get what they want from government regardless of what the public's preferences are.

To test the public's preferences hypothesis, we need data on the activities of interest organizations intended to affect the public's preferences, on the preferences themselves, and on legislative action. Should these data not support the hypothesis, we would also want data on alternative sources of influence on legislative action.

Unfortunately, the necessary data are rarely available, because those who study the impact of interest organizations on public opinion seldom follow through to consider the impact of both the organizations and opinion on policy, while those who examine the impact of public opinion on policy seldom analyze why public opinion changes (at least within the same study; compare Page and Shapiro 1983 with Page and Shapiro 1992). We do know that interest organizations sometimes affect public opinion within a given frame (Page and Shapiro 1992: 350–54), and that, probably less often, they can help reframe issues, getting the public to view the issues in a new way (as they apparently did with regard to affirmative action and nuclear power;

Gamson and Modigliani 1987, 1989).[7] And of course we also know that public opinion often influences policy. There are a few attempts to analyze the impact of both interest organizations and public opinion on policy, but more often than not they find that the organizations have no effect on public opinion (e.g., Burstein 1985; Burstein and Freudenburg 1978). Of the studies of which I am aware, only Anne Costain's analysis of the women's movement finds interest organizations having an impact on public opinion— but no direct impact on legislative action (1992: 150–55).

Other scholars have realized how important it is to consider how both interest organizations and the public affect legislative action, but unfortunately they often fail to distinguish between the substance of public opinion and the salience of the issue. Piven and Cloward, for example, see electoral concerns playing a key role in legislators' responses to social protest (1977: 31–32) and protesters working, at least in part, through public opinion. When they write that "[t]he events [civil rights protests] in the South also provoked broad support for civil rights demands among northern whites" (239), however, it is unclear whether they are suggesting that protest activities affected northern whites' opinions about civil rights or that they affected how strongly the whites felt about it; this matters because there is evidence that civil rights activities did affect salience but not substantive opinions (Burstein 1985).

Changing Issue Salience

Interest organizations may also affect legislative action indirectly by changing the salience of an issue to the public. Theoretically, this can be an effective tactic. As discussed earlier, public policy may move away from what the public would prefer when the public is paying little attention to the issue— the normal situation for most issues. Raising the salience of the issue to the public may lead it to notice the discrepancy between its preferences and public policy, and to then demand that the latter be made consistent with the former.

Increasing an issue's salience is a much more problematic tactic than changing the public's preferences, however. For one thing, the tactic will work only if such a discrepancy exists. Beyond that, though, raising the salience of an issue is actually risky for interest organizations. If interest organizations inadvertently increase the salience of an issue on which the public *opposes* them, ending the discrepancy would make the situation worse for them rather than better. What is worse, interest organizations that draw attention to themselves under these circumstances could even provoke repression by the government or a violent response by other organizations. Thus, the *issue salience hypotheses*: The greater the impact of interest organizations on an issue's salience to the public, the greater their (indirect) impact on legislative action, *provided that* there is a discrepancy between the public's preferences and public policy. The legislative action will favor the interest organizations only if the organizations' goals are consistent with the public's preferences; if they are inconsistent, the legislative action will move public policy away from the organizations' goals.

To test the issue salience hypotheses, we need data on the activities of interest organizations intended to affect the salience of the issue for the public, on the public's preferences, on existing policy, and on legislative action. Of course, many of the activities of interest organizations are intended to affect salience, the public's preferences, *and* the information being communicated to legislators, all of which should be considered in research on the impact of such activities.

The most direct test of this hypothesis is found in my work on the movement for equal employment opportunity (Burstein 1985). Civil rights protests had little direct effect on congressional action (as I have noted) and apparently little or no effect on public opinion on civil rights. They did, however, greatly increase the salience of the issue, particularly when they provoked a hostile public response in the South. The increase in salience, in turn, seems to have affected Congress so strongly that it enacted the Civil Rights Act of 1964 just after salience reached its peak. Yet it is crucial to note that Congress finally responded to the public at a time when most Americans had come to oppose racial discrimination. It is easy to imagine that had similar demonstrations produced a comparable rise in salience during the 1920s rather than the 1960s, they would have provoked repression rather than enactment of laws against discrimination.

I know of no other direct tests of the salience hypothesis, but an important controversy about the enactment of the National Labor Relations Act (NLRA) of 1935 provides some evidence consistent with it. In a spirited debate in the *American Political Science Review,* Goldfield (1989, 1990) argues that worker insurgency played a key role in getting Congress to act; Skocpol and Finegold (1990) disagree, emphasizing instead electoral politics and the discretion that those in government have to respond to pressure in a variety of ways. Neither side emphasizes the public's preferences or the impact of interest organizations on salience, but they do provide some relevant evidence. Addressing Goldfield's description of increases in labor militancy during the 1930s, Skocpol and Finegold argue that it is never necessary for governments to respond to such pressures with any particular concessions; alternative responses are always possible, including repression (1990: 1304).

When might governments respond favorably to such pressures (even if the exact form of the response cannot be predicted)? According to the salience hypothesis, governments would respond favorably if there were a discrepancy between the public's preferences and public policy *and* if the goals of the interest organizations were consistent with the public's preferences. According to Goldfield, there may have been such a discrepancy; public opinion had been moving to the left in the period before Congress enacted the NLRA, but labor policy had not changed significantly (1989: 1275). Thus, it is entirely possible that organized labor increased the salience of labor issues just as policies that labor wanted were winning majority public support.

Skocpol and Finegold disagree, contending that it was electoral politics—particularly Democratic victories in 1934—and not labor militancy that led to congressional action (1900: 1300). In the theory of democratic representation, however, there is no contradiction between the two views; the Democratic victories may be seen as evidence of the shift in public opinion, providing a context in which it would make sense for Congress to respond to public concern about labor with reform rather than repression.[8]

This chapter has focused thus far on legislative action. The enactment of legislation is hardly the end of the policy process, however; implementation must be considered as well.

Interest Organizations and Implementation

It has long been contended that, whatever the impact of interest organizations on legislative action, their impact on implementation is substantial. The popular notion that "the bureaucracy" and the courts are "out of control" is echoed in social scientists' claims that administrative agencies and the courts are unduly influenced by the interest organizations whose activities the public wants regulated. The theory of democratic representation provides some insight as to how this might occur. The public as a whole cannot sustain a high level of interest in very many issues and lacks the capacity to monitor closely how legislation is being implemented; thus, laws may be implemented in ways the public would disapprove of were it well informed.

Legislatures, too, have only a limited capacity for oversight, and therefore they delegate oversight of particular policies to their specialized committees. The members of these committees, however, may disproportionately represent districts whose citizens' preferences are very different from those of the public as a whole; congressional committees are proverbially made up of legislators who sought membership in order to win favored treatment for their constituents' particular interests. Finally, the judges and bureaucrats whose job it is to interpret and implement legislation are not elected and thus lack both the legislators' capacity to monitor public opinion and their incentive to do so. If a law is vaguely worded or grants much discretion to the administrative agencies or courts, it provides opportunities for interest organizations to influence its implementation, particularly when it has just been enacted and there are few precedents to constrain the judges or bureaucrats.

The theory of democratic representation also suggests that there will be limits to this influence, however. The legislature as a whole arguably needs to prevent implementation from departing so far from the public's preferences that it becomes an election issue; it will therefore exercise some control over the oversight committees and may amend the law if administrative or judicial decisions lead to public outrage. Apparently even the judiciary is affected to some extent by the public's preferences (Stimson, MacKuen, and Erikson 1995; Norpoth and Segal 1994; Mishler and Sheehan 1994). Thus, the *implementation hypotheses*: The lower the salience of an issue to the public, the greater the impact of interest organizations on the implementation of laws bearing on the issue. The greater the discretion available to administrative or courts charged with implementing or interpreting a law, the greater the impact of interest organizations on its implementation. To test the implementation hypotheses adequately, we need data on the salience of an issue to the public, on the public's preferences, on the amount of discretion granted administrative agencies and courts on the issue, on the activities of interest organizations intended to affect implementation, and on the relevant decisions made by administrative agencies and courts.

Although many studies highlight how administrative and judicial decisions are seemingly influenced by interest organizations, few carefully gauge how far such decisions depart from the public's preferences, and fewer still take salience into account. We have a sense that public outrage provoked by a series of administrative or judicial decisions may lead to legislative action overturning those decisions; the California tax revolt of the 1970s and recent changes in the implementation of affirmative action policies are good examples (Lo 1990; Burstein forthcoming). But far more systematic research is needed.

Few studies treat discretion as a variable (but see Lowi 1979). Again, however, it is fairly widely believed that administrative agencies and courts often have far more discretion when a law is newly enacted than they will later, when the precedents they themselves establish will exert great influence on subsequent decisions. The early, precedent-setting decisions in turn can be heavily influenced by interest organizations (see, e.g., Blumrosen 1993; Clark 1977; Zemans 1983).

Conclusions

I have argued in this chapter that if we are to understand how interest organizations influence public policy, we must analyze their activities in the context of theories of democracy and of how individuals and organizations function in complex, competitive environments. When we do so, we reach conclusions a bit different from those found in most works on social movements.

First, there is no theoretical justification for distinguishing between social movement organizations and interest groups. Gamson has contended that "the old duality of extremist politics and pluralist politics" was based on a mistaken premise; instead, "there is simply politics" (1990: 138). Similarly, the old duality of SMOs and interest groups cannot withstand scrutiny; there exist simply organizations—"interest organizations"—trying to influence public policy.

Second, because elected officials are intensely concerned about reelection, they must respond, first and foremost, to the wishes of a majority of their constituents. When these wishes are clear and strongly felt, interest organizations cannot directly influence policy.

But this does not mean that they cannot influence policy at all. The third conclusion is that democratic politics provides ways for interest organizations to affect policy even as it limits their impact. Together with limits on individual and organizational capacities, it provides opportunities for interest organizations to influence legislative action directly on those issues the public cares little about, and to influence policy indirectly by conveying information to elected officials, changing the public's preferences and the intensity of its concerns, and affecting the decisions of administrative agencies and judges.

These conclusions about the impact of interest organizations on public policy are necessarily very tentative, because little work on social movements tries to gauge their impact in the context of theories of electoral competition and legislative action. But the evidence supporting these conclusions certainly justifies further work.

I should also note a type of conclusion I have *not* tried to reach: conclusions about resources, strategies, and opportunities that enable some interest organizations to succeed while others fail. Those scholars studying social movements have been very much concerned with the success or failure of particular SMOs or, sometimes, particular social movements. At first, much emphasis was placed on discovering which tactics or organizational characteristics were associated with success—whether, for example, the use of violence helped SMOs or worked against them. More recently, attention has been devoted increasingly to the "political opportunity structure," those aspects of the environment which affect SMO success.

This is an important step in the right direction, for interest organizations are strongly affected by their environment. The more the environment is taken into account, however, the more complex the analysis becomes; for example, it becomes clear that the utility of particular resources for one interest organization depends very heavily on the resources available to other such organizations and the use they make of them (see Tarrow 1994: 170–71). Pursuing this line of analysis leads, I believe, to a conclusion already reached by the evolutionary biologists and economists who study complex, competitive systems—namely, that we can make broad predictions about what rates of change will be and how such rates are affected by circumstances, but not about which possible changes are most likely to occur or which agents of change (for us, which interest organizations) are most likely to win the battle for success. Democratic politics provides interest organizations the opportunity to compete for influence; and the complexity and intensity of the competition makes it virtually impossible to predict who will win.

Notes

1. It may seem odd to cite Gamson as saying both that challenging groups succeed and that they have little impact, that is, that democratic governments are both responsive and unresponsive. In fact, though, this ambivalence runs throughout his book and the work of others in this field (see Clemens 1993), perhaps because they have no explicit standard for gauging impact or responsiveness. These issues will be addressed later in this chapter.

2. Strictly speaking, organizations are intended to make government responsive to *citizens* who have the right to vote. In addition, we would expect government to be responsive mainly to *voters* rather than to all citizens. I will not consider the implications of these distinctions in this paper, and I will use the term *public* because it is the term used conventionally in so many of the works being cited.

3. Two other important reasons are constitutional and statutory restrictions on the power of majorities (for example, the limits on government power delineated in the American Bill of Rights), and problems in aggregating preferences by voting (for example, the problem of cyclic majorities).

4. McAdam, McCarthy, and Zald (McCarthy and Zald 1977: 1218; McAdam, McCarthy, and Zald 1988: 720) realize that the distinction between SMOs and interest groups is often hazy, but they stop short of arguing that such a distinction should be abandoned.

5. Neustadtl (1990) makes a somewhat similar argument in an article on campaign contributions made by interest groups.

6. See also Tarrow's arguments about how British government officials came to de-

pend on interest organizations for information as early as the late eighteenth century (1994: 51–55) and also about how disruptive tactics may become routine and cease to hold politicians' attention (112–14); Mansbridge (1992), too, emphasizes how important information provided by interest organizations is to legislative (and public) decision making.

7. It must be kept in mind that it is not easy to influence public opinion, partly because organizations trying to change it in one direction are often opposed by groups supporting the status quo or change in another direction (see Carmines and Stimson 1989; Kitschelt 1994; Page and Shapiro 1992; Riker 1982). Not only do organizations' attempts to change public opinion often fail, but sometimes they actually backfire, turning the public against the positions the organizations espouse (Page and Shapiro 1992).

8. It is interesting to note that in her analysis of the NLRA (Skocpol and Finegold 1990) Skocpol emphasizes the importance of electoral politics and downplays the impact of interest organizations, while with regard to mothers' pensions (Skocpol et al. 1993; Skocpol 1995) she does the reverse. It is possible that both conclusions are correct, but Skocpol provides no theory that could explain how.

2

Making an Impact: Conceptual and Methodological Implications of the Collective Goods Criterion

Edwin Amenta and Michael P. Young

The impact of challengers and their collective action in democratic polities is only rarely studied (Gamson 1975, 1990; Piven and Cloward 1977; McAdam 1982; Kitschelt 1986; Amenta, Carruthers, and Zylan 1992; Jasper and Poulsen 1993; Amenta, Dunleavy, and Bernstein 1994; Tarrow 1994: chapter 10; Burstein, Einwohner, and Hollander 1995; Kriesi et al. 1995: chapter 9; see review in Giugni 1994). The reason for this is, in part, that theorizing and analyzing the impact of challengers is different from theorizing and analyzing their mobilization, which has been the focus of attention in scholarly work on social movements and collective action. It comes as no surprise that the subjects receiving the greatest study have witnessed the greatest advances.

The relative lack of attention to the impact of challengers is due also to conceptual and methodological problems peculiar to the subject. As we identify and address these issues, we refer to the impact of social movements rather than widely employed alternatives—the "success" or "failure" of social movements or the "outcomes" of social movements. Because the alternatives confuse the conceptual and methodological issues we confront (the standard use of the term *success* tends to blur conceptual issues, and the standard use of the term *outcomes* blurs methodological issues), we develop analytical clarity around the term *impact*.

Ascertaining the impact of challengers requires conceptualizing what constitutes an important result of a challenge. The easy way out is merely to take the challenger's word for this—to speak in terms of success and failure. Doing that, however, means placing severe limits on an analysis. Although it would be foolish to ignore a challenger's stated goals, we argue that focusing on them alone would mean missing other important occurrences that might have resulted from the challenge. Often, moreover, many objectives of social movements are not clearly revealed. To speak of outcomes of social movements, however, is to presume what needs to be established by a researcher. Important developments sometimes happen in the wake of social movements and the collective action of challengers. But it is premature to call these developments the outcomes or results of challenges, because events that happen during or after a challenge may be due to forces other than the challenge. To ascertain or demonstrate the impact of a challenge, researchers must ascertain what might have happened in its absence. That basic methodological task, generic to all forms of causal analysis, is a difficult one for this subject matter, because the conditions that influence the rise of challengers may also independently influence both the goals sought by challengers and occurrences that might benefit those whom the challengers seek to represent.

In this chapter, we address some of the conceptual and methodological issues behind the study of the impact of social movements. We present and defend a definition of impact and methodological strategies to ascertain impacts. Neither of our approaches is particularly original. Our definition of potential beneficial impacts centers on collective benefits. Our methodological strategies, mainly ways to make plausible the causal claims of case studies, are also standard in social science. Here, though, we seek to apply the conceptual and methodological strictures to problems specific to research on the impact of challengers. The methodological problem, in essence, is to demonstrate that the actions of a given challenger resulted in collective benefits. We compare our definitions and strategies and their implications with others that are well known in the literature on social movements. We discuss these issues mainly as they pertain to state-oriented challengers, although we also argue that analogous thinking is required for challengers oriented to other targets.

We rely heavily on one particular example—the Townsend Movement. We use this case to provide recurrent illustrations of our categories and strategies. We also discuss other challengers from the American 1930s, as well as some cases from famous studies and recent history. Our effort here, though, stops well short of providing a theory of the impact of social movements. Nor do we try to establish that any of the challenges we discuss did or did not have an impact, as we define it. Our discussion here is preliminary to such analyses.

Before we jump into abstract issues, let us introduce the Townsend

Movement. Dr. Francis E. Townsend organized his mainly aged followers and made demands on behalf of the aged beginning in 1934. Peaking at about one million members in 1936, the Movement was centered on the so-called Townsend Plan: two hundred dollars per month for all Americans sixty years or older, to be funded by an earmarked sales tax, so long as the recipients did not work and spent the money within the month (Holtzman 1963). Though focused on the national level, the Movement also demanded changes in Old-Age Assistance laws in the states and, eventually, the enactment of "baby" Townsend Plans—flat, large, universal pensions in individual states. Nowhere was the Movement more active than in Townsend's adopted home, California. All the same, nowhere did a Townsend Plan pass. Instead the Social Security Act passed in 1935, creating Old-Age Assistance and Old-Age Insurance, the former a grant-in-aid program for states and the latter a national insurance program commonly known today as social security. All states adopted means-tested Old-Age Assistance programs by 1939, and the Social Security Act was amended in 1939 and 1950 in favor of the aged. By 1950, though, the Townsend Movement had deteriorated (Amenta, Carruthers, and Zylan 1992).

Thinking about the Impact of Social Movements

A crucial conceptual issue is how to think about the possible impact of challengers. We argue that the place to start is with the concept of collective goods—those groupwise advantages or disadvantages from which non-participants in a challenge cannot be easily excluded (Tilly 1978; Hardin 1982). Collective goods can be material, such as categorical social spending programs, or less tangible, such as new ways to refer to members of a group. Social movement organizations almost invariably claim to represent a group extending beyond the leaders and adherents of the organization, and most make demands that would provide collective benefits to that larger group. To our way of thinking, the greater the collective benefits achieved by the challenge, the greater its favorable impact. A focus on collective benefits is a simple enough starting point, but it is not the standard view. For this reason, we think it is worth exploring the advantages and disadvantages of our decision and alternatives to it.

"Success" and the Collective Goods Standard

The main alternative focuses on the program and the organization of the challenger. William Gamson's justly famous and influential study of American social movement organizations posits two forms of "success"—the realization of "new advantages" for the challenging organization and the "acceptance" of the organization as a legitimate mouthpiece for the group it claims to represent (1990: 29). By these means he divides his challengers into the famous two-by-two table, separating the cases into "full response"—two versions of partial success: "cooptation" and "preemption"—and complete failure, which he refers to as "collapse."

To ascertain what constitutes new advantages, the more influential of his two forms of success, Gamson focuses on the challenger's program. For him, success in gaining new advantages means the degree to which a challenger's stated program is realized. Correspondingly, if the challenger's program or demands are not mainly realized, the challenger is considered a failure on this dimension. Paul Burstein, Rachel Einwohner, and Jocelyn Hollander (1995) also make a strong case for determining success and new advantages by way of a close analysis of the degree to which a challenger's program is achieved. Examining success and defining it by way of the challenger's program has some definite advantages. It provides a sharp focus and draws attention to specific ends of collective action and the means devoted to attaining them.

However, the standard definition also has liabilities. Notable among these are the limits it places on the consideration of possible impacts of challenges. Most of all, it may be possible for a challenger to fail to achieve its stated program—and thus be deemed a failure—but still to win substantial collective benefits for its constituents. It is often premature or erroneous, moreover, to assume that the formal discourse and plans of social movement organizations represent the scope of the desires for change represented in a given social movement. Other goals may be present but ignored by a program-oriented analysis.

Some disadvantages of the standard definition can be illuminated by our example. From the standard perspective, the failure of the Townsend Plan implies the failure of the Townsend Movement (to win "new advantages"). Yet if the Townsendites were responsible for the collective benefits for the aged in the Social Security Act, as Frances Fox Piven and Richard A. Cloward (1971) notably suggest, the Movement should rightly stand as one of the most influential challengers in American history. This is because the Social Security Act ensured great collective benefits to the aged, the group that the Movement claimed to represent. Even if the Movement had merely won less substantial collective benefits for the aged, such as more generous and more easily accessible Old-Age Assistance benefits, it might still be considered influential. In short, a focus on program tends to overlook unintended results of challenges that may be beneficial to the followers of those challenges. If challengers of the state typically receive concessions other than their demands (Piven and Cloward 1977: chapter 1), a program-oriented analysis will regularly underestimate their impact.

Another problem with the standard application of the "new advantages" criterion is that aspects of a challenger's program may not provide collective benefits to a constituency. While challengers often make demands that would aid a larger constituency, so that the realization of those demands would produce collective goods as we define them, often, important parts of a challenger's program would provide benefits only to the leaders or participants in a challenge. More rarely, the program might incur costs on the beneficiary group. For instance, the Townsend Plan had a requirement that the aged retire. Winning only that goal might be viewed as a collective "bad" or cost and probably should not be counted as a benefit, despite the fact that it was part of the challenger's program. In other cases, it is unclear whether a challenger's program will do much good for the constituency. Gamson argues, in this vein, that Charles Coughlin's National Union for Social Justice, of the same era as the Townsend Movement, included a number of proposals that seemed unlikely to aid his unemployed and poor constituents (1990: 34).

This example highlights another benefit of our collective goods criterion—its range. A challenge that does not succeed in winning new benefits is accordingly considered a "failure" by the standard way of thinking and talking. Complete achievement of a program is the best outcome, and complete failure to achieve the program is the worst possible result. Indeed, often collective action itself is ignored or repressed, and so are the demands (Piven and Cloward 1977). Yet it is possible for challenges to do worse than merely fail to achieve goals. Collective action can backfire, resulting in negative consequences for the group that the collective action was supposed to aid (Snyder and Kelly 1979). Repression can go beyond harming those engaged in collective action; collective action can generate collective bads—laws passed restricting the material rights and benefits of groups as well as less tangible collective assets. The collective goods standard makes it easier to discuss and analyze collective action that might have harmed people represented by a challenger.

The Townsend Movement provides an example. In 1934, the Movement opposed the gubernatorial campaign of Upton Sinclair, whose platform was to "End Poverty in California," partly by way of fifty-dollar-per-month pensions for the aged. The reason for opposing Sinclair was that he had failed to endorse the Townsend Plan, unlike his far more expedient opponent, Frank Merriam, a conservative Republican who endorsed the plan. Merriam realized that his endorsement obligated him to do nothing for the aged in California (Putnam 1970). By aiding Merriam, the collective action of the Townsend Movement may have reduced collective benefits for the aged in California. Whether it did or did not is perhaps mainly an empirical question, one that we do not pursue here, but a collective benefits standard makes it easier to ask such questions.

Our concern with collective benefits to constituents diverges also from standard definitions of success employed in the sociology of organizations. The latter often focus on achieving operational goals and enhancing the survival of the organization itself (see, e.g., Gross and Etzioni 1985: chapter 2). Yet challengers differ greatly from other organizations, especially profit-making concerns, in their claims to represent a wider constituency—one that is typically disadvantaged by standard economic or political processes. We think it is worth making a distinction between the organizations and participants of a challenge and the constituents the challenge is representing.

The latter point suggests the limits of Gamson's second dimension—the use of access or acceptance as a criterion for the success, or what we would call a beneficial impact, of a challenger. As Gamson notes, the institutional acceptance of a social movement organization and its leaders as the legitimate voice for a constituency does not necessarily lead to new advantages, however defined. For instance, the Townsend Movement wanted the California legislature to ask, or "memorialize," the national Congress to pass the Townsend Plan. However gratifying to die-hard Townsendites, in themselves these "memorials" did little for the aged in California. It has been argued that, to the contrary, such action may have come at the expense of old-age benefits in California (Putnam 1970). As Piven and Cloward (1977: xv) argue more generally, access to elites won by organizations that develop within movements may blunt the impact of challenges by way of co-optation.

In short, whether a challenger's access to elites increases or decreases the likelihood of winning collective benefits for constituents is an issue that needs to be independently theorized and empirically assessed. For example, in Charles Ragin's reanalysis (1989) of Gamson's data, "access" is treated as a condition influencing "new advantages" or the lack of them. A focus on collective benefits may make it easier to keep separate the success of organizations that emerge within a challenge, and the impact of the challenge. Benefits or symbolic victories limited to activists and activist organizations do not constitute collective benefits in themselves, and should not be counted as a social movement impact unless they lead to collective benefits.

Implications of the Collective Goods Standard: Locating Beneficiary Groups and Alternative Goods

Entertaining impacts outside the stated goals of social movement organizations has implications for the assessment of challengers and their collective action. Radical movements in Western democracies invariably fall short of their stated goals (Goodwin and Skocpol 1989; Tarrow 1994). An analysis of success along the standard lines would consider all such movements as mainly failures by definition—even when they effect significant transformations of political, economic, and cultural institutions. A focus on collective benefits might lead to a more positive assessment. Such an emphasis also facilitates finer-grained analyses of the impacts of revolutionary movements outside capitalist democracies, instead of the standard all-or-nothing analyses that explain why some revolutions happened and others did not. Similarly, a challenge that tries for very little and achieves it would be assessed less positively by this standard. Another implication is that a challenger that has a tremendous impact, in terms of producing long-term and sustained collective benefits for constituents, but then disbanded would be evaluated more favorably than it would by way of standard practices.

We do not want to suggest that our definition is consistent only with rational-choice imagery and explanations. Scholars in this tradition typically try to explain collective action in terms of the benefits that might be gleaned from it. As with most studies of social movements, though, rational-choice scholars are typically attempting to explain contributions to collective action or mobilization. Rational-choice theorists often try to ascertain why individuals contribute money or effort to collective action—say, to a public television network—and assume that once the contribution is made, a definite amount of collective good—say, public television programming—will result. The issue is how to explain or induce sufficient contributions. Once that problem, often considered to be a free-rider problem or a prisoners' dilemma game, is solved or converted to a more manageable problem or game, collective benefits are expected to result almost automatically (see, e.g., Chong 1991). Collective action in real life, though, is often much messier and involves interactions that go beyond individual contributions, to efforts to achieve some collective benefit. For example, money or effort devoted to the Townsend Movement would not necessarily result in a standard amount of collective benefit—such as an increase in the old-age pension payment. The causal mechanisms linking collective action to collective benefits, we suggest, are complex and need to be theorized in their own right.

Our view of potentially beneficial impacts comes with its own problems, however, and we do not want to slight them. Foremost among them is ascertaining the constituency for any given challenger or social movement—the first task implied by our definition. Taking the claims of the challengers at face value may not solve the problem. The Townsend Movement, for instance, claimed to be helping everyone, as the plan was supposed to end unemployment and a number of other social ills. So even here the decision is not so simple as it seems. For the Townsend Movement, we would argue that the most important group represented was the aged, who provided most of the Movement's support and who constituted the main direct beneficiaries of the plan. Because the Townsend Movement was one challenger with a relatively coherent form of organization, it provides an easy case. Less well organized social movements may provide greater difficulty in isolating beneficiary groups. All the same, we think that these issues are worth thinking about and through, even if one definitive answer is impossible.

Another set of difficulties concerns the identification and assessment of collective benefits. How does one choose among the possible collective benefits to study? How does one assess the value of the collective benefits that may result from challenges? Most of all, how does one decide what is a collective benefit? In the end, to make that attribution means to posit that something is really in a group's interest—always a difficult task. In the debate over subjective and objective interests (Lukes 1974; Tilly 1978), we side with those who argue to take both into account. This does not mean ignoring the programs and demands of individual social movement organizations. We would suggest starting with those programs and demands and then analyzing the collective benefits inhering in them. A definition of beneficial results based on collective goods, however, makes it incumbent upon researchers to consider alternatives to the challengers' programs—other potential concessions—that might also be beneficial. Our view is that scholars need to do some hard thinking about the range of collective goods that would be beneficial for a group represented by a challenger. Unlike activists, who are forced to act on the spot and in a historical moment, researchers often have the advantage of hindsight and comparative knowledge in their analyses. We suggest only that these advantages not be dismissed out of hand.

To return to our example, if one can support a claim that the main beneficiary group of the Townsend Movement was the aged, the implications for research are relatively straightforward. The first would be to examine the plan for the collective benefits in it—the main one being the large and relatively unrestricted pension. The next step would be to examine other potential collective benefits, such as other forms of pensions for the aged. The researcher would focus on old-age pensions, evaluating the relative benefits in the provisions. The fact that the amount of pensions and aggregate of pensioners can be summarized in dollars and numbers simplifies the task. One would still need to ascertain how much of these benefits were attributable to the action of the Townsendites (more on that later). However, the challenge might have resulted in any number of collective benefits for the aged. These might include everything from a better image of the group provided by official statements and government publications or through public opinion, to a valuable and durable collective identity for the aged. Evaluating benefits that do not take a monetary form can, however, be difficult. We turn next to the subject of isolating and evaluating different types of collective benefits.

Types and Degrees of Potentially Collective Benefits

Most challengers, including our example, mainly target the state. Of the fifty-three groups studied by Gamson that represented the population of American challengers historically through 1945, thirty-three were state-oriented (1990: 21). Important examples of state-oriented social movements since then include the civil rights and women's movements. Because so many challengers and movements are centrally concerned with the state, it is key to categorize and assess potential benefits received by way of the state. Needless to say, however, many challengers and movements have targets mainly outside the state. Some prominent examples include labor movements, most of whose collective action is concerned with employers, and animal rights movements, which often confront businesses and universities. Some new social movements, hoping to create new collective identities, might be said to have no targets analogous to the ones just mentioned. Most challengers have some mix of state, private, and more diffuse targets. In what follows we discuss types of benefits available from those targets, starting with democratic states.

Collective Benefits from the State

We define states as sets of political, military, judicial, and bureaucratic organizations that exert political authority and coercive control over people living within the borders of well-defined territories. States engage in action, including taxation and social spending policies, that is binding on citizens and subjects, and the action is backed by the aforementioned organizations (Skocpol and Amenta 1986). Democratic states are those states whose leaders, forms, and policies are decided with key participation and input from everyday people, citizens rather than subjects; suffrage is relatively inclusive, citizens have the right to associate, and the state is significantly responsible to elected officials (Dahl 1971).

Scholars who have examined the potential impacts of social movements in relatively democratic states often suggest that there are different types and levels of impact. These types generally refer back to the new advantages and acceptance criteria of Gamson (1990). For instance, Kitschelt (1986) argues that social movements can achieve substantive, procedural, and structural gains, with the first two being analogous to Gamson's categories. The third type is a "transformation of political structures," which is expressed in Kitschelt's study as the rise of a new political party. Jenkins (1983) suggests a three-part scheme based on short-term changes in political decisions, alterations in decision-making elites, and long-term changes in the distribution of goods. The first and third are different forms of new benefits, while the second is a more general idea of access or acceptance.

We also propose a three-level approach, but each level refers ultimately to collective benefits and omits consideration of the recognition or acceptance of any challenging organization. From this perspective, the most minor impact is to win a specific state policy decision with no long-term implications for the flow of benefits to the group. The greatest sort of impact is the one that provides a group—but not necessarily organizations representing that group—continuing leverage over political processes. These structural gains are defined by the fact that they increase the returns to routine collective action. Most collective action is aimed at a more medium level—benefits that will continue to flow to a constituency unless some countering action is taken. In each case, new legislation is required to secure the benefits. The difference in impact is determined by the content of the legislation. Needless to say, much collective action in practice may be aimed at different levels, but these distinctions offer a basis for an analysis of the gains.

At the lowest level, challengers may win something specific for their constituency groups. A challenger may gain, for instance, greater respect, through official governmental representations, for the group represented by the challenger. An example for the aged would be to have them officially referred to as "senior citizens" in state communications. Another benefit at this level is a short-run pecuniary benefit. The attempt of American veterans' organizations to win the early payment of their World War I "bonuses" in 1936 instead of 1945 constitutes a case in point. These bonuses went to all who qualified for them at the time but had no implications for these World War I veterans in the future or for the veterans of future wars (Daniels 1971). The one-shot brand of benefit, however, has often been criticized as insubstantial (Lipsky 1968). From our way of looking at it, such a benefit implies a limited conception of rights for the categories of citizens to which the benefit pertains.

At the highest level, a challenger may gain structural reforms that give the represented group increased influence over political processes. For instance, winning the right to vote or the protection of that right for low-income or other disfranchised groups increases the productivity of future collective action by such groups. The winning of such rights increases the likelihood of gaining future pecuniary and other collective benefits (Meyer and Staggenborg 1996). The civil rights movement had as an important goal the enforcement of the right to participate in electoral politics (McAdam 1982). So, too, did women's suffrage movements (Banaszak 1996). Alternatively, collective action may win higher-order rights through the state that advantage a group in its conflicts with other groups (Skocpol 1985). The state may be used as a "fulcrum" in this sense (Tarrow 1994) by groups not mainly state-oriented. Labor movements, notably, often focus on the state to ensure rights to organize and engage in collective bargaining, as American labor did successfully in the 1930s (Plotke 1996). The general way to differentiate this sort of benefit from the other types is that it increases the probability of impact of collective action by a group—a kind of metacollective benefit.

It is at the middle level where most research has taken place and probably where most challenges aim to have an impact. Much of democratic state action concerns institutionalized benefits that provide collective goods in a routine fashion to all those meeting specified requirements. Once enacted and enforced with bureaucratic means, categorical social spending programs, notably, provide benefits in such a manner. The beneficiaries gain rights of entitlement to the benefits, and laws and bureaucratic reinforcement of those laws ensure the routine delivery of such collective benefits. Under these circumstances, the issue is privileged in politics and the political system becomes biased toward the group so favored. The issue is effectively removed from the political agenda in favor of the group. For the situation to change, it is incumbent on some other person or group to challenge the institutionalized benefits.

Such benefits were the kind that the Townsend Movement mainly attempted to secure. A legislative commitment to the Townsend Plan would mean that the aged would receive a large and equal pension from the federal government. The old-age legislation in the Social Security Act, possibly a result of Townsend mobilization, was also of this middle-level sort. Here there could be much variation in the degree, extent, and guarantee of the collective benefits. For old-age benefits, decisions have to be made about eligibility rules, benefit amounts, and the manner of their provision.

Benefits from Targets outside the State

Social movements can, of course, generate collective benefits other than through state policy. In Gamson's sample of fifty-three challengers (1990), twenty groups were occupationally based with, presumably, mainly private targets. Challengers with nonstate targets are not all so easily studied, though we think that the conceptual tasks remain the same—to identify beneficiary groups and potential collective goods and to attempt an estimation of actual gains. Some of these groups, like the Steel Workers Organizing Committee in Gamson's sample, were labor movements seeking concessions directly from employers. In many of these cases, the constituency of the challenger and the types and degrees of collective benefits are easily identified. In the case of labor movements organized by industry, all workers in the industry constitute the beneficiary group. Shorter working hours, better working conditions, increased job security, employment benefits, and, especially, higher wages are all standard collective goods sought by labor movements from employers and can be readily evaluated (Cohn 1993).

The same levels that apply for state benefits may hold for this sort of mobilization. Some concessions from employers may be of the one-shot brand of benefit and limited in impact. For instance, back pay for a period of work stoppage may be won, or discharged workers may be reinstated after pressure from the collective action of workers. At a higher level, structural reforms may be won that increase the likelihood of gaining future collective benefits as well as immediate gains. For instance, workers as a group may gain rights in decision making concerning the labor process or in investment decisions. At the middle level, workers may seek in a routine fashion contractual agreements insuring the provision of collective goods such as higher wage rates or improved benefit packages for all workers in a company or industry. As with state targets, it is at this level where most challengers bid for influence. In these relatively straightforward instances, all that remains is to ascertain how many of these concessions won from employers are attributable to the collective action of the challenger.

In collective campaigns against other nonstate targets, however, it is often far from obvious who should count as the beneficiary group, what should count as a collective good, and how such goods might be evaluated. Animal rights movements, for instance, constitute a special problem in identifying a constituency. Still, any analysis of impact would benefit from entertaining potential constituencies as a first step. Do animals count, or animal lovers? If one decides on animals, decreases in the harm done to animals would constitute the main collective benefit. If one decides on animal lovers, the perceived reduction of harm done to animals would be substituted. To further complicate matters, the targets of challengers—the persons or groups from which concessions are sought—can be many and varied. Animal rights movements often target businesses, private universities, and research institutions (Jasper and Nelkin 1992; Moore [this volume]). As with labor organizations, the concessions in these campaigns are likely to come directly from private targets, but they might also result from state intervention.

As is the case with state-oriented challengers, for challengers with non-state targets we would discount gains limited to movement organizations and participants. Access won from employers by union leadership does not automatically constitute a collective benefit. However, certain forms of institutionalized access might—such as collective bargaining rights implemented through democratic decision-making processes that include all workers in the industry, for the beneficiary group has been granted an influential role in determining its own working conditions. Of course, most occupationally based challenges, as well as animal rights movements, consumer activists, and environmental groups, have some mix of state and private targets. They may attempt to draw the state into their struggle with private targets in order to force concessions. In such cases, legislation that effects structural reforms favoring the beneficiary group in future dealings with the private target would be considered an impact of a high order.

Cultural Collective Benefits

In recent years the symbolic-expressive dimensions of challenges have come to the forefront, raising the question of the cultural impact of movements. Researchers claim that the development of a movement culture is a precondition to collective action (McAdam 1988; Melucci 1988; Tarrow 1992; Taylor and Whittier 1992). But most research concerning movements and culture also sees movements as vehicles for cultural change. As Doug McAdam (1994) argues, this research is devoted to showing that challengers may have a range of cultural effects, including transformations in belief systems or ideologies, new collective identities, innovative action repertoires, impacts on material culture (e.g., popular culture and language), and influences on the practices and culture of mainstream institutions (e.g., the curricula of universities). Each of these has implications for our collective goods criterion.

To illustrate the conceptual issues involved with studying cultural impacts, we focus on just one of these, new collective identities, which are sometimes seen as important consequences of collective action (Friedman and McAdam 1992; Inglehart 1990; Melucci 1989; Nagel 1995). After all, such identities are not necessarily confined to those participating in the challenge and may provide psychological rewards by countering shame and bolstering pride (Scheff 1994). Of course, new collective identities may not always be beneficial and might conceivably impose costs on a group by becoming the focus of a popular backlash against it or the cause of divisions that undermine subsequent bids for collective goods (Gitlin 1994). Needless to say, identifying and evaluating these benefits is more difficult than for some collective action, but not impossible. Although it may be difficult to assess the potential costs and benefits of a new collective identity, we believe it helpful for researchers at least to think through the potential costs and benefits that accompany new collective identities and other cultural impacts.

We also think researchers must establish that challengers have an impact on cultural patterns that extend past the network of movement participants. If alterations and innovations in shared identities are limited to circles of activists, then these changes are of limited impact. Through a network of local clubs, the Townsend Movement, for example, created something of a collective identity among its most avid followers. As Sheldon Messinger's study of the Movement in decline (1955) revealed, however, identification with the Townsend Movement remained narrowly confined to club members, centered on a weak hero worship, and did not extend to the beneficiary group. Although the Townsendite identity had very few implications beyond its challenge, this is clearly not true for, say, the black power or feminist movements. A rare example of a study that explores these wider ramifications is Joane Nagel's examination of the dramatic increase in Americans reporting an American Indian race in the census (1995). She argues that this resurgence in ethnic identity is, in part, the result of American Indian political activism.

Unlike pecuniary rewards from the state or material concessions from private targets, cultural impacts may be more closely delimited by the relationship between a challenger and its constituency than by a relationship with a third party. Collective identity is often considered self-reflexive in nature. However, we want to caution against ignoring the degree to which collective identities require a sort of ratification or affirmation from outside parties (Melucci 1985). Actors in civil society, particularly the mass news media (Gitlin 1980), as well as the state can be instrumental in the development of collective identities.

We suggest that the analysis of collective identity can be brought under an analytical scheme of levels of societal affirmation similar to the ones discussed earlier. At a low level, such affirmation may be episodic, with no long-term implications. At higher levels, affirmation becomes more routine and stable. We are not suggesting that affirmation in itself is a collective good. However, insofar as a challenger constructs a new collective identity that extends to a beneficiary group and provides psychological rewards such as pride, winning the affirmation of such an identity deserves attention as a potentially important concession. Finally, the identity sort of concession may be an important influence on subsequent collective benefits taking the form of pecuniary rewards or legal rights.

Establishing the Impact of Challengers: Methodological Issues

Studies of the impact of social movements need to go beyond specifying the benefits received by any group represented by challengers. Often neglected but also necessary are means to ascertain whether and the degree to which the mobilization and action of any challenger had an impact on collective benefits. Establishing a challenger's impact is straightforward in principle. It means to demonstrate that in the absence of the challenger, collective goods would not have appeared in the way that they did. The researcher has to show that the challenger realized the collective benefits, or the degree to which that might be true. We would argue that employing the language of "outcomes" of challengers tends to make people assume what needs to be established—that the challengers made an impact. Of course, not all researchers employing such language ignore causal issues (see, e.g., Giugni 1994; Kriesi et al. 1995). In the limited space remaining, we focus attention on analyzing the impact of state-oriented challengers.

Establishing the impact of a challenger, though seemingly simple, is an issue as complex as it is important. Challengers are rarely alone in pressing for collective benefits for a group and the effects of one challenger must be distinguished from the others. Other conditions may also influence outcomes beneficial to constituencies of challengers. Collective benefits may result for reasons that have little to do with challengers. This problem is troublesome in that economic crises or new political regimes may account for both the rise of challengers (McAdam, McCarthy, and Zald 1988) and what they attempt to effect. Research indicates, for instance, that various economic and political conditions and actors aside from challengers influence social spending policy (Huber, Ragin, and Stephens 1993). These other determinants have to be taken into account in assessing the impact of challengers on achieving collective benefits. It is possible, for instance, that when the United States or individual states adopted new programs benefiting the aged, the Townsend Movement did not cause them to happen. They may have been a result of other circumstances, such as the Depression itself or political changes.

The ways that the issue of establishing impact have been handled in the literature on social movements have not been completely satisfactory. Consider, one last time, Gamson's study (1990). He counts a challenger as having achieved new advantages merely if its agenda was mainly fulfilled within fifteen years of the challenge's demise. Calling a realized agenda a success without demonstrating that the organization made it happen, however, overstates the influence of a challenger. Declaring success in this way is the methodological equivalent of deeming phenomena that appear in similar times or places as challenges their "outcomes." It is always premature to make such a decision, for it disregards the potential that other conditions influenced both social protest and the collective benefits. Other researchers do worse by merely assuming that anything that happened somewhere close in time to a collective action campaign constitutes a result of it (see review in Burstein 1993). Often the connection is asserted by way of simple narrative devices on the order of, "Soon after the protests, Congress responded by . . ." Making such statements is like relying on bivariate correlations in causal analyses—not typically a satisfactory solution.

Gamson's pioneering research was constrained by his large number of cases and the need for devising consistent standards across all of them, and his project paid close attention to the views of movement participants and other contemporary actors engaged with particular challenges. Most contemporary researchers have neither such great constraints nor such high historical sensitivity. The tendency to attribute results to collective action without demonstrating that connection is mainly due to the fact that researchers are engaged in case studies (see Ragin and Becker 1992). Case studies in turn are typically beset by the so-called identification problem—too many potential causes chasing too few pieces of information (Lieberson 1991). For that reason, researchers of movement impacts need to employ techniques current in social science to extend case studies in order to make their claims more plausible. Most of these techniques employ historical or other comparisons (Giugni 1994).

Like any research involving causal statements, research on the impacts of challenges should be designed to appraise specific claims, either those devised by a researcher or those extant in the literature. To do this requires maximizing variation in the conditions deemed to be most influential (King, Keohane, and Verba 1994). Because theoretical arguments on the impact of challengers have lagged behind theoretical arguments concerning their mobilization, making precise methodological prescriptions is difficult. In research on state-oriented challengers, the claims that stand out most are the simple hypothesis that mobilization or collective action is effective in itself; that certain forms of mobilization or collective action are more effective than others (Gamson 1990); and, most of all, that combinations of specific forms of mobilization or action and specific political conditions are effective (Piven and Cloward 1977; Jenkins and Perrow 1977; McAdam 1982; Kitschelt 1986; Amenta, Carruthers, and Zylan 1992; Amenta, Dunleavy, and Bernstein 1994; Kriesi et al. 1995). For these sorts of claims, most standard methods for expanding the empirical dimensions of case studies seem applicable.

The most systematic way to ascertain the potential impact of challengers is by gaining information from a large number of ecological units (Snyder and Kelly 1979). Challengers typically attempt to have an influence in more than one place at a time; movements have been increasingly national and international in their scope. This approach relies on gaining information on variation in a movement organization's presence and activities, on other potential determinants of collective benefits, and on the benefits themselves. If information on each of these matters is available, all important potential causal conditions can be taken into account in attempting to explain variations in outcomes. Employing inferential statistical methods on these units makes it possible to assess the impact of a challenger relative to the impacts of other relevant conditions. For causal claims that are interactive or combinational, such as those described earlier, interactive specifications or like means should be employed. Such interactions can readily be modeled by way of qualitative comparative analysis (QCA), a technique that often can be employed in the absence of large numbers of cases (Ragin 1987, 1989; Amenta and Poulsen 1994). Either form of analysis can also incorporate a time dimension, as through pooled cross-sections and time-series or panel analyses or through time-sensitive measures for QCA.

Researchers with information on a smaller number of cases or with questions that cannot be easily addressed by large-scale research can always employ time-honored ways of making the most of these empirical materials (Amenta 1991). To appraise propositions, any number of small-N comparisons might be made. Some likely sorts include comparisons across units in which one challenger is mobilized, across challengers within a given unit, or across collective benefit outcomes in situations in which challengers are and are not mobilized or are mobilized in different ways. Making a choice among these sorts of comparisons would depend on the propositions being appraised.

In historical inquiries of the impact of one challenger, researchers can use some of the standard techniques in a limited way. These include juxtaposing the trajectory of the challenger's mobilization and collective action to outcomes of interest and, like Gamson, examining the views of participants, contemporary observers, and historians. A lack of a correlation between action and outcome probably would indicate a lack of impact. So, too, might a historical consensus that a challenger was ineffective. However, a positive correlation would not necessarily mean causation, and witnesses might be divided or biased in opinion. For these reasons, comparative methods are also typically needed.

We conclude this section with some observations about establishing the impact of a state-oriented challenger, our main subject. Analyses of the political process in the development of legislation can usefully be employed concerning the impact of social movements (Kingdon 1984; Burstein 1993). To make a convincing claim, any historical analysis would need to demonstrate that a challenger achieved one or more of the following: changed the plans and agendas of political leaders; had an impact on the content of proposals devised by executives, legislators, or administrators; or influenced disinterested representatives key to the passage of proposed legislation. Making such a case would require understanding political leaders' agendas and the content of legislative programs prior to challenges, and assessments of what legislators might have voted in the absence of the challenges.

Dividing new laws containing collective benefits into those components of the policy process simplifies analysis in ways that make it possible to judge the impact of challengers. If a challenger is successful in getting its issue onto the political agenda, we would argue that it has increased the probability that some collective benefits, whose value is unknown, will be incorporated in proposed legislation. As far as content is concerned, a challenger can work to increase the value of any collective benefits included in legislation on the issue. The type of collective benefit is also specified in a bill's content. Once a bill's content has been specified, moreover, challengers can influence individual legislators to vote for it and thus influence the probability of gaining specified collective benefits. To put it another way, a challenger's impact on any one of these processes would increase the expected value of collective benefits for the beneficiary group.

It follows that challengers might be effective in influencing some part of the process but fail to achieve new collective benefits. Getting an issue on the political agenda increases only the *probability* of action, and changing the content of a proposal influences only its *potential* value. Yet unless all three processes are negotiated successfully—placing the issue on the agenda, writing a bill with collective benefits, and passing the bill—no collective benefits will result. Even a successful negotiation of all three steps does not necessarily imply influence for a challenger, and very rarely is a social movement organization in a position to influence all of these processes. Thus, we are arguing that if a challenger influences the placement of an issue on the agenda, increases the collective benefits in extant legislation, or changes the probabilities that elected officials will support such legislation, each is a kind of beneficial impact in itself. It may, of course, be difficult to estimate the value of such partial victories.

Conclusion

In studies of social movements and contentious collective action, scholars have shown increasing interest in the results of social movements. After all, people engage in collective action at least ostensibly to gain collective benefits. All the same, studying the impact of social movements requires not only theoretical thinking that differs from that concerning mobilization, but also attending to new and difficult conceptual and methodological issues. Here we summarize the contrasts between the standard approaches to these issues and our own.

The first conceptual issue is to decide what counts as a significant impact. The standard view is to examine "success," as defined by new advantages and institutional access won by a challenger. In this view, new advantages are defined by the specific demands made by the challenger: the challenger is considered successful if the demands are mainly met, and unsuccessful if not. This definition, with its focus on specific social movement organizations, has the advantage of being relatively easy to understand and operationalize.

We advise instead, however, that researchers focus on potential collective goods in relation to the challenger's intended beneficiary group. This differs from the standard view, first, in that the only phenomena we consider to matter are new advantages. We do not consider the acceptance of a challenger as meaningful in itself, because, in itself, acceptance does not aid anyone and may lead to the selling out of the beneficiary group. By collective benefits, moreover, we mean groupwise goods from which it is difficult to exclude group members—the greater the value and type of such goods achieved by any challenge or challenger, the greater the impact.

Our collective benefits criterion has a number of implications. One of them is to examine a wider range of potential impacts than implied by the common understanding. According to that understanding, challengers succeed or fail. According to our point of view, challengers can gain greater or lesser collective benefits, but they also may cause collective bads for the represented group if collective action backfires. From our point of view, moreover, it is possible for a challenger to be completely successful in the standard sense but not have a major impact. Such would be the case if a challenger realized a program with only minor collective benefits. Correspondingly, a challenger that is mainly unsuccessful might have a large impact if the benefits inhering in the program were great but only partly achieved. Our standard is, of course, applicable to collective goods won by way of the state, but it also applies to benefits won from other targets and to cultural benefits such as collective identities.

The collective benefits standard also has implications for research. We suggest that researchers first think about the group that challengers represent. From there, researchers should examine the programs of challengers, separating the collective benefits from goals that are potential means to such ends and from goals that are only dubiously related to collective benefits. Researchers need to think hard, too, about potential collective benefits for the group not contained in the challenger's program.

Researchers must also go beyond the standard methodological strategies to ascertain the impact of challenges, which is typically assumed rather than demonstrated. The key methodological question to ask is what might have happened in the absence of the challenger. This problem is especially critical in studies of the impacts of challengers, because the conditions that influence challenges are likely to have some influence on the collective benefits for groups that challengers represent. Many standard social science methods can be employed to address this problem. In any historical analysis of collective benefits received from the state, moreover, we suggest that it is useful to separate the policy-making process into the components of agenda setting, the specification of the content of the legislation, and the enactment of proposal. This division makes it possible to analyze the degree of success of any challenger as well as the point in the process at which its impact took place.

None of these decisions, however, can substitute for theorizing about the impacts of challengers and social movements. Indeed, it is difficult to design research in the absence of theoretical propositions about such impacts. Nevertheless, theory and research on the impacts of social movements will no doubt advance the furthest and with the greatest speed by paying close attention to these conceptual and methodological issues.

Notes

We thank Vanessa Barker, Drew T. Halfmann, Kelly Moore, and the editors of this volume for comments and suggestions on a previous draft. This research was supported by National Science Foundation Grant SES-9210663.

3

The Impact of Social Movements on Political Institutions: A Comparison of the Introduction of Direct Legislation in Switzerland and the United States

Hanspeter Kriesi and Dominique Wisler

Political institutions have been considered the most stable elements of opportunity structures, almost beyond the reach of social movements. This is not surprising. The framers of political institutions purposely design them to last and make it difficult for challengers to change them. The stability and duration of institutions is a value in itself, since they allow for long-term planning. Moreover, institutions also have built-in mechanisms that make them self-perpetuating. They tend to generate patterns of beliefs and preferences that sustain them, because wants and desires are conditioned by the perception of available opportunities: by the mechanism of "adaptive preferences," one often dismisses as undesirable what is unattainable anyhow (Elster 1983, 1988: 311). Political institutions tend to channel preference formation into specific directions and to narrow the vision so that alternatives are not perceived as feasible. As Sunstein observes, the phenomenon of adaptive preferences joins with collective action problems to make significant change extremely difficult to achieve with respect to political institutions (1988: 351).

This is, of course, not to forget that political institutions have been a major area of contest in democracies. Our contribution will analyze one moment of the struggle for the institutionalization of democracy, namely, the struggle for direct legislation that constituted the main issue of the democratic movement in Switzerland during the 1860s and of its counterpart in the West of the United States from the 1880s to 1920. The case of direct democracy allows us to reflect more generally on the problem of how social movements achieve institutional change. We shall argue that institutional change implies a paradigmatic shift regarding the political system. Such a shift occurs only in periods of profound societal crisis, which open up the opportunity for fundamental social learning and the introduction of a new set of institutions, that is, a new political paradigm. This learning is, however, bound to people's past experiences, which is why, in order to impose itself, the new paradigm must "resonate" well with the political heritage of the past. Finally, we shall identify three additional conditions that facilitate institutional innovation and that have been crucial for the success of the democratic movements we are studying in this paper—federalism, the lack of institutionalization of the state, and the division of the political elite.

The Paradigmatic Shift and Its French Model

Institutional change constitutes a paradigmatic shift in the makeup of a polity. By analogy to Kuhn's argument about paradigmatic shifts in the history of science (1962), such a shift is triggered by "anomalies" that cannot be taken care of within the framework of the old paradigm, that is, established institutions. The paradigmatic shift institutionalizes a new set of rules that define a new framework for and establish a new era of "normal politics." In the case of direct democracy, the shift was from the old paradigm of "representative government" to the new paradigm of "direct legislation by the people."

The origins of this new paradigm go back to the ideas of Rousseau and Condorcet and their historical actualization in two successive constitutional projects of the French Revolution (Kölz 1992): the constitutions of the Girondists (February 1793) and of the Montagnards (June 1793). The Montagnard constitution had introduced a device for the legislative referendum whereby, for the first time, individuals rather than localities became the basis for the count of the vote. It is this mode of counting which truly echoed a new conception of citizenship and which constitutes the specificity of the modern paradigm of direct legislation (Kölz 1992; Curti 1885: 83). In the rapid course of revolutionary events, these constitutions were never implemented, and the Terror put an abrupt end to the new paradigm. Even if its flame was still kept alive by some French socialists, like Considérant and the review *La démocratie pacifique,* direct legislation became increasingly marginal in the French constitutional tradition and, according to Frei (1995), both constitutions came to be viewed as revolutionary utopias rather than practical solutions for the government of France.

However, the modern direct-democratic paradigm was given a new lease on life by two powerful social movements in Switzerland and the United States in the nineteenth century. These movements eventually succeeded in imposing this new paradigm in their respective polities. The 1860s constituted the crucial decade for the Swiss case, when the key canton of Zurich adopted what was later described as the most democratic constitution in Switzerland by introducing in a coherent way all direct legislation devices known at that time. Following the example set by the Swiss cantons and the Swiss federal government, the states west of the Mississippi adopted some of these instruments at the turn of the twentieth century.

Historiography describes the "democratic movement" in Switzerland as a social movement that used collective action to claim, above all, the right of direct legislation, especially the legislative initiative and the optional referendum in the 1860s. Other claims of the movement included the direct election of the executive and of government officials (such as judges and teachers), a tax reform, and the creation of a state bank. Although claims for more direct democracy had been made in Switzerland since the 1830s, those earlier movements were less successful and less extensive. Nevertheless, the so-called veto was first introduced in Saint Gall and Basel-Land as early as 1831–32.[1] Several cantons followed these examples in the early 1840s, but, according to Curti (1885), the wave was quickly stopped after the cantons dominated by liberals realized that the use of the veto could contribute to the fall of a liberal government, as it did in the case of Lucerne in 1841. A motion demanding the veto thus was turned down in Zurich in 1842. It was only in the 1860s that the democratic movement, a broad coalition of farmers, artisans, and workers, gained more momentum. After its initial success in the canton of Zurich in 1867–69, the paradigm of direct legislation spread decisively to the other cantons and, in 1874, was also introduced at the federal level.

In the United States, the movement for direct legislation started two decades later, in the 1880s, under the impulse of the populist movement, a coalition of farmers and workers. As in Switzerland, the referendum had already been used at the constitutional level—the constitution of Massachusetts was the first modern constitution to have been adopted by referendum, in 1778. Moreover, several states used the plebiscite, a referendum at the discretion of the authorities, for legislation from time to time. However, it was South Dakota that, under the impulse of the populist movement, first introduced the initiative and the referendum according to the new paradigm in 1898. Its example was followed mostly by states west of the Mississippi.

Two waves of direct-democratic constitutional amendments can be distinguished in the United States. The first impulse by the populist movement (1890s to 1920) was followed by that of the progressive movement at the turn of the twentieth century, a middle-class movement that made an attempt to replace corrupt practices and the patronage of political parties with "good government" reforms. In the struggle for direct democracy, Prohibitionists and suffragettes were usually allies during the first wave, and the movement was successful almost exclusively in states west of the Mississippi River (see, e.g., Price 1975). The second wave, which occurred during the 1870s, was linked to the rise of the new social movements. Although only Florida, Wyoming, and Illinois adopted some form of initiative during this second wave, direct democracy was also taken into consideration by many other states (Cronin 1989: 51).

The Crisis

Goldstone's reanalysis (1980) of Gamson's classical study (1975) found that social movement success is more likely in periods of crisis (e.g., major wars, economic or political crises). What applies to movements in general should be particularly true for movements making claims for institutional change. According to Siegenthaler, the core of an economic crisis is constituted by a loss of faith in the established set of rules (1993: 178). This loss of faith in the basic institutions of society does not bring about a crisis, but it is the characteristic feature of a crisis. It becomes probable as a consequence of increasing uncertainty, which is, in turn, a result of the distributional effects of stable economic development. In Siegenthaler's theoretical model, periods of structural stability are giving way to transitional or intermediary phases, crises in our terminology, when the structure, which is essentially a system of cognitive rules, becomes more malleable, processes of fundamental learning take place, and social organizations undergo change, are newly created, and relate to each other in unprecedented ways. In such periods, the institutional rules of the political system are subject to sharp conflicts and risk being changed. We cannot do justice here to this highly complex theoretical construct, but we believe that it provides an elaborate argument in support of the idea that institutional change is most likely to take place during periods of economic crisis.

Historical studies have well documented that both the Swiss democratic movement in the 1860s and the American populist movement in the 1890s arose in a period of deep economic crisis. Both movements grew out of an economic crisis that put an end to a period of considerable growth. The situation is described by Schaffner (1982) with regard to Zurich and by Blum (1977) and Epple (1979) with regard to Basel-Land, both crucial contexts for the development of the democratic movement. Schaffner draws attention to the profound social change that took place during the period of economic growth in the 1850s and early 1860s in the canton of Zurich. The expansion of the cotton and silk industries created new wealth but also an increasing industrial proletariat. In addition, the period of growth created new disparities between regions, especially between the city and the countryside, for example, in the context of the railroad question. Moreover, the transformations of the capital market profoundly changed the relationship between debtors and creditors. In the process, farmers lost their traditionally privileged position on the demand side of the capital market and were hard-pressed to adapt to its changing rules, which were no longer rooted in the rural world. In many ways, this period of growth undermined old certainties and created tensions that became fully apparent only at the moment of crisis.

This crisis in Zurich hit all sectors of society. As far as the farmers were concerned, they witnessed a series of bad harvests in the 1860s, which assumed catastrophic proportions in 1866–67. Rising interest rates, which were already at high mortgaging levels, and decreasing prices for grain put the farmers under enormous pressure. The two main industries of the canton—silk and cotton—also entered into a deep crisis starting in 1864, from which they recovered only in the early 1870s. The income levels of workers declined, and consumer prices went up at the same time. Finally, artisans suffered as well from the general lack of demand. Schaffner concludes, "The crisis concerned factory workers, day laborers, servants, farmers, and artisans all simultaneously" (1982: 133).[2] He argues that the "experience of the simultaneous setbacks in the primary and the secondary sectors sharpened the consciousness of the farmers, workers, and artisans who were hit by them for the profound transformations of their way of life, which had been going on for the last decades" (176).[3] In addition, the cholera epidemic of 1867, which coincided with the economic crisis in Zurich, not only aggravated the squalid living conditions of the urban working class but also drew the attention of a broader public to those living conditions and revealed in a most dramatic way the extent of social inequality.

As far as the American situation was concerned, Cronin states that the "boom-and-bust" cycles affecting frontier farmers and miners helped foment resentment toward elites in times of economic distress, sparking cries for economic and political reform (1989: 43). Such was the case with Daniel Shays's Rebellion, some Anti-Federalists, and, later, Jeffersonian Republicans and Jacksonian Democrats. The Grange, the Farmers' Alliances, single-taxers of the Henry George school, and the People's (Populist) Party were all populist-minded groups that became prominent in the period between 1875 and 1895, when prices for farm commodities dropped so low that in certain sections of the country farming was carried on at an actual loss:

These farmers and others suffering from economic hard times looked back to an earlier age when they believed they had been less exploited— a time when there were few millionaires and no beggars, few monopolies and no recessions. In short, the populist spirit was born of both nostalgia and genuine hope for a restoration of conditions prevailing before industrialism, large-scale corporate capitalism, and the commercialization of agriculture. . . . In the late eighties and early nineties the number of farm foreclosures skyrocketed. In some counties in Kansas, for example, 90 percent of the farms passed into the ownership of loan companies. The combination of denied credit, deeper debt, harsh taxation, and rising rail rates led the discontent to suspect a conspiracy by the moneyed interests of the country to enslave them in a web of economic servitude. (Cronin 1989: 44; see also Argersinger 1974)

Dibbern (1980), analyzing the social profile of the populist-minded farmers in one border county of South Dakota, found that, far from being nativists or the poor, they were usually immigrants who had arrived in the county during the great expansion of population and agriculture on the frontier in the 1880s. They became small property owners and invested heavily during the "boom" and the excellent climatic conditions of that period. Indebted as they were, these farmers fell victim to the "bust" caused by a subsequent decline in prices, population, and rainfall during the 1890s. "Without a successful harvest," Dibbern writes, "it was almost impossible for these farmers to meet their interest payments and to preserve their farms. Populism was rooted in this vulnerability" (1980: 214).

The crisis precondition is certainly crucial for those movements which Tarrow (1994) calls "early risers." For latecomers, as McAdam (1995) points out, the crisis may be less relevant, because other mechanisms come into play that facilitate the diffusion of a new political paradigm from one context to another.

Framing

Under conditions of liberal democracies, institutional change presupposes a process of social learning on the part of large sections of the population, except in the limiting case of a social revolution, where new institutions are imposed by force. This implies that ideas come to play a crucial role in the process (Hall 1993). As Siegenthaler (1993) has argued, a crisis increases the likelihood of fundamental learning of the required type. But, if it is likely that the crisis will give rise to a loss of faith in the established rules and to the widespread readiness for fundamental learning, it is by no means certain that the origins of the crisis can be attributed to the basic rules of the political game rather than to some elements of specific legislation or to the rules governing the economy or some other subsystem of society. Using Snow and Benford's distinctions between "diagnostic" and "prognostic" frames (1988), the old political paradigm is put into question only when people diagnose the problems they face as anomalies or deficiencies produced by the established political institutions and when they believe that the adoption of a new institutional paradigm will dramatically improve their situation. Elster has argued that consequential arguments for constitutional change—the "prognostic" frames—are likely to be speculative, because it is hard to know in advance the actual consequences of major institutional changes. This is why, he argues, a new political paradigm is typically justified by arguments from justice:[4] "If a reform is perceived as fundamentally just, people will be motivated to endure the costs of transition and the extensive trial and error procedures that may be required before a viable implementation is found" (1988: 319–20). Let us add, with Elster, that, like all norms, "those of justice and fairness are extremely context-dependent in the way they are interpreted and applied. They are, in particular, highly sensitive to framing and reframing" (316).

For the U.S. populist or progressive movement and the Swiss democratic movement, the diagnosis for the origins of the crisis was very similar. Both of them attributed the crisis to the deficiencies of the system of representative democracy. Both sought to overcome these deficiencies by the introduction of direct-democratic procedures, although other contemporary movements did not share these frames. To illustrate the framing in Switzerland, we shall restrict ourselves to the democratic movement in the canton of Zurich, which has been comparatively better studied than other cases. For the American case, we use generally secondary literature on the populist and progressive movements, in particular Cronin (1989).

The democratic movement in Zurich arose in a specific context. It mobilized against the liberals who had been governing the canton uninterruptedly for fifteen years. More specifically, it mobilized against the "system Escher," which took its name from the dominant liberal personality of the period, Alfred Escher, who not only was the head of one of the major banks and a crucial figure of the expanding railroad industry, but also was the dominant member of the Zurich government and a key figure in the federal parliament. Describing the "system Escher," an 1867 pamphlet of the Zurich democratic movement diagnosed the situation this way: "What kind of system is it that we are talking about? The system which brought to this canton the coalition of moneyed interests, credit powers and railroads, the clique and government behind the scene" (qtd. in Curti 1885: 219). Karl Bürkli, one of the leaders of the movement, defined it in these terms at one of the general assemblies organized by the movement:

> As "system" I understand the pernicious influence of the business interests, above all of the northeast railroad [dominated by Escher] which is their headquarters [and] the credit bank (also dominated by Escher). . . . The system, just like cholera, cannot be touched with your hands, but you can feel it in your limbs. If in 1830, the Uster day had to bring down an old, decaying, but legal city aristocracy, we have to topple now a new, luxuriantly growing, but illegal money aristocracy. (Qtd. in Gross 1983: 35)

Bürkli makes reference here not only to the cholera epidemic that was ravaging the Zurich population at the time, but also to the glorious days almost two generations before, when the liberal revolution had brought down the aristocratic regime that had been reestablished in Zurich after the defeat of Napoleon. Instead of "money aristocracy," democrats used the phrase "representative aristocracy," suggesting that the old aristocracy had in fact been substituted by a new aristocracy of big business interests that had captured the institutions of representative democracy. In a series of pamphlets, one of which sold more than 30,000 copies (in a polity with no more than 60,000 active citizens), the main agitator of the movement claimed that the republic had fallen prey to a clique of unscrupulous and greedy men who subordinated morality and justice to their own material interests (Schaffner 1982: 166 ff.).

The diagnoses made by the populist and progressive movements in the United States were very similar to the ones of their Swiss counterparts. Ray Billington characterized the populist perception of the situation in late 1870 as follows: "On the one side are the allied hosts of monopolies, the money power, great trusts and railroad corporations, who seek the enactment of the laws to benefit them and impoverish the people. On the other are the farmers, laborers, merchants, and all other people who produce wealth and bear the burdens of taxation" (qtd. in Cronin 1989: 44). Big business was framed as corrupting civil servants and legislators, and it was "a pathetic and tragic thing," as stated by the Wisconsin progressive Robert La Follette, "to see honest men falling before these insidious forces" (qtd. in Cronin 1989: 56), succumbing either to threats to their material situation or to the attraction of appointments to Washington jobs and bribes of money and women, even resorting to getting legislators drunk before a critical vote. Direct-democratic devices were thought to "diminish the impact of corrupt influences on the legislature, undermine bossism, and induce legislators to be more attentive to public opinion and the broader public interest" (Cronin 1989: 53). In a declaration issued to the citizens of San Francisco, who would eventually vote for the new city charter that introduced, in 1899, the initiative and the referendum at the city level, the Citizens' Charter Association asserted:

> We appeal to all good citizens to endorse the work of their freeholders elected last December and thus crystallize into low and honest effort to save San Francisco from the rule of the bosses, the water, lighting and railroad corporations and allied interests which have daily dealings with the city government and which have in the past and will in the future, unless they are restrained, debauch our politics, rob the people and paralyze the orderly operation of the law. (Qtd. in Oberholzer 1912: 352)

Direct legislation constituted the main plank of both movements' prognostic framing. Karl Bürkli wrote: "Where do we find the panacea against this [system]? We find it in direct legislation by the people, since the representative system was too permeable to the corrupt influences" (qtd. in Gross 1983: 33). Salomon Bleuler, another main exponent of the movement, used a pathological metaphor to frame the solution in his address to a general assembly in December 1867: "The extension of the people's rights hits the core and vital nerve of one of our main evils. It cuts through and destroys the one-sided economical interests, the superiority of one individual and his devout followers" (qtd. in Gross 1983: 28). The movement asked for the total revision of the constitution of the canton by a constituent assembly to be elected without delay by the citizens of the canton.

The paradigm of direct democracy was not invented by the democratic movement. As is observed by Ostrom, the particular set of rules that reformers contemplate "rarely contains all possible rules that might be used to govern an operational situation. The rules proposed are likely to be in a repertoire of rules already familiar to those who propose them" (1990: 209). In this sense, the structure of existing political institutions not only provides the incentive to look for alternatives but also constrains the possible search for alternatives. A similar idea is developed by Luthardt (1994). Thus, the new paradigm of direct legislation was inspired by older forms of direct democracy in Switzerland and in the United States and represented a modernization of those forms of government rather than a completely new invention. It had a high "narrative fidelity," because it resonated well with "the stories, myths, and folk tales that are part and parcel of one's cultural heritage and thus function to inform events and experiences in the immediate present" (Snow and Benford 1988: 210). As Kölz (1992) has documented, the liberal Swiss reformers of the 1830s and 1840s, who had already experimented with direct-democratic devices and had introduced rudimentary elements of direct legislation, such as the popular "veto" in some member states of the Swiss confederation, took their models from the constitutions of the French Revolution, without, however, explicitly acknowledging their sources. Neither did the French revolutionaries, in turn, create ex nihilo the paradigm of direct democracy. As we have already seen, it was the state of Massachusetts that first adopted a democratic constitution, in 1787, by referendum. Moreover, many authors (see, e.g., Auer 1989) attribute the resonance of direct-democratic procedures in the U.S. member states to earlier forms of town meetings in New England and to the Calvinist ideology of "common consent." Thus, leaders of the populist movement framed the new paradigm not so much as a new form of government but much more as a "restoration" of an older kind of self-government in the United States.

In Switzerland, the democratic movement radicalized liberal ideas and tied its claims for direct democracy to the older heritage of popular myths about the direct-democratic general assemblies *(Landsgemeinden)* in Alpine cantons and the general councils in city cantons such as Geneva, Lucerne, Fribourg, and Saint Gall (Battelli 1932).[5] The liberals and radicals had rejected this older Swiss tradition of general assemblies. As Kölz points out, they were afraid of political fragmentation, since in larger cantons only decentralized assemblies would have been possible (1992: 628). Moreover, they were skeptical about the readiness of the people to accept their progressive ideas. Finally, they wanted a strictly individualistic, liberal, and secularized democracy, not a cooperative or communal one. By contrast, the democratic movement explicitly built on the indigenous republican tradition. If Bürkli, "the most conscious protagonist" of the new paradigm (Curti 1885: 216), was also heavily influenced by the French constitutional models and by the ideas of such French socialists of the 1840s as Considérant, he and his colleagues also revived the memory of the traditional assembly democracies that had survived the aristocratic regimes of the seventeenth and eighteenth centuries and that provided an important emotional and ideological support for the democratic movement (Kölz 1992: 629). The ideologues of the democratic movement tried to frame the new paradigm as nothing but a modernization of tradition. Thus, Karl Bürkli wrote that "the old democracy, which had been taken away from the people by monarchist ignorance and blind faith in priests [*Pfaffenglauben*] should be won back by reason and science and modernized according to the changing times" (qtd. in Gross

1983: 39). It is no accident that the movement used the commemoration of the Uster day on November 22, 1867, to launch its campaign for a new constitution. And it is also no accident that it organized a series of public assemblies, which culminated, in December 1867, in four large general assemblies, called *Landsgemeinden* by proponents.

In Switzerland, as in the United States, direct democracy was perceived as a means to solve the problems created by the deficiencies of representative democracy. In both countries, the movements claiming direct democracy made similar additional demands, such as the creation of a state or cantonal bank to alleviate the credit squeeze of the farmers. In both countries, the respective movements created similar images of their adversaries: they mobilized against the world of "the boss," "the money," and "corruption." According to the imagery of both movements, the representative political system did not work either because it was in the hands of an oligarchy, a money elite—as symbolized in Zurich by the "system Escher"—or because it was responsive to powerful interest groups, such as the Southern Pacific Railroad Company in California. Direct democracy was seen as the only means to rectify the failure of the representative political system to address the needs of the people. The aim of direct democracy was to put an end to the influence of "the boss" on the political system (see Möckli 1994: 176–77).

The contrast between Swiss and U.S. socialists, on the one hand, and socialists from countries where direct democracy did not have any roots in political tradition, on the other hand, serves to illustrate our point about the crucial importance of the cultural resonance of a new master frame: while the former were optimistic about the possibilities for introducing social reforms by direct legislation and saw the referendum and the initiative as "bridges to the new world," the latter were much less sanguine about the promises of direct democracy and less inclined to attribute the predicament of the working class to the malfunctioning of the representative system. Thus, Karl Bürkli was rather isolated when he advocated direct legislation at the Fourth Congress of the International Workers' Association, held at Basel in September 1869 (Gross 1983: 40–41). Direct democracy was not officially debated at this congress and was discussed only in the Friday evening session at the very end of the congress week. The proposal was sharply attacked by the Belgian delegates, who maintained that the concept was not adapted to the Belgian and French political contexts and that socialists should not contribute to the legitimacy of those governments by participating in their politics. Although direct democracy had become part of the social democrats' program in Germany in the 1860s, Bürkli considered this development to be nothing but "decoration" (qtd. in Hernekamp 1979: 234). Direct legislation was in fact opposed by the fathers of the movement: Marx called it the "old world-wide known democratic Litanie," Engels saw in it nothing but "pure fashion," and Kautsky warned about the reactionary and conservative results of such devices (qtd. in Heussner 1994: 58). By contrast, the socialist movement in the United States was instrumental in bringing about institutional change at the state level, and direct democracy was adopted in the national platforms of the Socialist Labor Party as early as 1885 (Heussner 1994: 44) and the American Federation of Labor in 1902 (Cronin 1989: 164–65).

Structural Conditions

How was it possible that these movements could successfully impose the new paradigm? We believe that it was not enough for the claims of the movements to resonate well with the political culture of the U.S. and Swiss contexts. In addition, they met with similar political opportunity structures, which facilitated their success considerably but which were absent in other countries where the direct-democratic paradigm did not get implemented. We shall deal with two aspects of this political opportunity structure— federalism and the degree of institutionalization of the state.

Federalism

First of all, the federalist structure of Switzerland and the United States provided crucial opportunities for both of these movements. Generally, we argue that a federalist state structure reduces the start-up difficulties for a social movement attempting to change political institutions. Federalist decentralization constitutes a case of segmental differentiation based on territorial criteria. This type of differentiation implies that the different subsystems all fulfill the same functions. Moreover, they do so within the same overarching institutional framework, which is to say that they all function in more or less analogous ways. For purely probabilistic reasons, it is more likely that the conditions that facilitate the success of a movement for institutional change will be met in any one of the parallel subsystems of a federalist state than in the unique system of a unitary state. A social movement favoring institutional change may periodically monitor the behavior of the authorities in the different places and test the strength of their resistance to the new paradigm. The multiplication of parallel access points to the political system increases the likelihood that the system will yield at one point or another. This likelihood is increased by the possibility that the pressures exerted by social and economic conditions may be particularly strong in the context of a given subsystem. We have seen, for example, that in Zurich the economic crisis of the 1860s was accompanied by a cholera epidemic that contributed to the grievances of the population and sharpened its awareness of the desolate state of the local working class. This coincidence was unique to Zurich, and it would have mattered less had Zurich not had its own political system, which could be made directly responsible for the situation.

Moreover, it is the smaller scale of each one of the member states of a federalist state that facilitates the mobilization and the eventual success of a social movement. This, of course, was especially true in the nineteenth century, when transportation and communication were not as easy as today. As Schaffner reports, the contentious gatherings of the democratic movement in the canton of Zurich assembled no less than 15,000 people, about a fourth of the citizens having the right to vote (1982: 43). The petition that its leaders presented to the Zurich government at the end of 1867 was signed by 27,000 citizens. This enormous level of mobilization would not have been possible in a larger polity with the problems of larger distances and longer communication lines to surmount. In the absence of mass communications, telephones, and the Internet, people had to meet physically in order to give expression to their opposition to the government, to become informed about the new program, and to debate the proposals made by the leaders of the movement.[6]

If initial success for a member state of a federalist state is more likely than for that of a unitary state, the federalist structure also provides an opportunity for the *diffusion* of this initial success. With Ostrom, we would stress the incremental, self-transforming nature of institutional change: "Success in starting small-scale initial institutions enables a group of individuals to build on the social capital thus created to solve larger problems with larger and more complex institutional arrangements" (1990: 190). In other words, institutions that build on past experience and have been proven to work in similar contexts are more likely to be adopted than institutions that have not been used before. The federalist structure of the state allows this kind of small-scale experiment (see Aubert 1983), and the success of a movement in one context increases the likelihood that it will succeed in other, similar contexts within the federalist structure as well. In other words, the successful implementation of a new set of institutions in one context increases the "empirical credibility" of the new paradigm in other, similar contexts. As it has been defined by Snow and Benford, "empirical credibility" refers to the "fit between the framing and events in the world" (1988: 208). With Snow and Benford, we may grant that what constitutes empirical evidence for any particular claim is itself subject to debate. However, this does not imply that events are completely insignificant for the interpretative success of one paradigm over the other, as Gamson seems to suggest (1992: 69–70).[7] If citizens in a neighboring, very similar political system are able to participate in direct-democratic procedures, and if the political system is not destabilized by this innovation but rather becomes more stable by its introduction, it will be increasingly difficult for adherents of the old paradigm to argue to the contrary. The success of an "initiator" movement in one context has two additional effects on similar kinds of movements in other contexts of the federal state: they are put under pressure to achieve the same goal, and, at the same time, they learn from the successful movement how to go about doing this. As in Goertz's barrier model of diffusion (1994), we may expect that once the barrier of resistance against the new institutions has broken down in one context, its breakdown becomes much more likely in other, similar contexts and the new institutions are likely to spread rapidly to all of them.

The spread of the new direct-democratic paradigm in Switzerland confirms these expectations. Zurich was not the first canton to introduce the new instruments, but Zurich was unique for the scope of direct-democratic procedures it introduced. The success of the democratic movement in the canton of Zurich proved to be decisive for the further spread of the new paradigm to other cantons. Right after the adoption of the new constitution in the canton of Zurich in 1869, Thurgau, Solothurn, Bern, and Lucerne followed its example, and Aargau adopted a similar set of direct-democratic institutions the following year (see Gmürr 1948). Other cantons followed in the 1880s and 1890s. As we have already pointed out, in 1874, the optional referendum was introduced at the federal level, too.

In the U.S. case, a number of authors have pointed out the importance of local autonomy, newly acquired by cities, for the spread of direct-democratic procedures (Möckli 1994: 175). Auer found that decentralization and the adoption of the "home-rule" principle by states in the late nineteenth century was crucial for the development of direct democracy: "In the West everything seems to have begun in local communities and, more specifically, in big cities when they acquired, or better, conquered a certain level of organizational autonomy which freed them from the grip of the state" (1989: 111–12). Indeed, the first forms of initiatives are to be found at the local level in the United States. Oberholzer mentions many examples (1912: 387–88). Thus, Iowa introduced direct-democratic instruments first at the county level in 1897. Cities in Nebraska adopted the initiative and the referendum in 1898, fourteen years before analogous legislation was passed at the state level. Similarly, in California, direct legislation had been introduced at the county level (1893) and in fourteen home-rule cities between

1898 and 1910, before such legislation was adopted at the state level in 1911 (Key and Crouch 1939: 428).

Let us, finally, note that the Swiss example was instrumental for the spread of direct democracy in the American West. Rappard (1912: 129–32) counted more than a hundred writings published in the United States on the Swiss case between 1883 and 1898. One book was particularly influential in diffusing the new paradigm in the United States: J. W. Sullivan's *Direct Legislation by the Citizenship through the Initiative and Referendum*, published in 1893. Sullivan was a socialist leader and journalist who had studied direct democracy in Switzerland during two prolonged stays and returned to write a series of articles about the initiative and refendum from 1889 through the early 1890s. According to Cronin, "Sullivan was convinced that direct legislation was not an impractical, utopian scheme—*it worked there,* and he believed it would work well in the United States" (1989: 48). In other words, the Swiss experiment enhanced the empirical credibility of direct-democratic devices and "proved" that direct democracy was feasible even outside Switzerland. The positive results of direct democracy were clearly overstated by Sullivan, but the Swiss example contributed to the attractiveness of the new paradigm in the United States.[8]

Lack of Institutionalization of the State

Another striking similarity between the states of the United States and the Swiss cantons at the time of the democratic movements concerns their lack of institutionalization, in Badie and Birnbaum's sense of the term (1982). This implies, first of all, that both states and cantons were (and still are) very permeable to the influence of outside (mainly economic) interests. This was true for the Eastern states, too (see McCaffery 1993: 153–59), but it was particularly flagrant in the West, where the monopolistic railway companies exercised a tremendous power on legislatures and governors (Key and Crouch 1939; Shefter 1994). Moreover, the U.S. "spoils system" or "patronage state," which was attacked by the populist and progressive movements, made the administration dependent on the political parties ("machines"). The progressive movement in California was as much an "antimachine" movement as a movement for good government. This kind of state was vulnerable to charges of corruption and to the claim that the legislature should be made more accountable to the people through direct-democratic devices. In Switzerland, it was this lack of state autonomy that made the "Escher system" possible and that increased the government's vulnerability with respect to the framing of the democratic movement. More institutionalized states, such as France, or Germany since 1871, had a more independent, coherent,

and professional bureaucracy, which was better insulated from both monopolistic interests and the patronage of political parties. These strong states
were much less vulnerable to corruption frames (see Curtius 1919: 23).

But a weak state is not only more vulnerable to charges of corruption
and to claims for direct popular legislation, it is also less able or ready to resort to repression in order to defend itself against challenging movements.
Thus, a Swiss police intelligence was not developed before the turn of the
century and, when it did develop, was a concession, made reluctantly, to
pressures exercised by Bismarck to control foreign revolutionaries in Swiss
territory (Liang 1992: 10). It was not, at first, oriented toward local social
movements. The situation was certainly very similar in the new western
states of the United States. By contrast, France and Prussia had developed
early professional police forces, and they were better able to control ideas as
well as movements (see Liang 1992). Basically, in the 1860s, the only repressive force at the disposal of cantonal authorities in Switzerland was the local
militia—not a very dependable force in the face of a massive popular rebellion. Up to the 1840s, armed revolts against the capital, violent demonstrations, and bloody fights had belonged to the action repertoire of intracan-
tonal politics in Zurich and many other regions in Switzerland. Thus, in
1839, the government, solidly liberal at the time, had been toppled by an
armed rebellion of the countryside, against which it had been quite defenseless. By the 1860s, this type of political violence had disappeared from the
politics of most cantons, although it still existed in Geneva. However, memories of these events were still fresh, and the cantonal governments may not
have been sure about the readiness of the democratic movement to resort to
such tactics.

With the lack of coercive means and the fear of losing control over elections, the dominant strategy of the cantonal governments with respect to
political opponents was integrative. They tried to make limited concessions
and to co-opt the leaders of the social movements. This is illustrated by the
case of Johann Jakob Treichler, a leading socialist opponent of the 1840s and
1850s in Zurich. Treichler was co-opted into the government of the "Escher
system" and was, in fact, its president at the time when his former friend
Karl Bürkli headed the democratic movement in the late 1860s. Another example is the reaction of the Zurich government to the first campaign of the
democratic movement in 1863. Faced with considerable popular unrest, the
government declared its readiness to revise the cantonal constitution, but
once the revolt subsided, it took its time with the revision and finally introduced some limited changes that did not make any direct-democratic concessions and left the representative system essentially intact. This revision

was adopted by a popular vote in fall 1865. But the integrative dominant strategy is also illustrated by the governing liberals' reaction to the new, much more important campaign of the democratic movement in late 1867. Without delay, the liberal majority of the cantonal parliament accepted the movement's petition asking for the total revision of the cantonal constitution and fixed the date for a referendum about this question on January 26, 1868! Even if we grant that the governing elite seems to have miscalculated its chances in the popular vote (Craig 1988: 271), this was an extraordinary concession. As it turned out, the overwhelming majority of the citizens accepted the principle of the total revision and the call for a constituent assembly. The governing liberals still counted on winning the election of this assembly in spring 1868, but they got only about a third of the seats, while the democrats won enough seats to capture the presidency of the assembly and a majority in the committee that was to draw up the actual text. The final document, which implemented all of the demands of the democratic movement, was ratified in a popular vote in April 1869.

The fact that the states west of the Mississippi were almost the only ones to adopt direct-democratic devices in their constitutions (Cronin 1989: 47) is remarkable and may be partially explained in terms of their lack of institutionalization. These states were much younger than the eastern states, and their representative systems seem to have been penetrated to a greater extent by business interests. In fact, as in California, the Southern Pacific Railroad Company exercised a tremendous leverage on politics. According to Shefter, "The most powerful force in state politics during this period [the last decades of the nineteenth century] was not a party organization, but rather the Southern Pacific Railroad. The most influential political figure in California was not a party boss, but rather the head of the railroad's Political Bureau" (1994: 179). These states probably also lacked a strong civil service because of the youth of their institutions. Cronin attributes the adoption of direct legislation in these states to their "young age" and asserts that the eastern states could prove that the representative system had worked (1989: 165). In other words, according to Cronin, the representative systems of the western states could not count on an established state tradition and were, in that sense, much more vulnerable to the new paradigm.

In conclusion, the movements for direct democracy in the second part of the nineteenth century were more successful in poorly institutionalized states, which were more vulnerable to the new paradigm of direct legislation than states that had already acquired a stronger autonomy vis-à-vis business interests as a result of both the professionalization of politicians and the establishment of a strong and independent bureaucracy. The lack of institutionalization of the Swiss and U.S. member states made the diagnostic frames of the democratic and populist/progressive movements more credible. By contrast, given the high degree of institutionalization of the state in France and the strong French parties, it is no wonder that the only direct legislation that France has ever implemented has been initiated by the top in the form of the plebiscite, destined to legitimate the power in place rather than to bypass it (see Frei 1995; Luthardt 1994).

The Weakness of Political Parties and Elite Divisions

If lack of institutionalization makes a state more vulnerable to institutional change, such change becomes possible only if it is claimed by a social movement able to mobilize on a broad enough scope to impose it on the established political elites. Although it seems trivial, it is important to point out that, under conditions of liberal democracies, institutional change implies that a majority of the population is ready to support it. In other words, movements calling for institutional change need to be able to mobilize very broadly. This is possible only if the established political elite proves unable to control the masses of the citizenry. We maintain that, in liberal democracies, such a loss of control is most likely if the following two conditions are met: the political parties are weak and, thus, unable to integrate the masses into established channels of interest intermediation; and the political elite is internally profoundly divided and one of its segments stands to profit from an institutional change. Under these two conditions, the segment of the political elite favoring institutional change—the counterelite—may be tempted to bypass the arena of representative democracy, to appeal directly to the masses, and to mobilize them in a social movement.

The first condition was met by the western member states of the United States and by all the Swiss cantons. With respect to the second condition, we may note in the Swiss case that the call for direct democracy came from two types of counterelites: a conservative and a progressive one (Gilg 1951: 28). On the one hand, the conservatives no doubt hoped that, given the widespread conservatism of the people, the concessions made with respect to direct-democratic procedures would bring them long-term advantages at the polls.[9] On the other hand, it is conceivable that some progressive democrats not only wanted to increase the power of the people but also pursued some more opportunistic goals: they may have calculated that breaking the power of the money aristocracy by the introduction of direct-democratic devices not only could reinforce popular sovereignty but also could be instrumental for the electoral success of the progressive leadership that led the way in introducing them. In the American case, there is a correlation between the rise of the progressive movement and the 1896 change from a two-party to a single-party system (Shefter 1994: 75). Excluded from power, the counter-elite looked to social movements for an alternative to regain control of the political process.

The Weakness of Political Parties

In the case of the democratic movement of Zurich, we have seen that the crisis hit all sectors of society. This means that there was a latent potential for mobilization that extended to almost the entire population. On the basis of this widespread discontent and armed with its powerful master-frame, the movement was able to mobilize enormously. In fact, the movement mobilized the entire society. Everybody took part in the conflict: while participation in parliamentary elections had been down to no more than a third in the 1850s, the election of the constituent assembly in 1868 mobilized no less than 94 percent of the citizens. This mobilization was based on a network spanning the whole gamut of cultural and political associations of the time (Schaffner 1982: 43): monthly, Sunday, and Monday reading societies, permanent residents', elderly, and artisans' associations, and communal and district associations. There were also so-called political associations, the precursors of the future party organizations, the formation of which was sped up by the democratic movement. Schaffner counts no fewer than seventy-five assemblies organized by these associations in the three-month period between November 1867 and January 1868. In these "micromobilization contexts," the adherents of the movement met to form an opinion and to deliberate about the new paradigm. These assemblies constituted the "reasoning public" as it is conceived in the structural model of Habermas ([1962] 1990).

Even more important, perhaps, is the fact that the democratic movement was the first, according to Gruner (1968), to have developed a political "machine," that is, an organization designed to control the votes on a broad basis. Political parties in Zurich and in Switzerland in general had not yet developed their own organizational apparatus and rarely held conventions. Thus, it was only after their defeat in the 1868 elections that the liberals engaged in a process of counterorganization and created workers' associations. The introduction of direct-democratic devices in Swiss cantonal and federal constitutions accelerated this process of party building; thus, in the words of Gruner, political parties are truly "children of direct legislation" (1968: 581).

According to Shefter (1994), the weakness of political parties and their lack of organizational development before the rise of the populist and progressive movements is a major factor explaining the success of reforms for direct legislation in the United States, too. He argues that the success of the progressive movement in the western states of the United States was a result of the fact that, contrary to the situation in the East, political parties had not yet developed into strong and broad-based organizations. Shefter shows that before the crucial election of 1896, both abstention and the volatility of the votes were high in the western but low in the eastern states, where mass-based political machines were able to control the votes. In other words, in the West the populists and the progressives moved into a vacuum, whereas these movements proved unable to destroy the heavy political machines against which they mobilized in the East. Moreover, as is claimed by Clemens (1997), the party-centered system in the East also limited the impact of interest groups. In the West, the same interest groups could contribute, at a particular historical moment, to a broad movement for reform. Here, feminists, workers, and farmers, as well as specific business interest groups, flourished and constituted the organizational base for a strong movement that would mobilize successfully against the weak political machines.

Elite Divisions

The democratic movement of Zurich was led by a segment of the established political elite. At its head we find the ex-chancellor of the canton, Johann Jakob Sulzer, who became the president of the constituent assembly, and Salomon Bleuler, the editor in chief of the *Landboten,* the second newspaper of the canton. Among the leaders of the movement were several pastors and conservatives from the countryside, but it also had a very active left wing with, among others, Karl Bürkli (Craig 1988: 268–69). Based on the composition of the constituent assembly, we may note, with Schaffner, that the large majority of its members had already held a political office, either on the cantonal, district, or communal level (1982: 71 ff.). Moreover, the majority of those who had not yet held such an office were practitioners of the liberal professions—physicians, veterinarians, pastors—or were civil servants, teachers, or millers. Given that the constituent assembly was dominated by the democrats, these data indicate that the leaders of the movement represented a political counterelite that was already well integrated into the political system, rather than "new men" rising from below. The leaders of the movement constituted nothing else but the political opposition of the government dominated by the liberals. After the adoption of the new constitution, this counterelite won the cantonal elections of 1869 and was to dominate the cantonal government for the next ten years. In fact, as is pointed out by Craig (1988: 275), once the question of direct democracy was settled, the remaining differences between the liberals and the democrats were minor ones, apart from the fact that they were led by different personalities (1988: 275). Both parties were oriented toward the center, and both lacked a penchant for ideological polarization. In this sense, the Zurich democratic movement is a case of a deeply divided political elite, with the opposition having recourse to the mobilization of the masses in order to reinforce its own position and being able to mobilize on an impressive scale, given the lack of party organizations allowing the dominant part of the politial elite to control the masses.

In other cantons, direct legislation was supported by the Conservative Party in the opposition. Deploige mentions the case of Bern, where the radical majority had voted for subsidies for new railroads that exceeded the ordinary revenue of the state. The conservative minority thereupon called for the introduction of the financial referendum, with the explicit goal being to prevent any further increase of the budget deficit (1898: 83). Similarly, Epple (1997) points out that the democratic movement in Basel-Land combined its call for direct-democratic instruments with a call for tax cuts. Its goal was not only to save money but also to prevent the expansion of the cantonal state. The first attempt to introduce direct-democratic instruments in Zurich, in 1842, was actually made by the conservatives, who had just overthrown the radical government three years before. The conservatives in Zurich were determined to follow the lead of their conservative colleagues in Lucerne, who had successfully introduced the veto against the opposition of the liberals, who regarded the institution as reactionary.

Elite divisions have also been an important factor in the United States, and historiography traditionally describes the progressive movement in terms of the rise of a counterelite (see Clemens 1997). This movement split both the Democratic and the Republican Parties. Many prominent Democrats, such as Woodrow Wilson, supported its call for direct legislation. One important reason for the Democrats' support of direct legislation was its appeal to organized labor. The Democrats believed that they would be able to preempt socialism by implementing reforms for "good government" (Auer 1989).[10] In the 1896 presidential elections, the Democrats also supported the "silver movement" in an attempt to co-opt the populist movement, which by that time was controlled by the silver populists (Argersinger 1974). The movement for "good government" also split the Republican camp. In fact, one of the movement's precursors was the mugwumps, who constituted a wing of the Republican Party. In California, the progressive movement developed as a wing of the Republican Party and eventually took control of that party.

Shefter (1994) argues that until the emergence of the single-party system after the 1896 elections, progressives could play off one party against the other and try to implement reforms from within the two parties. However, with the emergence of the Republicans as the dominant party, the progressive counterelite was basically excluded from power, and it was this very exclusion that led it to look for alternatives outside and against the party system. "The emergence of a one-party regime after the election of 1896," Shefter observes,

> rendered the minority party useless as a vehicle through which individuals and groups without preferential access to the dominant party could challenge those within it; it was now impossible for them to pursue a balance-of-power strategy akin to the one the Mugwumps had employed. The political actors who found it impossible to advance their interests within the party system were joined together by the Progressives in an attack upon the party system. (1994: 76)

The progressive movement attracted these reform politicians who had been excluded from power and outsiders who did not benefit from the patronage system. The composition of the latter varied from state to state. They could be "shippers in states where the party was tied to a railroad, . . . firms that sold in national markets in cities where the machine was tied to businesses that sold in local markets, [or] . . . native middle classes where the party drew support from the ethnic working classes" (Shefter 1994: 76). They could also include workers (who were more or less equally excluded everywhere), suffragists (who lacked the right to vote in all the states), and farmers (Clemens 1997: 94).

Even more generally, at the turn of the century, party identifications were weakened by the fact that, after territorial expansion and industrial growth, the regional and the class bases of the two parties crosscut one another. As a result, "strains within the parties accumulated and undermined old loyalties and practices as the nineteenth-century party system was stretched to encompass new groups, new demands, and new techniques" (Clemens 1997: 23).

Conclusion

In our attempt to account for the rare occasions when social movements have brought about institutional change, we have followed Smelser's "value added" logic (1963). According to this reasoning, such change becomes possible only if a number of restrictive conditions are jointly fulfilled. We have developed the argument on the basis of a comparative analysis of the social movements that have successfully mobilized for the introduction of direct-democratic legislation in Switzerland and in the United States. The first condition for social movements to be able to transform political institutions is a societal crisis (typically an economic crisis) predisposing large parts of the population to fundamental social learning. The second condition consists of a master-frame that provides the citizens with a credible alternative to the existing set of institutions. We have argued that such a frame is particularly convincing if it succeeds in tying the new political paradigm, that is, the blueprint for the new institutions, to the cultural heritage of the population in question—if, in other words, it succeeds in presenting the nonincremental nature of the change as an incremental adaptation to changing conditions. Third, we have stated the obvious by pointing out that the success of the movement demanding institutional change crucially depends on the vulnerability of the existing institutions. According to our argument, federal systems and weakly institutionalized states are generally more vulnerable and therefore provide greater opportunities for institutional change than unitary and strong states. Finally, we have added that the movement for institutional change develops momentum only if the established elites prove unable to control the masses. We argue that this final condition crucially depends on the existence of both a split in the political elite and the weakness of political parties. Weak political parties fail to integrate the masses of citizens into established channels of interest intermediation, and divisions within the political elites weaken the control of the governing elite over the mobilizing masses and provide those masses with the ability to impose their claims for institutional change.

Notes

1. The veto was different from the referendum mainly in that the votes against a piece of legislation that was passed were counted as a percentage of the electorate and not of the turnout.

2. Here and in subsequent quotations, we have translated the original German text.

3. The same is argued by Epple with regard to the canton of Basel-Land: the agriculture, silk, and transportation trades—the three major economic sectors of this canton—found themselves in a structural crisis that was aggravated by conjunctural setbacks. The farmers were highly indebted and suffered from lack of credit and competitive pressures, the makers of silk lace in the putting-out system were hit by lack of work and income, and the transportation trade was about to lose its existing base with the spread of the railroads. The regions most concerned by the economic crisis—Sissach and Waldenburg, in the upper region of the canton—were also the ones that, according to Epple, mobilized most in favor of the democratic movement in this canton (1979: 112ff.).

4. As is observed by Sunstein, "The distinction between consequential arguments

and arguments from justice is hardly clear at all. Sometimes consequential arguments are arguments from justice, and vice versa" (1988: 350).

5. The general council was an assembly of citizens that voted on important matters and, as in Geneva, elected the four mayors of the city. As is convincingly argued by Liebeskind ([1938] 1973, 1952), the Genevan General Council was the inspiration for Rousseau's concept of the "general will" that became prominent in the French Revolution.

6. Today, this advantage of a federalist state may be less important, and it may be more relevant that the critical mass of people who are willing and able to contribute to collective action is, not only proportionately but also in absolute terms, smaller in a larger group than in a smaller one. The paradox of group size discussed by Marwell and Oliver states that "when groups are heterogeneous and a good has high jointness of supply, a larger interest group can have a smaller critical mass" (1993: 49).

7. As Gamson maintains, "It is not events that overcome frames but rival frames that do better at getting their interpretations to stick" (1992: 70).

8. Cronin: "Sullivan overstated the success of the Swiss initiative and referendum, yet in doing so he stirred the imaginations of would-be reformers in America. For Sullivan, the Swiss had 'rendered bureaucracy impossible' and shown the parliamentary system not essential to lawmaking: '. . . they have forestalled monopolies, improved and reduced taxation, avoided incurring heavy public debts, and made a better distribution of their land than any other European country'" (1989: 48).

9. This is an instance of an exchange of short-term concessions for long-term advantages, as discussed by Rothstein (1990, 1992).

10. A progressive editorial quoted by Auer (1989: 88) suggested around 1910 that "the conservatives blindly fight against socialism, while the progressives fight it intelligently by trying to improve the abuses and conditions which feed it."

4

Protest, Protesters, and Protest Policing: Public Discourses in Italy and Germany from the 1960s to the 1980s

Donatella della Porta

Public Discourse on Protest and the Effects of Social Movements

A main effect of social movements is their ability to focus the attention of the elites and public opinion on the issue of protest rights. By definition, social movements aim at producing or resisting changes in their environment. Social movements do not limit themselves to challenge public decisions, but they often criticize the ways in which decisions are taken, asking for more citizen participation in decision making (see, e.g., Rochon and Mazmanian 1993). More and more often, social movement organizations interact with the public administration, presenting themselves as representatives of a "democracy from below" (Roth 1994; see also Dalton 1994). They contribute to the creation of new arenas more open to the control of public opinion (Willelms, Wolf, and Eckert 1993). In short, they propose a new conception of democracy wherein citizens influence decision makers as more than electors (Offe 1985; Kitschelt 1993). While most existing studies usually have tried to assess the outcomes of social movements in terms of single policies or procedures, fewer have been written on the ways in which mobilization affects the political discourse (but see Gamson and Modigliani 1989).

In this article I analyze a particular field in which social movements contributed to an enlargement of the conception of democracy: the public discourse on the protest and the policing of protest. My assumption is that one of the main effects of social movements in the last few decades has been a change in the shared conception of the legitimate ways to protest as well as the legitimate ways for the state to control protest. These changes happened through an interactive process that can be understood only if we bridge political and cultural explanations, structures, and strategies. Let us start by briefly qualifying the main terms of these statements.

Analyzing the public discourse, I focus not only on the reality but also on the *perception* of the reality—assuming that the latter is one of the relevant intervening variables between structure and action. In social movement studies, this level of analysis has been quite marginal in the past two decades, when preferences, values, meanings, and beliefs have been considered as "given." As for the ideology, "some recognized its role in the social movement process, but their discussion of it seldom went beyond enumerating its functions and content, treating the latter as if it flowed almost naturally or magically from the movement's underlying strains" (Snow and Benford 1992: 135). More recently, however, there has been growing research on the development of cognitive processes of interpretation and, in particular, on movements' production of meaning. This article builds upon this literature, with a particular concern for the collective actors' interpretation of reality.

Protest is a political resource used by those who do not have direct access to policy making in order to mobilize influential public opinion (Lipsky 1965). Very often, in order to attract the attention of public opinion, protesters use illegal forms of action (e.g., blockades and occupations). Even when they do not, protest actions disrupt the public order. Most protest actions are therefore accompanied by the mobilization of police forces, whose task is to police the protest (della Porta and Reiter 1998). Needless to say, public discourse on legitimate forms of protest and protest policing is of great relevance for social movements, since it reflects widespread conceptions about the very right of expressing dissent through protest actions.

The article focuses on the public discourse on protest, protesters, and protest policing during the evolution of the left-libertarian movement family, a set of homogeneous movements, with similar basic values and organizational overlapping, that emerged in the 1960s "at the Left of the Old Left" (della Porta and Rucht 1995).[1] The study of public discourse during the *evolution* of a movement family seems particularly important. The transformation of protest repertoires during the evolution of the left-libertarian family is already known: protest started with symbolically innovative tactics and then shifted to mass actions that sometimes escalated in violent forms; when mass mobilization declined, the movements went back to more institutional forms of collective action, while small groups resorted to more radical forms of action (della Porta 1995; Tarrow 1994; Koopmans 1995). As for the evolution of the political discourse, it has been noticed that "the treatment of ideological factors in relation to the course and character of movements has been far from satisfactory" (Snow and Benford 1992: 135).

To help fill this gap, I am going to analyze the public discourses using one of the better-developed concepts for a cultural approach to movements: that of frame. According to Goffman (1974), frames are interpretative schemes that the various actors use in order to make sense of their world. In their studies on social movements, Snow and Benford define a frame as "an interpretative schemata that simplifies and condenses the 'world out there' by selectively punctuating and encoding objects, situations, events, experiences, and sequences of actions within one's present or past environments" (1992: 137). Master frames work on a larger scale, as "their punctuation, attributions, [and] articulations may color and constrain those of any number of movement organizations" (139). Applying this concept beyond the study of social movements, I aim at reconstructing the master-frames on public order that were used by the different political and social actors who intervened on the issue of protest policing—including those of police officers and protestors themselves. In particular, I focus on what could be defined as metaframes, that is, the frames referring not to protest issues but to the very right to protest. Both protesters and their opponents use the issue of protest policing to enlarge their respective coalitions of allies by delegitimizing their adversaries as those who violate the rules of the democratic game. During protest cycles, public order and protest rights become, in fact, the most relevant issues in the symbolic struggle between social movements and their opponents.

Frames can be distinguished according to their functions: defining a problem, giving solutions, providing motivations for action, stating identities, attributing blame, and so on. In my research, I concentrate on four types of frames, referring respectively to protagonist field definition, antagonist field definition, diagnosis, and prognosis. The first two frames set identities. As Hunt, Benford, and Snow observed:

> Identity constructions, whether intended or not, are inherent in all social movement framing activities. Not only do framing processes link individuals and groups ideologically but they proffer, buttress, and embellish identities that range from collaborative to conflictual. They do this by situating or placing relevant sets of actors in time and space, and by attributing characteristics to them that suggest specifiable relationships and lines of action. (1994: 185)

The protagonist field definition refers to "those individuals and collectivities who are identified as protagonists in that they advocate or sympathize with movement values, beliefs, goals, and practices, or are the beneficiaries of movement action." Conversely, the antagonist field definition refers to "persons and collectivities who are seen as standing in opposition to the protagonists' efforts, and are thus identified as antagonists" (Hunt, Benford, and Snow 1994: 186). While these definitions refer to social movements, I use them to study other collective actors as well.

The other two types of frames refer to the definition of problems and solutions. Diagnostic frames identify events or conditions as problematic and in need of amelioration and single out the culpable agents; the diagnostic frames are usually accompanied by prognostic frames that specify what should be done and by whom, defining at the same time specific targets, strategies, and tactics (Snow and Benford 1988).

A main peculiarity of the concept of frame is the definition of public discourse as an *interactive* process: movements, parties, media, governments, and state apparatuses (including the police) engage in a "politics of signification," that is, in "the struggle to have certain meanings and understandings gain ascendance over others, or at least move up some existing hierarchy of credibility" (Snow and Oliver 1995: 587). The process of framing denotes, therefore, a process of reality construction that is "active, ongoing, and continuously evolving; it entails agency in the sense that what evolves is the product of joint action by movement participants in encounters with antagonists and targets; and it is contentious in the sense that it generates alternate interpretative schemes that may challenge existing schemes" (587). In the evolution of their own frames, the various actors take into account the large range of frames present in the society as they develop strategies of frame alignment as well as frame dealignment. Frame alignment is defined as a micromobilization device, or rhetorical strategy, aiming at capturing consensus. Studying social movements, Snow and his collaborators (1986) suggest that movement organizations try to affect different audiences, adopting strategies that vary according to the perceived position of the targeted audience with respect to the movement's aims and means. Although expanding consensus is an important aim, social movement organizations—as well as other organizations—must keep a distinguishable identity; that is, they have to "exclude" others. There are, therefore, also processes of what we can define as frame dealignment, that is, processes that involve boundary framing or "attempts to situate one's own organization in time and space in relation to other groups" (Hunt, Benford, and Snow 1994: 193–94). From this "interactive" character of frames the need follows to study contemporaneously the evolution of the frames of the different actors who intervene on the topic of protest and policing. Besides those directly involved in the conflicts "in the streets," other social and political actors form civil right coalitions and law-and-order coalitions. Following Gerhards (1993), I assume that the communicative interactions between the various actors develop in different forums—that is, sectors of communications—each of which is composed of an arena, where the different actors interact, and a gallery, occupied by the public.

In what follows, I will suggest that, during the evolution of the left-libertarian movement family, each wave of protest focused the political discourse on protest rights. During this struggle over meanings and understandings, a civil rights coalition and a law-and-order coalition emerged and conflicted with each other over the degree of direct action that was to be considered legitimate in a democracy, and the proper means to control political demonstrations. This "politics of signification" was influenced mainly by two variables: the traditional political culture offered myths and interpretative schemata; and the configuration of power (Kriesi 1989) defined the strength and characteristics of the allies and opponents of the left-libertarian movements. If in the beginning there was a strong disagreement between those who supported a parliamentary conception of democracy and those who struggled for a participatory one, at the end of the process a larger convergence emerged on protest rights and limits. In this sense, social movements active inside the civil rights coalition produced a change in the political discourse on protest and the control of protest, but at the same time they were influenced in their conception of democracy by the political forces they interacted with.

To single out the evolution of the metaframes on protest and protest policing, the empirical research covers a quite long historical period, from the 1960s to the 1990s. Second, the research involves a cross-national comparison. As part of an ongoing research project and long-lasting interest, I selected Italy and Germany for this comparison. For an analysis of the left-libertarian movement family, the two countries offer a nice mixture of similarities and differences. In general, both countries are similar in size, degree of modernization, and political institutions; moreover, they both have had long experiences with authoritarian regimes in recent times, and strong social movements with visible radical wings. At the same time, however, they exhibit relevant differences in their party systems, the alternation of governmental coalitions, and the institutionalization of industrial relations, as well as in the cultural reelaboration of their past experiences with authoritarian regimes. While the similarities in the historical and cultural traditions allow one to stress, in both cases, the parallel effects of social movements as actors of a democratization process that developed with a similar timing, the differences in the party systems of the two countries permit one to analyze the influence of a different configuration of power in the "politics of signification" that developed around the metaissue of protest.[2] Third, the research is based on case studies, that is, on in-depth analysis of protest (and protest policing) events in various periods in the two countries, focusing on one particular form of protest—the march. Fourth, I analyze the debates in two arenas: the mass media and the parliament. The empirical research is based on qualitative content analysis of two types of sources for each event: articles in the press and debates on violent demonstrations in the parliament.[3]

The analysis that follows is organized into three parts, looking respectively at a first, a second, and a third wave of protest during which public discourse focused on protest and protest policing. Six protest campaigns of the left-libertarian movements are analyzed: the first escalation of the student movement in the late 1960s (spring 1967 in Germany and spring 1968 in Italy); a violent campaign of the youth "autonomous" movement, or *Autonomen* (spring 1977 in Italy and spring 1982 in Germany); and violent events involving residual autonomous groups in the late 1980s (spring 1987 in Germany and summer 1989 in Italy). In each part, I present the protagonist, antagonist, diagnostic, and prognostic frames of the law-and-order and the civil rights coalitions, concluding with some remarks on the peculiarities of each single period.

Protest and Democratization in the 1960s

In the late 1960s, a wave of student protest swept Western democracies. Together with the protest, the debate on protest rights also developed, in particular around some symbolically relevant events, such as the shah's visit in Berlin on June 2, 1967, when a student lost his life during a police charge, and the "Valle Giulia" battle in Rome on March 1, 1968, when for the first time students fought back a police charge.

In the second half of the 1960s, and especially after 1966, a long-lasting student mobilization, centered in Berlin, put the issue of freedom of demonstration on the agenda. The situation precipitated on June 2, 1967, when the Persian shah visited Berlin and the student organizations, together with Iranian refugees, organized a series of protests. Several times during the day, demonstrators and shah supporters clashed with each other, and the police charged and arrested the demonstrators. The most violent confrontations happened that evening in front of the Opera, where the Berlin authorities and their guests attended a concert, protected by about a thousand police officers. A few minutes after the performance began, the police charged the demonstrators with batons. Using what the police president defined as the "sausage" tactic, some police units pushed demonstrators on the front of the "sausage" and others charged them on its end. A plain-clothed policeman hunted one student, Benno Ohnesorg, into a courtyard; then the officer shot and killed him.

In the winter of 1967–1968, a wave of protest developed in the Italian universities. In February 1968, students occupied, among other schools, the University of Rome. One of the students' requests was a change in the examination system. After a long bargaining involving the academic authorities, on February 28, the *rettore* (the dean of the university) called the police to clear the premises. Later, a student march ended in fights between the demonstrators and the police. The next day, a student demonstration in front of the faculty of architecture culminated in the famous "battle of Valle Giulia." The demonstrators and the police fought each other when the students tried to enter the building, which the police were trying to "defend." According to official sources, about 3,000 demonstrators and 1,000 police were involved in a battle that lasted a few hours. The police used batons and water cannon; the demonstrators, clubs and stones. At the end of the day, there were 211 injured, 158 of them police officers. Moreover, 228 people were arrested and 4 imprisoned.

In this first escalation the discussion about protest and protest policing was heavily influenced, in both countries, by a traditional culture that was still very suspicious of direct forms of participation. As for the configuration of power, in Italy—because of the support of the Communist Party—the discourse about protest rights was embedded in the tradition of the "mass" labor movement and resistance against fascism, whereas in Germany—where the Social Democrats criticized the students—the discourse was centered around the rights (and risks) of a "radical minority."

Is Protest Democratic? The Discourse of the Law-and-Order Coalitions in the 1960s

In both countries, the discourse of the law-and-order coalitions in the 1960s shared two characteristics: the delegitimation of protest as the action of a minority revolting against democracy; and the claim that the internal opposition was allied with the external enemies. In Germany, the law-and-order coalition—formed by the two large parties, the Social Democrats (SPD) and the Christian Democrats (CDU)—identified with the warrantor of order. The protagonist master-frame indicates those who ensured (Western) freedom and civilization against the dictatorship of the Communist states. As the Social-Democratic member of the Berlin Parliament Theis stated, "We, and especially the Berliner workers, are those who suffered most in the struggle to provide the city with the necessary material bases for freedom and democracy" (AHB 1967: 140). The antagonist master-frame stigmatizes a radical minority. The students, or, better, the few who manipulated them, were puppets of the Communist regime—"*Radikalinskis* financed by the East" (reader's letter, in MOPO, June 8, 1967), the anarchist minority, professional demonstrators, *Berufsrevoluzzer*. They were those who "attempt against our freedom" (Christian-Democratic member of parliament Schmitz, AHB 1967: 139) using "the methods of Nazis" (reader's letter, in FAZ, June 7, 1967). The students' radicalism put them "outside the political system."

The diagnostic master frame attributes the disorders to a Communist conspiracy against democracy. According to this picture, the demonstrators wanted to produce chaos in Berlin in order to offer to the countries of the Eastern Bloc a justification for a military intervention that would bring the "quiet of a cemetery" (reader's letter, in MOPO, June 8, 1967). The catch-phrase is the "misuse of the right to demonstrate" (e.g., Berlin committee of the SPD, in MOPO, June 6, 1967). The prognostic master-frame emphasizes the need to limit the right to demonstrate to those who are "responsible" enough to know how to use it. In order to avoid the situation that had brought about Nazism, the politicians stated that—as the Berlin mayor proclaimed the day after the student's death—"we shall no longer allow a minority to terrorize us" (see Archive of the Institut für Bürgerrechte und öffentliche Sicherheit e.V.). A revealing comment published in the *Frankfurter Allgemeine Zeitung* suggested that "the students avoid for a certain period any type of demonstrations. Until the demonstrators learn to arm themselves with arguments instead of stones. . . . Until the youngsters understand that *political demonstrations are the most stupid and useless means of political participation*" (June 5, 1967; emphasis added). When the right of demonstration collides with the laws, the latter should prevail.

Also in Italy in the 1960s, the protagonist master-frame of the law-and-order coalition—which included the center parties (in particular, the Christian-Democratic [DC] Party) and the right (the Movimento Sociale Italiano [MSI])—refers to the defenders of the rights of the majority against left-wing extremists. As the minister of home affairs Taviani stated (P March 1, 1968), "The forces of order do not defend the position of the government, this or that political line. They defend the *stato di diritto*, the democratic state." "We are here not in a dictatorship, but in a democracy. The law must therefore be the same for everybody, and all have to respect it" (president of Rome University D'Avack, in T, March 1, 1968). The demonstrators, according to the antagonist master-frame, were left-wing extremists, party activists who manipulated the students, agitprops, political jailbirds. The Communists were the instigators of the protest—it was not by chance that the students met in the headquarters of the FGCI (the Federation of the Young Italian Communists): "The place they choose for their assembly—so the editorial of a Roman daily—demonstrates more than any argumentation that the communist party succeeded in controlling the student protest" (ME, March 2, 1968).

According to the diagnostic master-frame, the "extremists" wanted disorders in order to destroy democracy: "The disorders at the university are provoked for political reasons by those Moscovite or Chinese communists" (comment, in T, March 2, 1968). In fact, they did not protest or march; they rioted and provoked tumult; they did not stage democratic and civil demonstrations, but incoherent and indiscriminate rebellion (comment, CdS, March 4, 1968). The prognostic master-frame refers to the necessity of reestablishing public order and legality. The demonstrators' occupation of the university violated the rights of the majority of the students, who wanted to study: "The occupation is an illegal act that cannot leave indifferent those who believe in the validity of the democratic method of the exchange of ideas" (Christian-Democratic member of parliament Magrì, in P March 1, 1968); it was the violence of a minority against a majority. In order to "normalize the situation before it is too late" (ibid.), illegal protest had to be repressed.

Thus, in both countries the law-and-order coalition affirmed the defense of democracy against the use of illegal forms of protest by the puppets of a conspiracy against democracy. However, in Germany the turmoil was considered to be the evil deeds of a foreign enemy, while in Italy the enemy was an internal one: the Communist Party.

A Struggle for Democracy? The Civil Rights Coalitions and Protest in the 1960s

In both countries, a different conception of democracy was also present. In Germany, the civil rights coalition—extremely weak at the party level— identified with the real opposition in the battle against an authoritarian society in order to advance democracy. Facing the Grand Coalition (the alliance in government at the federal level between the CDU and the SPD), the students presented themselves as the only opposition. As stated in a reader's letter to the daily *Frankfurter Rundschau,* the demonstrators established "the basis for a democracy that still has to be built" (June 6, 1967). Their antagonist master-frame refers to the authoritarianism of the society and the political system, which was reflected in the brutality of a militarized police.

Professors, assistants, and researchers at various universities protested in numerous statements against the "brutal repression of the fundamental democratic rights" (Frankfurt and Giessen, in FAZ, June 8, 1967).

According to the diagnostic master-frame, the deep causes for the disorders lay, in fact, in the lack of a really democratic culture in Germany. The
democratization process was seen as still incomplete—especially in West
Berlin, where the concepts of freedom and democracy often overlapped with
that of anti-Communism. In the prognostic master-frame, the civil rights
coalition asked for democratization, including the defense and enlargement
of demonstration rights against repressive measures that "drastically reduce
important citizens' rights and menace in a fundamental way the freedom of
research and teaching in Berlin" (petition signed by about three hundred
professors, assistants, and researchers at the Free University and the Max
Planck Institute; see Archive of the Institut für Bürgerrechte und öffentliche
Sicherheit e.V.).

In Italy in the 1960s, the civil rights coalition—with the important
presence of the second largest party, the Communist Party (PCI) and even of
individuals within the Socialist Party (PSI, at the time PSU), a member of
the governmental coalition—identified with the progressive left. The students looked for a "connection with the struggle of the working class under
the slogan: No to the school of the capitalists, no to the classist school"
(Comitato di agitazione degli studenti romani, in ME, March 2, 1968). The
workers expressed "fraternal solidarity for the just struggle" (in PS, March 2,
1968); the democratic public opinion and the democratic professors manifested their solidarity with the students (PS, March 3, 1968). With a reference to the Resistance movement against fascism, the students were defined
as courageous rebels against an unjust authority: "The Young Courage of
the Students Humiliates Police Brutality," read a title in the left-wing daily
Paese Sera (March 2, 1968). The antagonist master-frame refers to the antidemocratic and conservative forces that responded with fascist methods to
the demands for reform. The government was too weak and unable to implement the long-overdue reforms.[4] The minister of home affairs was accused of behaving like the minister of a police state and of imposing the
"police power in the university"; moreover, "The *questore* [head of police]
did not realize that everybody has the freedom and the right to demonstrate"
(PS, March 2, 1968).

According to the diagnostic master-frame, the reactionary forces used
the police in order to block innovations—and, in fact, the police intervened
when the situation had started to change. The prognostic master-frame singles out the need for a deep reform, not only of the university but, more

generally, of the society. As stated by PCI member of parliament Natoli: "Responsible for the present serious tensions are those who believed that by the use of police forces they could break and destroy a movement that is rapidly spreading and that raises the *serious issues of renewal not only of the university but of the entire society*" (in P 1968; emphasis added). The reform had to include the defense and enlargement of democracy.

Thus, in both countries the civil rights coalitions stressed the need to promote democracy in the face of institutions that were still authoritarian. However, in Germany the opposition perceived itself as a small, enlightened minority, while in Italy it identified with the traditional left.

Public Discourses and the Legacy of the Past

Cross-national and historical similarities and differences in the political discourse on protest policing have to be located, first of all, in the context of the more general political culture. The political discourses presented in the preceding sections refer to some significant historical experiences that provide a repertoire of symbols and models to interpret political conflicts.[5]

In Germany, for *both* coalitions, the experiences of the Weimar Republic and the Nazi regime provide lenses for understanding the present situation. The use of these "lenses" can explain the dramatic polarization in the frame repertoire of the two coalitions. The main model setting of the law-and-order coalition is the *Weimarzeit*, a symbolic reference used by the public as well as by the politicians: "Those who lived in the time of the Weimar Republic and in the years that followed, they know it: it started in this way already once," stated a reader's letter (TSP, June 7, 1967). "It is not part of the conflict of ideas when somebody tries to impose his political belief upon others by throwing various objects. This is something we have already experienced. All of us, who lived the period before 1933, we know how it starts and how it ends," proclaimed the Social-Democratic member of parliament Theis (AHB 1967: 140).

In the model setting of the civil rights coalition, the legacy of the past explains police brutality—a position exemplified by the widely quoted discourse of the dean of the philosophical faculty at the Free University, who stated:

> The form of common life that with more or less consensus is called democracy does not yet have in our country the roots necessary in order to grow and flourish. Unluckily, we need time to transform a mentality of loyalty to the authority, that is centuries old and has been

cultivated for generations. . . . The years of national socialism brought an already deep-rooted inclination to its most horrifying and terrifying forms. The so-called reeducation after 1945 had some success, but democracy remained in our country a small and tremulous branch, that needs care and attention. (In MOPO, June 9, 1967)[6]

Often-used catchwords are *Widerstandsrecht,* the right to resist against an unjust authority, and *Polizeiterror,* in order to consolidate democracy, the police have to be *entfaschistisiert* (de-Nazified).

In the same period in Italy, the historical legacy of the breakdown of democracy and fascism was also present, though with different understandings, in the two coalitions, both claiming to represent the heritage of the Resistance. As for the civil rights coalition, not only did the reactionary forces behave now "like the fascists," but the problems of even the university derived from the legacy of the fascist regime: "The fascist legacy," a group of physicists stated, "is in the fascist legislation that still now suffocates the university structures" (communiqué of professors of physics, in PS, March 3, 1968). Unable to pass a reform, the government was accused of responding with the "arms of the fascists": "Faced with the claims of the student movement, [the government] sent the Public Security agents and the carabinieri; it predisposed an enormous repressive apparatus (that went from the batons to the hydrant), deliberately tramping on legality and democracy in the same moment in which it said to defend those values" (PS, March 1, 1968). On the other side, the law-and-order coalition recalled that "the weakness, the incertitude of the forces of order was one of the components of the sunset of democracy and the advent of fascism" (Minister of Home Affairs Taviani, in P March 1, 1968).

Moreover, in both countries, the political discourse was influenced by a configuration of power marked by the polarization of the cold war. It is not surprising that this polarization was particularly strong in Berlin, where the law-and-order coalition used the East-West opposition to align its frames with all those who believed in Western civilization. In their discourse, the students used symbols that indicated their subordination to the German Democratic Republic: "Red flags were the symbols under which the popular rebellion of June 17th was repressed and the wall was built" (*Bild,* June 3, 1967). The demonstrators were criticized for the very fact that they protested against those who ensured them the right to demonstrate, that they used their freedom to discredit those who granted them freedom. As the Gewerkschaft der Polizei (the largest police union) stated, they misused demonstration freedom insofar as they demonstrated against democracy (in MOPO, June 4, 1967). In a similar way in Italy, the student movement was perceived as being manipulated by the Eastern Bloc. However, while in Germany the whole party system was aligned with the "coalition for freedom," in Italy the party system was split, with the endogenous Communists perceived as the "third column" of Moscow in the Western world.

In both countries, the result was a profound reciprocal mistrust between the members of the two coalitions, which did not entrust each other with respect for the rules of the game. This reflects a deep disagreement on the conception of democracy: it was limited to parliamentarian forms for the law-and-order coalition; it was "democracy in the street" for the civil rights coalition.

Polarization or Depolarization? The Political Discourse during a Second Wave of Protest

The deep differences in the conception of democracy that separated civil rights and law-and-order coalitions in the 1960s were not quick to disappear. Far from it; new waves of protest tended to fuel the disputes on democratic rights. This was the case, at least, in the public discourse around the two events I will analyze next: the disorders that followed the prohibition of a march in Berlin against the first visit of President Ronald Reagan of the United States during a cycle of protest against the deployment of cruise missiles in Europe; and the wave of violent youth protest during the spring of 1977, which culminated in Rome in the death of two police officers and a demonstrator.

During a journey in Europe on June 11, 1982, the president of the United States, Ronald Reagan, visited Berlin. In several European cities, Reagan's visit had been met by large marches organized by the peace movement to protest against nuclear armament and, in particular, the deployment of nuclear rockets in Europe. In Berlin, in a climate of tension that had already escalated during the evolution of the so-called squatters' movement, the police prohibited two demonstrations that were to take place during Reagan's stay in Berlin. While the large coalition of demonstrators decided to move the demonstration to the day before the visit, the Alternative List (AL; that is, the Berlin Greens) stuck with the decision to organize the prohibited demonstration, joining the radical *Autonomen*. The march on the day before Reagan's visit was peaceful, and the task of the police was limited to traffic control. But the next day, a series of fights involved the police and the demonstrators. The result was 87 wounded police officers, 40 hospitalized people, at least 200 people who were treated by the fire brigades and another 200 by the "autonomous Red Cross," and 242 demonstrators arrested.

In the spring of 1977, the wave of protest that had started in March around university issues rapidly escalated. In Rome, after a long series of violent street battles between radical protesters and the police, on April 22, autonomous militants killed two police officers during a street battle near the university. The government's immediate reaction was a prolonged prohibition of any kind of political demonstration in the capital, suspended only for the traditional march on Labor Day. A few days later, on May 12, the authorities prohibited a concert organized by the Radical Party and the New Left. In the afternoon, the police encircled the Piazza Navona, where the concert was to have taken place. A small group, including members of Parliament, staged a sit-in; the police and the carabinieri charged the protesters. Street battles went on the whole afternoon. According to official sources, eight people were injured (one of them with firearm); in the evening, a bullet killed Giorgiana Masi, a young activist of the Radical Party and the feminist movement.

In both countries, the legacy of the traditional political culture, together with a configuration of power that isolated the (radical) wings of the social movements, maintained a polarized climate. However, if we look carefully, we can also see the beginnings of some convergence between the discourses of the two opposing coalitions.

The Law-and-Order Coalition: A Selective Acceptance of Demonstration Rights

In both countries, the public discourse of the law-and-order coalition emphasized the respect of lawful procedures, which should bind both police and demonstrators. In Germany, the protagonist master-frame of the law-and-order coalition—which again allied the SPD and the CDU, this time together with the liberal Free Democratic Party (FDP)—refers to the defenders of the *Rechtsstaat,* of respect for the law and the right to "order." The police were described as efficient and successful. The Social Democrats and the liberal FDP, however, claimed that the state monopoly of force found its boundary in the law and in the proportionality of the means to the aims. The antagonist master-frame describes the violent demonstrators as terrorists, *Chaoten* who came from outside Berlin looking for trouble. The most widespread metaphors were those of the "criminal" type: hooligans, criminal mobs, brutal street butchers, rampagers, rioters, rioting youth, troublemakers.

The diagnostic master-frame stresses the demonstrators' violation of the rules of representative democracy. The young autonomous demonstrators were accused of attacking internal security and international depolarization (Social-Democratic member of Parliament Paetzold, AHB, 1982). The problem lay in the existence of groups of violent young people considered to be "enemies of the *Rechtsstaat* who want to transform the state in a battle field" (the police union Gewerkschaft der Polizei, in TSP, June 12, 1982).

The diagnostic master-frame is a quite pragmatic combination of repression and integration. A military solution was supported especially by those who employed an emergency frame (mainly the CDU, part of the liberal FDP, and the police trade unions), stating the need for new police armament and/or legislation more restrictive toward demonstration rights.[7] There is, however, another frame (present mainly in the SPD and part of the FDP), which denounces the military solution as counterproductive because "the violent hooligans want counter-violence" (Social-Democratic member of Parliament Rasch, AHB 1982). Besides "normal" repression, therefore, the need for "political education" against the use of violence and against the belief that the aims justify the means was expressed—a need that was particularly urgent for the parliamentary AL, the Berlin equivalent of the Greens.

In Italy, the law-and-order coalition—this time including also the PCI—defined the protagonist as the constitutional forces, that is, those responsible forces that defend the democratic and republican order. They protect the right to freedom and a peaceful living together; they stand by the citizens. "The workers, the labor movement," as the PCI member of Parliament Spagnoli put it, "must avoid that a group of provocateurs and ravagers engage in an armed war against the democratic state, putting at risk those conquests that cost us years of struggle and sacrifice" (P 1977: 7533). The police were also considered democratic, it was "well understandable" that the police officers—young people, children of workers, and part of the working class— were exasperated and sometimes overreacted. In a parallel way, the antagonist master-frame states that the main enemy was the antidemocratic, terrorist forces that refused to comply with the democratic institutions. The antagonists were "notorious autonomous" terrorists who demonstrated on the street, provocateurs, destroyers, addicts to the P38 gun. The prohibition to demonstrate derived from "the painful acknowledgment of the existence of a group of criminal provocateurs" whose aim was the "search for the fight and the tragedy, in the hope of triggering a process of chain reactions that drags the community into a state of fear and rage" (minister for home affairs, in P 1977: 7515, 7517). They were extraparliamentary forces, and, for this reason, dangerous: the frame opposes the "piazza" the institution.

The diagnostic master-frame locates the problem in the conspiracy against the democratic republic born out of the Resistance. The situation was one of emergency; there was a "plot" against democracy,

> an aggression of armed bands, an attack of terrorist groups that has the clear and expressed aim of throwing the country into chaos, into paralysis, and to hit the very bases of the democratic regime and of civil life altogether. . . . We believe that there is a design that intends to hit the democratic state and subvert it, and humiliate it. (The Communist Spagnoli during the parliamentarian debate, in P 1977: 7531–32)

The use of plainclothes and armed police officials, the most criticized police strategy, was framed as a normal way of collecting information on crimes. The Communist leader Pecchioli, renouncing the traditional Communist proposal of an unarmed police force, stated that the police must carry guns, even at demonstrations, for their own security (in R, May 18, 1977). The prognostic master-frame indicates the necessity of a large unity of the democratic forces in order to pass emergency measures and to save democracy. The defense of democracy was possible only with "a strong unitarian involvement," "a large and democratic solidarity," "the unity of all the constitutional parties," a large consensus, or, to quote the Communist mayor of Rome Argan, "democratic vigilance in order to isolate the violent provocateurs" (in PS, May 15, 1977).

Thus, in both countries the law-and-order coalitions presented themselves as the defenders of the democratic state against the provocation of violent minorities. These minorities, however, were described mainly as nonpolitical hooligans in the German case, and as political terrorists in the Italian case. The main solution was a military one, but the integration of the "less radical" social movement organizations into the democratic process was also considered.

The Civil Rights Coalition: Between Violence and Nonviolence

In the public discourse of the civil rights coalitions in both countries, we find a sense of exclusion but at the same time a debate on the "right" way of protesting, with an emerging criticism against the use of violent repertoires. In Germany, the protagonist master-frame of a civil rights coalition that has a small presence in Parliament with the AL is that of a second society: the real democrats were outside the traditional party system; they wanted to affirm the right to demonstrate, a right that cannot be constrained. They identified their struggle with that of other movements. Rewording John F. Kennedy's famous statement "We are all Berliners," the commentator of the left-wing daily *Tageszeitung* wrote: "Women and squatters, autonomous and alternatives, peace movement and left parliamentarians: we are Berliners too" (June 12, 1982). While the most radical part of the movement identified with the "freedom fighters of the whole world" (Autonomous and anti-imperialist groups, in TAZ, June 18, 1982), others proposed a self-definition based on "a nonviolent resistance to traditional politics" (member of AL Wendt, AHB 1982: 1527). The antagonists were those who were part of the "established politics." The most direct enemy was the police: they hunted isolated demonstrators, devoted themselves to an "orgy of batons," "went wild," and brutalized. Most of the police comprised "criminal elements" and "militant fighters"—although a few commentators admitted that even among the police there were "human beings."

The diagnostic master-frame states that the authorities provoked in order to repress, because they did not recognize the democratic right to demonstrate dissent (the AL leader, in TSP, June 13, 1982). Although the main cause of violence remained the unwillingness of the political system to respond to the needs of the so-called minorities, a secondary diagnostic frame refers to the so-called *Chaoten*, infiltrated by "professional street fighters." They constituted a social problem that was "part of our time" ("Humanistische Union," in TAZ, June 14, 1982), reflecting economic depression, the legitimacy crisis, technological risks, and the "growing divergence between misery and waste" (member of AL Jaenicke, AHB 1982: 1529). The solution to political violence was the recognition of an unconstrained right to demonstrate when and where one wanted to. However, an increasingly successful prognostic frame refers to the need to find a way to demonstrate nonviolently but with fantasy. As one activist put it, "The nonviolent demonstrators need more courage; the militants have to be wiser" (Kunzelmann, in TAZ, June 14, 1982).

In Italy, the civil rights coalition—represented at the parliamentary level only by the small Radical Party (PR) and the Democrazia Proletaria (DP), allied with other groups of the New Left (among them the Partito di Unità Proletaria [PdUP] and Lotta Continua)—defined the protagonists as the left-wing movements: workers, youth, students. They were the democratic and progressive forces of the lay left that defended constitutional rights in the struggle for freedom and democracy. In order to defend the basic liberal freedoms, including the right to demonstrate on the street, they affirmed the duty to disobey an unjust order (*Nuremberg* is a catchword). If, for most of the New Left, the self-definition relied upon a belief in "the possibility of a revolutionary alternative" (LC, May 14, 1977), the PR stressed instead the use of nonviolence (see, e.g., PR member of Parliament Pannella, in P 1977:

7524). According to the master-frame, the antagonist is the state of the mas-
sacres. Asks the Radical member of Parliament Pinto:

> What is pending upon this parliament? Which shadows accumulate
> upon it? . . . The massacre of Piazza Fontana, the massacre of the
> Italicus, the massacre of Brescia, the comrades and youth killed on the
> street by the fascists, the massacres carried out by the secret services
> that had to defend the freedom of the Italian people, and instead
> depended directly from the government, from the various Christian-
> Democratic governments, and plotted day after day against the free-
> dom of the workers. (In P 1977: 7540)

The antagonists were those who represented the authoritarian conspiracy
tendencies always present in the Italian republic; the DC and its allies in an
"authoritarian, violent and clerical-fascist regime"; the "regime of the mas-
sacres"; and those who carried on a "violent and authoritarian design" aiming at destabilization.

According to the diagnostic master-frame, the prohibition to demonstrate is a provocation planned in order to produce chaos; it belongs to a
strategy of tension. The police followed, in fact, a precise plan aiming at producing disorders and violence so that repression could harden. This was part
of the conspiracy of the bourgeoisie against the working class: "Special
squads had the task of provoking a death in order then to be able, in the
name of this death, to pass under silence much more serious things, aiming
at repressing (with the alibi of the autonomous and the fetish of the P38)
the whole movement, the working class, its conquests, in terms of both freedom and welfare" (PR member of Parliament Pinto, in P 1977: 7540). The
provocation of the regime aimed at "precipitating a situation that was prepared for a long time with the main aim of cementing a moderate public
opinion through terror and the constant threat of a civil war" (LC, May 17,
1977). The language was a military one: catchwords were *civil war* and *terror, state of siege* and *state of emergency, war of gangs* carried out by the government, *military presidium,* and *terrorism* ("The police kill, the government
claims responsibility"). The police were so brutal that even the bourgeois
press had to admit it. However, not the police officers but their political
leaders were responsible for the escalation. There was, in fact, an attempt to
produce tensions inside the police forces, to block the changes that emerged
with the demands for police unions. The new techniques of repression included reactionary and fascist repression, together with the advanced instru-
ment of social consensus, based on the use of the PCI to produce a call for
law and order, even in the progressive masses. The cause of violence lay in

the Christian-Democratic government and its "antidemocratic intolerance." The main task of the movement, the prognostic master-frame states, is the defense of the liberal and bourgeois democracy. "When a historical crisis reaches a head, the defense of democracy becomes the most important task," states a communiqué of the PdUP (in M, May 15, 1977). The secretary of Lotta Continua confirmed, "The everyday activity of the government and of the forces that support it aims at the abrogation of democracy, even bourgeois democracy" (LC, May 17, 1977). The defense of democracy required mass unity, vigilance, and especially the mobilization of the working class. The defense of democracy implied a democratization of the police.

In both countries the civil rights coalitions presented themselves as the only defenders of democratic rights in the face of authoritarian tendencies. While in Germany, however, there was an emphasis on an "alternative," second society, in Italy the reference was still to the (real) left.

Between Radicalism and Moderation

The new escalation brought about the return of "old" frames on protest and the police, frames deeply rooted in the traditional political culture. In Germany, reference to the Weimar Republic and the *Nazizeit* was still present in the discourse of both coalitions, although it was weaker than in 1967. Also in Italy, the political discourse had very dramatic tones, stressing once again a situation of emergency. The historical experience of the Resistance provided symbols to both coalitions: the unity of the constitutional forces for the law-and-order coalition, and the right to oppose an unjust authority for the civil rights coalition. In both countries, a pessimistic zeitgeist, together with some resilient frames from the 1960s, helped ensure the survival of black-and-white images. As for the configuration of power, one reaction to the previous waves of protest and their legacy of radical groupings was the enlargement of the law-and-order coalition.

Besides these continuities, there were also some changes, indicating that the "struggle over signification" that emerged in the 1960s had consequences for the political discourse. On the side of the civil rights coalitions, in both countries there was a growing criticism against violent forms of action and violent autonomous groupings, which were considered more and more to be a social problem. Violence was, in fact, criticized. From the most instrumental perspective, as was often stated in Germany by members of the AL as well as by readers of the alternative *Tageszeitung*, violence produced isolation (people were scared and did not go to demonstrations that were expected to turn violent), and this damaged the goals of the peace movement. Also in

Italy, radical autonomous groups were perceived as a "contradiction," a "moment of confusion" in the youth movement.

On the side of the law-and-order coalitions, there was a more and more selective approach, with a stigmatization of some forms of protest—the autonomous groups were described more often as terrorists, with the frequent use of a metaphor of war—and an increasing acceptance of others. Related to this are the very similar reactions that we find in the 1970s and 1980s in Germany and Italy apropos of those movement-parties that entered the parliamentary arena. For the German law-and-order coalition in 1982, the AL constituted a political problem, since it held seats in Parliament but only partially recognized the rules of parliamentary democracy (Social-Democratic member of Parliament Vogel, AHB 1982: 1523). The problem was evident in its very self-definition as a mainly *ausserparlamentarian* (out-of-parliament) force: AL members' belief in direct democracy brought them to justify violence (Christian-Democratic member of Parliament Rzepka, AHB 1982).

Similarly, in Italy in the 1970s, the law-and-order coalition stigmatized the "malicious" behavior of the small parties of the left. In fact, even if they held seats in Parliament, they behaved like *extraparlamentari*—that is, they did not "accept the rules of a democracy, with a majority and a minority, with a government that has the right to govern" (in P 1977: 7529); and "a member of the parliament, according to the government, cannot and must not endorse, even with his mere presence, actions that are in contrast with order, with legality" (minister for home affairs, in P 1977: 7516). In both countries, the law-and-order coalitions called on the former "extra parliamentary" groups to accept the parliamentarian rules of the game.

Normalization or Criminalization? The Evolution of the Discourse on Protest

With the diffusion of forms of unconventional political participation in different groups of the population, a larger consensus was achieved on protest rights and policing techniques. Although in times of intense protest several elements of the traditional "polarized" discourse on protest and policing reemerged in both coalitions, the past interactions had also produced a learning process with increasing similarities on some basic points. For both coalitions, violence was excluded as a political means, but peaceful demonstrations were accepted as a basic democratic right. This was visible, for instance, in the political debate that followed some violent encounters between demonstrators and the police during a visit of the U.S. president Ronald Reagan in June 1987 in Berlin, and in the demonstration that followed a police intervention to clear a squatted youth center in August 1989 in Milan.

On June 12, U.S. president Ronald Reagan was again expected in Berlin, this time on the occasion of the celebration of the 750th anniversary of the foundation of the city. Once again, for the peace movement, Reagan's visit was an occasion to protest against the U.S. policies on rearmament. As in 1982, the police prohibited marching on the day of Reagan's visit, and the majority of peace groups agreed to demonstrate on the day before. On June 11, about 80,000 people took part in a massive peaceful demonstration against U.S. rearmament policies, organized by about 140 groups. During the march, the police distributed leaflets warning the protesters not to use violence and wishing them a peaceful demonstration. This time, however, a large group of the radical *Autonomen* participated in the mass demonstration. Fights with the police developed at the end of the march and continued later on in different parts of the city, in particular in the district of Kreuzberg, where a large number of squatted houses constituted an important infrastructure for the alternative milieu. Autonomous groups and the AL had announced various protest initiatives for the next day, but the administrative court confirmed the police prohibition. When a few hundred demonstrators converged in the city center, the police built cordons and encircled a group of about three hundred people. The authorities suspended most public transportation from Kreuzberg, and the police controlled all cars headed out of the district. For two nights, there were several incidents during this massive police patrol in Kreuzberg.

The history of the "youth centers" in Italy is a very long one. Founded during the youth protests of the late 1970s, the youth centers developed as important places for the establishment of a new culture, where, in particular, new musical fashion was experimented with. However, they also held radical political positions, often engaging in increasingly ritualized struggles with the police, especially when police forces were sent to clear occupied buildings. These confrontations were particularly frequent in the case of the Leoncavallo Center in Milan. It was after one police intervention to clear the headquarters of the Leoncavallo that the militants of the youth centers converged in Milan and staged a march that ended up in violent confrontations.

The Limits to Protest: Law-and-Order Coalitions and Protest Discourse in the 1980s

In both countries, violence was stigmatized more as a social problem than as political extremism or terrorism. In Germany, the law-and-order coalition, which was centered on CDU, identified with the champions of Western freedom. As "real" democrats, coalition members defended the demonstration rights that were attacked by those who used violence. As the federal minister for home affairs Zimmermann declared, in order to assure the right to demonstrate for nonviolent people, it was necessary to avoid the "misuse" of the same right by the *Chaoten* (in FAZ, June 13, 1987). The antagonist master-frame refers to juvenile gangs: the antagonists were *Krawalmacher, Vermummten,* rioters, punks, criminals. Moreover, they were, as in 1982, *reisende,* traveling people—or, to use the expression of the senator for home affairs, "vagabond and criminal bands" (in TSP, June 16, 1987) with no political aims.

The diagnostic master-frame refers to a state of emergency produced by the rioters. The explanation includes the unplanned effects of an escalation. If, according to the senator for home affairs, the police succeeded in achieving their main goal, criticism against police decisions was expressed from inside the coalition (e.g., in AHB 1987). The prognostic master-frame refers to the need to defend democracy against those who are not ready for it; this on the basis of the principle of the *wehrhafte Demokratie,* a democracy that has to limit some democratic principles in order to defend itself (Christian-Democratic mayor Diepgen, AHB 1987). As in 1982, there were a few demands for changes in demonstration rights.[8] Even the law-and-order coalition emphasized, however, that the presence of a "potential for violence" could not be solved just with the police, and it warned against a "purely" law-and-order solution.[9] The police tactics that were considered more favorable were those that avoided escalation. In the attempt to reestablish a basic consensus, the AL and the SPD were asked to criticize violence so that an agreement could be reached among the democratic forces (Christian-Democratic member of Parliament Buwitt, AHB 1987).

In Italy, the law-and-order coalition, gathered around the Socialist Party and the neofascist MSI, emphasized its role as law enforcer. "First of all there are the rules, and they have to be enforced," declared the socialist mayor of Milan Paolo Pillitteri, later involved in a corruption scandal (in LN, August 22, 1989). Coalition members were the "defenders of the defenseless citizens," who fought drug addicts and extremists. The antagonists, the "Autonomous" groups, were considered to be hooligans who practiced violence for its own sake. On the one hand, in the descriptions of the fights between the "forces of order" and the protesters, the language of the 1970s emerged anew: "guerrilla war," "last Autonomous bastions," "anarchists." The young demonstrators were autonomous and wanted to impose their will using violence instead of ideas (G, August 19, 1989). On the other hand, with their extravagant clothes, green hair, studs, and safety pins, they resembled punks more than terrorists. Unlike in the 1960s and 1970s, they did not qualify as "political demonstrators"—they were "*incivili, e basta.*"

The diagnostic master-frame explains escalation as a result of protesters' marginality. The *Autonomen* represented, in the words of *Il Corriere della Sera,* "a smaller and smaller area of irreducible marginal people who decided to 'stay out' of a social context they do not accept and to fight against with all possible means" (CdS, August 17, 1989). In the 1980s, even if "the molotov strategy survives," "the Autonomous merges with the punk, with the marginal youth, those who smoke marijuana, take drugs and behave antisocially. . . . [They are] forever marginalized, and self-marginalized, because of their indomitable need for rebellion" (CdS, August 19, 1989). They "resist reality, more than the police" (G, August 17, 1989). For this reason, the prognostic master-frame suggests a "decisive" police intervention against the troublemakers. The "orders from above" that forced the police to tolerate violence, thus embittering the police, are criticized (G, August 20, 1989). As the Milan Christian Democrats declared, to help the "violent ones" would imply discrimination against the "law-abiding" people (LN, September 9, 1989). However, repression had to go together with social help for those who accepted the rules.

In both countries, the law-and-order coalitions emphasized the need for a "selective" repression of violent groups, which were considered to be neither political actors nor organizations that mobilized social claims. However, this position was expressed with more emphasis in Germany than in Italy, where the law-and-order coalition appeared, in fact, quite silent.

How Much Protest? The Civil Rights Coalitions and Protest Discourse in the 1980s

In both countries, the civil rights coalition condemned violence but considered it a social problem that could not be solved with police repression. In the late 1980s in Germany, for the civil rights coalition, composed of the SPD and the "alternative" groups, the master-frame refers to the protagonists as those who defended demonstration rights, which could not be constrained because of a small minority of violent demonstrators. Conversely, the antagonist master-frame refers to the conservative forces that defined political and social problems in terms of a public-order emergency. The antagonist frame is, however, a differentiated one. For instance, if the SEK (*Sondereinheiten,* or special corps) was considered particularly evil, even the left-wing *Tageszeitung* reported on criticisms from inside the police against the brutality of some colleagues (June 15, 1987), as well as on the internal divisions in the government over the way to deal with protest. Moreover, an additional antagonist frame refers to the violent groups inside the youth movement.

The diagnostic master-frame singles out a political failure to face social problems, which brings about escalation. In this interpretation, social inequalities, unemployment, alcoholism, drugs, and misery were the main causes for the "lack of perspective" that led youth to violence (see, e.g., letter to the authorities from evangelist pastors, in FR, June 16, 1987). An additional component of the discourse emphasizes the risks of escalation when the solution to social problems is left to the police. The main causes for the escalation were, however, located in the very dynamics of police-radical confrontations in the Federal Republic as well as in Berlin. With a telling appropriation of the term, a leader of the AL in Kreuzberg accused the police of destroying the work that had been done to "normalize" the situation in his neighborhood (in TAZ, June 16, 1987). The prognostic master-frame is the quest for a political solution to the social problems that produce violence. The AL and the SPD suggested establishing a dialogue with the violent groups (and in particular with the *Autonomen*) in order to find out the causes for the potential for violence and *Staatverdrossenheit* (mistrust toward the state). As the Social-Democratic leader Paetzold stated during the parliamentary debate, "It is unwise to try to react to violence only with the police"; it was instead necessary to set up a dialogue with the radicals: "Those who trust only the police and do not look for political solutions, they are responsible before this city" (AHB 1987: 3250).

In Italy, a civil rights coalition that was again enlarged to include the PCI presented itself as a "guardian" of the correct application of democratic rights for peaceful protest. It emphasized its "responsibility." The antagonists were singled out as the irresponsible police officers, and the problem was in the wrong or imprecise indications by the government that risked increasing tensions and reducing trust in the democratic state. If the police intervention against the autonomous center was criticized as following "a logic of war," the main responsibility nevertheless lay with the dominant economic groups that, with their value system oriented to profit and success, "push the marginals into a deeper and deeper marginality" (M, August 18, 1989). The "cannibalism" of the dominant social groups "destroys even the smaller stronghold of difference" (M, August 20, 1989). At the same time, the "provocation of small groups of Autonomous" was stigmatized. The "new Autonomous" were described by the left as a "prepolitical generation," the "hippies of the seventies," "existentialists," and "rebels." However, even among the "boys and girls" of the Autonomia, there were responsible ones who tried to calm down the comrades who threw stones, inviting them to use "only eggs and tomatoes" (R, August 21, 1989). In fact, the "youth social centers" were described as "those who try to fight against heroin and marginality keeping together the wise and the crazy ones, the crushed and the furious ones" (M, August 23, 1989).

In the diagnostic master-frame, the "brutal" police interventions are considered mainly as unplanned results of "old and disgraceful techniques" and poor training. The government was therefore accused of renouncing a strategic conception of peacekeeping that would avoid escalation and keep demonstrations peaceful. Some rhetorical questions were asked in the Communist daily *L'Unità*: "Is it fair to solve the problem of marginality with the police? . . . Was it not possible to face the terrible Autonomous with a political proposal?" (August 17, 1989). In fact, "criminalization" risked an increase in social tensions that must instead be eased through social reforms. The prognostic master-frame includes the need for social reforms that would help integrate the disenchanted youth into the society. Among these "political solutions" was the offering of public space to the autonomous centers, considered to be a type of grassroots organization that was extremely useful in countering the diffusion of heavy drugs—"an interesting and potentially very positive form of aggregation in the periphery of the big cities, which should not be closed down but multiplied" (Luigi Cancrini, responsible for the struggle against drugs in the PCI shadow cabinet, in U, August 19, 1989).

Thus, in both countries the civil rights coalitions presented themselves as defenders of protest rights against the political failure of the conservative forces in government to solve social problems. In both countries political violence was described as a sign of social disease. In Italy, a paternalistic overtone reflected a traditional attitude by the Old Left to co-opt and represent any social claim.

A Selective Enlargement of Protest Rights?

In the 1980s, political discourse became more pragmatic. In the law-and-order coalitions there was a larger acceptance of demonstration rights and an outspoken criticism of the more radical protest forms advocated by the civil rights coalitions. In Germany, encumbering historical memories (the Weimar Republic, the Nazi regime) no longer dominated the symbolic field as part of the traditional political culture, providing the metaphors for reading contemporary events; in Italy, references to the "years of lead"—the "heavy" and "gray" 1970s—and terrorism were more often used for stressing the differences than for singling out similarities. In both countries, in a depolarized configuration of power and with the Old Left again inside the civil rights coalition, the discourses of the two coalitions had more in common: for both coalitions, violence was mainly an indicator for social problems; and for both coalitions, demonstration and protest rights were inalienable civil rights that tended to prevail over concerns for law and order. The police defined their task as the protection of demonstrators, and they emphasized de-escalation. As for the master-frame on demonstration rights, the "normalization" of some forms of protest goes along with the stigmatization of others.

This "depolarization" in the political discourse resulted from an interactive framing process during which, in the long run, each coalition came to accept part of the discourse of the other, and adapted its frames accordingly. A typical example is the image of the *reisende Chaoten* (traveling hooligans) that the law-and-order coalition proposed in Germany in 1982 and that the civil rights coalition incorporated in 1987. The political discourse evolved, therefore, through processes of frame alignment and dealignment, tradition and innovation. The effect of this "depoliticization" of the adversary was the denial of political rights. As the law-and-order coalition stressed in Germany, the *Chaoten* refused to express any political opinion when they chose to go around with balaclavas on their faces in the so-called *Vermummung,* or "masking." Along this line, the senator for home affairs referred to the decision of the Constitutional Court on demonstration rights to explain why the "hooligans" were excluded from this right:

> Demonstrations, according to the terminology of the Constitutional Court, belong to the human right to express one's opinion in the street. . . . Men and women can in this way clarify their opinions, even their deviant opinions. But when somebody hides his face behind a mask, that has nothing more to do with the expression of an opinion, . . . or of anything related with demonstration or the right to demonstrate, but a lot to do with violence and terrorism. (Kewenig, AHB, 1987: 3230)

The *Chaoten,* who attacked the right to demonstrate, were nondemonstrators: the very fact that they were masked showed that they did not want to communicate (Christian-Democratic mayor Diepgen, AHB 1987). Similarly, in Italy, the use of violence—even when eggs and tomatoes were substituted for stones—was considered a sufficient ground for excluding those involved in it from any negotiation with the authorities. Openly distinguishing between "good" and "bad" people, the public administration declared that it would help those who "deserved" its help. "We do not negotiate with the violent," "We do not discuss with them," stated the Milan city government (in LN, August 30, 1989; see also della Porta 1998).

On the other side, the civil rights coalition asked for a dialogue. In Italy, the Communist Party stressed the need for "reasoning and dialogue" instead of "force and authoritarianism," and Don Mazzi, a priest involved in the struggle against heroin, declared: "We should not marginalize all those who do not accept the city-shop window, that refuse it because they cannot, or do not want, because they think that being normal is not interesting. Do we have to leave them in the hands of the judges and the police?" (U, August 18, 1989). Similarly in Germany, Social-Democratic leaders claimed to be against the use of the police to solve the causes of violence. "We have to be self-critical," the Social-Democratic mayor of Berlin Momper declared in Parliament, "and look for the social reasons for the lack of confidence in the state and violence proneness in part of the youth. We have to look for a dialogue" (AHB 1987: 3236). In both cases, "violence" was considered an anomic reaction to social problems.

Protest and Protest Discourse: A Summary

In this article I have tried to assess the evolution of the frames on protest rights and policing from the 1960s to the 1980s, as they appeared in the press and in parliamentary debates. As I suggested in the introduction, these changes were the effect of a "politics of signification" on demonstration rights. During waves of protest, the political discourse focused on the metaissue of democracy. With their very action, social movements polarized the political and social forces. Their opponents gathered in law-and-order coalitions; their allies joined in civil rights coalitions. The traditional political culture influenced the frames chosen by the two coalitions, whose composition reflected the configuration of power available to the social movements. The effect of these protracted symbolic interactions was a change in the political discourse of all the actors who participated in them. Through an interactive process, social movements stimulated a political discussion on the conception of protest rights, contributing to a change in the political culture on the issue.

Summarizing our results, in the political discourse on protesters, the control of protest, and protest rights in the evolution of the left-libertarian movement family in Italy and Germany, we observe the following evolution. Identity frames (both protagonist and antagonist frames) switched from political ones (progressive versus conservative) to Manichaean ones (good versus evil) and then to pragmatic ones. For the law-and-order coalitions, demonstrators in the 1960s were puppets of an international menace (an "external" one in Germany, an "internal" one in Italy); during the second escalation, the political image faded away, leaving space for the label "terrorists"; in the third wave, violent demonstrators became increasingly conceived as socially marginal people. In a parallel way, for the civil rights coalitions, the government and the police in the 1960s were actors of a reactionary design; in the second wave, they were enemies of a long-lasting war; in the third, they were simply unprepared to solve social problems.

In both countries, there were increasingly differentiated frames—with a "normalization" of several protest forms and a stigmatization of others. As for the law-and-order coalition, we suggest the existence of a polarization between the "good" image of a large part of the demonstrators and the "bad" image of a minority, between good demonstrators and bad demonstrators. Peaceful protest was increasingly considered to be normal politics, violent protest to be crime. In parallel fashion, a differentiation appeared in the civil rights coalition between "good" and "bad" strategies for handling protest, with the acceptance of the need for some control. In the diagnostic frames, there is an evolution from a metaphor of political conflict to a metaphor of war and then to a metaphor of disease.[10] For the law-and-order coalition, violent protest in the late 1960s was considered, in general, a degenerated expression of a political conflict. Later on, violent protest came to be seen as a sort of war (more internally produced in Italy, more imported from outside in Germany). More recently, political violence came to be framed in terms of social problems. Similarly, for the civil rights coalition, police brutality was more and more perceived as an effect of escalation and/or bad training rather than planned provocation.

In the prognostic frames, there seems to be a shift from the definition of a differentiated solution (reform and repression), to a military solution related through the metaphor of war,[11] to a social "cure" prescribed by the metaphor of disease. As for police tasks, the emphasis shifted from law enforcement to peacekeeping and from force to intelligence and specialization. The growing refusal of physical violence also pushed the police to "justify" their tactics primarily as "de-escalation."

This process developed interactively. The traditional political culture offered myths and models for understanding protest and protest policing. In both Italy and Germany, the legacy of recent experiences with totalitarian regimes was a mistrust of democratic procedures. The traditional political culture, however, was transformed during a symbolic struggle over the very conception of democratic rights. In both countries, a civil rights and a law-and-order coalition formed around the issue of protest rights. Unlike in Germany, where there was a larger "basic consensus" between the main political parties, in Italy the polarization of the political system around the left-right cleavage was reflected in a political discourse in which the left and the right reciprocally accused each other of refusing the rules of the democratic game.

In both countries, however, we notice a shift from a formalistic view of democracy as the right of the majority (where demonstrators were called a "minority" and the police, the institutional defender of the majority rights) to a more participatory conception of democracy. At the same time, violent forms of protest were more and more unanimously stigmatized. We can therefore conclude that the evolution of movement families brought about important changes in the very frames that refer to demonstration rights. This evolution was a complex one, involving processes of alignment and dealignment, polarization and depolarization. Eventually, the new understanding of demonstration rights was more "liberal" than the older one, but at the same time there was a growing exclusion of violence as a form of protest. Peaceful demonstrations were considered to be basic rights that the police had the responsibility to defend; violent ones were considered to be "nonpolitical" events. This seems to confirm Snow and Benford's hypothesis that cycles of protest bring about innovative master-frames: "Associated with the emergence of a cycle of protest is the development or construction of an innovative master-frame" (1992: 143). One of the main innovative master-frames refers to democracy itself. After first waves of protest polarize public opinion, during following waves symbolic interaction brings about a new "basic" consensus on a new definition of protest rights and on how to handle them.

Notes

I thank Mario Diani, Pierpaolo Donati, Marco Giugni, and Sidney Tarrow for their comments on previous versions of this chapter. For the research on the German case, I used the rich archives of the Institut für Bürgerrechte und öffentliche Sicherheit e.V. in Berlin. I am particularly grateful to Heiner Busch and Norbert Pütter for their help.

    1. Herbert Kitschelt (1990: 180) suggested the term "left-libertarian" to single out a certain type of political party that is "leftist" because it asks for equality, and "libertarian" because it supports direct democracy.

    2. For more references on the choice of Germany and Italy in cross-national comparisons, see della Porta (1995: chapter 1).

    3. As for the press, I sampled six dailies for each country and each event, including both local and national press and newspapers with different political inclinations. For these dailies, I systematically analyzed all the articles referring to each of the chosen events for one week after each event. As for the parliamentary debates, I analyzed the debates referring to the chosen events in the Italian Chamber of Deputies and in the Berlin Parliament. For both sources, my unit of analysis is the statement, which I consider as a discourse unit involving a subject, an object, and a predicate. I collected all statements referring to the protagonist, antagonist, diagnostic, or prognostic frames. The statement is,

in my research, "reconstructed." I wanted not to measure the "degree of presence" of each statement but to single out the various frames of different actors. The code sheet I used included, besides the sources and the date of each statement, the definition of the actor who expressed the statement, its object, and its content. To reconstruct the frame, I reported the storytelling, metaphors, and model settings connected with it. See the end of this chapter for a list of the sources and abbreviations. All translations from the dailies and parliamentary debates are my own.

4. The members of parliament Codignola and Santi, of the governmental party PSU, denounced, in a parliamentary interrogation, "the insufficient engagement of the political power in order to respond to the situation with reforms instead of repression" (in ME, March 2, 1968).

5. Reference to the disaster of the Weimar Republic, for example, explains the deep stigmatization of violence in Germany; the myth of the Resistance explains why, for a long time, violence was not such a taboo in Italy.

6. Along the same lines, there was mention of the "ever present difficulties of the German character with the masses: fluctuation between brutality and helplessness. [The German police officer] never [has] the natural authority of a Bobby. It is not by chance that the policemen appear in Germany as more militaristic than the very soldiers" (reader's letter, TSP, June 7, 1967).

7. The demands of this coalition included arms that could be used from a long distance, such as rubber bullets and CS gas, the return to the old *Landfriedenbruchparagraph* (which considered it a crime to take part in a prohibited demonstration that had turned violent, even if personal responsibilities were not proved), and the introduction of the crime of the dangerous formation of a mob.

8. The Gewerkschaft der Polizei asked for distance arms (in TAZ, June 13, 1987); the federal minister for home affairs Zimmerman (in FAZ, June 13, 1987), the conservative Gewerkschaft der Polizei in Deutscher Beamtenbund, and the former Berlin senator for home affairs Lummer called for the introduction of the *Vermummungsverbot* (according to which the use of any form of mask during public demonstrations was a crime) and for the prohibition of demonstrators to carry "passive arms" (such as helmets).

9. As the senator for home affairs stated, the police would not have intervened against the three hundred masked *Autonomen* during the demonstration of June 12, 1987, even if a *Vermummungsverbot* had already existed, since the police had always to balance two principles: the respect of the law, and the security of the citizens (Kewenig, in AHB 1987).

10. According to Rein and Schoen, "A great deal of contemporary policy tends to organize events in terms of a health metaphor in which worries are interpreted as outcroppings of social pathology" (1977: 241).

11. To quote Rein and Schoen, "The generative metaphor may be one of battle and victory. If it is possible in the situation to identify villains, victims and heroes, then the problem setting may be construed in terms of doing battles with the villains and winning" (1977: 242).

Sources and Abbreviations

Germany

Dailies:
Berliner Morgenpost (MOPO): 1967, 1982, 1987; *Bild*: 1967, 1982, 1987; *Frankfurter Allgemeine Zeitung* (FAZ): 1967, 1982, 1987; *Frankfurter Rundschau* (FR): 1967, 1982, 1987; *Tagesspiegel* (TSP): 1967, 1982, 1987; *Tageszeitung* (TAZ): 1982, 1987; *Telegraph* (TELE): 1967.

Parliamentary Acts:
Abgeordnetenhaus von Berlin (AHB), *Plenarprotokoll,* June 8, 1967; June 24, 1982; June 18, 1987.

Italy

Dailies:
Il Corriere della Sera (CdS): 1968, 1977, 1989; *Il Manifesto* (M): 1977, 1989; *Il Messaggero* (ME): 1968, 1977; *Il Giornale* (G): 1989; *Il Tempo* (T): 1968, 1977; *La Notte* (LN): 1989; *La Repubblica* (R): 1977, 1989; *Lotta Continua* (LC): 1977; *L'Unità* (U): 1989; *Paese Sera* (PS): 1968, 1977.

Parliamentary Acts:
Parlamento della Repubblica (P), Camera dei deputati, *Resoconto delle sedute plenarie,* March 1, 1968; May 13, 1977.

5

Political Protest and Institutional Change: The Anti–Vietnam War Movement and American Science

Kelly Moore

After taking a backseat to analyses of the emergence of political protest, the effects of widespread contentious politics are garnering renewed interest. Most studies of outcomes, however, still focus on the causes of policy outcomes, especially the state's provision of economic goods and legal rights to protesting groups and their constituents (Amenta, Carruthers, and Zylan 1992; Burstein and Freudenburg 1978; Burstein 1979; Clemens 1993; Gamson 1990; Gelb and Palley 1987; Isaac and Kelly 1981; McAdam 1982; Piven and Cloward 1979; Schramm and Turbett 1983; Tilly 1978). Typically left unexamined are challenges to nonstate institutions such as medicine, art, science, law, and education. Although institutions are distinguished from states by their lack of routinized access by everyday people, they serve smaller sets of constituencies, have less ability to create and use law, and have little ability to use violence and repression to stifle dissent, thus making them more likely to be responsive to challengers than would the state.

This chapter examines the conditions under which institutions change as a result of challenges from protest movements. The main argument is that two conditions matter: the existence of disruptive challenges that make the day-to-day reproduction of institutional action impossible; and, more importantly, institutional vulnerability to challenge that results from rapid growth, ties to the state, a high level of dispersion, and a dependence on client relations among professionals within the institution. I also identify and explicate the mechanisms through which change takes place in institutions. Changes are seen to take place through the actions of mediators, who, as simultaneous members of institutions and movement participants, translate challenges into concrete changes in institutional rules. Changes in normative rules for association with nonmembers of institutions are identified as the most important aspect of institutional change for social movement challengers, for such changes open up long-term possibilities for affecting institutional action.

Substantively, the chapter considers why science was vulnerable to challenge by anti–Vietnam War activists in the 1960s and 1970s, and how specific mediators—liberal and radical scientists who were also participants in or sympathetic to the antiwar movement—translated that challenge into changes in taken-for-granted rules about proper subjects, activities, and participants in science. As a result of these challenges and vulnerabilities, the relationship between scientists, scientific knowledge, scientific practices (i.e., the institution of science) and the American public changed dramatically. Among the most dramatic shifts was, first, the astronomical increase in citizen access to reliable information about the dangers and benefits of technologies, indirectly through the mass media and, more importantly, directly from scientists themselves, through public interest science organizations. Second, no longer was the relationship between intellectuals, citizens, and governments cozy and uncritical, as it had been in the 1950s. Leading the charge in scrutinizing science were intellectuals, especially academics, who developed analyses of science that were highly critical, rather than sympathetic and deferential. One of the main ways in which this stance has been formalized is through the development of science and technology studies programs and departments in universities in the United States. Although some of these programs are supportive of science, most are dominated by intellectuals with highly critical, and sometimes hostile, views of science. In turn, scientists have struck back, charging that critics are naive and sometimes incompetent, spurring what some observers have called the "science wars."

The antiwar movement was not single-handedly responsible for all changes in the relationships between scientists and everyday people, nor for those between scientists and other intellectuals. But it was the first of a series of challenges to scientific authority that took place beginning in the late 1950s by women, recreational drug users, and radical ecologists. In this chapter, I examine the features of science that made this earliest challenge possible.

Protest and Institutional Vulnerability

Protest and criticism are ongoing features of all democratic states, yet they do not always result in changes in institutions. Characteristics of protesters and their activities are important determinants of movement success in challenges to the state. Challenges that are nationally based, that last for several years or more, and that have multiple targets are most likely to be successful. Like states, institutions are big and unwieldy, containing groups with vested interests in stability; without consistent prodding, force, and pressure, they are unlikely to budge. And since, like states, institutions are constantly negotiating demands for monies, status, and power among members and allies, those who do not have leverage, in the form of something to exchange, are bound to fail. The Metropolitan Museum of Art, for example, may add one exhibition on Asian American artists in response to protest from Asian Americans, but without consistent, disruptive pressure, Asian Americans are unlikely to be routinely included. For those who are not bona fide members of an institution, leverage comes from disrupting multiple aspects of an institution so as to provoke multiple responses. Similarly, if protest is constant over several years but at the same time innovative, institutions will be more likely to act than if protest is simply a one-shot action. Like challenges to the state, then, challenges to institutions must avoid short-term, symbolic changes in limited areas, and this can be done in part by mounting disruptive, widespread, long-term challenges.

Yet, as students of social movements know, the actions of protesters are only one determinant of social movement outcomes. Equally important are the characteristics of targets. States and organizations have clearly received the lion's share of attention from scholars of movement outcomes; here I want to shift the focus to a mid-range entity: social institutions. Institutions are social groups that bound action by providing taken-for-granted prescriptions for what is a proper object of action (representational rules), for who can legitimately engage with that object (constitutive rules), and for what kinds of actions are appropriate and permissible vis-à-vis a particular subject of action (normative rules; Scott 1994: 68). They are composed of organizations, networks, people, objects, money, and other resources. What makes them distinctive is that they are organized around a specific subject (e.g., art, education, medicine, religion, or science), and the rules that guide action around that subject endure over time. Their edges are usually blurry, as some people, subjects, and activities may be seen as only partially legitimate, or may be seen as shifting from legitimate to illegitimate (midwifery and midwives, in relation to American medicine, provide one example).

The term *institution* is sometimes used in a lay sense to refer to a specific organization, especially a large organization such as General Motors or Harvard University, or to describe an organization, person, object, or activity that has been in existence for such a long time that it becomes taken for granted as a permanent element of social life in a particular area. Thus, the

New York Yankees baseball team may be called a New York institution. Although there is some overlap between these usages and the more standard
sociological concept of an institution, they are mainly distinct ideas. It is
worth noting, though, that the notion of an institution as permanent and
meaningful (the second lay sense of the word) is related to the sociological
conception of an institution. Institutions in both senses are taken for granted as permanent because of their political and/or cultural power and because
their origins are obscure or forgotten.

Institutions are also sometimes confused with organizations. The former are much larger, being composed of many organizations, networks, and
people, not just one formal organization; and are organized around the production of a socially and culturally recognized product, such as, but not limited to, aesthetic goods (art), knowledge and products for controlling the
natural world (science), and knowledge and products for controlling human
health (medicine). In contemporary industrialized societies, institutions are
usually dominated by professionals, and the subjects that they address are
usually taken for granted as distinctive and separate elements of significance
in a given society. For example, religion, in most Western industrialized
democracies, is seen as different from science.

Institutions differ from the state in significant ways vis-à-vis the potential influence of social movements. A central difference is that there are no
standard and direct mechanisms for the influence of everyday people on institutions comparable to elections and other democratic processes that citizens have to influence the state. Institutions might be thought of as more
like benevolent, nondemocratic states. Other key differences are the localized nature of institutions (including their localized legitimacy) and their
ultimate reliance on the state as regulator (Fligstein 1992: 314–17).

It should be noted that the relationship between institutional vulnerability and protest is interactive: vulnerabilities to protest will not mean
much without persistent, widespread, and disruptive protest; neither will
protest mean much against a target that is impervious. Vulnerability should
not be considered a dichotomous category such that institutions are or are
not vulnerable, or that there is something permanent about them across
time or place. Few aspects of institutions are static in the sense that they
emanate from a constitution or other set of formal laws. In fact, this is what
makes them so distinctive and fascinating: important rules and relationships
that constitute them are *not formalized* and are thus constantly subject to negotiation from within and without. There are few, if any, static aspects of institutions, except in the most banal sense (e.g., religion is about something
extrarational; medicine is about healing the sick). I want to make the strong

claim that other than those bases, institutions are constantly shifting, and that it is the speed and content of those shifts that ought to be the subject of analysis.[1]

Just as there are more opportune times than others to challenge the state, there are better times than others for challengers to press their claims against institutions. Simply put, institutional vulnerability makes institutions susceptible to challenge from clients. There are four characteristics of institutions that determine their relative vulnerability. The first is rapid growth in organizations, infusions of money, or especially members. Growth is inherently destabilizing, because it makes change more normative for participants and thus more likely. It also increases the sheer numbers of people and units that have little investment in business as usual. Newer members, like newer organizations, are likely to seek advantageous positions for themselves (whether these are moves higher up in a hierarchy or simply moves to other positions), for multiple reasons: prestige, personal satisfaction, a wish to occupy a position in which they can assist more people, money, selfishness, and other motivations. Rapid growth in funding means that patterns of funding distribution are unlikely to be settled and routinized, encouraging jockeying for monies through new political claims-making.

Second, the relative diffuseness of an institution makes it more vulnerable to challenge. A diffuse institution is one that lacks consistent, centralized control over members or participants (both individuals and organizations), in which members gain monies and status from multiple sources, and in which there are multiple pathways of entry. Another way of saying this is that institutions that have organizations, networks, and individuals with a relatively high level of autonomy are, by definition, hard to control. This means that individuals or organizations may respond to challenges and opportunities in unique ways, as they see fit.

American medicine, for example, is presently less vulnerable than art, because medicine exerts tight control over membership and has a relatively small number of professional organizations, and because sites of work must be licensed. Art, on the other hand, has weak control over membership and has hundreds of professional organizations, and work may be done at any number of sites. The multiple points of entry and lack of control over members mean that art, as an institution, is much more vulnerable.[2]

A third element of institutional vulnerability is the link between clients and professionals within an institution. All institutions are led by professionals.[3] Professional legitimation claims (and hence claims to monies, status, and political power) are typically based on expertise and on service to a client or clients. To the extent that professionals claim to serve specific, organized clients and receive benefits (such as money) on this basis, they are vulnerable to challenge. The type of link matters significantly in determining vulnerability. On the one hand, all professionals depend on clients to help legitimate their activities, in that clients help support the claim that nonprofessionals cannot perform certain services and tasks as well as professionals. But on the other hand, professionals are even more vulnerable when clients are in a position to provide monies or other material support. Finally, organized clients are more threatening than those who are unorganized.

Finally, it is ironic that ties to the state may also make an institution vulnerable to protest by social movements. The main point here is that, to the extent that institutions are connected to the state, they are vulnerable to the same processes that give movements influence over the state. Alliances with the state can be useful during historical periods when there is little dissent, but close allies of the state may be vulnerable during periods of intense protest against the state. Institutions may be thought of as allied with the state (or, more properly, state agencies) when they receive a significant portion of their funding from the state or when an agency that is targeted by protesters has been captured by an institution. Thus, alliances with and benefits from the state may sometimes be sources of political and economic power for a group, but they will be disadvantageous during periods when the state, or parts of the state, are targeted by social movements. One of the important ways in which state-institution ties may be established is through laws. Thus, some institutions with strong legal and informal ties to the state—such as law—are more vulnerable than those with few of these ties.

What Changes When Institutions Change?

Political protest potentially affects three features of institutions. Institutions are routinized ways of organizing the actions of a particular set of people vis-à-vis a set of subjects of action. Institutions, then, are mainly about *rules and assumptions* that shape *who* can do what in regard to a *subject*. Protest may change any of these three aspects: when it changes all three in fundamental ways, challenges may be thought of as most successful; when none change, challenges may be thought of as failures.

In examining whether or not change has taken place, then, we should look, first, for changes in the social or demographic characteristics of people within the institution. To follow on the example from medicine, only those licensed by the state can legitimately practice medicine. Protest may change who counts as a healer by including new groups or excluding others. These rules are often the targets of protest groups: AIDS activists, for example, have challenged the taken-for-granted rule in medicine that the only legitimate judges of the effectiveness of AIDS drugs are physicians (Epstein 1996).

Second, we should also look for changes in the taken-for-granted rules for subjects that gain the attention of institution members, especially the attention of professionals, who tend to have the most power in institutions. What are the problems or subjects with which they engage? What sorts of things do they deem appropriate subjects, and which do they ignore?

Finally, rules with regard to sorts of action around a particular subject and with regard to specific types of persons may change. These are normative rules, rules that determine what kinds of contact people may have with each other and what kinds of action they may perform on subjects. Since professionals within institutions often claim to serve clients, changes in normative rules encompass changes in the sorts of typical or routine actions that take place between them. Alternatively, normative rules also shape the kinds of routine forms of action (advice, neutrality, or brokerage, for example) that institutional members have with other powerful groups, such as the state. Examples might be changes in scientific researchers' treatment of laboratory animals as a result of animal rights protest (but not the abandonment of the practice of experimenting on animals altogether), and the (hypothetical) widespread elimination of entry fees for museums.

How much do participants, objects, and forms of action matter, comparatively? For the most part, normative rules are the most important, just as laws that guide action are usually the target of state-oriented challengers. For example, consider three different sorts of goals that a movement might pursue: one-time changes in who can participate in an institutional activity, a change in a subject of institutional activity, and changes in rules for access and representation by nonmembers. All three are concerned with the rules that govern relations between members and nonmembers, between products and clients, and between subjects, clients, and professionals. But in the long run, changes that affect the form of the relationship between those who are inside an institution and those who are outside are of central importance, for herein lies the key to the power of institutions: professionals within them set rules, while those outside typically do not. Having routine, permanent access to institutions provides nonmembers with access to rule making.

Mechanisms of Institutional Change

Understanding how vulnerable institutions shift subjects, personnel, and activities demands knowing how challenges are translated into change. At the most basic level, people and organizations within institutions respond when public, disruptive protest takes place at the site of the public reproduction of an institution and when widely circulated verbal and written criticisms take place. It is not enough to challenge institutions in private—members do this all the time. Criticisms must be undertaken in such a way that the ongoing reproduction of normal, everyday relations is undermined. Underlying this hypothesis is the assumption that members of institutions, especially professionals, value business as usual both as an end in itself that legitimates institutional action, and because it leads to continued flows of monies and personnel.

Disruptive challenges coupled with institutional vulnerability are translated into changes when mediators—individuals who are members of a movement and also professional members of an institution—initiate changes in actions in organizations within the institution. Usually theories of social movement treat challengers and polity members as distinct, separate groups, but there is ample evidence to suggest that there is overlap between these two groups. Such mediators are likely to occupy marginal, rather than central, positions with respect to institutional membership, movement membership, or both. Mediators, who occupy this middle ground between institutions and movements (or between movements, or between movement networks) are in a good position to translate the claims of protesting groups into changes in practices, norms, and members. Gay doctors who are participants in or sympathetic to the claims of AIDS activists, for example, have been extremely important in challenging the medical community's treatment of AIDS patients (Epstein 1996).

It is difficult to discount claims of institutional members—after all, they have already been legitimated—so they are less likely than outsiders to be dismissed as kooks or quacks. Intermediaries also promote change because they have access to rule-making bodies, resources, and people, while those who are simply movement members do not. Finally, mediators are multilingual: they can translate concerns of a movement into language acceptable and understandable by institutional members.[4] The next section of this chapter considers these general propositions through an examination of the vulnerability of science to antiwar activism, and of the way scientist-activists who were participants in the anti–Vietnam War movement precipitated changes in the activities and subjects of science.

Science in Post–World War II America: New Opportunities, New Vulnerabilities

In the decade following World War II, scientists were celebrated mainly for their discovery of atomic energy and weapons, which promised Americans a safe and prosperous life. Americans now had a monopoly on a source of energy "too cheap to meter" and were the beneficiaries of the ongoing production of weapons and material goods that made America the most prosperous and perhaps most highly armed nation in the world. Because they were thought to be able to address political questions objectively, scientists were seen by many politicians as keys to the "end of ideology" in political debate. Economic policy makers also viewed research and development as the engine of the American military and industrial economy.

More concretely, federal confidence in and enthusiasm for science resulted in an unprecedented rise in funding for science after 1945. Federal funds for science were considerably less than $100 million in 1930, but by 1945 they had increased tenfold, to $1 billion. That figure had doubled by 1954, with the United States spending well over $2 billion a year on science research and development (Price 1965: 35). State sponsorship was especially crucial to the state's military needs. In 1959, 59 percent of the federal research and development budget went toward defense-related research (National Science Foundation 1977: 34), and those agencies most closely tied to military needs received the lion's share of the monies. Conversely, those federal agencies receiving the lowest percentages of federal funding were the National Science Foundation (NSF) and the National Institutes of Health (NIH).

Newly available funds also spurred the growth of scientific knowledge. Scientists formed new associations to keep up with developments in ever more specialized fields. While physics was still the "queen of the sciences" as the discipline with the clearest understanding of the basic building blocks of matter and at the same time the most capable of building useful goods, by the middle of the 1950s, biologists were contesting that position, starting with the discovery of DNA by Watson and Crick in 1956 (Keller 1992). Professional associations grew like weeds: in 1945, 153 new professional science organizations were founded; in 1955, 185; and in 1960, 216 (*Encyclopedia of Associations* 1992).[5] The federal government also formed new organizations to sponsor research, including the NSF, the NIH, and the Atomic Energy Commission. Because federal sponsorship was to be directed toward major research institutions, not divided equitably among all colleges and universities, universities quickly sought to build up their research capability and to portray themselves as better than competing universities. This meant that scientists' intellectual attentions were focused on narrower and narrower slices of the natural world and on the opinions and interests of a smaller number of scientists, so that there was no real centralization to scientific research as there had been during the Manhattan Project.

Finally, as funding for research grew, so did the number of scientists.

Although the number of science doctorates awarded rose at the same rate as other disciplines, the number within particular scientific disciplines rose more quickly. Biology grew at a faster rate than any other major scientific discipline, followed by physics. Not only were these fields thus likely to be destabilized, they were also populated by younger scientists than other fields (National Research Council 1950–1970). Scientists also became more heterogeneous. Jewish scientists, some of whom had escaped Nazism and rarely shared American scientists' apolitical ethos, increased their numbers after 1945 (Hollinger 1996), and more and more middle-class men joined the ranks of scientists. Scientists worked at a wider variety of work locations, too; whereas in the 1930s the largest employer of scientists was industry, by 1960, the federal government employed nearly as many scientists as did the private sector. Colleges and universities experienced the highest rate of increase, although scientists there were numerically dwarfed by industry and government science employees (U.S. Department of Labor 1973).

Between 1945 and 1960, then, science expanded rapidly and dramatically. New ideas were being developed, monies poured in, and there were opportunities for those who would take them.

In this case, growth was also accompanied by decentralization. Conventional wisdom tells us that American science, because it was funded mainly by the state in the postwar period, was fairly heterogeneous and centralized (Mukerji 1989; Lapp 1965; Lasby 1966). Yet this is clearly not the case. As I argued earlier, it is clear that by the early 1950s, biologists did not see themselves as subordinate to physicists in the pecking order of science but instead saw themselves as on the verge of the fundamental discoveries about life that would surpass those of physicists (Keller 1992). More importantly, there was no central organization that guided the certification of scientists or their public or private behavior; even multidiscipline organizations such as the American Association for the Advancement of Science (AAAS) were not in control of scientists' actions so much as they coordinated information exchanges among them. Nor did the National Research Council or the National Academy of Sciences dictate the behavior or subject matter of scientists, as the American Medical Association was more likely to do for physicians (see Starr 1982; Wolfle 1989).

Rapid growth and differentiation was one consequence of the state's interest in the material goods that science could produce and scientists' reciprocal interest in funding. Yet there were other ties to the state aside from intellectual and financial ties that served the interests of scientists throughout the 1940s and 1950s and made them vulnerable in the 1960s. First, there were strong political ties. Scientists had emerged from the Second World

War as strategic elites, a group with special knowledge and skills of value to the state (Lasby 1966: 267). Through their participation in advisory boards and ad hoc committees in the executive and legislative branches, scientists participated in political decision making (Lapp 1965). In 1958, one of the most politically significant formal political alliances between the state and science was created through the formation of the Jason program of the Department of Defense Institute for Defense Analysis, whose purpose was to bring the best and brightest physicists to work on classified problems of national defense (Cahn 1971).

Cutting across intellectual, political, and financial relationships between the state and science was the development of military research centers on university campuses. These centers were usually created by universities to attract research monies from government, especially through specialized programs, such as Project Themis, that were designed to provide research monies for universities and to facilitate collaborations with local industries that themselves were the recipients of defense grant monies from the government (Heineman 1993: chapter 1). Among the largest and most prominent of these centers were the Stanford Research Institute and MIT's Lincoln Laboratories and Instrumentation Laboratory (Leslie 1993). Lucrative university-military collaborations were located not only at prominent private universities, including California Institute of Technology, Columbia University, Harvard University, Cornell University, and Johns Hopkins University, but also at public schools, such as the State University of New York–Buffalo, the University of Wisconsin–Madison, the University of Arizona, the University of Michigan, and Pennsylvania State University (Heineman 1993).

In the late 1950s and early 1960s, these programs, and related ones such as Jason, were seen by scientists, university administrators, and military officials to mutually benefit all parties. Scientists received steady funding and often saw themselves as engaged in basic research that served the public interest, administrators received large overhead, and the state received weapons and goods. As Mukerji (1989) has observed, this arrangement placed scientists at the political disposal of the state, making them into a kind of reserve army of labor that would readily defend state projects in the language of objective observers, as well as produce weapons.

Finally, the financial and political attachment to the state was seen by scientists as serving the interests of their main clients: all Americans. States were supposed to represent the interests of citizens, and thus, by extension, ties to the state could plausibly be seen to serve broader interests (see Grodzins and Rabinowitch 1963 for a collection of articles that reflect this supposition from the *Bulletin of the Atomic Scientists,* the main intellectual journal concerned with science-society relations in the postwar period. At the same time, it was a rare professional science organization that had a committee or program that linked the interests of scientists with those of ordinary people. Even the few that did exist before 1969, such as the AAAS Committee on Science for Human Welfare and its precursor, the Social Aspects of Science Committee, worked mainly on promoting public appreciation for the economic, political, and cultural value of scientific products and activity but never solicited input from citizens or were attentive to citizen concerns (Kuznick 1994; Wolfle 1989: 234–36).

These conditions were not to last, however. In the 1960s, more people began to challenge this arrangement, asking whether or not the tie between science, the state, and universities was morally correct, democratic, or in the national interest. That this arrangement was successfully challenged was in part due to the fragmentation in the institution of science, which ironically was a result of the state's interest in science.

The Anti–Vietnam War Movement and Science

Although the United States had been involved in fighting nationalist Vietnamese forces on behalf of France as early as 1954, American involvement took a decidedly large step in 1965, when President Johnson took action on the Gulf of Tonkin resolution, dramatically increasing the bombing of North Vietnam. Unlike the earlier "ban the bomb" movement, which had been led mainly by professionals, some scientists, and a handful of pacifists, protest against American involvement in Vietnam was led by students (DeBenedetti 1990). Science was not an early target of campus-based protesters organized against the war, but it became so as a coincidence of student protests that not only took place on college campuses but were increasingly directed against universities themselves, which were seen as full partners in facilitating the war in Vietnam. It is a truism that people tend to protest against the nearest objects, and the military-science alliance on college campuses was quite visible. For many students it was no great leap to begin to ask questions about the relationship between universities and the "military-industrial complex" that Dwight Eisenhower had identified in 1958. There were also more ideological and intellectual reasons for attacking universities and their faculty: members of Students for a Democratic Society (SDS), who on many campuses acted as leaders of antiwar protest, took seriously the work of Frankfurt school philosopher Herbert Marcuse, who argued that repression in capitalist societies was located not only in the overt actions of the police and courts but in the very institutions, languages, and cultures of a given society (Ehrenreich and Ehrenreich 1969: 34–35).

Increasingly, students targeted military recruitment programs and research laboratories that received funding for research that was ultimately used by American troops in Vietnam. Between 1965 and 1970 on at least eleven major college campuses,[6] military-supported research buildings and laboratories were sites of antiwar protest and were associated with some of the most dramatic events of the period: the 1970 bombing of the Army Math Research Center at the University of Wisconsin, which killed a researcher; the 1970 Kent State University killings; and the 1968 sit-in at Columbia University. In each of these cases, protesters directed their actions against the physical representations of the alliances between universities and the military, usually Department-of-Defense-sponsored laboratories and programs. At Kent State as early as 1968, student protest was directed against the Liquid Crystals Institute, which developed motion detectors used in Vietnam (Heineman 1993: 37) and at Stanford, against the Stanford Research Institute, which was created explicitly to attract defense contracts and upon which Stanford was economically dependent, though the institute was nominally separate from Stanford University. At Columbia University, the 1968 campus occupation was sparked mainly by Columbia's association with the Institute for Defense Analysis, which poured millions of defense dollars into scientific research on campus. Similarly, the bombing of Sterling Hall at the University of Wisconsin in 1970 was motivated by anger toward the university's alliance with the military (Bates 1992; DeBenedetti 1990; Heineman 1993).

More generally, protesters considered the war foolish, cruel, and stupid, perpetuated by authorities—including scientists—who were out of touch with citizens. The main charge against scientists was that they had failed to take responsibility for using scientific knowledge and goods for socially useful, rather than deadly and destructive, ends. The attack on science and technology was so widespread that at a White House ceremony for the National Medal of Science Award, President Johnson was compelled to defend scientists: "An aggrieved public does not draw the fine line between 'good' science and 'bad' technology. . . . You and I know that Frankenstein was the doctor, not the monster. But it would be well to remember that the people of the village, angered by the monster, marched against the doctor" (qtd. in Kevles 1978: 400). This larger questioning of authority placed scientists directly in the line of fire, since they had earlier laid claim to status based on political authority and on their role in keeping America safe (DeBenedetti 1990; Kevles 1978; Lapp 1965; Leslie 1993). In conjunction with the direct and public attacks on the alliance between science, universities, and the war in Vietnam, antiauthoritarian challenges made scientists' claims to serve humanity increasingly implausible.

It is possible that universities, professional science associations, scientists, and others might simply have ignored these protests. Yet that is not how the story unfolded.

Mediators and Institutional Change

As I have argued elsewhere, scientists did not simply respond to protest but were also participants and initiators of it. Some scientists—especially Jewish biologists and physicists—were well aware of the Faustian bargain they had made with the state—exchanging weapons for money—and were greatly concerned that human political capabilities had been exceeded by technological advances. Even before the development of the atomic bomb, some American scientists were expressing moral concerns, and some had pressed President Roosevelt not to drop the bomb at all (Smith 1965). After the Second World War, some had formed groups such as the Federation of Atomic Scientists and the American Association for Social Responsibility in Science (based on a British group) and had published the widely read *Bulletin of the Atomic Scientists*. In 1948, scientists gathered for the first annual Pugwash Conference, in Pugwash, Nova Scotia, to seek ways to encourage international cooperation.

During the middle and late 1950s, scientists (again, often led by Jews) could be found as leaders of peace groups: Albert Einstein, Linus Pauling, and Albert Schweitzer were instrumental in the founding and launching of SANE (Committee for a Sane Nuclear Policy); others, such as Manhattan Project scientist Leo Szilard and Washington University biologist Barry Commoner, were active in other peace and "ban the bomb" groups, such as Scientists for Survival and fallout information groups (Commoner 1958; O'Neill 1971). Still others, such as Eugene Rabinowitch, were outspoken advocates of international control of nuclear energy (Grodzins and Rabinowitch 1963).

It was this tradition of scientific activism, which had been submerged and muted during the 1950s, that was revived by scientists during the anti–Vietnam War movement. On college campuses, liberal (and, more rarely, radical) scientists, usually physicists and biologists who were often Jewish and usually either full professors or graduate students (Moore 1996), sought to find ways to reconcile their political and scientific commitments. These scientists were usually affected by the antiwar movement in one of two ways. First and more commonly, they themselves were antiwar activists who, in conjunction with antiwar activities, came to espouse the critique of science as captured by military interests. The other, more rare pathway through which scientists participated in antiwar activities was via recruitment by science graduate student activists, who pressured faculty to act (Moore 1996).

These mediators, or activist scientists, usually sought to join their political and professional interests, first, by making use of existing professional associations. Usually, members of these associations either found involvement with popular politics incompatible with the promotion of the professional interests of scientists, or engaged in small symbolic acts, such as adding sessions on "science and society" to their annual meetings. As a result of the intransigence of professional associations, scientists initiated what would become one of the most important outcomes of the antiwar movement: the formation of science-based organizations that sought to communicate directly with, and work on behalf of, liberal and radical individuals and citizen political groups by providing them with scientific information and expertise. The most important of these were the Union of Concerned Scientists (1969), Science for the People (1969), the Center for Science in the Public Interest (1972), and Computer People for Peace (1969). Other public interest groups that were formed in part by scientists and in part by lawyers included the Natural Resources Defense Council and the Environmental Defense Fund.

The most important effect of these organizations was that they changed rules in science.[7] From the 1950s through even the late 1960s, publicly providing scientific information and legitimation critical of industry and the state was viewed as out of bounds for scientists (see Fox 1985: 298 for a good example of scientists' attacks on Rachel Carson for her publication of *Silent Spring*). But by the middle of the 1970s, scientists were falling over themselves to find ways to study subjects of importance to the public, even narrow segments of the public, not just the state or industry. At least five new books by scientists analyzed their responsibility to the public and made suggestions about how they could assist the public in winning political battles with industry and the state.[8]

The Union of Concerned Scientists (UCS) perhaps did more than any other group to legitimate this form of action. After producing a report about citizen challenges in the Boston area air pollution hearings in 1970, the demand for its services skyrocketed (Union of Concerned Scientists 1970). In July 1971, UCS released the first independent safety report on nuclear power; because it was aimed at a lay audience, it received substantial attention from the media, including CBS and NBC news organizations (UCS 1984). Over the next ten years, UCS continued to play an important role in linking citizens with the state, by providing information about power plant sitings and safety rules and by attacking the Atomic Energy Commission's Emergency Core Cooling System (Downey 1988). Its activities also led to more public awareness of the dangers associated with nuclear power; for the first time, major news sources reported on nuclear power issues.

Over the next ten years, virtually every major professional science organization (and most minor ones) adopted platforms, committees, or adjunct organizations that sought to do just what public interest science organizations were doing: linking scientific research and action with the interests of citizen groups.[9] Physics, biology, and mathematics associations led the way. Recall that physicists and biologists, and to a lesser extent mathematicians, were most likely to be involved in antiwar activism and to challenge their own professional associations to engage in socially responsible activities. The pathway through which institutional change took place, then, was this: scientist-activists found professional associations unresponsive to such activities, but when they founded their own public interest organizations, these same activities were then adopted by the professional organizations.

If these groups, with their new subjects (problems of concern to citizens, rather than to the state or industry) and a new kind of action (direct communication with the public), had been the only effect of the antiwar movement on science, it would have been a significant victory for activists. But changes made by scientists were also complemented by changes in the intellectual and academic treatment of science by nonscientists. If the changes scientists made in science came in the relationship between science and other aspects of social life, humanist intellectuals (mainly sociologists) acted in a parallel fashion. They were influenced by leftist critiques of science (including Marcuse), new developments in the philosophy of science that showed that science was a social and political creation, and experiences with antiwar and civil rights activism that illuminated subtle and not-so-subtle ways in which science was linked to projects of domination. Philosophers and sociologists of science located on just a few campuses formed new intellectual networks and formal organizations devoted to emphasizing, rather than obfuscating, the social and political determinants of scientific knowledge and action. The main organization was the Society for the Social Study of Science, founded in 1975 at Cornell University. New degree-granting academic programs under the rubric of "science and technology studies" were also formed. The first two in the United States were at MIT and Rensselaer Polytechnic Institute in Troy, New York. While at some universities these programs have acted as boosters for science, the dominant attitude of most faculty has been critical of science, rather than wholeheartedly respectful, as earlier generations of scholars were.[10] As with any discipline, the number of journals devoted to this subject has mushroomed. The dominant one is still *Social Studies of Science,* founded in 1971.

Conclusions: Critiques, Protest, and Change in Science

Antiwar protest affected science because it was already vulnerable. The ability of protesters to obtain a response from scientists was due to the fact that scientists themselves were also activists and were responsive to critiques of the politicized nature of science in America. These mediators were able to translate the challenges of protesting groups (which rarely included scientists) into changes in the rules of action for scientists through the formation of new kinds of socially responsible organizations, whose activities were also adopted in modified form by major professional associations throughout the 1970s.

Why were these mediators able to make changes? Science was vulnerable ideologically as well as organizationally. The rapid growth of science meant that there was no single center of power; hence there were multiple locations of challenge and access for protesters and dissenting scientists. As a result, efforts at change by mediators took place through challenges to university-military ties and professional associations, and in some cases through the refusal of individual scientists to accept military funding. Rapid growth also meant that there were many newcomers to the field whose interests were not the same as those scientists who had made their careers from the 1940s through the early 1960s, when the cold war was arguably at its height.

Liberal scientists, mainly younger physicists and biologists who worked on college campuses, and Jews of all ages on those campuses sought ways in which they could reconcile commitments to science and to their political beliefs. Why were these groups' interests so different from both those of their predecessors and those of their more hawkish and conservative peers? On the one hand, the sheer numbers of people engaged in science made it more likely that there would be differences of opinion. But, on the other hand, it is also the case that new groups of people—émigré scientists, especially Jews and younger scientists—had political experiences that made them suspicious of strong military-science ties. Rebuffed by professional associations, with their largely conservative leaders, these scientists began their own organizations. Their activities were eventually adopted, first in a modified form by the very organizations that had initially ignored their requests, and later, by 1975, by most major and minor professional science organizations.

At the same time, academics who were also participants in the antiwar movement and were engaged in studying the sociology and philosophy of science came to similar sorts of conclusions: that science was deeply entrenched in war making and domination. Like academic activist-scientists, these intellectuals sought to explicate this relationship through ethnographic, historical, and philosophical analyses of science, collectively called the social studies of science.

I will conclude by identifying a few of the ways in which the form and causes of changes in nonstate institutions are similar to and different from those of changes in the state. They are similar in that for activists to acquire their goals, the timing must be favorable. In protest targeted against the state, this means that activists must have allies—usually elected or appointed officials—or they must be able to offer something in return for support of their goals (monies or votes, usually). Similarly, without an incentive to change, groups within an institution are unlikely to do so. The second point of similarity is that, in both cases, those who do not hold positions of power (within the state or an institution) usually need to use extraordinary means to acquire a hearing, and even more so to force change. These points of comparison are not particular to social movements or to politics—they are more general comments on most power relations.

The similarities between state-targeted and institution-targeted protest are overshadowed in significant ways by the differences between them. Most importantly, challenges to institutions are more difficult for activists, because it is not clear where power is centered in an institution. Although some institutions are more centralized than others (medicine more so than art, for example), their fluidity and diversity make changes more difficult to promote (as well as to observe). Second, elected officials have considerable power in the state, although they obviously also share it with bureaucrats. This means that activists can withhold votes from elected officials and use standardized procedures in conjunction with direct and disruptive action to acquire their goals. Not so with institutions. Although professionals within institutions usually hold the most power, and although they have prestige and informal power in part because they claim to serve clients, not just their own self-interest, in reality there are few ways in which clients can routinely affect the behavior of professionals. In the long run, this means that groups challenging institutional behavior, membership, and subjects cannot use the usual track that most American movements have used in challenging states: direct legal and electoral action combined with innovative and disruptive action. Using a different tack—innovative and disruptive action, and the use of allies who can act as mediators to translate goals and to pressure institutional leaders—is more likely to lead to collective benefits for challengers.

Notes

I am most grateful to Edwin Amenta, Lynn C. Chancer, Marco Giugni, Doug McAdam, David S. Meyer, Duane Oldfield, Francesca A. Polletta, Walter W. Powell, Steven Valocchi, and Gilda Zwerman for invaluable comments on earlier drafts of this paper. Outstanding research assistance was provided by Barnard College students Bari Meltzer, Sonia Qadir, and Marie Segares.

1. In comparing the relative vulnerability of institutions within the same state during a specified period of time, emphasis is likely to be placed on differences between institutions. Yet a cross-national comparison of several institutions (say, medicine and art in France and Japan) will likely focus the researcher's attention on the *similarities* among institutions within a given country. Thus, to what a given institution is compared will affect a researcher's judgment about the relative vulnerability of an institution over time.

2. However, diffusion and autonomy as elements of vulnerability are inversely related to the ability of a challenge to make dramatic changes across an institution. To the extent that institutions are diffuse, changes are likely to take place only in small segments and locations, not across all aspects or "from the top down."

3. Professionals are those occupational groups which monopolize the access to and the creation of a body of knowledge and which have some sort of code of ethics that they claim to adhere to in order to gain the confidence of the public or clients, a system of licensing, peer control (only specialists can judge one another's work); and professional associations that uphold these relationships and activities.

4. The importance of "middle-persons" for the spread of ideas, members, and tactics and for coalition building across movements is examined in Meyer and Whittier's article on social movement spillover (1994).

5. These numbers actually underestimate the numbers of organizations founded, because they include only those organizations which were still in existence in 1992.

6. Pennsylvania State, SUNY–Buffalo, Kent State, Georgetown (Heineman 1993: 196, 214–17, 228), Columbia (Avorn 1969), MIT, Stanford (Leslie 1993: chapter 4), Berkeley, Chicago (Lyttle 1988), Wisconsin (Bates 1992), and Northwestern (Porter 1973).

7. Except in some particular cases (the American Physical Society, for example), there was little change in the kind of scientists engaged in particular scientific activities as a result of the antiwar movement. This, simply put, was because antiwar protesters typically did not level charges related to the social characteristics of scientists.

8. The most widely read book of this sort was *Advice and Dissent: Scientists in the Political Arena*, by Joel Primack and Frank von Hippel (1974). Others include *Science for Society* (proceedings from the National Conference on Goals, Policies, and Programs of Federal, State, and Local Science Agencies), edited by John E. Mock (1970); *The Social Responsibility of the Scientist*, edited by Martin Brown (1971); and *The Social Responsibility of Scientists* (Annals of the New York Academy of Sciences, vol. 196, art. 4), edited by Philip Siekevitz (1972).

9. These groups, in order of their founding, were the American Physical Society (1969), the American Society for Microbiology (1969), and the American Association for the Advancement of Science (1970).

10. Sal Restivo, 1995–96 president of the Society for the Social Study of Science, made this observation in a conversation with me on October 15, 1995.

6

The Biographical Impact of Activism

Doug McAdam

It has been common in recent years for movement scholars to lament the lack of systematic research on the impact or consequences of social movements (see McAdam, McCarthy, and Zald 1988: 727). But, as Marco Giugni's introduction to this volume makes clear, there has actually been a great deal of scholarship on the general topic of movement outcomes. When one surveys this work, however, one is struck by the unevenness in the coverage of various kinds of impacts. Some kinds of consequences have been accorded a great deal of attention, while others have received short shrift. To oversimplify a bit, the bulk of work on movement outcomes has been focused on the political institutional impacts that have followed from movement activity. Much less attention has been paid to the wide range of unintended social or cultural consequences that could plausibly be linked to social movements. Within this latter category I would include those biographical or life-course consequences that have been empirically tied to movement activity.

In this chapter I want to distinguish between two very different kinds of demographic effects of social movement activity. The first concerns the biographical consequences that appear to follow from sustained individual activism. The second, and potentially more consequential, effect centers on the role of movements as sources of aggregate-level change in life-course patterns. In the next section, I will review the various follow-up studies on 1960s activists that attest to the biographical impact of movement participation. The balance of the chapter will then be given over to a report of recent research by some colleagues and me that appears to support the contention that a good many of the demographic changes we associate with the "baby boomers" may, in part, betray the influence of the political and cultural movements of the 1960s.

The Biographical Consequences of Individual Activism

Before turning to the few systematic follow-up studies of former activists that have been completed to date, permit me a word or two—some of it of an editorial nature—about the popular media's interest in the topic. The relatively meager scholarly output on the topic contrasts sharply with the volume of popular media attention in the United States devoted to the question, where are the 1960s radicals today? Based on countless newspaper and magazine articles and television news shows, many in the general public feel certain they "know" what happened to the 1960s activists. And in knowing what happened to the 1960s activists, they presume to know something more general about the consequences of movement participation. What they "know" can be gleaned from popular media portraits of the contemporary lives of former activists.

What emerges from these stories is the image of the former " '60s radical" as opportunistic yuppie. The contemporary lives of former activist "stars" such as Jerry Rubin and the late Eldridge Cleaver are routinely offered as evidence to support this generic story line. Rubin's reincarnation as a Reagan-era stockbroker and Cleaver's conservative, born-again views on life in contemporary America provide good copy and serve as reassuring evidence of a kind of moral and political maturation claimed to be typical of many 1960s "radicals." So often have stories on these two appeared in the popular press that their lives now serve as a general account of the contemporary biographies of yesterday's activists. Thus, the collapse of the New Left in the early 1970s allegedly set in motion a period of wholesale generational sellout that found the lion's share of former radicals embracing the politics and lifestyles of the Me Decade.

Given that Rubin and Cleaver are virtually the only former activists to receive widespread media attention, why do these images of generational sellout persist? The answer may lie in the larger depoliticizing function of the story line. If most of the 1960s radicals grew up to become yuppies, then their earlier radicalism can be largely written off as a product of youthful immaturity and faddishness. By having grown up to espouse mainstream values and hold conventional jobs, figures like Rubin and Cleaver reassure the public that it need not take their earlier radical politics seriously. From this perspective, the long-term biographical consequences of 1960s activism—and, by extension, movement participation more generally—appear to be minimal.

Despite the popular appeal of the dominant media account, there are several reasons for doubting its generalizability. First, after Rubin and Cleaver, it is hard to identify many other prominent 1960s activists who fit the story line. Second, the account rests on a dubious assertion of continuity linking the shifting patterns of cultural and political allegiance characteristic of the baby boom generation. Probably no more than 2 to 4 percent of the generation took an active part in any of the movements of the mid to late 1960s. It therefore seems likely that today's yuppies are drawn not from the activist segment of the generation but from the other 96 to 98 percent of their baby boom cohorts. Third, and most relevant to this review, the popular media account is woefully out of sync with the few systematic follow-up studies that have been conducted on 1960s activists.

Though far less extensive than the literature on movement recruitment, there does exist a small body of follow-up studies of former activists that have sought to assess the biographical impact of movement participation. These studies are remarkable for the consistently contradictory portrait they draw of the former activists relative to the media account I have described. Before sketching this scholarly portrait, let me first briefly describe the major studies that constitute the scholarly literature referenced here.

The first major study to examine the impact of movement participation was one conducted by Jay Demerath, Gerald Marwell, and Michael Aiken. In 1965, these researchers conducted "before and after" surveys with 223 volunteers who took part in that summer's SCOPE project, a voter registration effort sponsored by Martin Luther King's Southern Christian Leadership Conference. Four years later, the researchers supplemented this initial wave of data collection with follow-up interviews with 40 of the SCOPE volunteers. The results of these various efforts were summarized in 1971 by Demerath, Marwell, and Aiken in their book *The Dynamics of Idealism*. Then, in 1984, the same researchers returned to the field to assess the longer-term impact of participation in the SCOPE project. This time they surveyed 145 of the project participants and published their results in a *Public Opinion Quarterly* article in 1987 (Marwell, Aiken, and Demerath 1987).

Next off the mark was James Fendrich, whose own participation in civil rights activity in Tallahassee, Florida, granted him unique access to his subjects. To date, no one has published more on the topic of biographical consequences than Fendrich. For much of this published work, Fendrich relied on data collected in 1971 from 28 white and 72 black civil rights activists. In certain of these articles, Fendrich focuses only on the data from the white activists (Fendrich 1974; Fendrich and Tarleau 1973). In others, he uses the data on white and black activists comparatively (Fendrich 1977). Like

Demerath, Marwell, and Aiken, Fendrich also revisited his subjects at a much later date to gauge the longer-term impact of their experiences. In 1986, Fendrich resurveyed 85 of his subjects. These new data served as the empirical cornerstone of an important article in 1988 (Fendrich and Lovoy 1988) as well as Fendrich's book *Ideal Citizens* (1993), summarizing the overall thrust of his nearly twenty years of research and reflection on the question of the biographical impact of individual activism.

The next major entry into this line of research came from two political scientists, Kent Jennings and Richard Niemi, who, in 1973, used survey data on 216 former activists to look at the question of biographical conse- quences (Jennings and Niemi 1981). Besides the large sample size, the Jennings and Niemi study was unique in two other respects. First, their sub- jects varied widely in the extent of their movement involvements. Second, these involvements spanned a much longer time frame (1964–1972) than was true in any of the other studies.

Next came a study in 1977 of 30 activists involved in the 1967 People's Park demonstrations in Berkeley, California. Conducted by Alberta Nassi and Stephen Abramowitz, the study used survey techniques to assess the lasting impact of the earlier demonstrations on the subjects' lives. The results of this study were reported in two articles, published in 1979 (Nassi and Abramowitz 1979) and 1981 (Abramowitz and Nassi 1981).

Jack Whalen and Richard Flacks weighed in in the early 1980s with their own focused follow-up study of 11 student radicals arrested in Santa Barbara, California, in connection with the burning of a Bank of America branch near the University of California–Santa Barbara campus. Eschewing survey techniques, Whalen and Flacks used hours of interviews to fashion rich profiles of their subjects. These profiles formed the core of their book *Beyond the Barricades* (1989), as well as two earlier articles (Whalen and Flacks 1980, 1984).

Finally, my own follow-up study of those who applied to take part in the 1964 Mississippi Freedom Summer project bears mention in this review. Conducted between 1982 and 1985, the study relied on surveys, depth interviews, and an analysis of original project applications to compare the experiences of 212 volunteers and 118 no-shows in the years following the Freedom Summer project. The principal findings from the follow-up por- tion of the study were reported in the book *Freedom Summer* (1988), as well as in an article that appeared a year later in the *American Sociological Review* (1989).

These various studies are not without their methodological shortcomings. The first problem concerns the timing of the research. Several of the studies

(Demerath, Marwell, and Aiken 1971; Fendrich 1974, 1977; Fendrich and Tarleau 1973; Jennings and Niemi 1981) were conducted at the peak of the 1960s "protest cycle," making it hard to know how much of the political continuity evident in the lives of the subjects was a product of their earlier activities and how much was a function of the turbulent times.

A second issue concerns the small number of subjects involved in many of these studies. Only the research by Jennings and Niemi; Marwell, Aiken, and Demerath; and McAdam consistently involved more than 40 subjects. Third, most of the studies drew subjects from only a narrow geographic area, sometimes a single city (cf. Whalen and Flacks). This makes it difficult to generalize the results of the studies.

Another weakness of these studies is their failure to make use of non-activist control groups. Without such groups, one cannot establish a behavioral or attitudinal baseline against which to judge the effects of activism. Four of the aforementioned eight studies failed to employ a control group. Finally, with only three exceptions (Demerath, Marwell, and Aiken; Marwell, Aiken, and Demerath; and McAdam), the studies also lack "before and after" data on the activists. The usual procedure has been to gather contemporary information on former activists and then to infer the effects of participation from the data collected. But without prior information on the subject, it is hard to determine the extent and significance that changes in participation may have brought about.

These methodological shortcomings would be a good bit more worrisome were it not for the remarkable consistency in the findings reported in the various publications I have noted. Taken together, these studies suggest a powerful and enduring effect of participation on the later lives of the activists. Unlike Rubin and Cleaver, the subjects in these studies display a marked consistency in their values and politics over the course of their biographies. Specifically, the former activists

- had continued to espouse leftist political attitudes (Demerath, Marwell, and Aiken 1971: 184; Fendrich and Tarleau 1973: 250; Marwell, Aiken, and Demerath 1987; McAdam 1989: 752; Whalen and Flacks 1980: 222);

- had remained active in contemporary movements or other forms of political activity (Fendrich and Lovoy 1988; Jennings and Niemi 1981; McAdam 1989: 752);

- had been concentrated in teaching or other "helping" professions (Fendrich 1974: 116; McAdam 1989: 756);

• had divorced or remained single in far greater numbers than their age peers (McAdam 1988, 1989).

It would be hard to imagine a set of findings that would contradict the popular image of the 1960s activist more than the one presented here. Unlike the figures profiled in the popular press, the subjects in these systematic studies have evidenced a remarkable continuity in their lives over the past ten to thirty years. They have continued not only to voice the political values they espoused during the 1960s but to act on those values as well. Many of them have remained active in movement politics. Moreover, in a variety of ways they appear to have remained faithful to that New Left imperative to treat the personal as political. Indeed, both their work and their marital histories appear to have been shaped to a remarkable degree by their previous activist involvements. All of this underscores the central point of this survey: that intense and sustained activism should be added to that fairly select list of behavioral experiences (e.g., college attendance, parenthood, military service) that have the potential to transform a person's biography.

The Broader Life-Course Impact of Movement Activity
While the follow-up studies reviewed above have produced consistent findings attesting to the long-term impact of individual activism, it is reasonable to question the general significance of these findings. That is, given the highly select nature of the subjects in these studies, one could reasonably argue that, while the findings are interesting, they have few, if any, implications for the general population and the aggregate patterning of life-course events. In the remainder of the chapter I want to take up these issues. Specifically, I want to report on recent research in which some colleagues and I are currently involved that would seem to attest to the broader life-course significance of movement activity.

The central goal of the recent research is to assess the relationship between people's "political experiences and orientations" during the 1960s and 1970s and their subsequent life-course choices. The period in question was marked not only by widespread political and cultural turbulence but also by growing deviation from a good many of the normative conventions that had previously structured the life-course. The question is, to what extent were these two trends linked? Are nontraditional political experiences and orientations during these years linked to later deviations from the normative life-course (e.g., nonmarital cohabitation, childlessness among married couples, off-time birth of first child)?

The Sample

To get at this question, we conducted a randomized national survey of U.S. residents born between 1943 and 1964. Subjects were obtained through a multistage phone screening process. Working from a random national sample of phone numbers, interviewers first determined whether the number was, in fact, an operational residential number. If so, the interviewer then determined whether the person she or he was talking to (or anyone else residing at that number) fell within the specified range of birth years. If more than one resident was eligible to take part in the study, the interviewer selected, by methods worked out in advance, a single subject to take part in the study. Having identified the subject and obtained his or her consent to take part in the study, the interviewer then asked for an address to which we might send the questionnaire. In all, 2,253 subjects were identified in this manner. All were mailed questionnaires within a week of the initial phone contact. Follow-up cards and an additional survey were sent to all subjects who failed to respond within three weeks of our initial mailing. Completed surveys obtained from 1,187 subjects were distributed fairly evenly across the twenty-two cohorts.

By usual social-science standards, receiving responses from 53% of those to whom questionnaires were mailed is marginally acceptable. However, given the special difficulties we faced in identifying age-eligible subjects, the time demands we placed on our respondents—the questionnaire required 45–60 minutes to complete—and the sensitive nature of many of the survey items, we were quite pleased by the overall response rate achieved. Still, a 53% response rate invariably raises questions concerning the sample's representativeness. As a gauge, I compare the distributions of several sample characteristics to those found in other established samples or censuses. The first characteristic considered is age, given its centrality to the focus of this research. Comparing the single-year distribution of respondent age in the sample to that in the 1990 U.S. census produces an index of dissimilarity of 7.77%. This implies that fewer than 8% of the cases in the sample would need to be shifted to another category in order to make the two distributions exactly equivalent. This number is not exceptionally small, but neither is it so large as to cause concern. The sample does not fare as well on other demographic characteristics. For example, 59.8% of the sample is female, while the census shows that only 51.3% of the U.S. population is female. The sample is 92.3% white, whereas the U.S. population is 80.3% white. In terms of education, 97.3% of the sample completed high school and 43.2% graduated college, compared to figures of around 80% and 22% respectively in the population.

Given these percentage differences, we will need to exercise caution in generalizing our findings, but, on balance, we are not overly troubled by the numbers reported here. While undesirable, discrepancies between sample and population are especially problematic only if they can be shown to have biased systematically the characteristics of the sample that are of primary interest to the researchers. In our case, we are especially interested in the shifting political orientations and behaviors of our subjects. Interestingly, the discrepancies we noted would not seem to have undermined the representativeness of our subjects on these latter two dimensions. Consider political orientation. At the time of the survey, 26.0% of the sample claimed to be "liberal" to some degree, 32.8% "moderate," and 41.2% "conservative." By comparison, the 1991 General Social Survey (GSS) estimates the population to be 27.8% liberal, 40.0% moderate, and 32.1% conservative. A more detailed set of response categories were available on the GSS than on our questionnaire, although both have been collapsed for this comparison. Depending upon the approach to disaggregating categories, the two samples can be made to look quite similar or slightly dissimilar. Given the difficulty in comparison, however, this result could be overstated. A related indicator that is easier to validate and perhaps more reliable because of its behavioral basis is voting behavior. When asked for whom they voted in the 1992 presidential election, 40.4% of our sample claimed to have voted for Clinton, 38.4% for Bush, and 21.2% for other candidates (including Perot). According to the National Election Survey, the comparable figures are, respectively, 43.0%, 37.4%, and 19.6% for the population.

In summary, the sample appears to lack somewhat in its demographic representation of the U.S. population, especially with respect to race/ethnicity and education. However, this does not appear to translate into a dramatic political difference between the sample and the population as a whole. More importantly, the purpose of obtaining this sample was not to estimate percentage distributions in the population but rather to examine the *relationships* among various demographic and social or political characteristics. Even where basic demographic distributions differ from those in the population, there is no reason to believe that the relationships that are the focus of this research will be affected. The results of 1992 polls measuring voting behavior provide indirect support for this belief. In short, we are confident in using our sample to examine the relationship between life-course factors and political orientations among recent U.S. cohorts.

Key Variables

Data generated from the questionnaire include detailed life-course histories as well as various measures of our subjects' "political experiences and orientations" during their formative adolescent and young adult years. In creating measures of these political experiences and orientations, we relied exclusively on retrospective behavioral rather than attitudinal or self-characterization items, because there is good reason to suspect that the bias inherent in the former kind of item is lower than in the latter. Retrospective claims about what kind of person someone was earlier in her or his life are inherently problematic, because they are not only ambiguous but also subject to continual reevaluation and change. In contrast, the likelihood that someone will deny or forget engaging in a general class of behavior is considerably smaller. With this in mind, we asked respondents whether they had ever participated in "political demonstrations" in connection with any of the following:

- civil rights
- opposition to the war in Vietnam
- the women's movement

A positive response to any of these behavioral items was coded as a "yes" on our dichotomous New Left variable.

In order to assess the predictive power of this variable in relation to the life-course choices of our subjects, we designated certain life-course outcomes as "deviations" from previously "normative" patterns. These deviations include the following items:

- NOKIDS—subject has no children (biological or adopted)
- COHABIT—subject lived with a sexual partner before marrying for the first time
- NEVERWED—subject has never been married

These variables were treated as dichotomous, and their relationship to our measure of New Left activity was assessed by means of logistic regression.

In addition, we used proportional hazard models to study the link between New Left activity and two other continuous time variables. These were the subjects' age at marriage and their age at the birth of first child. Here, too, we were interested in assessing the degree to which those of our subjects who had engaged in any New Left activity had deviated from the age-specific life-course norms associated with these events.[1] I will present these various analyses in the next section. The two questions we hope to answer concerning our dependent variables are to what extent are variations in these life-course "deviations" linked to prior participation in "New Left politics," and what factors mediate their diffusion over time? I take up the question of movement links first.

Results

To assess the relationship of our key independent variable to the various life-course deviations noted in the previous section, I make use of three types of analysis: simple bivariate comparison, logistic regression, and hazard rate analysis. I begin with a series of t-tests to assess the significance of the percentage differences between those subjects who did and those who did not engage in New Left activities in terms of each of our three dichotomous dependent variables. Table 1 reports the results of these tests.

Table 1. Percentage Differences between Those Who Did and Those Who Did Not Engage in New Left Activities, by Dependent Variable

	Yes (N=192)	No (N=897)
Cohabited before marriage (COHABIT)	48%	32%**
Never married (NEVERWED)	18%	13%*
Has not had children (NOKIDS)	35%	23%*
Mean age at marriage	23.41	21.98***
Mean age at birth of first child	26.89	24.26***

$*p < .05$ $**p < .01$ $***p < .001$

In all cases, participation in New Left activities was associated with significant differences in the frequency of life-course deviations. I also used t-tests to see whether the mean age at first marriage and the birth of first child was significantly different for our New Left and non–New Left subjects. In both cases, the differences in mean age were significant at the .001 level. For those New Left subjects who had married by the time of the survey, the mean age at which they had first done so was 22.9, as compared to 21.2 for non–New Left subjects. At the birth of first child, the age comparison was 26.6 for those who had taken part in any New Left activities and 24.3 for those who had not.

As suggestive as these results are, they are limited in two very important ways. First, I have looked only at the bivariate relationships between our key dependent and independent variables. It remains to be seen what effect other relevant independent variables will exert on the relationship between New Left activity and the various life-course alternatives under study here.

Second, to this point, I have failed to examine the time order of our two classes of variables. That is, all I have shown is that there is a strong association between our key independent and dependent variables. But our argument posits a specific time order to this relationship. We hypothesize that it was *prior* New Left activities that encouraged our subjects to deviate from various life-course conventions. To redress this latter deficiency, I will hereafter recode the New Left variable to include only those instances of activism which precede the life-course outcome in question. To transcend the limits of bivariate analysis, I turn first to the technique of logistic regression. The technique of logistic regression allows me to test for the simultaneous effects of various independent variables on our dependent variables. The results of this analysis are reported in table 2.

As one can see from the table, the inclusion of other variables does little to erode the strength of the association between the various life-course deviations and our key independent variable. In all cases New Left activities exert a significant positive effect on the likelihood of life-course deviation. These

Table 2. Estimates of Effects of Selected Independent Variables on Deviations from Traditional Life-Course

Independent Variable	Model 1 (COHABIT)	Model 2 (NEVERWED)	Model 3 (NOKIDS)
Prior New Left activity	0.882***	1.336***	0.626**
	(0.225)	(0.290)	(0.220)
Gender (1 = male)	0.245	0.620**	0.445**
	(0.154)	(0.209)	(0.162)
Parents' class ("lower" category omitted)			
Upper (1 = upper)	0.070	-0.132	0.219
	(0.228)	(0.291)	(0.230)
Middle (1 = middle)	0.092	-0.376	-0.048
	(0.167)	(0.236)	(0.181)
Year of birth	0.100***	0.118***	0.103***
	(0.013)	(0.020)	(0.014)
Race (1 = Caucasian)	-0.228	-0.625	-0.484
	(0.357)	(0.451)	(0.366)
Attained college degree	-0.221	0.343	0.696***
	(0.163)	(0.218)	(0.168)
-2 log likelihood	1021.940	597.540	944.725
Degrees of freedom	7	7	7

*$p < .05$ **$p < .01$ ***$p < .001$

results hold despite our inclusion of the variable "year of birth," designed to assess the effect of cohort sequence on life-course outcomes. Predictably, given what we know about the increasing-over-time incidence of all of our dependent variables, birth year is highly predictive of all of three outcomes shown in table 2. Yet, net of these predictably strong cohort effects, the positive associations between New Left politics and our dependent variables remain undiminished.

Before I move on to an analysis of our continuous time variables, let me say a word or two about the findings presented in table 2. Suffice it to say that, net of the impact of New Left activity, the results are entirely consistent with past research. Given the normatively older age at which men typically marry and have children, the positive relationship between gender and NOKIDS and NEVERWED makes sense. The positive relationship probably has more to do with the fact that our male subjects still "have more time" to enter into these life-course statuses than it does about men being ultimately less likely than women either to marry or to have children. The strong positive association between college degree and NOKIDS should probably be interpreted in the same way. That is, attending college for at least four years has no doubt had the effect of delaying the entrance into parenthood for some number of our subjects—especially our younger subjects. In fact, we were surprised to find no significant effect of college degree on NEVERWED, though the relationship is positive and borders on being significant at the .10 level.

The results reported in table 2 strengthen the case for movement participation as a force shaping individual life-course choices. But to take full advantage of the retrospective time-series data, I employ event history models to see whether involvement in prior New Left activities is linked not simply to deviance from the normative life-course but to the timing of movement through the life-course.

Table 3 reports the results of a single event history model applied to each of the aforementioned life-course outcomes.[2] The results merely amplify the central conclusion to emerge from the logistic regression. Prior involvement in New Left politics exerts a powerful influence not only over the structure of various life-course statuses but also over the timing of these life-course events. Indeed, the predictive power of prior New Left activity as regards our two "timing" variables is on a par with the well-established demographic influences reported in table 3, even taking these influences into account in our model. Again we see the powerful effect of birth year and gender on the timing of both marriage and parenthood.

These results are especially impressive in light of the consistent strong effect of college education on the dependent variables. Consistent with much

Table 3. Estimates of Effects of Selected Independent Variables on Timing of Two Life-Course Outcomes

Independent Variable*	Model 1 (Age at Marriage)	Model 2 (Age at First Birth)
Prior New Left activity	-0.662***	-0.666***
	(0.133)	(0.013)
Gender (1 = male)	-0.426***	-0.309***
	(0.074)	(0.074)
Parents' class ("lower" category omitted)		
Upper (1 = upper)	-0.163	-0.293*
	(0.111)	(0.113)
Middle (1 = middle)	-0.032	-0.098
	(0.079)	(0.078)
Year of birth	-0.033***	-0.037***
	(0.006)	(0.006)
Race (1 = Caucasian)	0.312	0.234
	(0.201)	(0.194)
Attained college degree	-0.382***	-0.552***
	(0.078)	(0.078)
-2 log likelihood	9558.453	9846.614
Degrees of freedom	7	7

$^*p < .05$ $^{**}p < .01$ $^{***}p < .001$

previous research (e.g., Rindfuss, Bumpass, and St. John 1980; Rindfuss and St. John 1983; Bloom and Trussell 1984; Marini 1984b), commitment to higher education typically delays marriage and the onset of parenthood. But this strong association between college graduation and the delay of marriage and parenthood does nothing to erode the predictive power of prior New Left activism. Net of college attendance, involvement in New Left politics has the effect of increasing the age at which subjects first married and had children. This is significant insofar as one might have presumed that the strong positive association between New Left politics and these two life-course outcomes was a spurious by-product of college attendance. We ourselves wondered whether, among our New Left activists, the delay in the onset of these two life-course events was largely a function of the activists' propensity to attend and graduate from college. These results provide a powerful refutation of this interpretation. During the period in question, New

Left activism appears to have exerted a powerful and consistent effect on the timing, as well as the content, of subsequent life-course events.

However, before we wholeheartedly embrace the findings reported in tables 2 and 3, let us consider one other possibility: that the relationships between prior New Left activity and our various life-course measures are spurious; and that both owe to some underlying disposition to nonconformity that masks the nature of the true causal dynamics involved in the unfolding of life-course events. In raising this possibility, I should say at the outset that better than a quarter of a century of careful empirical research on the link between individual-level personality or dispositional factors and movement participation has generally confirmed the predictive poverty of such approaches (McPhail 1971; Gurney and Tierney 1982; Wicker 1969). Accordingly, in recent years, theories of movement participation have moved away from such "personalogical" accounts of activism to stress instead the prospective recruits' prior structural relationship to the movement (R. Gould 1991, 1995; Klandermans and Oegema 1987; Marwell, Oliver, and Prahl 1988; McAdam and Paulsen 1993). But if such approaches have generated little empirical support and have minimal theoretical resonance in the contemporary study of social movements, they nonetheless have been a powerful staple of life-course research. It is therefore incumbent on me to use what data I have to speak to the issue of spuriousness.

I do so rerunning the analyses reported in tables 2 and 3, this time adding five variables designed to measure crudely our subjects' *prior* generalized disposition to nonconformity. The five variables are as follows:

- liberal/left mother—subject identified his or her mother's political orientation as liberal or left during subject's high school years;
- liberal/left father—same as above, but in regard to subject's father;
- prior use of marijuana—subject reported use of marijuana prior to either New Left activity or entrance into any of our life-course events;
- early sexual activity—subject reported "early" sexual activity (operationalized for males as having intercourse before age sixteen and, for females, before age seventeen);
- life different—subject was asked whether, at age eighteen, he or she had hoped that each of four different aspects of life—work, education, marriage, and family—"would be

different" from that of his or her same-sex parent. Taken together, these four "life different" items constitute a scale with values ranging from 0 to 4.

The results of the new models incorporating these five "dispositional" variables are reported in tables 4 and 5. Table 4 reports the results of new logistic regression models predicting the three "deviant" life-course statuses, while table 5 shows coefficients for hazard models predicting the timing of first marriage and parenthood for our subjects.

The results of these new analyses do little to undermine our confidence in the relationships reported in tables 2 and 3. In all five of the models, prior New Left activity remains highly predictive of the dependent variable. Moreover, in only one of the five cases does the introduction of the dispositional variables significantly weaken the relationship between our key independent variable and the relevant life-course measure. The lone exception is NOKIDS, where the test for "spuriousness" reduces the significance level of the New Left–life-course relationship from .001 to .05.

The stability of the hypothesized relationships takes on added significance when we reflect on the significant independent effects that some of our dispositional measures have on the life-course variables. To me, the most interesting of these effects centers on the consistently strong demonstrated association between liberal/left mother and four of our five life-course variables. Apparently, being raised during these years by mothers with liberal/left political views tended to exert a powerful influence over our subjects' subsequent life-course trajectories.

Relative to the impact of liberal/left mother, the rest of the dispositional measures were not consistently predictive of the life-course variables. Having a liberal/left father exerted only a weak and generally conforming effect on our subject's life-course choices. Our two behavioral measures of generalized nonconformity—prior use of marijuana and early sex—were generally unrelated to our life-course variables. The one notable exception was cohabitation, to which both of these behavioral measures were highly related. The same was true for the "life different" variable. Only in regard to cohabitation was a strong desire to see one's life as different from the same-sex parent related to a "deviant" life-course status.

Whatever the interesting relationships the new models turned up involving the dispositional and life-course measures, the bottom line is that none of these relationships serve to weaken seriously the general impact of New Left activity on the structure and timing of life-course processes. There is no evidence in the data to suggest that these latter relationships are in any way spurious.

Table 4. Estimates of Effects of Two Sets of Independent Variables on Deviations from Traditional Life-Course

Independent Variable	Model 1.1 (COHABIT)	Model 1.2 (COHABIT)	Model 2.1 (NEVERWED)	Model 2.2 (NEVERWED)	Model 3.1 (NOKIDS)	Model 3.2 (NOKIDS)
Prior New Left activity	0.880***	0.824***	1.334***	1.354***	0.626***	0.546*
	(0.204)	(0.216)	(0.290)	(0.297)	(0.220)	(0.227)
Gender (1 = male)	0.262	0.233	0.620**	0.611**	0.445**	0.478**
	(0.139)	(0.148)	(0.209)	(0.217)	(0.162)	(0.168)
Parents' class ("lower" category omitted)						
Upper (1 = upper)	0.230	0.449*	-0.132	-0.012	0.219	0.343
	(0.203)	(0.220)	(0.291)	(0.302)	(0.230)	(0.239)
Middle (1 = middle)	0.164	0.372*	-0.376	-0.366	-0.048	-0.004
	(0.152)	(0.165)	(0.236)	(0.244)	(0.181)	(0.188)
Year of birth	0.086***	0.074***	0.118***	0.119***	0.103***	0.109***
	(0.013)	(0.013)	(0.020)	(0.021)	(0.014)	(0.015)
Race (1 = Caucasian)	-0.163	-0.181	-0.625	-0.659	-0.484	-0.415
	(0.332)	(0.353)	(0.451)	(0.459)	(0.366)	(0.375)
Attained college degree	-0.223	-0.129	0.343	0.354	0.696***	0.643***
	(0.147)	(0.158)	(0.218)	(0.227)	(0.168)	(0.174)

Table 4. Continued

Independent Variable	Model 1.1 (COHABIT)	Model 1.2 (COHABIT)	Model 2.1 (NEVERWED)	Model 2.2 (NEVERWED)	Model 3.1 (NOKIDS)	Model 3.2 (NOKIDS)
Liberal mother	—	0.228 (0.253)	—	0.828* (0.327)	—	0.867*** (0.260)
Liberal father	—	0.352 (0.289)	—	-0.116 (0.428)	—	-0.688+ (0.354)
Smoked marijuana	—	1.058*** (0.153)	—	0.020 (0.224)	—	-0.014 (0.174)
Had sex at a young age	—	0.304* (0.198)	—	-0.323 (0.278)	—	-0.310 (0.216)
Desired own life to be different from parents' at age 18	—	0.184*** (0.043)	—	-0.005 (0.062)	—	0.074 (0.049)
-2 log likelihood	1249.492	1162.437	597.540	620.601	944.725	960.588
Degrees of freedom	7	12	7	12	7	12

+p < .10   *p < .05   **p < .01   ***p < .001

Table 5. Estimates of Effects of Two Sets of Independent Variables on Timing of Two Life-Course Outcomes

Independent Variable	Model 1.1 (Age at Marriage)	Model 1.2 (Age at Marriage)	Model 2.1 (Age at First Birth)	Model 2.2 (Age at First Birth)
Prior New Left activity	-0.662***	-0.648***	-0.666***	-0.572***
	(0.133)	(0.136)	(0.113)	(0.129)
Gender (1 = male)	-0.426***	-0.454***	-0.309***	-0.374***
	(0.074)	(0.076)	(0.074)	(0.077)
Parents' class ("lower" category omitted)				
Upper (1 = upper)	-0.163	-0.190	-0.293	-0.344**
	(0.111)	(0.115)	(0.113)	(0.117)
Middle (1 = middle)	-0.032	0.036	-0.098	-0.101
	(0.079)	(0.082)	(0.078)	(0.081)
Year of birth	-0.033***	-0.037***	-0.037***	-0.042***
	(0.006)	(0.006)	(0.006)	(0.006)
Race (1 = Caucasian)	0.312	0.293	0.234	0.252
	(0.201)	(0.202)	(0.194)	(0.195)
Attained college degree	-0.382***	-0.346***	-0.552***	-0.493***
	(0.078)	(0.080)	(0.078)	(0.080)
Liberal mother	—	-0.369**	—	-0.482**
		(0.144)		(0.143)
Liberal father	—	0.121	—	0.311*
		(0.160)		(0.153)
Smoked marijuana	—	-0.062	—	-0.059
		(0.077)		(0.077)
Had sex at a young age	—	0.204*	—	0.286**
		(0.098)		(0.098)
Desired own life to be different from parents' at age 18	—	-0.010	—	-0.047*
		(0.021)		(0.021)
-2 log likelihood	9558.453	9547.506	9846.614	9820.727
Degrees of freedom	7	12	7	12

$*p < .05$ $**p < .01$ $***p < .001$

But what about the aggregate impact of New Left activism on the structure of the American life-course? Having demonstrated a general link between individual activism and various life-course outcomes, I turn to the second goal of the research project: assessing the role of 1960s movements in the onset of the distinctive demographic patterns characteristic of the baby boom cohorts. I begin with a general discussion of the topic.

In the post–World War II period, demographers came to characterize a particular sequence of life-course statuses as defining the "normative" transition to adulthood. While there was never universal conformity to the pattern, general adherence to the sequence was certainly the rule. The sequence began with completion of formal education and proceeded as follows: entrance into paid employment, marriage, and the onset of parenting (Elder 1978; Hogan 1981; Marini 1984a, 1984b; Modell 1989).

Over the past ten to fifteen years, however, evidence has accumulated suggesting that this sequence is being experienced by a decreasing proportion of young adults (Rindfuss, Swicegood, and Rosenfeld 1987). Deviation from this "normative" sequence is especially characteristic of the baby boom cohorts.

How can we account for the marked deviation from normative patterns among the baby boom cohorts? Reflecting the relative lack of interest among life-course researchers in the question of aggregate-level change in life-course patterns, few scholars have sought to answer this question. One notable exception to the rule is the economist Richard Easterlin. In his provocative book *Birth and Fortune* (1980), Easterlin argues that these deviations were largely a function of the size and sequence of the baby boom cohorts. Benefiting from the rapidly expanding boom-fueled economy and the relatively small size of the Depression and World War II cohorts, the early boomers confronted unprecedented occupational opportunities that, in turn, allowed them to conform to the normative sequence defining transition to adulthood. The younger boomers were not so lucky. Confronting an increasingly stagnant economy and intense competition for any available position, the younger boomers found paths to satisfying full-time employment blocked, thereby delaying their entrance into other adult roles.

Easterlin's account is a powerful one and no doubt tells us much about the unique demographic profile of the baby boomers. We are convinced, however, that it is not the whole—nor perhaps even the most important part—of the story. What troubles us is the demographic determinism inherent in Easterlin's account and his failure to grant any causal importance to the broader political, cultural, and social dynamics of the period in question. After all, the baby boom comprised cohorts who grew up or matured during the 1960s and 1970s, years of significant political and cultural change in American life. At the center of much of this turbulence were the various social movements that made up the New Left. Those movements and the "counterculture" they helped spawn embodied an explicit critique of marriage, the nuclear family, the notion of a traditional career, and the very way of life that had previously defined "normal" adult status in American society. What we are suggesting, in contrast to Easterlin, is that some number of the baby boomers may not have been forced, by demographic and market pressures, to postpone entrance into conventional adult roles, so much as they *chose* to do so, on the basis of their affinity with New Left politics or the countercultural practices of the period. This argument raises the more general issue of the link between social movement processes and aggregate-level changes in the content, structure, or timing of life-course events. Yet, for all the implicit claims about the significance of movements as important vehicles of social change, very little systematic research on the topic has been undertaken by movement scholars. This certainly holds true in the area of demographic change. Movement scholars have never sought to study systematically the link between social movement processes and aggregate-level changes in the life-course. We hypothesize just such a link between the political movements of the 1960s and 1970s and the shifts in life-course patterns associated with the baby boom cohorts. What is the nature of this link?

We think Easterlin's account of the demographic and market sources of deviation from the "normative" transition to adulthood is not wrong so much as incomplete. While demographically produced market pressures no doubt had something to do with the distinctive life-course patterns that emerged among the baby boom generation, a great deal of attitudinal and economic heterogeneity remains within these cohorts (Cooney and Hogan 1991; Elder 1978). Indeed, we suspect the effects of cohort size were mediated by the values and the political and cultural experiences of the baby boomers. Our own reading is that the rise of the New Left and the attendant development of a "youth counterculture" exposed a good many baby boomers (and some preboomers) to very different socialization processes than the ones that had previously sustained the traditional transition to adulthood. In turn, these new socialization processes granted those exposed to them very different images of the life-course. Thus, the political and cultural ferment of the period selectively altered socialization practices, resulting in more heterogeneity in life-course images and outcomes. Modell (1989) has interpreted this process as one in which large numbers of persons born during this period were beginning to take personal control over their life-course processes. Or it may be, as we are inclined to suspect, that this segment of the baby boom generation were not taking demographic control of their lives so much as they were conforming to alternative life-course patterns.

Where did these alternative patterns come from? We do not know for sure. We can, however, sketch a plausible answer to the question based on the current research as well as work we have done in the past (McAdam 1988, 1989; McAdam, Moore, and Shockey 1992). We suggest a three-stage process by which these alternative patterns were first established and later made available to a significant minority of the baby boom and later cohorts. The first stage involved the conscious rejection of life-course "norms" in favor of more "liberated" alternatives. The architects of these alternatives were pioneering activists in both the political and countercultural movements of the period. Drawing upon a diverse strand of critical perspectives on mainstream America—those of the New Left, the Beats, the black nationalists, Eastern philosophy, the human potential movement, and so on—these activists sought to make the personal political by fashioning what they came to regard as more humane, just, or personally fulfilling alternatives to the traditional life-course statuses. Many of the Freedom Summer volunteers gave explicit voice to this process, acknowledging that such life-course "deviations" as nonmarital cohabitation, childlessness (or communal child rearing), and episodic work histories were consciously chosen as alternatives to traditional patterns that they perceived to be personally constraining or politically suspect (McAdam 1988, 1989, 1992).

The second stage of the process involved the embedding of these alternatives within that diverse set of geographic and subcultural locations that came to be the principal repositories of the "'60s experience" within the United States. In their capacity as centers of New Left activism and countercultural experimentation, college campuses—especially elite public and private institutions in the North and West—came to serve as home to the new life-course alternatives. So, too, did self-consciously countercultural neighborhoods—Haight Ashbury in San Francisco, Greenwich Village in New York—in virtually every major city in the country. Gradually, upper-middle-class suburbs—first on the two coasts and later elsewhere—also came to embody the new alternatives through the socializing force of older brothers and sisters away at college.

In the third stage of the hypothesized process, through broad processes of diffusion and adaptation, these alternative patterns became available to an increasingly heterogeneous subset of American youth. In the process, however, the alternatives were largely stripped of their original political or countercultural content and came instead to be experienced by those exposed to them as simply a new set of life-course norms. Thus, the increasing heterogeneity in life-course patterns noted by researchers owed, we think, more to variability in the options to which different subgroups of young people were exposed than to any significant increase in the percentage "taking control" over their lives. Those who were exposed early on and fairly intensively to the alternatives were apt to conform to them; those who grew up in settings where the traditional patterns remained intact were likely to adhere to those traditional patterns. This is the process, we hypothesize, by which the broad social movement dynamics of the period came to reshape the normative contours of the life-course. However, it remains for us to subject this account to systematic empirical scrutiny.

Here we want to move from an analysis of the origins of these alternative patterns to an exploration of those factors which mediated their spread through the general population. Here we are interested principally in identifying those structural locations which may have increased or decreased our subjects' exposure to these alternative patterns. Based on simple bivariate comparisons within each of three broad cohorts (1943–49, 1950–56, 1957–64), three such locations emerged as potentially significant in this regard. Two of these locations appear to have placed our subjects at greater risk of adopting the new life-course patterns. These are attendance at an "activist" college after 1969, and residence in a "liberal state" at age fifteen. In contrast, a third "location"—weekly church attendance at age eighteen—appears to have discouraged the adoption of these life-course alternatives.

In examining the mediating effect of all three variables, we were particularly interested in assessing their effects for the last two of our three cohorts. In our thinking, these two cohorts are contemporaneous with stages 2 and 3 in our hypothesized diffusion process. Recall that in stage 2 we expected the new life-course patterns to grow beyond their early embedding in activist and countercultural communities. We expected the spread to be mediated by specific structural locations, such as those we identified earlier. In contrast, by stage 3 we felt that the patterns would have diffused so widely in society as to have muted the effects of those variables which mediated the spread in stage 2.

To test these general propositions, we once again turn to the technique of event history analysis. Tables 6 and 7 report, for both the full sample and for each of the three large cohort subgroups, the results of a single proportional hazard model testing for the effect of our various mediating variables on age at marriage and age at birth of first child.

Do the effects of these "mediating factors" vary as hypothesized over the three cohorts? With a few exceptions, the answer is yes. As expected, for the oldest cohort, the introduction of the new variables does little to alter the general pattern or strength of the relationships we have documented. For those born between 1943 and 1949, none of the "mediating" variables have any predictive significance for either age at marriage or age at birth of first child.

Table 6. Estimates of Effects of Selected Independent Variables on Age at Marriage for Full Sample and by Birth Cohort (Two-Tailed Test)

Independent Variable	Full Sample	Birth Cohorts 1943–49	1950–56	1957–64
Prior New Left activity	-0.640***	-0.914***	-0.392*	-1.628**
	(0.138)	(0.269)	(0.196)	(0.513)
Gender (1 = male)	-0.452***	-0.269	-0.653***	-0.526***
	(0.078)	(0.168)	(0.134)	(0.134)
Parents' class ("lower" category omitted)				
Upper (1 = upper)	-0.201	-0.193	-0.296	-0.104
	(0.126)	(0.252)	(0.216)	(0.198)
Middle (1 = middle)	-0.036	-0.024	-0.207	0.096
	(0.084)	(0.164)	(0.145)	(0.147)
Year of birth	-0.040***	0.041	-0.082*	-0.083**
	(0.007)	(0.042)	(0.034)	(0.030)
Race (1 = Caucasian)	0.283	-0.033	0.502	0.264
	(0.208)	(0.377)	(0.440)	(0.320)
Attained college degree	-0.375***	-0.389*	-0.502**	-0.226
	(0.096)	(0.182)	(0.173)	(0.167)
Liberal mother	-0.400**	-0.558+	-0.386	-0.081
	(0.147)	(0.291)	(0.252)	(0.258)
Liberal father	0.135	0.476	-0.266	0.251
	(0.162)	(0.330)	(0.288)	(0.267)
Smoked marijuana	-0.069	0.143	-0.167	-0.104
	(0.080)	(0.163)	(0.134)	(0.144)
Had sex at a young age	0.171+	0.702**	0.040	0.125
	(0.102)	(0.266)	(0.175)	(0.155)
Desired own life to be different from parents' at age 18	-0.019	-0.026	-0.058	0.003
	(0.022)	(0.041)	(0.041)	(0.037)
Attended church weekly at age 18	0.096	0.127	0.062	0.046
	(0.087)	(0.152)	(0.153)	(0.166)
Attended church irregularly at age 18	0.242*	-0.142	0.319	0.261+
	(0.097)	(0.254)	(0.153)	(0.151)
Attended an activist college post-1960s	0.006	0.241	-0.258+	0.010
	(0.098)	(0.238)	(0.155)	(0.159)
Attended a nonactivist college post-1960s	-0.006	0.163	0.122	-0.229+
	(0.101)	(0.230)	(0.166)	(0.156)

Table 6. Continued

Independent Variable	Full Sample	Birth Cohorts		
		1943–49	1950–56	1957–64
Residence in liberal state	0.156	0.228	-0.276⁺	-0.053
at age 15	(0.106)	(0.206)	(0.158)	(0.186)
Residence in moderate state	-0.004	0.088	0.206	-0.298*
at age 15	(0.082)	(0.162)	(0.144)	(0.144)
-2 log likelihood	9024.019	2029.492	2654.498	2688.148
Degrees of freedom	18	18	18	18

$^{+}p < .10$ $^{*}p < .05$ $^{**}p < .01$ $^{***}p < .001$

Table 7. Estimates of Effects of Selected Independent Variables on Age at Birth of First Child for the Full Sample & by Birth Cohort (Two-Tailed Test)

Independent Variable	Full Sample	Birth Cohorts		
		1943–49	1950–56	1957–64
Prior New Left activity	-0.521***	-0.544*	-0.446*	-0.662⁺
	(0.132)	(0.246)	(0.221)	(0.354)
Gender (1 = male)	-0.348***	-0.197	-0.342*	-0.613***
	(0.080)	(0.154)	(0.136)	(0.142)
Parents' class ("lower" category omitted)				
Upper (1 = upper)	-0.328**	-0.449⁺	-0.355⁺	-0.280
	(0.122)	(0.239)	(0.209)	(0.214)
Middle (1 = middle)	-0.122	-0.011	-0.374**	-0.075
	(0.083)	(0.149)	(0.143)	(0.152)
Year of birth	-0.039***	0.004	-0.019	-0.072*
	(0.007)	(0.037)	(0.033)	(0.031)
Race (1 = Caucasian)	0.301	0.040	0.704⁺	0.102
	(0.201)	(0.374)	(0.367)	(0.337)
Attained college degree	-0.472***	-0.580***	-0.530**	-0.368*
	(0.097)	(0.172)	(0.176)	(0.180)
Liberal mother	-0.501***	-0.565*	-0.535*	-0.302
	(0.146)	(0.256)	(0.259)	(0.277)
Liberal father	0.292⁺	0.288	0.402	0.333
	(0.157)	(0.280)	(0.286)	(0.279)
Smoked marijuana	-0.007	0.031	0.101	-0.145
	(0.080)	(0.151)	(0.134)	(0.151)

Table 7. Continued

Independent Variable	Full Sample	Birth Cohorts		
		1943–49	1950–56	1957–64
Had sex at a young age	0.284**	0.602**	0.166	0.166
	(0.101)	(0.224)	(0.176)	(0.159)
Desired own life to be different from parents' at age 18	-0.046*	-0.077+	-0.072+	-0.003
	(0.022)	(0.040)	(0.039)	(0.038)
Attended church weekly at age 18	0.218**	0.157	0.352*	0.169
	(0.087)	(0.142)	(0.155)	(0.172)
Attended church irregularly at age 18	0.203*	0.112	0.314+	0.337+
	(0.098)	(0.222)	(0.168)	(0.198)
Attended an activist college post-1960s	-0.078	0.128	-0.157	-0.342+
	(0.105)	(0.220)	(0.171)	(0.191)
Attended a nonactivist college post-1960s	-0.049	0.080	0.072	-0.255
	(0.106)	(0.226)	(0.171)	(0.186)
Residence in liberal state at age 15	0.098	-0.010	0.256	0.017
	(0.104)	(0.185)	(0.183)	(0.192)
Residence in moderate state at age 15	-0.098	-0.058	0.131	-0.373*
	(0.084)	(0.152)	(0.147)	(0.150)
-2 log likelihood	9238.777	2365.158	2729.637	2494.683
Degrees of freedom	18	18	18	18

$+p < .10$ $*p < .05$ $**p < .01$ $***p < .001$

The pattern of effects for those born between 1950 and 1956 is quite different. Though New Left activity remains predictive of our dependent variable, it now shares the explanatory spotlight with a number of other variables, including two of the mediating factors we have reviewed. Attendance at an "activist college" significantly delayed the onset of marriage for those in the 1950–56 birth cohort, while church attendance had the opposite effect on childbearing for the same cohorts.

But the effects for our last cohort are the most interesting and most confirming of our general perspective. Here New Left activity remains only weakly related to our dependent variables, while the full array of mediating variables comes into play. This is especially true for age of marriage, where all three of our mediating structural locations bear a significant relationship to age at marriage. Weekly church attendance lowered the age of first marriage, while both residence in a "moderate" state and attendance at a "nonactivist" college delayed the onset of marriage. The latter two relationships hold for the birth of first child as well. The new life-course patterns have indeed spread far beyond their movement origins. By the time those in cohort 3 reached their formative years, the alternative life-course patterns had diffused through much of society and were now being influenced by a wide range of variables, including the kinds of structural locations under examination here.

Discussion and Conclusion

What do we make of the results reported in the previous section? The combined weight of our findings would seem to suggest two important implications. The first concerns the specific set of influences that shaped the rather dramatic restructuring of the life-course we associate with the baby-boom cohorts. From a dramatic rise in nonmarital cohabitation to the eschewal of childbearing, the last thirty or so years have witnessed a series of significant changes in the content and timing of the kinds of life-course patterns that characterized the two decades following World War II. To date, there have been few systematic attempts to discern the source of these shifts in the organization of the life-course. One exception is Easterlin's book *Birth and Fortune*. While our research in no way constitutes a systematic "test" of Easterlin's thesis, our findings clearly bear on his argument, and, in general, they tend not to support its central conclusions.

At its most basic level, the Easterlin argument relies on a form of demographic determinism in which the size and sequence of the baby boom cohorts shaped the broad contours of the life-course through two intervening mechanisms. The first of these mechanisms was the job market. Benefiting from the rapidly expanding postwar economy, the early "boom" cohorts enjoyed lucrative occupational prospects that allowed them to make a rapid transition into adult roles. By contrast, the later boomers faced a more stagnant economy and increased job competition, thereby delaying their entrance into full-time employment, marriage, and parenthood. The second mechanism stressed by Easterlin as mediating the relationship between cohort sequence and life-course choices was the baby boomers' socialized expectations as regards their economic fortunes. The generalized affluence of the postwar years raised the expectations of the boomers, especially the later boomers, who witnessed the success of parents and older siblings alike. The lucrative job market allowed the early boomers to meet their expectations, while the more stagnant economy confronting the later boomers did not "match" their heightened expectations. This mismatch between expectations and job prospects grew more severe with each succeeding cohort, prompting ever larger numbers to deviate from the normative life-course.

Quite apart from whatever theoretical issues one might raise with this account, the simple fact is that our results do not accord well with the Easterlin argument. For example, it is hard to reconcile several of our co-efficients with Easterlin's stress on the mediating effects of socialized expec-tations. According to Easterlin, these expectations are "largely the uncon-scious product of the environment in which they [the baby boomers] grew up. In other words, economic aspirations are unintentionally learned, or 'internalized,' in one's parents' home. And this environment is very largely shaped by the economic circumstances, or income, of one's parents" (1980: 40-41). Given the argument summarized earlier, the implication of this quotation is that among the baby boomers we should expect those from ad-vantaged backgrounds to have had the highest and thus most "mismatched" expectations when confronted with the increasingly stagnant economy of the late 1960s and early 1970s. Social class should thus also be related to the various life-course deviations under study here. It is not. Only in regard to the age at birth of first child does class background matter, and then only in some models and at marginal levels of significance.

At the very minimum, it would seem clear that the argument advanced by Easterlin fails to explain as much of the era's changing life-course dynam-ics as he claims it did. So what other influences would seem to be implicated in these changes? Based on our results, the broader turbulence of the era needs to be accorded a much more central role in the aggregate-level changes in the life-course noted by Easterlin. This brings us to the second major im-plication of our findings. While social movement scholars have long as-sumed the potency of social movements as vehicles of social change, rarely have they sought to study their long-term effects systematically. And where they have done so, they have generally confined themselves to an assessment of a given movement's success or failure in attaining its stated goals. Here we have tried to look beyond the explicit aims of the 1960s movements to their broader impact, both on the lives of those who took part in the struggles and in the current structure of the American life-course. Both bear the clear im-print of those struggles. At the individual level, prior participation in New Left activities is significantly related to all five of the life-course outcomes ex-amined here. But, as the separate cohort models show, the strength of this relationship declines over time, supporting at the aggregate level the general model of demographic diffusion stressed throughout the chapter. For our oldest cohorts, New Left participation is among the strongest predictors of the new life-course patterns. Over time, however, the strength of these rela-tionships declined. As the new patterns diffused with each passing cohort, the predictive power of movement activity was supplanted by an increasingly broad mix of structural and attitudinal factors.

These findings suggest an impact that transcends the lives of the activists who disproportionately appear to have "pioneered" the various life-course alternatives. Whatever the force of the "normative" life-course in the immediate postwar period, its influence appears, in our data, to have waned with each succeeding cohort. Given the relative youth of our youngest cohort, this conclusion must be voiced tentatively as regards the central life-course events of marriage and parenthood. But even here the data speak, at the very least, of great changes in the timing of these outcomes, if not their normative force.

Table 8. Percentage of Respondents Who Had Never Married and/or Had a Child, by Birth Cohort

		Never Married		Never Had a Child	
Birth Cohort	Total N	%	(N)	%	(N)
1957–1964	412	23.1	(95)	37.4	(154)
1950–1956	361	10.2	(37)	19.5	(80)
1943–1949	316	6.3	(20)	12.7	(41)

Using the same three cohorts described earlier, table 8 reports comparative data on the percentage of subjects in each group who have yet to marry or have children. Not surprisingly, the percentages, in both cases, increase steadily across the three cohorts. The figures for the youngest group, however, are the most striking. Nearly a quarter of those in the cohort had yet to marry, and fully 37% had yet to have children. Keep in mind that the subjects in this group were aged twenty-nine to thirty-four at the time of the survey. To appreciate the magnitude of the change embodied in these numbers, consider that in 1960 the median age at marriage stood at 20.1 for females and 23.1 for males, while the median age at first birth was 21.5 for females and 24.8 for males. Thus, even if a majority of those in our youngest cohort go on to marry and have children, they will bear witness to a significant change in the temporal structure of the life-course that has taken place over the past thirty or so years. Our guess, however, is that, given their relatively advanced ages, the percentage of these respondents who never marry or have children will significantly exceed the comparable figures for the other two cohorts. What these data appear to reflect is the solidification of a broader range of life-course options with each passing cohort.

This "relaxation" or broadening of what was previously experienced as a fairly narrow set of life-course parameters—both normatively and temporally—has, of course, been noted by others (Modell 1989). But what these other accounts have failed to provide is any systematic empirical sense of the processes that have shaped the emergence of this broader set of life-course options, and especially the role that the political and cultural movements of the 1960s appear to have played in this process. By our findings, we hope to encourage more empirical work at the intersection of these two subfields. We hope that our work will reinforce that branch of life-course research which has long recognized the demographic significance of broader historical events and processes (see Elder 1974; Buchman 1989; Elder and Caspi 1990). At the same time, we encourage social movement scholars to pay more attention not only to the impact of social movements on the structure and timing of the life-course but also to the role of life-course dynamics in shaping both the onset of protest cycles and the ebb and flow of individual activism. Only by combining the theoretical insights and empirical methods of both fields can scholars in each hope to understand fully the phenomena of interest to them.

Notes

1. In 1960, the median age at first marriage was 20.1 for females and 23.1 for males. The median age at first birth was 21.5 for females. Thus, our operationalizations of "lateness" (of marriage and parenthood) clearly hold face validity with respect to the post–World War II version of the normative life-course which provided the socialization context for our older cohorts. Our operationalization is intended to be sensitive to these gender differences and historical trends. Presently (U.S. Bureau of the Census 1990), the median age at first marriage is 23.7 for females and 25.5 for males. Even with these age increases, "lateness" is still captured by the ages we use. However, our concern is less with incorporating these recent trends than with explaining them.

2. The modeling approach we use incorporates the temporal aspects of our hypotheses by looking directly at the elapsed time between various life-course markers, such as entry into first job, first marriage, and birth of the first child. Specifically, we consider two time-based life-course outcomes: the subject's age at the birth of his or her first child, and the subject's age at first marriage. In each case, we seek to predict the overall "risk" that the second marker or event (first child, first marriage) will occur at a given moment in time (measured as the time elapsed since the first marker) and the extent to which New Left activities influence this risk.

More formally, the dependent variable is defined as the "hazard rate," or the probability that the second event will occur with exactly time t having elapsed since the first event, given that the second event has not yet been observed.

$$h(+) = \lim_{\Delta t \downarrow 0} \frac{P(t + \Delta t \geq T \geq t \mid T \geq t)}{\Delta t}$$

Here T is the random variable denoting the length of time elapsed since the first event, that is, the period during which a respondent is "at risk" for the second life-course marker defined for a particular dependent variable (Allison 1984; Tuma and Hannan 1984; Yamaguchi 1991). The relationship between the set of independent variables $(X_k, k = 1, \ldots, K)$ and the hazard rate is defined exponentially (or log-linearly) as:

$$h(t) = h_0(t) \exp(\textstyle\sum_k b_k X_k)$$

The baseline hazard function $h_0(t)$ accounts entirely for any variation in the risk attributable to time. One advantage of the proportional hazards model is that estimation of the effects of the K independent variables is possible without having to specify the nature of the baseline time function (Yamaguchi 1991). However, the proportionality assumption inherent in the model requires that none of the X_k terms change in their *relationship* to the hazard over time. This assumption can be examined and relaxed if necessary. The SAS procedure PHREG (SAS Institute 1996) was used to estimate the hazard models reported here.

Part II
Comparative Perspectives

7

Feminist Politics in a Hostile Environment: Obstacles and Opportunities

Joyce Gelb and Vivien Hart

During the 1980s and 1990s, the women's movements of the United States and the United Kingdom have shared the experience of presenting a feminist agenda in an era of antifeminist governments. In this review of women's movement activism in the late twentieth century, we contend that new stimuli and new opportunities have been important alongside the evident obstacles to achievement of movement goals. Both movements have indeed been severely challenged. Both can nonetheless claim changes in the political agenda and the achievement of policy goals that in some respects have advanced, not just defended, women's political aspirations. Neither movement is the same as it was twenty years ago. There have been new organizational developments, especially in Britain, and new issues are featured on the agendas of both movements. Cultural change is particularly evident in the United States, while policy achievements can be attributed to feminist influence on both sides of the Atlantic.

Change within movements, whether to new forms of mobilization, to new alliances, or to new relationships with the state, is not in itself an "outcome" of the same kind as goal achievement. The recent goal achievements of these women's movements, however, cannot be understood without their connection to structural changes within the movements and external relationships with other organizations and with the state. Our account describes a pattern of sustained dynamic interaction in which these movements' forms and agendas have both facilitated and responded to internal and external change. There is no simple cause and effect by which movement structures are determinant of outcomes. The examples of policy outcomes discussed here, however, do endorse the importance of the interrelationship between mobilization, agenda formulation, and effectiveness in policy making and changes in values and consciousness.

This chapter addresses change within the women's movements of Britain and the United States. The next section briefly outlines the picture of second-wave feminist organization that was standard in the early 1980s and the new political environment that appeared to challenge movement survival. We then review change in the movements themselves, in the United States and in Britain, in preparation for our core discussion of policy outcomes in three important arenas—abortion, economic equity, and domestic violence. If a movement is to achieve secure and lasting change, however, it must hope for more than success in winning individual items on a legislative agenda. We therefore also examine briefly some evidence of value and consciousness change to assess the extent to which movement goals may have become more widely diffused into everyday norms and practices.

Our cautiously optimistic conclusion is strengthened by comparative evidence contrasting the United States with Britain. Zald has presented the U.S. movement as arguably the social movement with the best staying power of social movement groups founded in the 1960s and 1970s (1988: 10–41). Burk and Hartmann were more critical when they wrote that, like many other social and political movements, the U.S. women's movement has found it difficult to respond to changing (economic) times (1996: 19). However, Bashevkin has hypothesized of Britain that, contrary to a logical expectation that the movement might "disappear under the strain of prolonged Conservative rule," it might instead have managed to "sustain and to some extent transform itself" (1996: 526). The two movements have shared the experience of a hostile political era and social and economic changes that have harshly affected women. In the late 1990s, access to a second-term Democratic administration in the United States and the advent of a Labour government in Britain make timely an appraisal of the ways in which these movements have survived and transformed themselves. Of course, the two movements have developed, since the early 1980s, from somewhat different starting points and within different institutional and cultural environments. It may nonetheless be asked, for example, how the impact of strident American ideological antifeminism compares with the equally severe structural and official antifeminism experienced in Britain. To what extent and by what means has either movement retained its support and its ability to advocate change, and retained a margin of influence and success in making feminist public policy?

Movement and Context in the Early 1980s

The standard picture of the American feminist movement has been of a well-established and professional network of national organizations coordinating a mainstream reformist movement with liberal equality goals. The American movement has also had a vigorous, if less visible, set of locally organized grassroots movements, which have combined advocacy and service delivery in negotiating with bureaucratic and elected policy makers. Through coalitions, membership organizations, and other cooperative relationships that have developed between local and national levels, American women have interacted with the state in policy advocacy and delivery, litigation, and campaigns for representation. At its most effective moments, this arrangement has permitted maximum flexibility and opportunity to pursue shifting and varied goals and priorities (Gelb 1995: 130).

In the early 1980s, British feminism had developed no equivalent superstructure. Women gained access to national policy making primarily as minority members of male-dominated organizations—parties, unions, professional associations—or on gender-specific grounds through the Equal Opportunities Commission (EOC), a government agency with semi-autonomous status. The movement was characterized by a marginality to or an ideological rejection of the "high politics" of the centralized parliamentary state. This history underlies the British understanding of movement politics as distinct from and outside of women's mainstream party and interest group activity (Byrne 1996: 57–59). At the local level, however, British women were no less vigorous than Americans, within a "decentralized, localized and anti-elitist—sometimes described as an anarcho-libertarian—" universe of groups (Gelb 1987: 267). These groups pursued their own agendas of liberation or broad social or specific political change, forming only occasional temporary coalitions on both local and national issues. National anti-statism was moderated by tolerance for a "local state" more willing to collaborate on the provision of services along the nonhierarchical, communal principles of the movement (Cockburn 1977).

The U.S. political context—the backdrop against which its movement politics must be evaluated—has been characterized by the absence of a strong leftist, labor-based party (unlike "Old Labour" in Britain), the reluctance of the state to intervene in the "private family" except to correct the behavior of those considered the unworthy poor (a tendency Britain increasingly shared under Conservative rule), a modified pluralist structure in which interest groups are often more powerful policy makers than parties (unlike Britain's party dominance), and multiple obstacles to policy adoption and implementation of legislation due to the separation of powers and federalism. U.S. feminist groups, unlike their counterparts in Sweden and, to some extent, Britain, have tended to organize gender-based groups outside established political structures. For the British movement, the structural problem has been how to penetrate the parliamentary hegemony in order to influence public policy.

Since 1980, movements in both nations have faced right-wing, antifeminist national regimes. Republicans occupied the American presidency for twelve years beginning in 1981. The Republican Party controlled the Senate for six years under Reagan, then both houses of Congress after 1994. Republican policy impacts in areas such as deregulation and welfare have confronted the American movement with escalating problems and diminishing resources. The American feminist movement has also had to contend with a political backlash against its agenda, embodied not only by the Republican Party from Reagan through Gingrich but also by such right-wing groups as the Christian Coalition, the Eagle Forum, Concerned Women of America, and the right-to-life movement. As Bashevkin suggests, the virulence of the antifeminist movement in the United States has no counterpart in Britain (1994: 670). Is its vehemence a reaction to the relative success of the better-coordinated and politically integrated feminist movement in the United States?

The British Conservative Party, in office from 1979 until May 1997, usually eschewed strong rhetoric while espousing more nebulous "family values" embodying a traditional view of women's roles. But in the name of free-market ideology, Conservative governments implemented both structural and policy changes directly affecting the women's movement to a degree paralleled in the United States only by the transfer of federal power to states in the 1996 welfare reforms. In Britain, with no separation of powers, decision making became yet more centralized. Central government severely pruned the discretionary powers and financial autonomy of local government and the education sector, circumscribed the rights of unions, and subjected the EOC to budget cuts and unsympathetic appointments. Privatization of public-sector functions diminished public accountability, adversely affected women's employment, and threatened women's support services and funding. Overall, access diminished while women's social disadvantage was exacerbated. With one-party rule, dissent among Conservatives often mattered more than conflict between parties, giving greater power than the numbers suggested to a right-wing minority view on social issues.

Movement Change: The United States

"The story of the women's movement in the US is one of transformation, expansion and diversification" (Wolfe and Tucker 1995: 436). Probably one major accomplishment of the movement by the late 1990s is the creation of new and enduring feminist structures of all kinds at all levels of politics. Ferree and Martin have contended that feminism can no longer easily be classified into collectivist or bureaucratic forms or, for that matter, liberal or radical categories (1995: 5). The movement is characterized by the coexistence of groups with seemingly disparate goals and strategies, some of which retain a commitment to more radical, alternative goals and others which behave more like reformist interest groups with a feminist agenda.

On a continuum of strategies, some movement groups utilize lobbying, litigation, and campaigning to reform the system; they may be mass-membership-based and staff- or board-run. Other groups, including many local and some national groups such as the National Coalition against Domestic Violence, have struggled with contradictions between the need for financial survival, interaction and tension with bureaucratic rules and processes, and commitment to feminist ideals. This struggle has led some in the direction of "modified collectives" and continual reassessment of priorities and structures. U.S. movement groups are especially conscious of the need to confront conflict and continually to renegotiate organizational structure and goals, perhaps helping to account for their relative longevity (Disney and Gelb forthcoming).

The importance of the feminist movement in the United States may be seen in several ways. From the 1970s onward, one manifestation of the movement, a feminist presence, was established in Washington, D.C., to advance a new public policy agenda and to mobilize support for legislation. Washington-based feminist groups increased from 75 in 1982 to about 140 in 1995, and increased cooperation shows in the formation of such new coalitions as the National Network to End Domestic Violence, the Coalition on Women and Job Training, and the National Coalition on Pay Equity. Because of the importance of the judicial system in the United States, a network of feminist legal advocacy groups has been crucial in litigating precedent-setting cases, following the example of black civil rights groups. Political action committees that raise money for feminist candidates have also become an important feature; EMILY's List, begun by one wealthy woman, enjoyed phenomenal growth in the 1990s, claiming 36,000 members in 1996. Through legal groups, PACs, policy research centers, and national membership groups, feminists have developed important policy advocacy momentum in national politics.

The movement has emphasized network and coalition building across issue and ideological lines. One consequence of organizational proliferation and defensive adaptation to the adverse political environment of the 1980s and 1990s has been the emergence of new submovements concerned with such issues as domestic violence, women's health, rape, and reproductive rights. New groups that mobilized in the late 1980s with a direct-action agenda, such as Third Wave, the Women's Action Coalition, and Women's Health Action Mobilization, were predominantly composed of twenty- to thirty-year-old women (Gelb and Palley 1996: xvi). While tendencies toward fragmentation have been offset to some extent by the Council of Presidents, which represents more than one hundred women's organizations, fragmentation has been inevitable as each group has differentiated itself in order to raise money from foundations and other sources and to gain members and contributors. Riger (1994) has argued, nonetheless, that there is relatively little competition among service and advocacy groups for limited funding, because of the "issue niche" approach, through which each group concentrates on a relatively narrow activity or goal. To secure funding, the movement has developed ties with the extensive American philanthropic sector, obtaining about 6 percent of foundation donations in the mid-1990s. Community-based women's foundations have created an additional source of support for local feminist and women's groups in most large cities. Most movement groups rely on "conscience constituencies" or contributors for their resources and staff for both day-to-day decision making and long-term strategizing (Gelb 1989: 46). While Walker (1991) and others once stressed the success of feminist groups in gaining grants and contracts from public- and private-sector groups in comparison with other social movements, in recent years Disney and Gelb (forthcoming) have found that these groups have sought to lessen dependence on outside sources, diversifying support and seeking to increase membership-based funding. Overall, at local and national levels and among different kinds of groups, it seems that the feminist movement has gained from a general mobilization against the right. According to one activist in the early 1990s, quoted by Bashevkin, "We had more momentum and more public support than ever before" (1994: 693). The Senate hearings of 1991 in which Supreme Court nominee Clarence Thomas was accused of sexual harassment by former employee Anita Hill also proved to be a bonanza for women's groups, highlighting both sexual harassment and the absence of women in powerful positions. Membership groups such as the National Organization for Women (NOW), the National Abortion and Reproductive Rights Action League (NARAL), and the National Women's Political Caucus (NWPC) have found membership increasing with the perception of crisis: in the aftermath of the *Webster v. Reproductive Health Services* abortion decision in 1989, which modified the liberal interpretation of women's right to choose, NOW's membership increased from 160,000 to 270,000, and its budget to $10.6 million (Brenner 1996: 33).

Far from being dead, the feminist movement has become more diffuse; it is organized everywhere, albeit sometimes "unobtrusively" in churches and synagogues, corporations, state legislatures, other social movements, universities and unions (Katzenstein 1995; Wolfe and Tucker 1995). Through cultural feminism, a woman's culture has been advanced through bookstores, art galleries, publishing companies, and cooperatives. In 1996, early radical feminist journals still survived: *Sojourner* and *off our backs* claimed circulations of about 25,000 (Brenner 1996: 57). Movement-related groups—influenced by the feminist ideology of empowerment—may be found at the neighborhood level through the National Council of Neighborhood Women, organized in 1975, and the Coalition of Labor Union Women (CLUW), half of whose leaders are women of color (Brenner 1996: 35). Liberal feminists, too, have been creative in expanding notions of sex discrimination to include sexual harassment and violence against women, continuing commitment to their original goals while greatly expanding the sweep of issues they consider crucial to the feminist agenda. Feminist groups at the local level have responded to specific issues in women's lives that directly affect women's oppression, including rape, domestic violence, health care, and the displacement of homemakers. Local advocacy groups continue to exist, though they are often found in a tense relationship with funders, both foundation- and government-based, and bureaucracies that seek to modify their goals and behavior. Nonetheless, it is fair to say that feminists themselves have modified bureaucratic norms and values, even as feminist structures themselves have been modified (Reinelt 1995). Groups have struggled with the dual demands of providing service and continuing advocacy, although they have proven that the two are not mutually exclusive. They have expanded their scope of action through efforts related to immigrant women, victims of gender-based violence, HIV and AIDS, housing and homelessness, and economic and environmental justice. While concerns about generational carryover are great, large numbers of young women joined the February 1996 Expo '96 for Women's Empowerment in Washington, D.C., to explore issues related to women's empowerment.

After the 1992 U.S. congressional election and the election of Democrat Bill Clinton, movement veteran Jo Freeman concluded that the movement had gained control of the agenda but also noted that "the two major parties have completely polarized around feminism and the reaction to it" (1993: 21). Some critics have decried the movement's preoccupation (however necessary) with pro-choice issues to the detriment of advocacy of other important concerns such as child care or attacks on poor women and children through the welfare reform enacted in the Personal Responsibility and Work Opportunity Reconciliation Act of 1996. One lesson to be drawn is that political isolation from one party was surely a limiting factor in ensuring the political momentum of American feminism. Anticipating the divided government occasioned by the 1996 election, Burk and Hartmann deplored the development of a competitive "flea market feminism" within the movement. They asked "how women's organizations in the short space of twenty years lost political power and came to be perceived as irrelevant (or even hostile) to the common woman" (1996: 19). While this harsh judgment is not universally shared, Nelson and Carver contend that, "in the current context, women's organizing—especially feminist organizing—has many voices but few vehicles for translating demand into sustained action" (1994: 739). The problem for contemporary feminism, and indeed all social movement groups that would oversee change, is one not of articulation but rather of implementation. Burk and Hartmann's approach may be more an indictment of the political system, in fact, than of feminist politics.

Movement Change: Britain

Rowbotham has claimed that "if feminism as an influence has been pervasive in Britain, feminism as a movement has become even more elusive" (1996: 13). The movement has indeed changed, but in some respects feminism appears more prominent, not less. In British national politics in the late 1990s, the old antistatism is on the wane. Seventeen years of state-sponsored antifeminism demonstrated the power of the state against outsiders. Women have achieved leadership positions in the Labour Party, and the Labour Party has formed the government since its May 1997 election victory. All political parties have sought new formulas to appeal to both activists and voters. Movement activists have been involved in Labour Party politics since the rise of second-wave feminism. Perrigo (1996) recounts how women have changed within the Labour Party and how they changed the party prior to the 1997 election, generating proactive programs to increase their representation and to communicate their issues. The Liberal Democrats, professing a policy of equality of opportunity, have also sought to increase women's presence and to campaign on women's issues (Squires 1996: 73). Conservatives remain torn between their traditionalist female constituency and newer and more articulate constituencies of conservative professional women; for the latter, they have supported legislation on stalking and have set gender targets for public appointments.

    Labour women are well connected to a network of national voluntary-sector organizations. Some have held office in civil liberties and social policy advocacy groups such as Liberty, the National Council for Single Parent Families, and the Child Poverty Action Group, which have included feminist causes in their broader agendas. In turn, these women and groups are becoming linked to newly effective national feminist coordinating organizations. Revitalized groups like the Fawcett Society (founded in 1866) and new ones like the National Alliance of Women's Organisations (NAWO, founded in 1989), although shoestring operations compared with the American NOW, are providing the machinery for coordinated action on both national and international feminist issues. The Fawcett Society is a membership organization that raised numbers from about four hundred members in 1990 (UK Cabinet Office 1990) to almost two thousand in 1996. NAWO is an umbrella organization for two hundred groups and associations representing five million women. Both operate with a handful of staff, teams of volunteers, and spartan budgets (both well under $500,000), but they maintain extensive lobbying, educational, and media campaigning activities (Fawcett Society 1996b; National Alliance of Women's Organisations 1996). Fawcett initiated a nationwide constituency-based election campaign in 1997 to lobby and to keep a wide range of women's issues prominent in debate and media coverage. NAWO's 1996 "Womanifesto" is a comprehensive policy agenda on the economy, violence against women, the arts and media, and special issues ranging from the ordination of women to family law, aging, rural women's problems, racism, and immigration. National coordinating groups with a more specialized agenda, such as the Rights of Women or the National Abortion Coalition, have also become respected players in their areas of expertise (Griffin 1995). The internationalization of many women's issues is evidenced by NAWO's membership in the European Women's Lobby, and NAWO's joint pressure with Fawcett and other groups for the implementation of the UN Beijing resolutions.

Local movement groups, like their national counterparts, have shed much of the ideological factionalism that sometimes was a diversion from women's needs. The key change in the local movement has been recognition of and response to diversity. Ethnic women's groups, especially in Asian British communities, have acted on particular needs in education, health provision, marriage, and violence. The Southall Black Sisters (SBS), founded in 1979 to meet the needs of women in an ethnically mixed and economically disadvantaged London borough, exemplifies the broadening agenda of such groups. The original service-providing Southall Centre remains a major local resource. But in a national advocacy role, SBS now works with "groups like the Women's Institute and the Townswomen's Guild as well as Justice for

Women to reform the law on provocation," which has often protected men, but not women, accused of domestic violence. SBS works with immigration groups, education groups opposing separate Muslim schools, and antiracist campaigns. SBS is also a cofounder of Women against Fundamentalism, is part of a group fighting for social change in South Asia, and has sent representatives to New York and Beijing to address human rights issues (Griffin 1995: 79). Ethnic and other causes spill over into each other, as do local and national issues. Similarly, the National Group on Homeworking represents the lowest-paid women in the workforce, many of whom are minorities; the Leeds-based organization publishes information on wages and conditions in Panjabi, Urdu, Gujarati, Bengali, and Mandarin Chinese. Justice for Women campaigns nationally to change the law on intimate homicide as a result of a case originally raised locally by SBS and a Sussex Women's Aid branch. A mutually reinforcing interaction exists between national policy agendas and the social-change goals and service provision of local organizations.

The local state was a particular target of the Conservative government's structural reforms. Discretionary powers and funds were savagely cut, the most extreme example being the abolition in 1985 of the Greater London Council (GLC). The GLC had become the flagship of feminist organization; at its peak, its Women's Committee had a staff of ninety-five and controlled an average annual budget of £6 million. With its demise, power was scattered to smaller local boroughs. Two-thirds of these had a women's committee or initiative in the 1980s, but by 1994 only two remained. Women might have expected otherwise as Conservative councils lost elections (nationally by 1996, only 12 out of 457 authorities remained in their control); but parochial local Labour parties have often given only grudging support to equality and women's issues (Lovenduski, Margetts, and Abrar 1996: 11–12; Lovenduski and Randall 1993: chapter 5). Advances such as an overall increase in the number of both elected and appointed women in local government and the survival of practical and financial support for women's groups may owe more to women's networks, for example, the Women in Local Government Network of women in management positions (Lovenduski, Margetts, and Abrar 1996: table 4 and 19–23). Local groups have had to cast more widely for premises and for funding, from the National Lottery and the voluntary sector, for example (Russell, Scott, and Wilding 1996). In one respect, the Conservatives' decimation of public services has helped; the privatization of welfare has transferred state funding to services commissioned from the voluntary sector (Griffin 1995: 7). SBS, running referral and advice centers, support groups, language classes, and children's summer projects, and lobbying locally and nationally on domestic violence and immigration issues, receives more than half its annual budget of £150,000 from the London borough of Ealing, with most of the rest raised from foundations and charities (Southall Black Sisters 1996).

Approval within the movement of such considerable changes as the decline in antistatism, ideological softening, recognition of diversity, and professionalization has not been universal. To Lynne Harne, a self-described revolutionary feminist, "the autonomous women's liberation movement seemed at an all-time low by the end of the 1980s," because "municipal feminism has risen and then fallen" and the movement "has been shaken apart by the need to take on board the issues of class, race and disability; and in the process it seems almost to have destroyed itself" (Harne 1988: 65, 69). Feminists among "Thatcher's children"—those who grew up under Conservative governments—are unexpectedly optimistic. It is particularly among younger women that diversity is seen as positive rather than divisive: "'Women's Liberation' as an organised (inter)national movement no longer exists, but feminism is all-pervasive. Many gains have been made, especially in terms of putting the experiences of a diversity of women—working-class women, Black women, lesbians and women with disabilities—on the 'women's agenda'"(Pegg 1990: 159).

Structurally, the British women's movement in the late 1990s is in the midst of transformation, enforced by the hard times of the Conservative era, encouraged by social and professional advances made by women, and adaptive to new opportunities even as old ones close down. It may be more stratified into elite and local segments than in earlier years, but it is also more interactive across that and other dimensions of diversity, and more professional altogether. To a degree, particularly at elite national levels, it is following the pattern developed by the American movement of entry into and lobbying of government, a trend visible even before the 1997 election. These developments may be valued as successes in mobilization and thus are important within the movement. But such changes are also integral to the effective achievement of policy goals, enabling a reflexive response to new circumstances, new alliances for new agenda items, and new strategies to foster or to cope with the opening of new channels. The movement formation and change described thus far are a part of the explanation of the policy changes to which we now turn.

Feminist Impact on Policy Change: The United States and Britain

The success of a movement may be measured in several ways: through movement mobilization, policy impact, and cultural change; or change in collective consciousness and discursive politics, which may create resources for further mobilization and change. Tarrow (1994) has argued that movement success, in addition to policy change, depends on the range and flexibility of the "tactical repertory." In the policy sphere, a major contribution of the American feminist movement has been to change federal and state policy through legislative and judicial decisions. The movement has achieved recognition as a legitimate participant in decision making.

A major factor in the achievement of feminist goals in the United States has been the dramatic increase over the past two decades in the number of women seeking and elected to office. This change is largely a consequence of the politicization created by the women's movement and specific efforts to increase women's representation in order to achieve greater equity. Of particular significance in aiding the feminist political agenda is the fact that a large number of women elected to political office in the United States are members of women's groups and women's rights organizations; one study found that 40 percent of all elected women belong to a women's rights organization (Darcy, Welch, and Clark 1995: 37). In addition, women legislators owe their election in part to the activities of women's movement groups. Such groups supply money and volunteers, and women legislators are far more likely than their male counterparts to identify such support as crucial to their electoral success. Groups such as EMILY's List have joined others, including the Feminist Majority, the Republican WISH List, the Women's Campaign Fund, and Voters for Choice, as well as the NWPC, an earlier movement organization. According to one account as many as forty-two PACs represent women's interests in making funds available to feminist candidates (Brenner 1996: 69 n. 79). The NWPC has also been responsible for training candidates to aspire to electoral office. Reflecting the interests of their support base, women legislators are more likely than their male colleagues to endorse policies that are liberal and feminist. (Center for American Women and Politics 1995: 2; Carroll 1985: 171). Their presence is felt even more at the state and local levels, where they hold more than 20 percent of seats.

In addition to seeking change through legislative politics, feminist groups have sought to increase the appointments of women to executive and bureaucratic office. By 1994, in partial recognition of women's support for his candidacy, Clinton had appointed seven women to cabinet-level positions and a record thirty of ninety-one appointments to the federal judiciary. In 1996, after his reelection, which was marked by even greater support from women voters than in 1992, and under pressure from the Council of Presidents, representing more than a hundred women's groups, he appointed other women to high office, including Madeleine Albright as secretary of state. U.S. feminists have employed "insider/outsider" strategies, utilizing the support of influential power holders within the system as well as movement mobilization from outside (Staggenborg 1991: 155; Spalter-Roth and Schreiber 1995).

British movement activists anticipated presence and visibility as government insiders following the Labour election victory of 1997. Labour deliberately nominated women candidates for winnable seats, but the huge increase from the preelection 37 Labour women MPs to 101 was as unexpected as Labour's total of 419 seats. Altogether, there were 120 women MPs in the new Parliament, up from 62 and forming 18 percent of the total. Many of the new members were young and had recent experience in movement politics and local activities. The numbers of women receiving public appointments to commissions and the all-important quangos that have taken on much policy implementation in the last seventeen years, had been rising for some time. Although women still made up only about one-third of the total in 1996, this compares with less than one in four as recently as 1991 (*Equal Opportunities Review* 1996 [no. 67]: 6). The 300 Group, which monitors appointments as part of its aspiration to see three hundred women in Parliament, maintains lists of hundreds more women who are as qualified for public jobs as men.

Feminist pressure has contributed to this development. Labour required women-only candidate short lists in the 1990s until, in 1996, an industrial tribunal found this practice a breach of sex discrimination law. The Liberal Democrats had women on all their selection lists, and both parties were urged on by increasingly active national movement groups like the Fawcett Society. After the 1992 election, a new phenomenon to Britain, EMILY's List UK, was established to recruit, train, and fund feminist candidates. The success of earlier campaigns for equality in higher education and the professions has created a larger recruitment pool of experienced women. Women comprise 15 percent of top civil servants and almost half of qualifying solicitors, and significant percentages in other professions (*Equal Opportunities Review* 1996 [no. 67]: 6; Moss 1995: 172). Opportunity 2000, a business-sponsored initiative for equality in management, had 61 business organization members in 1991 and 305 in 1996, though in 1996 women comprised still only 12.3 percent of managers, in comparison to about 40 percent in the United States (*Equal Opportunities Review* 1996 [no. 68]: 4).

With five women in the first Labour cabinet and fourteen more as junior ministers, and with the professionalization and coordination of national organization, in 1997 the British movement possessed the characteristics of the insider/outsider politics described by Staggenborg and proven effective in the

United States. One aspect of such politics is "access to many skills and re- sources which facilitated institutionalized types of mobilizing activities and persuasive rather than confrontational collective-action tactics" (Staggenborg 1991: 30). A second aspect is the connection of insiders to outsiders. In Byrne's phrase about the movement, the insiders are "like icebergs—the visible 10% is important, but without the underlying 90% it will melt away" (1996: 71). Influential Labour women in government have connections to the organized 90 percent in the parties and groups outside, through links to women's, civil liberties, and social advocacy organizations that advise and support them and bolster their feminist commitment.

Even under optimal conditions, policy impact may vary according to many conditions and is best assessed by looking at a set of comparative examples. We will do so by examining three—abortion, economic equity, and domestic violence—and contrasting the evidence of movement impact on each.

Abortion

In the United States, abortion and reproductive choice have been highly visible issues in a highly politicized context since the Supreme Court's 1973 decision in *Roe v. Wade*. An active and strong pro-choice feminist movement that coalesced behind the decision has been countered by virulently anti- abortion, pro-life groups, which have challenged abortion rights in the courts and in Congress, mounted violent attacks on abortion providers, and effectively limited access to abortion services. These forces have gained new legitimacy through their acceptance within the Republican Party. The scope of conflict has expanded, supporters and opponents have been highly mobi- lized, and symbols have been manipulated by both sides in an attempt to control the debate. Efforts to maintain access to abortion have been spear- headed by NARAL, NOW, Planned Parenthood, and the Reproductive Freedom Project of the American Civil Liberties Union (ACLU). Movement tactics have combined legal strategies, mass rallies in Washington, D.C., leg- islative lobbying, and efforts to target antichoice legislators at the ballot box. In 1989, pro-choice forces suffered a setback when the Court, in *Webster v. Reproductive Health Services,* upheld a woman's right to have an abortion but replaced the trimester principle of *Roe v. Wade* with that of fetal viability, in effect drawing a line between legal and illegal abortion (Gelb and Palley 1996: 221). In a second setback, in 1992 in *Planned Parenthood of South- eastern Pennsylvania v. Casey,* the Court upheld a wide disparity of options limiting access to abortion in the states as not placing an "undue burden" on pregnant women. The Hyde Amendment, initially adopted in 1976, bans

Medicaid funding for abortion except in highly restrictive circumstances, while the "right-to-life" strategy of seeking to limit access to abortion in every possible way continues, although it has been unsuccessful in passing a constitutional amendment.

Despite the continuing conflict over this issue and the extraordinary diversion of energy and resources demanded by continued pressure, the pro-choice movement survives as a relatively strong movement capable of responding in several arenas. In April 1989, as a response to the *Webster* decision, between 300,000 and 600,000 participants marched in Washington, D.C., in protest. The movement estimate of participants in a 1992 march was approximately 500,000, including many young women and women of color. NARAL's membership grew from 200,000 in 1989 to 400,000 in 1990, and Planned Parenthood and the ACLU, allies in the pro-choice struggle, saw significant increases in membership and contributions. However, after the election of President Clinton, NARAL membership dropped from almost 350,000 to just 100,000 (qtd. in Brenner 1996: 33). Burk and Hartmann's argument that President Clinton's election "undermined the central core" of the movement, causing abortion rights activists in particular to believe their cause was won (1996: 20), is given some credence by these figures. Clinton did advance a pro-choice agenda from the outset, largely in response to support from women voters. He lifted the gag rule that prevented doctors in federally funded clinics from providing abortion counseling, lifted the ban on fetal tissue research, and repealed the policy that denied U.S. funding to countries that provided abortion counseling. Clinton also signed into law the Freedom of Access to Clinics Act and permitted research on the RU 486 "morning after" pill that could transform abortion policy. On several occasions from 1996 to 1998, he vetoed a controversial congressional bill banning late-term abortions.

The abortion issue has never been the central, polarizing issue in British politics that it has been in the United States, although it generated one of the first permanent national coordinating organizations. The National Abortion Campaign (NAC), founded in 1975, led resistance to each attempt to restrict the effectively broad rights won in 1967 to abortion with the consent of two doctors under certain medical and social conditions. In the 1970s, NAC organized large demonstrations, but by 1990, its tactics had shifted toward more professional lobbying and smaller marches (Byrne 1996: 62, 65). In 1990, pro-lifers sought to roll back the time limit on legal abortions from the twenty-eighth to the eighteenth week of pregnancy. For the first time, pro-life MPs persuaded the government to give its own parliamentary time (though not its endorsement) to a clause added to the Human

Fertilization and Embryology Bill. After that pro-life success in agenda building, NAC's coalition regarded the eventual vote for a twenty-four week time limit as a relative victory.

The principal pro-life organizations, the Society for the Protection of the Unborn Child (SPUC) and LIFE, have copied American tactics to try to create a high and emotional political profile for abortion. SPUC has brought in American advisers, including a team from Operation Rescue, while LIFE has waged media campaigns around emotive cases of multiple pregnancies and has unsuccessfully sought an injunction to prevent the termination of one pregnancy. The usually low profile of the issue in Britain despite these efforts is partly due to the different political environment. Abortion has not been a party or electoral issue. Party business fills parliamentary time, and the party whips allow a free vote on abortion. Direct intervention by religious bodies has been rare in British politics. Pro-lifers have, however, tried to change both the nonpartisan status of the issue and the detachment of the churches. In the buildup to the 1997 election, Catholic prelates demanded a ban and attacked Labour leader Tony Blair as a sham Christian for failing to commit the party to an antiabortion position. The newly formed Pro-life Alliance ran close to fifty candidates against prominent politicians and in marginal constituencies. These attempts to force the issue onto the electoral agenda have been rejected by the political party leaders, even by many pro-life parliamentarians, and by the electorate, but they have undoubtedly given new prominence and energy to pro-life organizations (*Observer*, January 5, 1997).

Economic Equity

Burk and Hartmann's prescription for the recovery of the women's movement follows from their belief that the movement has failed to "make the priorities of women the focus of the women's movement." Women's priorities, from poll evidence, are "economic issues (pay equity and pensions), health care (which is economic), and violence" (1996: 20). Economic equity was a priority for the national organizations of second-wave feminism in the United States, which gained from the inclusion of women in the Civil Rights Act of 1964 and won further progress with the establishment of the Equal Employment Opportunity Commission (EEOC) and through affirmative action and comparable worth programs. British legislation was later and lesser in scope, but the Equal Pay Act of 1970 and Sex Discrimination Act of 1975, which established the British Equal Opportunities Commission, were "greatly influenced by the pattern of US legislation from the 1960s and early '70s" (Lester 1996: 25).

A quarter century of slow progress is shown by the crude basic indicator of pay equity. From a 1970s U.S. average of fifty-nine cents earned by a woman to each dollar by a man, and British women's average hourly earnings of 62.9 percent of men's in 1970, both figures rose above 70 percent in the late 1990s ("Through a Glass Darkly" 1996: 51; *Equal Opportunities Review* 1996 [no. 70]: 34). Some victories for some women have been won on other work-related causes, notably pensions, with persistent advocacy from women's legal organizations in the United States and the EOC in Britain (Goldstein 1988: 513–36; Collins and Meehan 1994: 385–87). The U.S. legal strategy has clearly benefited women through access to higher education and managerial and professional employment (Kessler-Harris 1994: 73). Race-conscious affirmative action programs have also enhanced access to some nontraditional jobs, like construction and engineering. In 1987, the Supreme Court authorized gender-conscious affirmative action programs when it upheld the hiring of Diane Joyce as a road dispatcher for the Santa Clara County Transportation Agency. In this case, the amicus brief submitted by the NOW Legal Defense and Education Fund (NOW LDEF) and an alliance of thirteen other feminist and civil liberties groups contrasted with the Reagan administration's Justice Department opposition to all affirmative action (Goldstein 1988: 562–82).

Alongside these achievements, however, the movement must address continuing and insistent inequities. For middle-class women, access to the professions is but one step toward equity; thus, the Glass Ceiling Commission established in the Civil Rights Act of 1991 began to probe the next step, promotion (Gelb and Palley 1996: 235–36). The stratified and gendered structure of the low-skilled labor market has proven resistant to change. Part-time work, with worse conditions and fewer benefits than full-time work, is 62.3 percent female in the United States, 85.4 percent female in Britain. As Kessler-Harris has noted, the outcome of American affirmative action programs is ambiguous for "less-educated and less-skilled women," including many women of color (1994: 73–74). Legislative campaigns and programs of service provision by organizations such as Wider Opportunities for Women, to improve access to skills training and to nontraditional unskilled employment, to provide employment services, and to network with union groups such as CLUW in working for the lower-paid sector, remain relatively low-profile and, in terms of service provision, just "drops" in the ocean of need (Spalter-Roth and Schreiber 1995: 124). Women benefited in the past from the carryover of rights from race- to gender-conscious programs; now they are vulnerable to decisions whittling away at race-conscious programs. The women's legal community did not intervene in several 1995 Supreme Court cases that, respectively, shifted the burden to individual proof of discrimination *(Adarand v. Pena),* loosened the standards for affirmative action implementation *(Missouri v. Jenkins),* and rejected race redistricting *(Miller v. Johnson)*; nor in *Hopwood v. State of Texas* (U.S. Court of Appeals for the Fifth Circuit, 1996), where race was rejected as a criterion for college admissions. But feminist legal groups, including NOW LDEF, joined the fight against the anti–affirmative action Proposition 209 passed in California in 1996.

Equal rights, however, will remain a prime terrain of contest for the American women's movement. The centrality of the equal protection clause of the Fourteenth Amendment to American political culture and to the resolution of issues of social and economic equity, and women's long tradition and expertise in constitutional politics ensure that setbacks will not end debate. A more radical challenge in the sphere of economic equity is presented by the welfare reforms signed into law by President Clinton in 1996, with their five-year cap on benefits, restriction of benefits to legal aliens, and work requirements. Analysts of "the feminization of poverty" have long pointed out that welfare is also an issue of economic equity (Pearce 1990). The 1996 legislation lays bare this connection and the urgency to develop woman-friendly policies for the many unskilled women of color and white women who are already marginal workers in the economy or will become so as recipients of the new "temporary assistance for needy families."

In the 1970s, Britain imported the American model of equality legislation and an EEOC into a polity where parliamentary sovereignty precluded claims for judicial review of legislation or administration. At that time, Britain also lacked a culture of rights politics; economic issues were the province of class conflict or corporatist negotiation. Recession, the growth of a part-time, low-paid, privatized, and increasingly female workforce, restrictions on unions, and a regime committed to perfecting a free-market system then exacerbated problems. In the 1990s however, British women have made gains in economic equity through litigation *and* have developed new coalitions to fight with and for low-paid women. Changes in mobilization, strategy, and agenda have interacted to produce results in an apparently bleak social situation.

European litigation strategies fostered these developments. In the 1970s, an expert recalls, "it did not occur to us that *European Community law* would play a crucial part" (Lester 1996: 25). Britain joined the European Economic Community in January 1973, signing the Treaty of Rome, whose Article 119 enshrines a right to equal pay for women. In 1976, in *Defreene v. Sabena,* the European Court of Justice ruled that such European equality principles could be claimed by individuals in their own national courts to overrule national legislation or even to require legislation where none existed. Since then, this route has been used to combat direct and indirect discrimination in pay, pensions and retirement ages, hiring and firing protections, and the rights of part-time workers, winning significant changes in women's economic position (Collins and Meehan 1994). In the process, the British women's movement has forged new alliances, offering one of the clearest examples of the interaction of mobilization and goals in achieving policy change. A formal complaint to Europe in 1994 that abolition of minimum wage legislation breached European treaty obligations, for example, was brought by the EOC and Trades Union Congress together, backed by organizations for gender interests (the Pay Equity Project), nonunionized low-paid workers (the Low Pay Unit), and ethnic workers (the National Group on Homeworking) (Hart 1994). The Fawcett Society has undertaken to lead a campaign against low pay. Both Fawcett and NAWO participate in the European Women's Lobby and European Social Policy Forum, in a developing European network of economic equity organizations. This network is also proactively pushing the narrow economic conception of European law to encompass policy on sexual harassment, reproductive rights, and family law (Elman 1996; Meehan and Collins 1996). Litigation and European lobbying are technocratic forms of politics, but the emerging networks of experts and advocacy groups for the most deprived women are achieving the same kind of insider/outsider coalitions as those which Spalter-Roth and Schreiber (1995) find significant for economic equity policy in the United States.

Domestic Violence

The issue of domestic violence represents the emergence, in Britain and the United States, of a locally based feminist issue onto the national agenda. Its acceptance as a legitimate issue of public policy represents a triumph for the more radical branch of feminism, which has defined this "personal" issue as a political one and has been able to obtain legislative and judicial intervention in family relationships by the state. In both nations, the movement has demonstrated that service delivery and advocacy need not be contradictory or mutually exclusive goals.

The first movement response to the issue in Britain was a practical one: the establishment of two refuges in 1972 in London. In 1975, thirty-five groups running refuges formed the National Women's Aid Federation (NWAF); today the English federation alone represents about two hundred refuges. The NWAF became an active legislative lobby, testifying to the

parliamentary committee in 1975 that authoritatively defined domestic violence as a social, not an individual, problem. Legislation won in 1976 and
1978 provided for injunctions to restrain or exclude abusing partners from
the home, and the Housing (Homeless Persons) Act of 1977 guaranteed
public housing for women fleeing violence (Lovenduski and Randall 1993:
305–8). In the United States, following the British model, a shelter for battered women was first opened in 1974 in Minnesota (and still exists today).
Initial efforts at legal reform and funding came at the local level, the latter
augmented by foundation support. In the 1970s, national women's movement groups in the United States began to mobilize around this issue. The
NOW Task Force on Battered Women/Domestic Violence was founded in
1976, the National Coalition against Domestic Violence (NCADV) in 1977.

A challenge for shelter providers in the United States and Britain has
been to maintain financial security without surrendering feminist principles
of organization and goals including the empowerment of battered women:
"The battle we all face is the need to develop strategies which make it possible for the feminist agenda to reverberate through non-feminist organizations; to make them take on our political agenda rather than us taking on
theirs" (Foley 1996: 174; see also Reinelt 1995). The NCADV, which still
survives in the United States in the late 1990s, is a coalition of service
providers; this group has maintained itself even as it has struggled to develop
an autonomous women's voice and to speak to controversial positions while
relying on government and foundation funding. Because the group's guidelines specify that if a funding agency refused to support its agenda the funding must be turned back, twice the NCADV returned large grants, one to
the U.S. Department of Justice and one to Johnson and Johnson. A 1992
conference scheduled in Colorado was also canceled at considerable cost, because of that state's endorsement of an anti–gay and lesbian proposition.
The movement's survival despite these funding losses illustrates the earlier
point that funding sources have been diversified, in NCADV's case with no
more than 30 percent deriving from any one source (Disney and Gelb forthcoming). The group's structure has also been modified, with continued commitment to consensus decision making; class, race, and sexual diversity; and
a reconstituted smaller steering body.

The British movement has faced the same dilemma in a context where
its primary source of funding, housing, and other social service provision has
been the local state. A study of Welsh refuges in the mid-1990s found that
overall funding increased during the 1980s and the number of refuges grew.
Local authorities remained the main source; Welsh Women's Aid, an um-
brella body, received most of its funding from the central government Welsh

Office (Charles 1995: 626–28). Refuges now fill a statutorily mandated function, which helps guarantee funding. Nonetheless, here, as in other funded services for women in both Britain and the United States, concern about and alertness to funding unattached to a feminist analysis remains (Radford and Stanko 1996: 70; Foley 1996: 174). Welsh activists believe they have sustained their autonomy partly because their role is both distinctive and authorized in law. For state social services, according to a parliamentary select committee, "what is involved" is "not the plight of a particular category of unhappy women, but the future of families, involving men, women, and—most important of all—their children" (qtd. in Dobash and Dobash 1992: 128). Women's groups can define their role differently, an unnamed refuge worker explained to Nickie Charles: "We're unashamedly one-sided. . . . A woman's been subjected to violence, that's all. We may be the only people that do that. You know, the social worker, the health visitor, doctor, may all be sympathetic, but they'll all be trying to help them as a family" (Charles 1995: 628).

While domestic violence gained national attention in the late 1970s, passing national legislation in the United States proved difficult due to the ascendancy of right-wing groups in the Republican Party after the 1980 election. A "family protection act" was even introduced in Congress in 1981 by these forces, to prohibit funding for any domestic violence programs, although it failed to pass (Gelb 1983). During the next decade, most states passed legislation related to battered women, providing some funding for shelters and improved intervention by the criminal justice and judicial systems. Some states used surcharges on marriage licenses to finance these new initiatives. Local- and state-level efforts were spearheaded by women's groups through class-action civil suits, pressure on responsive locally elected officials, and the presence of a large number of professional women in the justice system itself. Lessons learned by feminist groups at the local level were later employed in the federal arena, including the creation of broad-based coalitions, bipartisan support, and neutralization of right-wing efforts through the use of nonthreatening concepts such as saving the family and protecting victimized women (Dobash and Dobash 1992: 206–7).

A developing feminist discourse and analysis has had some impact on the U.S. legislative process in the 1980s and 1990s. In 1984, the Violence Prevention and Services Act was signed into law, following six years of pressure and activism by the feminist movement. It provided, and continues to provide, limited funding for shelters. According to Dobash and Dobash, the passage of this legislation was "a monument to the energy, hard work, increased political sophistication, alliance building and tactics" of the women's movement, particularly notable during the ascendancy of the Reagan ad-ministration's antifeminist and regressive social policy agenda (1992: 144). In 1994, after another extended period of prodding Congress, the Violence against Women Act was passed as part of an omnibus crime bill. Perhaps the most significant legislation enacted with regard to the feminist agenda in the 1990s, this law was a testament to the successful use of the insider/outsider strategy employed by the feminist community and its allies. In a telephone conversation on April 26, 1996, Pat Reuss, legislative director of the NOW Legal Defense and Education Fund, explained:

> Insiders included Senator Biden, chairman of the Senate Judiciary Committee, and numerous bipartisan supporters in Congress. Out-siders were represented by a coalition of feminist groups led by the Violence against Women Task Force organized by the NOW Legal Defense and Education Fund, and with strong participation by NOW, the National Women's Law Center, NCADV, Women's Legal Defense Fund, and the newly organized National Network to End Domestic Violence. They worked with a much broader coalition, including the Junior League, Catholic Charities, General Federation of Women's Clubs, and Feminists for Life.

Grassroots mobilization was undertaken by local activists and union mem-bers, and coalition participation extended to supportive law enforcement of-ficials and lawyers. The focus of the legislation is primarily on crisis preven-tion through judicial and police protection. The law mandates interstate enforcement of protective orders, a national domestic violence hotline, training for state and federal judges, civil rights remedies for gender-related crimes, and some aid for battered immigrant women. Special support is given to strengthen local law enforcement and police and prosecutorial training. In addition, the law provides for some additional federal money for shelters (Gelb and Palley 1996: 230). A total of $1.6 billion was allocated to support these activities through the year 2000.

Violence against women is equally a national issue in Britain today. Its potency as a movement rallying call was demonstrated in November 1996, when a conference on "violence, abuse, and women's citizenship" drew two thousand participants, more than half from Britain, including many young women and many from ethnic minorities. The event was organized by a uni-versity women's unit and sponsors including NAWO, the Women's Aid Federations of England and Wales, the SBS, and other ethnic, women's, chil-dren's, and development groups. The spread of the Zero Tolerance Campaign, a public awareness initiative on violence against women, from its creation by the Edinburgh Women's Committee in 1992 to local initiatives across the United Kingdom is another indicator of the vitality of the movement on this topic (Mackay 1996). Its prominence is equally evident in recent campaigns to educate law enforcement and judicial officials, to reform procedures, to improve existing legislation, and to bring in new measures on stalking.

Dobash and Dobash contrast the American policy debate on domestic violence with that in Britain. In the 1970s in the United States, feminist discourse was accompanied by the call for civil rights and legal protection. British MPs ignored feminist social and cultural analyses of the problem, preferring to attribute domestic violence to "individual inadequacy and poor family background," but then accepted the activists' pragmatic proposals for refuges, housing, and social services. In effect, "the solution was adopted while the nature of the problem was denied or transformed" (1992: 100). Subsequent British action has followed three lines: continuation of the original concern to provide material resources, especially housing, to ensure women safety and independence; new campaigns, like those in the United States, for legal reforms and better treatment by law enforcement agencies; and a broadening of debate from domestic violence to all forms of violence against women. For example, the issue of rights of residence in, and exclusion of violent partners from, the family home has recently been debated. A legislative initiative to confirm long-standing rights to residence that applied to married and unmarried partners alike mobilized a relatively small but well-connected conservative pro-family lobby. Although it was the Conservative lord chancellor (who heads the judiciary and holds both legislative and executive positions) who introduced the Family Homes and Domestic Violence Bill in 1995 to codify these rights, the bill was a flashpoint for a small group of right-wing Conservative MPs, including several women, who saw in it a threat to the entire institution of marriage. A last-minute but successful parliamentary and media campaign killed the bill. Although some of the lost provisions were incorporated in the 1996 Family Law Act, the same opponents forced a compromise that gives judges discretion to discriminate between married and unmarried partners in granting access to the home, "to have regard to the fact that [unmarried cohabitants] have not given each other the commitment involved in marriage" (*Current Law Statues* 1996, c. 27).

The Women's Aid Federation of England (WAFE) led a movement lobby to recover the lost domestic violence bill and in the process raised

British women's professionalism and involvement in policy making to a new level. The staff of two activated refuge workers and local volunteers coordinated a national network of other organizations and briefed the media. They became directly involved in the legislative process in ways that are not normal British practice, drafting thirty amendments to the bill, briefing MPs and the lord chancellor, and monitoring the key committee stages. As a counter to the "family values" campaign in Parliament and the right-wing press, they were extremely effective. The eventual compromise meant that, as in the United States, the legislation was loaded with support for the traditional family and marriage. But WAFE staff argued that the destruction of the 1995 bill showed that the "forces of reaction work within government" and thus that women must do the same. It seemed to them that outright rejection of compromise would have created powerful enemies and probably would have resulted in worse, or no, legislation. As it was, WAFE won a codified set of remedies and did extend protection against violence. The compromise allowing discrimination against unmarried partners was at least only discretionary. The proof of the pudding would be in how the courts used their discretion; hence, the next step by WAFE was to file an application to sit on the committee drawing up the regulations (Harwin and Debbonnaire 1996).

Monitoring implementation draws attention to police practices and the judicial system. The Domestic Violence Act of 1976 gave magistrates the power to attach arrest warrants to injunctions against violent men, but police remained reluctant to intervene in domestic disputes. Discontent with the police grew during the 1970s and 1980s, and feminists critiqued their conduct in domestic violence and rape cases and the racial bias and violence against, as well as failure to address the needs of, ethnic women. These critiques generated prolonged pressure to implement legislation on injunctions and exclusion of violent men from the home, but only in the late 1980s did shifts in police practice begin to occur (Hester and Radford 1996). Home Office guidelines in 1985 and 1990 responded to feminist critiques from WAFE, Women against Violence against Women, and the Women's National Commission (which in 1986 issued a report, *Violence against Women*) (Radford and Stanko 1996: 74). By 1993, sixty-two of sixty-nine Metropolitan Police divisions in London had domestic violence units, as recommended by the 1990 Home Office guidelines, as did twenty of the forty-two other police forces in England and Wales (75, 85). "Despite limited and uneven progress there has been an increasingly vocalized acceptance of women's right to police protection from violent male partners" (Hester and Radford 1996: 85).

As in the United States, there are examples of new integrative, multi-service models of service provision and police intervention, such as that in the London borough of Islington, where women councillors joined with the Women's Committee, and in Manchester, where feminist groups joined with police and health authorities to create a sexual assault center (Foley 1996: 168). Together with domestic violence groups such as WAFE, feminist groups such as Rights of Women, Women against Rape, and rape crisis groups have campaigned persistently for such improvements. Rights of Women, Justice for Women, and a number of ethnic groups, especially SBS, have also been at the forefront of pressure on judges to review both court procedures and, after several high-profile homicide cases against abused women, the law itself (Bindel, Cook, and Kelly 1995). Most recently, the vulnerability to deportation of immigrant women who flee abusive marriages has forged a new alliance of feminist, ethnic, civil liberties, and refugee organizations to fight the "one-year rule," which leaves them unprotected (Southall Black Sisters 1996). As Julie Bindel of Justice for Women has observed, "Violence against women could be said to be an area of feminist 'success' in that the issue is now one of intense public concern, and many of our particular criticisms have been accepted as valid" (Bindel, Cook, and Kelly 1995: 65). Success in building an agenda leading to policy change thus inevitably challenges the movement to sustain that success by building organizations and resources for the long-term and day-by-day routinization of implementation and monitoring procedures.

Consciousness and Value Change

The final area for analysis of movement success is that of the impact on public consciousness and value change. In the United States, a survey conducted for the Center for Women Policy Studies in 1993 found that most women indicated that the women's movement had expanded their job opportunities, had made possible more roles for women, and had increased their self-esteem and self-confidence (Wolfe and Tucker 1995: 457). Attitudes toward the women's movement have become steadily more positive. In 1970, 40% of women favored efforts to strengthen and change the status of women; in 1980, the figure had increased to 64%, and in 1990, 77% of women supported such efforts. A 1989 survey reported that 89% of women thought that the women's movement had given them more control over their lives, and 82% thought that the movement was still improving the lives of women. Approximately one-third of women in the United States identify themselves as feminist, and 65% think that NOW is "in touch with the average American woman." Moreover, about 4.5 million Americans, including many young women and women of color, claim to have made a contribution at one time to the women's movement (Ferree and Hess 1994: 192, 199).

There is considerably less evidence of the changing views of British women. A 1992 poll found that "the majority of both women and men viewed feminism positively (57 and 56 percent respectively)" (Lovenduski and Randall 1993: 357). Surveys since the 1980s have found a strong majority of women and men supporting equal opportunities—92% in the mid-1980s. A clear majority also emerged in a recent survey of ten thousand women by the Women's Communication Centre, which noted that respondents "echoed many of feminism's original concerns," viewed women still as second-class citizens, and sought "equality of opportunity for all" and an end to gender stereotyping (*Guardian*, July 1, 1996). Lovenduski has cautioned, however, that there is only slight evidence of general attitudinal change within key decision-making circles:

> On the one hand there is evidence of change, a slow improvement in women's presence in politics, of the establishment of some sex equality policies. . . . On the other hand, [wider] policy and organisational gender biases appear to be under no immediate threat. Only occasional sensitivities to the gendered implications of public policy are evident; cultural change in organisations is rare. (Lovenduski 1996: 16)

Britain's cultural feminism has also taken some knocks, with, for example, the demise of feminist publishing house Pandora Press, the struggles of its counterpart Virago, and the disappearance of *Spare Rib* from the newsstands. Although women's studies programs have spread to most universities, women remain a tiny minority of professors in those institutions (Griffin 1995, chapter 14).

In electoral politics, the "gender gap" in the United States—the difference between the way in which male and female voters think and behave—owes a great deal to the consciousness of gender at the ballot box created by the women's movement (Mueller 1988). First observed in 1980, when men were eight percentage points more likely to support Republican Reagan for president, the difference has ranged from 4% to 7%. The issues that elicit a more Democratic, progressive vote among women are not always or even usually feminist issues, but rather those reflecting concern with public-sector spending and intervention related to employment and other policies that may involve self-interest (Erie and Rein 1988). However, on occasion, candidate and partisan stands on abortion and affirmative action do cause female voters to provide a swing vote in state and congressional elections. One example occurred in Oregon in January 1996 in a U.S. Senate by-election, where women voters provided the 1-percent margin of victory through turnout and a gender gap that favored the liberal Democratic candidate (*EMILY's List* 1996: 1).

The gender gap played an even more central role in the 1996 national election than it had in 1992, with an unprecedented gap of 11% between male and female voters, with even higher gaps among unmarried women (49%–62%) and working women (35%–56%) (Connelly 1996). Black and young women supported Clinton in large numbers. In 1996, the women's movement saw efforts by the Democratic and Republican Parties to appeal to women voters as an important swing constituency. It is the Democratic Party that has reaped the major benefit from the gap; the Republican Party, as noted earlier, has continued to support antichoice and antiaffirmative action policies despite the efforts of moderate and pro-feminist Republicans to modify these stances.

A gender gap has developed rather differently in Britain. A seventeen-percentage-point gap, with women in favor of the Conservatives, was standard in the 1950s. This gap dwindled to a mere 1% in 1987, grew in 1992 to 6%, and fell again to less than 1% in 1997. Norris (1996), however, found what she labels a "gender-generation" gap in the 1990s. Among voters under thirty years old, young women created a fourteen-point gap in favor of Labour; the 30–64 age group showed eight points in favor of the Tories; and the disproportionately female group aged sixty-five and older favored Conservatives by eighteen points. This gender-generation gap grew dramatically in 1997, with a 35% gap in favor of Labour among women under thirty, and only those over sixty-five favoring the Conservatives. But the strongest political response of women reflects the unattractiveness and irrelevance of national party politics to their lives. A Fawcett report noted that more than half of women (52%, compared to 35% of men) simply did not know which party they would trust the most; that many called for "a Parliament that is less concerned with one party bashing the other"; and that young women in particular felt that politics was a self-interested and futile activity (Fawcett Society 1996a). Responding to these feelings, an early promise of senior Labour women after the 1997 election was to change what Minister for International Development Clare Short has called the "yah-boo" male culture of the House of Commons. And our account has shown that a figure of less than 7% of women declaring themselves "very interested" in politics need not mean apathy. Women have been busy in other forms of politics than the "men's club" of Parliament.

Conclusion

The Relationship between Movement Strength and Continued Success in a Hostile Political Environment

In the 1980s and 1990s, both the American and British women's movements have faced hostile antifeminist political regimes and countermovements. Yet there is evidence that both have survived and expanded. Rather than just holding on in the face of adversity, they have seen positive changes: movement expansion and redefinition and enlargement of goals, diversification of membership and targeting of services, efforts at recruiting a new generation of political activists, and new forms of public representation. All underpin the effective formulation and adoption of feminist policies. This analysis has been premised on the concept that collective movement mobilization and action have led to changes in policy and attitudes. Therefore, the survival and continued strength of movement politics are essential to ensuring continued movement success.

Even as feminists have succeeded in establishing issues on the public agenda, however, the problems of women have increased through political, economic, and social changes, some attributable to government action and some beyond its control. Simple parallels between the two nations underestimate complex political and social differences but can also highlight important trends. Comparable labor-market developments have added urgency to cross-class agendas attentive to the needs of disadvantaged women workers and have created new networks, notably in Britain. Yet in both Britain and the United States, voters elected antifeminist candidates and parties—although not necessarily with antifeminist issues as their electoral priorities. There is some evidence that the presence of hostile regimes can enhance movement recruitment, although in both nations movement membership demonstrates cycles of decline and resurgence. In both countries, challenges to the institution of the family, particularly abortion and domestic violence, have engendered the most opposition, possibly an ironic indicator of success in agenda building and policy change. In the United States, antifeminism has been longer-lived, more organized, more strident, and strengthened by its association with a right-wing movement inside and outside government. The recent activism on family values and abortion in Britain is minor by comparison; but it nonetheless fits Marshall's categorization of a countermovement in formation, gaining visibility and attempting to gain a foothold in legislative politics (1995: 334).

As Tarrow suggests, during the conservative years of the Reagan administration (and thereafter), through personal networks and secondary associations, activist women kept the flame of feminism alive by keeping in touch (1994: 185):

> American women first mobilized in the shadow of the civil rights move-
> ment, combined a rich and varied repertoire, a meaningful discursive
> politics, a network structure embedded in society and institutions and
> an electoral advantage that have made the women's movement among
> the most successful in American social history, effecting—among other
> things—a profound shift in political culture. (184)

The strength of the American women's movement is in its broad, varied, and continually expanding network structure, ranging from informal women's collectives, to women's studies programs in universities, to more structured professional organizations such as NOW and the NWPC. Even the major defeat of the Equal Rights Amendment in the 1980s and subsequent challenges experienced by the movement have not shattered the networks that comprise it nor signaled a decline in mobilization for antidiscrimination legislation, broadly defined. There has been change in the grassroots, self-generated, and largely volunteer branches of the movement, which now are more likely to be service-oriented and more dependent on government and charity funding than was true at the outset.

While the story of the American movement is one of sustained mobilization and presence, that in Britain is one of transformation. There have been two clear trends: a decline in antistatism, leading to increased professionalization and entry into political institutions; and the local survival of a multiplicity of active groups, still determined to retain feminist autonomy but now responding to social as well as ideological diversity. In Britain, although not in the United States, the rollback of state service provision has had the unexpected impact for some feminist groups of increasing funding for their provision of material assistance, advice, and comfort—but as the welfare state has dwindled, this increased funding has been accompanied by increased demand for such services. British and American women have in common the resulting struggle to raise funds without compromising their principles and to sustain a critical advocacy role alongside an accountable service function. As this chapter has shown, the strong links in both countries between the local and national levels of feminist politics have contributed to movement sustainability under pressure.

According to Tarrow, the American women's movement took a long time to bear fruit, but it has emerged as a major factor in American politics (1994: 183). It has developed a shifting and uneasy alliance with the party system, through the gender gap gaining access to the Democratic Party platform and challenging the Republicans to follow suit. The close relationship of the feminist movement to only one party has limited its ability to have an impact on the entire system of fragmented government. British feminists have also been closely associated with only one of the two major parties, the Labour Party, and this alliance left them outside the unitary, centralized state controlled from 1979 to 1997 by Conservatives. This made it harder to get feminist claims onto the agenda, but if that first step can be achieved, legislation is more likely to emerge from a unitary and tightly managed legislative process. Thus, the crucial factor in movement effectiveness may not be association with one party or many. American structures allow and respond to multiparty influence at multiple points of access. Parliamentary government calls for pressure targeted upon the majority party in the national Parliament, and the extent to which the movement has survived and even matured during the outsider years of Conservative government will be tested by its ability to win policy demands from a more friendly regime. It has also been contended that it is easier to articulate demands in the divided American system than it is to implement them effectively. On the one hand, as with policy making, the federal structure and separated powers may make the task of monitoring and reporting on bureaucratic implementation more complex and more difficult than in the unitary British system. On the other hand, the difficulties imposed by such structural complexity may be offset by at least three other factors in comparison to Britain: the greater number of women already within the system; the greater number of political appointments to administrative and legal positions, permitting more interchange between insiders and outsiders; and the tradition of open government and information sharing.

Policy Success

It is possible to list an impressive number of major pieces of congressional and parliamentary legislation that can be tentatively credited to feminist action and classified as feminist in content (Bashevkin 1994: 682, 684; 1996: 535–36). The feminist agenda in both nations has certainly expanded and has become more central to the public program. The issue of violence against women is the prime example of this phenomenon. The adoption of the less threatening term *domestic violence* to replace *wife beating* helped feminists present the issue in a more inclusive, less threatening manner (although the use of the more value-neutral term *pro-choice* in the abortion arena has not had similar results). This approach, borrowed from the area of child abuse, proved successful in gaining action through the presentation of a social problem that was widespread and that cut across class lines (Gelb and Palley 1996: 228). Linking efforts to deal with domestic violence to the larger issue of crime control proved especially effective in the American context. Moving from "domestic violence" to "violence against women" widened the policy arena even further, integrating issues such as rape and stalking and preventative measures such as housing and transportation planning, as well as the reform of police and judicial procedures—thus approaching an inclusive policy analysis of the pervasive problem of violence.

It is notable that the issue of domestic violence in the United States, first introduced as major legislation in the Violence against Women Act (VAWA) in the Senate in 1990, was "initially considered a radical package and a political hot potato" (qtd. in Carroll 1995: 14). Four years later, the successful crime bill including this legislation was seen to benefit primarily women and children. VAWA seemed to slip through the process quietly, with little public attention and no major controversy: "VAWA had become a virtual sacred cow which no one cared to question or oppose" (Carroll 1995: 14). It is certainly arguable that issues of the protection of women, as opposed to their empowerment, carried the day at variance with the initial goals of the battered women's movement. Nonetheless, the movement of the once totally private issue onto the public agenda in a period of conservative dominance is nothing short of remarkable. In both the United States and the United Kingdom (where measures against stalking won all-party support in a similar attainment of public recognition), support for shelters and particularly efforts at reform of judicial and police practice have been undertaken in coalitions with law enforcement officers, law and order advocates, and social work professionals, among others. Even initially opposed right-wing women's groups, including the antifeminist Eagle Forum, had adopted the issue of wife battering by the mid-1980s (Brenner 1996: 56).

In the case of abortion and reproductive choice, the impact of a hostile environment continues to be a dominant factor in limiting options and further progress, particularly in the United States but, in the late 1990s, in Britain as well. In the United States, the federal system and Supreme Court rulings ensure that state legislatures, as well as the Congress, will remain battlegrounds on this issue for years to come. Because in the United States abortion politics is linked to a broader conservative worldview and political movement, the politics of resentment and fear there is more threatening to feminism than it is in Britain (Brenner 1996: 44). Some have contended that the narrow emphasis of the American pro-choice movement on a single-issue-based individual right is insufficient to deal with larger social and economic issues related to unwanted pregnancy. Such movement critics, who recognize the centrality and significance of bodily autonomy, nonetheless seek to build new and broader coalitions based on the impressive outpouring of activism that continually supports efforts to keep abortion legal.

Issues of equity and equal treatment have remained a central terrain on which feminists in the United States and now also in Britain engage the state. The initially central cornerstone of the American liberal feminist movement—equal rights—remains primary, even as new issues of economic equity have gained ascendancy in both nations. In this policy arena, Britain's traditional class consciousness and the linkage of feminism and socialism have fostered a continuing spillover of membership and collaboration between gender- and class-based groups exploiting the new European politics together. However, it is arguable that in the United States, social welfare legislation related to balancing the demands of work and family and attacking the causes of women's poverty has languished and even fallen further behind. The passage of the 1993 Family and Medical Leave Act, which provides for unpaid leave of up to twelve weeks, has not led to any further demand for paid leave. Comparable worth legislation has been stalled, particularly at the national level, and poor women have increasingly been victimized by new assaults on welfare programs. In Britain, too, despite progress in protecting basic work conditions, the problems that have been the core agenda of the women's movement since the revival of second-wave feminism—inequality, dependence, poverty, racism, violence, and lack of control of women's own lives and bodies—have not disappeared.

Finally, there remains the problematic evidence of change in culture and values. Numerous analysts have argued for the importance of the diffusion of feminist values in the United States, even as opposition has been sustained (Wolfe and Tucker 1995). Surveys and the gender gap phenomenon provide evidence of support for feminist goals and values. The "unobtrusive mobilization" of feminist constituencies in professional associations and other mainstream institutions, including churches, is another manifestation of the pervasiveness of feminism in the United States. Parallel developments in Britain have included the rise of women's professional organizations. In the heart of the establishment Church of England, the Movement for the Ordination of Women has attained its goal, and the traditionalist Mothers' Union has also taken up women's issues. These developments suggest that timing, rather than structural factors, may explain some apparent differences between Britain and the United States (Griffin 1995). Rowbotham's belief in the pervasiveness of feminism in Britain may also be demonstrated in the hope for equal opportunities expressed by 90% of Britons. But hope coexists with Lovenduski's warning that the policy-making process has yet to manifest an automatic gender consciousness (1996: 16). As more women in Britain move into leadership positions, it will become clearer whether the cultural foundations as well as the organized movement groups are strong enough to sustain pressure to carry through feminist goals.

Across the dimensions of movement success, we have identified evidence of the survival of women's movements. Positive signs include sustained mobilization and recruitment of a new generation of women into diverse local and national organizations. Vitally, networks of women have been sustained locally and nationally and also across differences of ethnicity, nationality, sexuality, and class. The evolution of rights and litigation strategy in Britain has been responsive to new European opportunities. In the United States, through exploration of the limitations of a sole dependence on this route, women are beginning to move beyond rights politics to incorporate broader social issues. The expansion of the agenda and foregrounding of the issue of violence against women in both nations epitomize women's continued presence and effect in the policy arena. While they are broadly similar in many developments, Britain and the United States inevitably evidence differences in their political contexts and cultural traditions. Their most important common ground is that into the second decade of right-wing and antifeminist political strength, both movements have not only survived but have continued to sustain their principles, develop dialogue, innovate organizationally and strategically, win at least some important battles, and position themselves for new opportunities.

8

How the Cold War Was Really Won:
The Effects of the Antinuclear Movements of the 1980s

David S. Meyer

The cold war, a bipolar standoff between the United States and the Soviet Union that dominated international relations for more than forty years, ended suddenly in 1989. One by one, citizens in the former "buffer" states of Eastern Europe overthrew state communist governments, and the Soviet Union refused to intervene to enforce discipline. In November 1989, East and West Germans danced atop the Berlin Wall, the most visible symbol of the oppression of the cold war. Just two years later, the Soviet Union itself dissolved into component republics.

The nuclear arms race, the centerpiece of the superpower rivalry, took a downward turn a little earlier. In 1987, the United States and the Soviet Union signed an arms control pact that reduced the number of intermediate-range nuclear missiles that each side could place in Europe—the first time in the history of arms control that an agreement mandated actual reductions, rather than future ceilings, in the number or types of weapons either side could deploy. Of the four former Soviet republics with nuclear weapons, all but Russia explicitly renounced their possession of nuclear weapons, and the United States began downsizing its nuclear deterrent as well. Progress on multilateral accords on such issues as a comprehensive nuclear test ban, always slow, has accelerated, although numerous compliance issues must be resolved in difficult future negotiations. Nonetheless, the course that the nuclear arms race has taken, and that of the cold war more generally, has featured a series of apocalyptic turns that no policy maker would have predicted even twelve years ago.

Nearly ten years earlier, however, not a few of the critics of those policy makers, had offered a vision of the end of the cold war in which the blocs would begin to disintegrate (e.g., Forsberg 1984; Havel 1985; Kaldor 1983; Kaldor and Smith 1982; Michnik 1982; Myrdal 1982; Thompson 1982; Thompson and Smith 1981). Historian E. P. Thompson, in an activist role, argued passionately and effectively that citizen-activists could force their governments to disarm and break down the cold war bloc system by mobilizing opposition both to new nuclear weapons and to the cold war more generally. Established political leaders dismissed this vision, trumpeting the stability of nuclear deterrence instead, and accused Thompson, as well as the peace and antinuclear weapons movements that spread throughout the West during the early 1980s, of (at best) naïveté or (at worst) servility to Soviet tyranny.

The dramatic events of 1989, unsurprisingly, inspired a raft of reanalysis and rewriting, for most analysts of international relations not only had not predicted the end of the cold war but also had missed the mechanisms that brought about that end (Hopf 1993). Those peace movement activists who had some inkling of what they meant to do were slow to claim credit for their efforts (but see Cortright 1991, 1993; Meyer 1990–91; Thompson 1990). In contrast, their political opponents rushed to proclaim their version of the story (e.g., Fukuyama 1989; Gaddis 1989; Krauthammer 1989; Weinberger 1990), ascribing the end of the cold war to a variety of factors, such as great men like Mikhail Gorbachev or Ronald Reagan, long-wave economic cycles, inherent weaknesses in controlling inventories in demand systems, and Western stalwartness.

That strong peace and nuclear disarmament movements preceded the actual process of nuclear disarmament and the end of the cold war by less than a decade does not prove the political influence of those movements; the connection between causality and correlation is a familiar chimera in social-science research. Nor does the fact that antinuclear activists were able to come up with a better narrative much earlier than their opponents mean that their efforts actually made a difference; there is a distance between pre-science and politics. And, at least at first glance, the case for peace movement influence seems weak: by the middle of the 1980s, antinuclear movements had largely faded, and the parties they supported in elections almost always lost national elections throughout the West (but not in New Zealand). Their supporters were poorly positioned to make claims of influence at the end of the decade. A few academics, however, using mostly historical process-tracing methods, have found that elements of the peace movement influenced critical security debates and decisions in both the East and the West in the late 1980s (see Evangelista 1995; Knopf 1993; Meyer and Marullo 1992;

Risse-Kappen 1991a, 1991b), but larger puzzles about the influence of social movements on matters of foreign policy remain.

In this chapter I will use the peace movements of the early 1980s and their influence on national security policy in order to address more general theoretical questions about the influence of movements on policy. I begin by briefly reviewing relevant literature on political outcomes in order to look at the influence of movements on foreign policy as a particularly difficult theoretical problem. I then outline the general mechanisms by which a social movement might influence a state's decision on a matter of foreign policy. I next offer three brief case studies of peace movement influence in the early 1980s: the nuclear disarmament movements in three liberal-democratic states—(West) Germany, the United States, and New Zealand. These cases reflect three Western polities facing very different security problems and distinct routes to political influence. (Peace movement allies in New Zealand helped win an important national election; in West Germany they helped lose one; in the United States they exhibited only an electoral threat.) I conclude by returning to the general question of movement influences on foreign policy.

I mean to make an empirical argument about the movements and the end of the cold war and to argue that these findings call for an expansion of theoretical understandings of movement outcomes. The empirical argument is that the peace movements played a role in ending the cold war in a number of different ways. In one case, a movement won a short-term victory by directly altering government policy. More significant, however, the movements constrained policy by altering political alliances and political culture, making the maintenance of an aggressive security policy politically untenable. They also promoted policy alternatives that percolated into public policy over a longer period of time. The theoretical argument stresses the international constraints on the outcomes of political movements on foreign policy, and the interplay of movements and state policies.

Social Movement Influence and Foreign Policy

Although activists always behave as if their efforts might matter, the scholarly literature on movement outcomes, particularly in the area of public policy, is somewhat less certain. To be sure, analysts of the policy process (e.g., Baumgartner and Jones 1993; Kingdon 1984; Stone 1988) acknowledge the role that social movements can play in setting the public agenda and suggesting alternative policies. At the same time, however, the factors that give rise to social movements, particularly what McAdam (1982) describes as "expanding opportunities," also create additional pressures for policy reform that may be independent of anything activists within a social movement do. In other words, the conditions that produce changes in policy may concomitantly produce social movements calling for those changes. Disaggregating movement influences from movement causes is no easy matter in the best of circumstances, for the analyst must suggest the counterfactual case, as if there had been no movement.

Further, just as policy is affected by more than social movements, movements may affect more than policy, and even the process by which policy reforms take place is more complicated than it initially seems. It is useful to begin by looking at three distinct but interdependent levels of effects—public policy, culture, and movement participants (following Meyer and Whittier 1994)—before returning to consider the special difficulties of assessing foreign policy effects.

Policy

Every study of movement influence on policy derives in some way from the critical work of William Gamson (1975, 1990), who identified two distinct components to movement organization success: recognition as a legitimate actor in politics, and new advantages to a group or its beneficiary constituency. Broadly speaking, these measures refer to the substance (new advantages) and process (recognition) of public policy. Subsequent scholars operationalized the outcomes differently but accepted the general distinctions in studying movement influence. Piven and Cloward (1971, 1979) traced the influence of poor people's protest on national social welfare expenditures. Button (1978) tracked appropriation by city, relating federal government spending to civil unrest in the United States. All of these studies neglected the mechanisms by which challengers influenced policy, citing government adoption of movement claims as evidence of influence, even if such adoption took place well after the peak of a challenge. It is important to add that movement challenges can affect the policy choices not only of governments but also of other institutions, such as parties and interest groups, businesses, churches, schools, and essentially any other venue in which the public can be engaged.

Culture

Movements struggle on a broad cultural plane, of which formal government policy is only one parameter (Gusfield 1980). Thus, the civil rights movement sought not only to win changes in rules and procedures that made political inclusion appear more possible to black Americans, but also to change the attitudes about racial integration that were prevalent in mainstream society. In its efforts, the movement drew from available symbols in dominant culture, such as the flag and the Constitution, and appropriated others from African American communities, bringing church spirituals, for example, into popular political parlance. Within mass culture, the civil rights movement was responsible for altering the cultural climate so that television network executives, for example, thought it appropriate to give black actors recurring roles on prime-time television.

Culture constrains policy. It is unthinkable today that government could effect the sorts of formal restrictions on participation in American life by blacks or women that were common two decades ago. A number of scholars (Breines 1989; Gusfield 1980; Rochon 1997) have argued that the cultural effects of movements, though often neglected by analysts, are often longer-lasting and farther-reaching than the more narrow short-term policy victories and defeats.

Participants

Movements also affect those who participate in them. By engaging in the social life of a challenging movement, an individual's experience of the world is mediated by a shared vision of the way the world works and, importantly, the individual's position in it. By engaging in activism, an individual creates himself or herself as a subject, rather than simply an object, in history and—contrary to popular myth—is unlikely to retreat to passive acceptance of the world as it is. In his studies of the veterans of the civil rights project Mississippi Freedom Summer, McAdam (1988, 1989) found that participants in the project were far more likely to be engaged in social-change movement activities than a matched group that chose not to participate. Similarly, Whittier's work on veterans of the radical women's movement (1995) indicates permanent changes in the way activists saw themselves and presented themselves to the outside world, changes that affected conduct even in the absence of overt social protest. Individuals who have forged a worldview through the struggle of a social movement will make different kinds of decisions in all sorts of contexts in the future.

At the most general level, then, movements can affect not only the political landscape but also material and cultural resources available to themselves and to other challengers (Meyer and Staggenborg 1996). In challenging policy and the policy-making process, movements can alter the structure of political opportunity, or external environment, that new challengers face. This approach outlines a broad variety of potential influences and suggests numerous mechanisms of influence over an extended period of time. The variety of mechanisms also mandates a more flexible approach to assessing movement outcomes, particularly in regard to the timing of policy changes. A movement that loses a battle on a matter of policy may alter the policy agenda such that its influence extends to subsequent, although often uncredited, victories.

In looking at foreign policy, particularly strategic nuclear weapons policy, challengers face an especially unlikely area in which to exercise influence—and scholars have an especially difficult time in sorting out the influences of political movements (Meyer 1991). Most people know little about their governments' foreign policies and are particularly ill informed about the strategy underpinning policy decisions and the hardware used to execute policies. Further, factors exogenous to domestic politics and protest, especially the conduct of other nations, substantially influence the policy environment. Nonetheless, in assessing movement influence, scholars have followed the same general approaches used by those studying other domestically oriented social-protest movements. Small (1988) interviewed decision makers in the Johnson and Nixon administrations, explicitly asking whether protests against the war in Vietnam influenced their decisions. Cortright (1993) conducted a similar case study on the impact of the nuclear freeze movement on national security policy.[1] Other scholars (see Knopf 1993; Joseph 1993; Marullo 1994) have supplemented interviews with other historical process-tracing efforts to ascertain the role a movement may have had in setting the political agenda and in making some decisions more attractive or less available than others. Historians and memoirists have differed in their interpretations but generally focus on the same two questions: Did domestic unrest influence the content of foreign policy decisions? Did protest bring new actors into the policy-making process?

In order to understand whether citizen movements influence policy, we need to disentangle the causes of peace movements from their effects. This is possible only if we understand the circumstances in which such movements emerge. Citizens rarely pay much attention to the politics of national security, for obvious reasons: national security issues rarely intrude upon the lives of most citizens in advanced industrial democracies. Although peace activists are always trying to put their concerns about military policy, spending, and nuclear weapons on the public agenda, only occasionally are they able to do so. Social-protest movements on national security issues emerge only when government policy and the international context allow these issues to become salient to large numbers of people.

Since World War II, antinuclear movements have waxed and waned in response to the perceived urgency of the threat of war. Sometimes through cooperation and sometimes in response to the same international factors, movements throughout the Western alliance have generally faltered or flourished in concert. Immediately after World War II, a scientist-led movement to ban the bomb challenged the morality of relying on such a powerful weapon, but this movement was waylaid by the beginnings of the cold war when fear of the Soviet Union replaced fear of nuclear weapons. Shortly afterward, antinuclear protesters in the West remobilized, this time in a campaign that focused on ending nuclear testing; this movement abated when the United States, Great Britain, and the Soviet Union negotiated a partial test-ban treaty. The most recent mobilization, the focus of this chapter, was the most coordinated and broadest-based internationally, although it took distinct forms in different countries. In most Western countries, peace mobilization subsided by the middle of the 1980s and was shortly followed by the unraveling of the bipolar cold war international system (Meyer 1993).

To examine the influence of these movements, it makes sense first to identify the potential ways that subnational movements *could* affect international politics.[2] A peace movement might exercise influence on international policy through three distinct routes: direct and indirect influence on state policy from within the state, direct influence on foreign governments, and indirect influence on foreign governments by alliance with movements in other countries.

First, a protest movement may directly influence the policy of the state in which it operates by bringing elite attention to certain political problems; bringing new people into positions of power in government; suggesting and supporting policy alternatives; increasing the difficulty and costs of policy implementation to such an extent that the government alters its conduct; and/or changing coalition conditions and thus altering the government's policy options. Movements may indirectly influence the policies of their own government by changing political discourse within their country and altering perspectives on politically viable solutions; purposefully altering the emphasis on selected themes within the value system of the dominant culture; and providing new experiences for the citizenry that alter its perceptions (see Gusfield 1980).

Second, peace movements may influence the policies of their own governments by changing the behavior of foreign governments in much the same way as outlined in the preceding paragraph. They may also serve as conduits for ideas, as foreign governments can use activists as unofficial channels to explore ideas for political negotiations.

Finally, movements can influence international politics by changing the content of proposals that leaders consider. Proposals may arise from below and be passed transnationally through conferences and informal contacts.[3]

As an example, Evangelista (1990) makes a convincing case that international conferences between Soviet and American scientists, specifically the Pugwash meetings, influenced the Soviet scientists' view of antiballistic missile (ABM) systems and that the scientists then influenced the Soviet Union's posture in subsequent arms control negotiations. Activists may draw public attention to peace and antinuclear movements in other countries, thus strengthening them and weakening governments' capacities to claim consensus. In the cases that follow, we will see influence at all of these levels but in different contexts.

Western Peace Movements in the 1980s

Antinuclear movements have emerged in the past in response to some apparent new and threatening development in the nuclear arms race; they have subsided when the perception of that threat declined, often as a result of an arms control agreement or change in policy. The peace campaigns of the 1980s, like their predecessors, emerged when the arms race became more expensive and threatened to become much more dangerous. More than their historical antecedents, however, most recent campaigns developed as coordinated transnational campaigns, allied across Western Europe and the Atlantic and in concert with sympathetic movements in Eastern Europe.

The precipitating factor of the 1980s movements was the "dual-track" decision of the North Atlantic Treaty Organization (NATO) in 1979, ostensibly in response to the Soviet deployment of new nuclear missiles, the mobile multiple-warhead SS-20s. NATO would deploy U.S. Pershing II and ground-launched cruise missiles carrying nuclear warheads in Western Europe, while simultaneously conducting arms control negotiations to reduce intermediate-range missiles in Europe. President Jimmy Carter's December 1979 announcement of this policy spurred an immediate response in the countries scheduled to host the weapons. The dual-track decision provided both an impetus and a focal point for peace movements across Western Europe (Cooper 1996; Johnstone 1984; Kaldor and Smith 1982; Risse-Kappen 1988, 1991a; Rochon 1988). It also presented activists in the West with a critical political challenge: to oppose the new NATO missiles, they also had to find some explicit way to respond to the weapons those missiles were meant to counter, or risk political marginalization. The movements considered in this chapter developed distinct ways of dealing with the problem of symmetry that were contingent upon their national contexts.

In November 1980, the American presidential election underscored the issues of concern. Ronald Reagan, running far to Carter's right, defeated the incumbent and, in a landslide, brought the Republican Party control of the Senate for the first time in nearly thirty years, a situation that provided a legislative base of support for Reagan's initiatives in domestic and foreign policy.[4] Reagan sought to manage none of the grievances that peace activists had addressed to Carter and, in fact, disdained even the most modest efforts at arms control, staffing the significant bureaucracies in the departments of State and Defense with ideological conservatives who had vigorously opposed previous arms control agreements. Importantly, this largest and most visible faction within the Reagan administration was dubious about the prospect of arms control altogether. Thus, the dual-track decision rapidly became only a plan to deploy new nuclear missiles in Europe. Additionally, the Reagan administration offered new initiatives in strategic nuclear missiles, including new nuclear weaponry featuring land-based intercontinental ballistic missiles, nuclear missiles on submarines, and nuclear bombs and missiles on new strategic bombers. In conjunction with buildups in conventional weaponry, the strategic buildup drove the U.S. military budget to levels previously unmatched in peacetime. Finally, issuing reckless rhetoric about the likelihood and consequences of nuclear war,[5] the Reagan administration undermined public confidence in its willingness and capacity to manage the security posture of the Western alliance. Citizen movements across Europe and the United States accelerated their efforts and found increasing numbers of sympathetic allies in an increasing diversity of settings. I will briefly review three of these campaigns and their outcomes.

West Germany

Germany's division in the wake of World War II, along a border that separated the West from East, meant that superpower confrontation and nuclear weapons would always be salient public issues. NATO's dual-track decision was in fact primarily a response to German concerns about an imbalance in forces in Europe, forcefully articulated by West German chancellor Helmut Schmidt.[6] Missiles in Germany would keep the Soviets out and the United States in. To avoid German exceptionalism and to share the political burden of the new missiles, NATO also planned to deploy new missiles in Italy, Belgium, Great Britain, and the Netherlands. The government decisions to accept weapons in each of these countries reflected political realities, including the dissident movements, that were peculiar to each country.

Whereas Schmidt's predecessor, Willy Brandt, often articulated peace movement positions, Schmidt left considerable room for opposition on his left, both within and outside his Social Democratic Party (SPD). The announcement of the NATO decision provoked what Cooper describes as "the largest extraparliamentary coalition of political activists ever to launch sus tained protest [in West German history]. It also spread farthest into the mainstream populace, in terms of both passive support and grassroots participation" (1996: 135).

The emergent movement in West Germany was both large and diverse. Early opposition to the new missiles came initially from local activists who traced their roots to the student left of the 1960s. In the 1970s, aided by German law and the federal system, these activists had staged a series of citizen initiatives focused mostly on environmental issues and nuclear power, but also articulating feminist concerns and an explicit commitment to democratic processes as well as outcomes. In addition to site-based protests directed at American military bases, movement partisans contested local elections, forming a new political party that initially was a coalition of local parties, the Greens. For party activists, opposition to the new missiles, as well as much of the extraparliamentary opposition, was grounded in this larger vision of grassroots or "base" democracy.

With very few exceptions, activists were also vocal in condemning the new Soviet missile deployments, explicitly rejecting NATO's modernization while vigorously criticizing the Soviet Union at the same time. Typically, demonstrators called for an end to all nuclear missiles in Europe. German dissidents were careful in portraying their efforts as less a retreat from NATO than an assertion of independence and alternatives. As a result, activists also sought to discover and project alternative models and means of pursuing national security, grouped under the rubric "peace research." Starting in the 1970s and often funded by the SPD, small peace research institutes began to spring up, conducting research on the causes of war and of peace. By the time the movement of the 1980s had emerged, peace researchers had developed visions of alternative defense arrangements, most often based on "nonoffensive" and sometimes nonviolent defenses. They used the burgeoning movement of the 1980s to project their visions. The movement, then, was largely responsible for creating these new institutions. In addition to thriving in alternative institutions, peace activism grew rapidly within already established institutions, including both the Catholic and Lutheran churches and the SPD. The mainstream churches formed new organizations that coordinated both grassroots and national protest activism.

Activists within the SPD pressed Chancellor Schmidt to ensure, at minimum, that both elements of the dual-track strategy were pursued vigorously, which meant emphasizing the newly neglected element of arms control. In this context, Schmidt proposed a "zero option," in which the West would forgo its deployments if the Soviet Union would dismantle its SS-20 missiles—a proposal that came directly from the banners of the peace movement.[7] Schmidt, however, presided over a coalition government that depended upon the support of the centrist Free Democratic Party (FDP) to form majorities. FDP leaders also pressed Schmidt to alter his policies, albeit in different directions. Facing increasingly unmanageable tensions in his coalition, Schmidt called for early elections in March 1983 and watched the FDP desert its thirteen-year partnership with the SPD to forge a successful electoral alliance with two large conservative parties (Markovits 1983). Although the peace movement lost the election, it won the SPD. Freed of the responsibilities of governance and coalition, peace activists quickly gained substantial influence within the SPD on foreign policy. The party did not articulate movement positions exactly, but it did criticize vigorously the imposition of the NATO decision SPD leader Schmidt had orchestrated, as well as any further modernization of NATO's nuclear forces in Europe generally, and Germany in particular. The political turmoil in Europe created by the fallout from the dual-track decision made the planned modernizing deployment of follow-on short-range nuclear missiles politically untenable (Huygen 1986) and forced both the German and American governments to project serious-seeming efforts at détente and arms control. In West Germany, the conservative-center alliance led by Chancellor Helmut Kohl also pressed for arms control and opposed subsequent nuclear modernization.

The peculiarities of the German situation also afforded unusual opportunities to West German dissidents. On the front lines of the cold war, few West German peace activists saw state communism in the East as a benign phenomenon, and they sought to draw attention to human rights activists in East Germany. Peace and human rights activists, often affiliated with the transnational group END (European Nuclear Disarmament), publicized and supported dissident efforts in the East, providing public forums for exiled dissidents such as Rudolf Bahro and Wolf Biermann. They explicitly neglected the official state-aligned peace council to promote independent and dissident activists who saw necessary links between peace and human rights.

By the middle of the 1980s, the West German Greens held regular meetings with the independent peace movements in East Germany, even adopting the East's "swords into ploughshares" emblem in much of their own literature (Tismaneanu 1989: 104). Such meetings strengthened the resolve of Eastern activists, legitimating their efforts and building their confidence. When the Germanies were united, the Greens negotiated an electoral alliance with the independent Civic Forum, including many of the activists who actually started the October revolution, although both wings of the alliance did badly at the polls (Ash 1991; Pond 1990). Both the Greens and the democratic activists of the East were upstaged by conservative Chancellor Kohl, who promised rapid unification and economic growth.

The loss of important elections in 1983 and after the end of the cold war obscures the influence of the peace movement on German politics and policy, particularly given the serious constraints the international context placed on West Germany. The peace movement played an important role in altering the terms of the debate about national security, as well long-standing political alliances. Although the movement suffered an immediate defeat on policy, it won victories in rhetoric and political culture that conditioned subsequent discourse and public policy. Within just a few years in the early 1980s, both major parties changed their positions on national security issues substantially. After leaving government in 1983, the Social Democrats went from supporting controlled modernization of nuclear forces to opposing all new nuclear weapons and supporting alternative defense. The conservative alliance, which has controlled the national legislature since 1983, went from criticizing the old SPD from the right, pressing for faster modernization and closer ties with the United States, to supporting arms control and détente and serving as a brake on NATO initiatives to modernize its nuclear force. Piggybacking on the popularity and mobilization of the peace movement, the Green Party entered the national Parliament as well as many state governments (where it sometimes governed in coalition with the SPD), bringing with it not only visible concern for traditional peace movement positions but also an institutional voice for activism on environmentalism, feminism, and protecting the rights of immigrants.

United States

Although European activists focused on the United States as well as their own governments (after all, NATO planned to deploy U.S. nuclear missiles in Europe, and the United States would negotiate on NATO's behalf with the Soviet Union), American activists were initially less successful in reaching the public with their message.[8] A large demonstration planned by a coalition of antinuclear groups to mark the United Nations' first Special Session on Disarmament drew only fifteen thousand people to New York City in 1977. Ronald Reagan's election in 1980 changed the possibilities for movement action.

In the same 1980 election, a nonbinding referendum question calling for the United States to negotiate a bilateral freeze on the development, production, and deployment of nuclear weapons won large majorities in three state senate districts in western Massachusetts. The freeze idea had circulated for a few years among peace movement organizations, but until 1980 it was but one among many ideas for activist attention. The success of the proposal at the polls in districts that voted for Ronald Reagan suggested its viability as a goal for political mobilization. The proposal quickly won the endorsement of a large number of activist organizations and served as the centerpiece of peace activism for most of Reagan's first term. The explicit bilateral nature of the demand was a critical part of the appeal of the freeze proposal. It allowed activists to avoid both assessing blame for the cold war and the arms race and discussing particular weapons, yet still to press the government for policy change. Bilateralism, however, would later prove to be a tool that the administration could use in co-opting the movement for its own purposes.

The freeze quickly and easily won broad support in public opinion polls, town meetings, and state and local referenda. Lacking other visible alternatives or initiatives from government, arms control groups and congressional supporters flocked to it in 1982—not necessarily to endorse its aims but to lodge criticism against the Reagan administration. At its height the movement included an exceptionally broad range of political activity, including civil disobedience and direct action, lobbying in and campaign contributions to Congress, large demonstrations, and broad educational programs. In June 1982, one million people assembled in New York's Central Park to demonstrate for a nuclear freeze and to mark the United Nations' second Special Session on Disarmament. During the same period, public attention to nuclear weaponry reached a level rivaled perhaps only by the period immediately following the first use of atomic weapons in 1945. Nuclear weapons were the subject of symposia, public education programs in colleges and universities, magazine and journal special issues, concerts, movies, books, television specials, and situation comedy episodes. In the fall of 1982, peace organizations claimed credit for significant Democratic Party gains in the House of Representatives.

In 1983, the House of Representatives overwhelmingly passed a nonbinding nuclear freeze resolution, which it had debated vigorously for more than a year. The following year the Democratic Party nominated a presidential candidate who ostensibly embraced the freeze proposal (six of seven Democratic hopefuls endorsed the freeze resolution). More significantly, the Reagan administration was compelled to respond to the broad concern about nuclear weapons that the freeze demonstrated. Reagan refused to allow the movement to demonize him and his policies. He and his administration backed away from the cavalier rhetoric about nuclear warning shots, recallable missiles, improvised fallout shelters, and limited nuclear war that had characterized the early years of the administration and animated the movement. Instead, they learned the utility of guarded language about options and flexibility.

The administration engaged in a propaganda war to rob the freeze of the political space it commanded. One front involved playing on fears of the Soviet Union by accusing the Soviets of chemical warfare and treaty violations, explicitly suggesting that bilateralism was impossible. At the same time, responding to both domestic pressure and the concerns of European allies, the administration reopened arms control talks with the Soviet Union, proposing treaties such as a "zero-zero proposal" for intermediate nuclear forces in Europe and START (the Strategic Arms Reduction Talks). One proposal called for deep (yet what the administration thought were unacceptable) cuts in the Soviet arsenal in exchange for modest reductions in U.S. plans. This proposal came from Schmidt in response to the German peace movement, and it immediately encountered strong opposition within the Reagan administration. Recall that top-level officials distrusted arms control generally and wanted to ensure a political link with Europe by deploying new weapons. The administration finally decided to propose its "zero" option, which could mean forgoing intermediate-range missile deployment, only when its officials were convinced that the Soviets would not accept the proposal (Risse-Kappen 1988; Talbott 1984). The final piece of the Reagan political strategy was the Strategic Defense Initiative ("Star Wars"). On March 23, 1983, Reagan abandoned talk of prevailing in nuclear war and instead asked Americans if it wouldn't be "better to save lives than to avenge them" (qtd. in Meyer 1990: 221). Taken together, the administration's approach, stoking deep-seated public fears of the Soviet Union while simultaneously softening its rhetoric and proposing arms control, prevented the 1984 election from serving as a referendum on Reagan's nuclear policy. Reagan proclaimed his mammoth reelection landslide a mandate for arms control, and, ironically, he was right.

The Reagan who campaigned in 1984 was substantially different from the one who took office in 1981. In January 1984 Reagan announced his intention to resume arms control negotiations with the Soviet Union, and he was defensive about his failure to meet with any Soviet leaders, promising to do better in his next term. He no longer spoke of "winnable" nuclear wars. Indeed, he memorized and frequently repeated the phrase "nuclear war cannot be won and must never be fought" (Bundy 1989: 6). Between the freeze campaign and his own Star Wars plan, Reagan had become convinced that the system of mutually assured destruction was morally intolerable. Importantly, this took place well before Mikhail Gorbachev ascended to power in March 1985.

The president's conscience was not the only constraint on policy. The arms control caucus in Congress was stronger, better educated, and more aggressive than ever before. The House of Representatives pushed for restraint in military spending, antisatellite weapons development, research on star wars projects, and deployment of first-strike weapons such as the MX missile. Senators and representatives also consistently pressed the Reagan administration to pursue arms control more actively (Fascell 1987; Magraw 1989). Members of Congress had good reason to be more concerned about nuclear weapons and arms control. The freeze groups remained active locally and held representatives accountable to the wishes of their districts. Political leaders could no longer count on ignorance or apathy about nuclear issues among their constituents. They had to be more aware themselves, and more responsive. As a result of raised awareness and activism in both Congress and mass public opinion, Reagan's initial approach to nuclear weapons and foreign policy was no longer possible. The freeze disappeared from public discourse after Reagan's reelection, but so did the strategic posture it criticized. United States military spending peaked in 1985, a result of the 1984 budget, and began to decline. When Soviet general secretary Gorbachev accepted the zero-zero proposal for nuclear weapons in Europe, a proposal the Reagan administration had designed to be rejected, Reagan had no alternative but to negotiate, and those negotiations made subsequent reform and disarmament possible. In this case, the movement visibly lost on its central demand, the end to the nuclear arms race. At the same time, however, it won large changes in rhetoric and culture that subsequently translated into different policies.

New Zealand

Whereas West Germany was the front line of the cold war and the United States the motor of Western nuclear modernization, New Zealand operated within the Western alliance but on the periphery of most security debate.[9] This position, thousands of miles from nuclear weapons and from the scene of most imagined nuclear confrontations, afforded peace activists the latitude to affect government policy far more directly than their allies elsewhere could. From the middle 1970s onward, United States Navy ships visiting New Zealand were commonly met by citizens on surfboards and in kayaks, dinghies, and yachts, aggressively and ineffectively trying to stop them from reaching port (Clements 1988; Graham 1989). The strategy was not peculiar to New Zealand, but what was unusual was that the government ultimately endorsed the protesters' claims.

In 1984, as the antinuclear movements faded elsewhere, the newly elected Labour government of New Zealand announced that henceforth its waters would be nuclear-free. Unlike other ostensibly nuclear-free states,

New Zealand would not allow nuclear-powered ships or ships armed with nuclear weapons to visit its harbors. New Zealand also banned ships that *could* carry nuclear weapons unless certain that they were not doing so. This new policy presented a direct challenge to the long-standing United States naval policy neither to confirm nor to deny the presence of nuclear weapons aboard its ships. The New Zealand policy also represented a clear political victory for the peace movement in that country.

Neither superpower has assigned much strategic significance to the nation, which is roughly the size of Japan but far more sparsely populated and geographically isolated. As a result, New Zealanders have seen more of the negative consequences of the arms race, particularly fallout from nuclear testing, and much less of the purported benefits of nuclear deterrence. Historically, antinuclear activism has focused on two issues: radioactive fallout from United States, Soviet, and French nuclear tests in the South Pacific; and port visits from U.S. warships that might carry nuclear weapons. The antinuclear movement mobilized on these issues from the 1950s through the 1970s, sometimes with the support of government (when the Labour Party was in power).

In the late 1970s, the antinuclear movement continued its efforts, focusing most of its activity against port visits, the most visible aspect of the arms race in New Zealand. In the early 1980s, the Reagan administration's policies, particularly a naval buildup including new ship-based nuclear weapons, provoked more activism. The peace movement in New Zealand conscientiously sought to build on the efforts of allies abroad, sponsoring tours of international activist visitors including Helen Caldicott and Richard Falk. In addition to public education and petition campaigns, activists staged large demonstrations and protests against port visits, in August 1983 actually stalling a visit by the USS *Texas*. Importantly, New Zealand's strategic location on the periphery of the cold war allowed both the activists and the government more autonomy in crafting proposals. The movement did not feel constrained by bilateralism as its counterparts in West Germany and the United States did, for activists could credibly argue that their nation could withdraw its (admittedly minimal) participation in the nuclear arms race without materially affecting the outcome. Reflecting this reality, activists focused on nuclear-free zones and began creating them from the grassroots up, in houses, churches, and small communities. By early 1984, more than 65 percent of all New Zealanders lived in self-declared nuclear-free zones (Clements 1988: 116). The Labour Party actively endorsed the nuclear-free-zone concept and increasingly pressed the issue as the movement grew.

The antinuclear movement was but one of many problems plaguing the

National Party government, led by Prime Minister Robert Muldoon, but it was the one that brought the government down. A Labour minister introduced a nuclear-free bill into Parliament in June 1984, gaining the support of two National Party MPs and threatening Muldoon's working majority. After the government killed the bill, Muldoon called snap elections. Port visits by nuclear-armed ships were a visible issue in the electoral campaign; all the contending parties but the National Party supported some kind of ban (Macmillan 1987; Pugh 1989).

The United States government, unlike the New Zealand public, saw the nuclear-free promises of the Labour Party as the most significant issue in the campaign, viewing any kind of "defection" from the alliance as a threat. On June 25, 1984, in a speech at the University of Pennsylvania, Assistant Secretary of State Paul Wolfowitz emphasized the importance of access to New Zealand ports to United States security interests. Within the next few days, members of the United States Congress suggested that sanctions in international trade might be an appropriate response to a port visit ban (Landais-Stamp and Rogers 1989: 61–63). This clumsy attempt at influence could only hurt the National Party by raising the salience of what had started as a relatively minor issue. Expressly antinuclear parties received 62 percent of the vote.

Labour won the election handily and, upon taking office, focused on economic issues, adopting market-oriented reforms of the New Zealand economy. Prime Minister David Lange initially sought to moderate the party's policy on nuclear ships but was pressed by Labour leadership to hold to all its campaign promises. Domestic political pressures loomed far larger on the horizon than U.S. pressures.

In October 1985, Lange consulted with U.S. Secretary of State George Shultz to arrange joint naval exercises for the following March, Lange looking for a way to bring U.S. ships into port without mobilizing the antinuclear movement. At his urging, the United States requested a port visit for a frigate, the USS *Buchanan,* which had visited to minimal protests in 1979. Days before the announcement of the visit, however, a peace group, the Coalition against Nuclear Warships (CANWAR), anticipating the request, published a list of all nuclear-powered and nuclear-capable ships in the U.S. arsenal. Lange asked the United States to declare that the *Buchanan* would not be carrying nuclear weapons or to select another ship, but the United States refused (Clements 1988: 132; Jackson and Lamare 1988: 174).

Lange unsuccessfully asked his cabinet to permit the visit, noting that the *Buchanan* would probably not carry nuclear weapons. Since Labour's election, the New Zealand peace movement had become better organized as a whole and more intensely focused on both port visits and the nuclear-free-zone idea, and it likely could punish Labour for failing to uphold the ban. Rounds of criticism from the United States, Britain, and Australia increased public support for the ban—and for Labour—in New Zealand (Landais-Stamp and Rogers 1989: 73–75). The United States canceled the joint military exercises; although New Zealand explicitly continued to support ANZUS (the alliance between Australia, New Zealand, and the United States), the United States declared that an alliance without joint exercises or port visits was in fact no alliance at all. The United States instituted sanctions reducing the extent of cooperation and flow of intelligence to New Zealand, but it never imposed, nor apparently seriously considered, trade sanctions. The low costs of the ban economically, in conjunction with the national independence it represented for New Zealand, enhanced political support for the ban and for Lange. Public approval of the ban moved from roughly 50 percent of New Zealanders in 1982 to 76 percent in March 1985 (Macmillan 1987: 34).

Lange himself, initially less enthusiastic about the ban, grew increasingly committed to the proposition of a nuclear-free New Zealand as he saw the political benefits of this posture both in New Zealand and internationally (see Lange 1985). In a debate with conservative American religious leader Jerry Falwell at the Oxford Union in March 1985, Lange spoke for the proposition that nuclear weapons were "morally indefensible." Before and after each speech, he received standing ovations as he emphasized the rights of nations not to be protected by nuclear weapons: "We are actually told that New Zealanders cannot decide for themselves how to defend New Zealand but are obliged to adopt the methods which others use to defend themselves. . . . To compel an ally to accept nuclear weapons against the wishes of that ally is to take the moral position of totalitarianism, which allows for no self-determination" (qtd. in Landais-Stamp and Rogers 1989: 85–86). The nuclear-free policy allowed New Zealand to carve out a distinct international identity and a different, actually less marginal, position in international politics. The favorable responses at Oxford and elsewhere underscored the possibility of stronger political and cultural ties with an alternative social and political network. New Zealand gained heightened visibility and prestige within the Western alliance, if not among all of the NATO governments.

The harsh United States rhetorical response, in conjunction with minimal sanctions outside of defense matters, encouraged New Zealanders to see the nuclear issue as a matter of self-determination—an assertion of national pride rather than a strategic risk. In contrast to the other two cases, in New

Zealand a policy change became a source for cultural change. In July 1985, two French citizens working for the French government blew up the Greenpeace ship *Rainbow Warrior,* which was in port in a New Zealand harbor, killing a Greenpeace worker aboard. This action reinforced New Zealanders' sense of the need to assert national independence and confirmed politically the coalition supporting the port ban. In September of the same year, Labour passed legislation reinforcing the ban, and ANZUS dissipated. In 1987, Labour extended its electoral and governing majority, the nuclear issue being a minor one in the campaign. In 1992, after the cold war, the United States Navy announced that it would now not normally place nuclear weapons on its surface ships. In New Zealand, politicians discussed the prospects of reconstituting ANZUS on the nonnuclear terms they had proposed nearly a decade earlier.

Conclusion

The three cases described in this chapter suggest both the difficulties of evaluating the impact of protest movements on foreign policy and the diversity of ways in which movements can influence policy. Immediately we must recognize that, at least in matters of national security, nations are not ecological units influenced only by domestic or international considerations. Rather, there is an interplay of domestic and international policy (see Knopf 1993), with movements in one country responding to, and often influencing, the conduct of not only movements but also governments in another country. The election of an American president, for example, served as provocation for peace movements throughout the Western alliance. The West German peace movement criticized both its own government and that of the United States, and its mobilization led the United States to offer arms control initiatives. New Zealand's Labour Party learned that carving out an independent security policy produced not only electoral security at home but visibility and prestige abroad. Transnational contacts between movements and governments must be considered as both opportunities and outcomes for social-protest movements. Activists built tactics and claims transnationally, altering political culture and discourse even in the face of policy defeats. Further, victories by one movement were claimed by allied activists operating in different national contexts.

The three cases also suggest different routes to political influence, in which movement claims and ultimate outcomes are contingent not only upon activist strategies and claims and national political structures, but also the international context in which the nation is embedded. Activists and governments in the United States and West Germany were more directly challenged by Soviet activists and the front line of the cold war than were their counterparts in New Zealand. This made the process of policy reform more difficult. In New Zealand, policy reforms coincided with, or even preceded, cultural changes. In the United States and West Germany, victories in rhetoric and political culture came more easily than policy reforms.

The story of the peace movement in New Zealand is initially the simplest. National security policy was normally a low priority issue for governments in New Zealand, primarily because of New Zealand's geographic isolation from the centers of global conflict. Seeking electoral support, however, the Labour Party seized upon the issue when out of power and promoted it aggressively as a means of attacking the governing National Party. The movement won the support of the Labour Party, and when Labour won an election, it implemented the policies it promised—policies the National Party had explicitly neglected. The movement was able to win a policy victory quickly, which led to cultural and rhetorical victories, and not only in New Zealand. The movement's influence in promoting the nuclear-free-zone idea extended beyond the boundaries of New Zealand, as activists in other Western countries adopted the idea as a strategy for organizing.

In the West German case, peace activism clearly precipitated the fall of a government unfriendly to activist concerns and initially led to the election of a much *less* friendly or responsive government. Shattering the thirteen-year-old coalition between the SPD and the FDP, however, allowed the SPD considerably more flexibility in exploring and promoting alternative foreign and security policies. The SPD's rhetorical and financial support of peace research led to the promulgation of new ideas about security in Germany, as well as elsewhere in Western Europe and in East Germany. The zero option came from the movement particularly through the Schmidt government, and ultimately to the United States. Here the movement lost the initial policy battle but made large gains in political culture. The transnational contacts between peace activists in West Germany and human rights activists in East Germany, particularly, led to greater visibility for the Eastern dissidents and important support for reformers in the East.

Meanwhile, government policy also changed in response to the movement. Although Chancellor Kohl and a conservative-centrist alliance have governed (first West Germany, then a unified Germany) since the election of 1983, from the start government ministers were committed to preventing nuclear weaponry from reemerging as an electoral issue. This meant that the Kohl government was able to press the United States and NATO more strongly for arms control efforts than had the Schmidt government it replaced. Thus, the peace movement lost this electoral battle but may well have won the war. Intermediate-range missiles were deployed for a very short time, but the entire category of weaponry was soon eliminated under the Intermediate Nuclear Forces (INF) Treaty of 1987. Subsequent nuclear modernization was politically untenable. Here the movement's short-term losses on matters of policy nonetheless affected the subsequent policy debate.

The German case also provides evidence for a movement's "spillover effects" (Meyer and Whittier 1994). Without doubt, the peace issue provided the necessary cohesion for the Green Party to emerge as a significant player nationally. Entering the national Parliament for the first time in 1983 by surpassing the 5 percent electoral threshold, the Greens used the resources of government, not least national visibility, to address a range of other issues, particularly environmental protection and immigrants' rights. At the state level, the Greens frequently won electoral representation and sometimes shared in governance with the SPD.

Evidence for spillover effects in the United States are less apparent, but changes in policy and discourse are evident. Although the nuclear freeze was unable to defeat its primary target, incumbent president Ronald Reagan, despite commanding upwards of 70 percent support in public opinion polls, its presence on the national landscape changed the contours of nuclear weapons policy and discourse. The president and his advisers altered the way they spoke about nuclear weaponry, and the change in discourse affected more than symbolic presentations of security. The Reagan administration, seeking to cultivate public support, offered arms control initiatives it hoped the Soviet Union would spurn. When Gorbachev accepted one of these proposals, the zero-zero option, the Reagan administration was essentially trapped by its own rhetoric; despite its best efforts, the administration could not find a way to reject its own proposal.

Domestic unrest in the United States and Western Europe influenced Western policy, particularly that of the United States and NATO, circumscribing further military buildups after 1984 and forcing leaders to adopt a more conciliatory posture toward the Soviet Union, resurrecting an arms control regime in the process. Clearly, Pershing II and cruise missiles were deployed in Western Europe, an unambiguous defeat for the European movements. Neither the nuclear freeze nor the ambitious reformulation of United States policy it demanded has been implemented in the United States. Failing to bring about central demands, however, does not demonstrate lack of effect; rather, it suggests a more complicated process of exercising influence, one involving short-term marginal impact and long-term changes in political culture.

Notes

1. In both cases, the findings were intriguing, tentative, and ambiguous; policy makers are generally and understandably loath to credit extra-institutional protest with influencing their decisions on important policy matters (Meyer 1991).

2. The scholarly literature on the influence of movements on foreign policy is generally underdeveloped, but for a synthetic overview, see Risse-Kappen (1991a).

3. John Kennedy, for example, asked antinuclear activist and editor Norman Cousins to explain the U.S. position on a nuclear test ban. Cousins's shuttle diplomacy early in 1963 proved critical in bringing the two U.S. and Soviet leaders together later in the year to negotiate a treaty (Seaborg 1981: 207–8).

4. I have devoted considerable attention to these changes in policy and politics elsewhere (e.g., Meyer 1990: chapters 2–4; 1993, 1995).

5. Scheer (1982) provides a disturbing compendium of misstatements on nuclear weapons.

6. There is much writing on the dual-track decision and German politics. This section draws on Johnstone (1984), Cooper (1996), Risse-Kappen (1988), Pond (1990), and Rochon (1988).

7. Importantly, the zero option was designed less as a strategy for national security than as a means of mitigating the domestic pressures of the peace movement. Schmidt also tried to push the United States to offer arms control proposals that sounded viable. See Talbott (1984: 56 ff.) for details.

8. This section draws from a number of studies of peace protest in the United States generally and of the nuclear freeze in particular, including Kleidman (1993), Lofland (1993), McCrea and Markle (1989), Meyer (1990), Rochon and Meyer (1997), Solo (1988), and Waller (1987).

9. I have dealt with the New Zealand case more extensively in Meyer (1994).

9

The Impact of Environmental Movements in Western Societies

Dieter Rucht

Like the labor movements that raised "the social question" during the second half of the nineteenth century and beyond, a new kind of movement has put "the environmental question" on the agenda of the last third of the twentieth century—and probably beyond. Whereas in retrospect it is obvious what impact the labor movements had, the effect of the environmental movements is less clear. Though much has been written about the environmental movements, no comprehensive study of their impact has been carried out yet.[1] What are the relevant dimensions to be taken into account? Does the movements' impact differ significantly across countries in the Western world? If so, which factors could explain such differences? These are the key questions to which this chapter tries to offer some tentative answers.

"Tentative answers" should be taken not as an understatement but as an indication of the difficulties and limits of such an enterprise. In part, these difficulties stem from the nature of the problem, that is, to conceptualize and assess social movement impact.[2] Moreover, this impact may be multidimensional and dependent on many mediating factors. Another difficulty results from the very scope and complexity of the special topic addressed in this chapter. Environmental movements are composed of many groups and engage in a large variety of issues. No wonder that the few existing analyses on environmental movement impact are limited to case studies, in which it is easier to overview the factors that come into play.

Therefore, this chapter should be understood as an essay in the literal sense of the word. Other scholars who are more experienced in the study of policy outcomes or who have a better knowledge of particular issues and/or countries in question than the author has may engage in improving and elaborating on this preliminary approach.

The Paradox of Environmental Movements

When compared to the long existence of some other social movements, the environmental movements are a recent phenomenon. "Environmental movements" denotes the network of nongovernmental groups and organizations that aim, by means of political and social intervention, including collective protest, to prevent the exploitation and/or destruction of natural resources. In their attempts at strategic intervention, environmental movements can be distinguished from the traditional and predominantly apolitical conservationism that prevailed until the late 1960s. Whereas conservationist groups focused mainly on local and sectoral issues without embedding them into a broader approach, environmentalism tends to have a more dramatic and more coherent perception of the problem ("Save planet Earth"). Even when mobilizing at the local level, environmental actors perceive their mobilization as part of a worldwide movement according to the slogan "Act locally, think globally" (Rucht 1993).

What has the impact of the movement been so far? Leaving aside all territorial and thematic variations, we are confronted with a remarkable paradox: On the one hand, the brief history of the environmental movement can be read as an amazing success story. This success becomes apparent when we consider the movement's growth and consolidation, its role as an agenda setter, its impact on individual attitudes and behavior, and its contribution to the establishment of a new polity and a new industrial sector. On the other hand, however, the movement has been largely unsuccessful in halting environmental deterioration. This paradox of success and failure needs to be explained in more detail.

The Success Story

Within less than two decades, the environmental movement experienced spectacular growth in the number of activists, adherents, and sympathizers, as well as in terms of financial and organizational resources. In most countries of the Western world, preexisting environmental organizations were revitalized, and a considerable number of relatively large new movement organizations were created. Beyond mere growth, several other trends contribute to the image of a successful movement. First, the movement has diversified with regard to various issues, thus covering, by and large, all aspects of perceived environmental problems, including nuclear power production, toxic waste, the destruction of tropical rain forests, and human-made climate changes. This specialization has been accompanied by the acquisition of sophisticated knowledge that often matches that of experts within industry and the state administration. Second, partly related to this trend, the movement has shown a growing tendency toward professionalism and institutionalization, for example, by creating its own apparatuses, scientific bodies, institutes, and journals in which a growing number of professionals serve the common cause. Third, the movement has become a truly international network, with intense cooperation across borders, the formation of international alliances and networks, and the establishment of coherent supranational organizations (Princen and Finger 1994; Wapner 1996). Among the latter, Greenpeace and the Worldwide Fund for Nature claim to be among the world's largest nongovernmental organizations. Whether or not this is true, certainly they can be counted among the organizations that have exhibited the most spectacular growth rates in recent history.

Probably still more impressive than its growth, institutionalization, and internationalization is the movement's success as an agenda setter. In the aggregate, environmental problems, in spite of the ups and downs of specific issues (Downs 1972), are among the most intensively and most continuously debated political problems in recent decades. Moreover, environmentalism is highly valued. Hardly any relevant social group, hardly any important political party, can afford to reject the goal of environmental protection. Even those industrial branches and corporations which, on concrete issues, act as opponents of environmental groups rhetorically embrace environmentalism and try to gain a "green and clean" image.

The prominent role of environmentalism in public debates is echoed at the level of individual attitudes. Even though support for the environmental cause may be lower at this level when compared to the mainstream of public opinion, overall we find a high degree of esteem and sympathy for both the environmental cause and the movement that represents this cause most forcefully. Observers have called this striking level of attitudinal support the "miracle of public opinion" (Dunlap and Scarce 1991: 651).

Support for environmental protection also manifests itself in public administration and state policies. Here one should consider numerous laws and other regulations to protect the environment. Recently, even attempts to declare environmental protection part of the constitution have been undertaken in some countries. In addition, the task of environmental protection has resulted in the creation of state departments, environmental agencies, advisory boards, communal public services, programs of environmental education, and the like.

Finally, both societal and state-centered efforts at environmental protection are flanked by the establishment of a growing environmental industry that has a financial interest in strengthening environmental concerns and thus presents itself as an ally to the movement. Not all these trends can be attributed to the environmental movement, but the movement certainly helped breach the wall of ignorance and passivity and served as a catalyst.

The Failure

This success story stands in stark contrast to the movement's tangible outcomes. After all, the movement's growth, public support, and institutional impact are only means to reach the movement's central goal, that is, to halt further deterioration and, eventually, to improve the state of the environment. Even while acknowledging the measurement problems, gaps, and flaws of statistical reporting, it is safe to say, in summary, that the movement has not achieved its ends. Globally speaking, in spite of the movement's impressive mobilization, the state of the environment has worsened during the last decades, according to various sources (Porter and Brown 1991; Worldwatch Institute 1992; Wissenschaftlicher Beirat der Bundesregierung 1996).[3] Consider just a few telling indicators:

- Natural resources continue to be exploited, probably on a larger scale than ever before in history.
- The number of species of flora and fauna continues to decline.
- Territories in which human intervention is absent or scarcely destructive continue to shrink, because of the growth of the population, intense agriculture, urbanization, logging, road construction, and other factors.
- Pollution of air, water, and soil increases steadily and, consequently, people are confronted more and more with harmful substances that can cause disease, pain, and even death.

A More Complicated Story

Though I would maintain that this crude picture of striking success in terms of means and striking failure in terms of goals holds true, it has to be differentiated in various ways. Most obviously, success and failure vary across issues and regions. When looking at the state of the environment as an ultimate measure of the movement's success, one could easily point to various improvements and, in this sense, to partial gains made by the movement, although its actual contribution to these gains may remain unclear.

Particularly when regarding some of the most economically developed countries, one could stress the reduction of water pollution in many lakes and rivers, the decrease of some harmful substances (e.g., carbon) in the air, the expansion of nature reserves, the "renaturation" of pieces of formerly cultivated land, and the decrease in energy consumption. At least in part, these improvements can be attributed to the mobilization of environmental groups (Jänicke and Weidner 1995). One could also point to individual cases in which environmental groups succeeded in stopping specific programs and projects that were supposed to have detrimental environmental impact, such as nuclear power stations and the construction of new airports, highways, and dams. Some of these successful cases are documented (e.g., Caldwell, Hayes, and MacWhirter 1976; Jänicke and Weidner 1995). Probably the issue that has been most closely examined in cross-national comparisons is that of nuclear power (Rüdig 1990; Midttun and Rucht 1994; Rucht 1995). Some environmental battles were won even in countries such as France, where environmentalists are usually confronted with considerable resistance (Rucht 1994). Also, some environmental gains at the transnational and even global levels should be acknowledged. For example, oil tankers have been essentially prevented from cleaning their tanks with seawater that is then spilled into the ocean. Moreover, plans have been abandoned to divide up and then economically exploit the resources of Antarctica.

Overall, however, these countervailing examples are too marginal and too scattered to compensate for the negative trends. Even when we take into account that in environmental conflicts, aside from a few complete successes and probably more complete failures, the movements often achieve partial successes, we have to consider that these successes tend to be marginal and are sometimes purely symbolic. This skeptical assessment is also shared by many environmental activists who tend to admit their powerlessness frankly. A German researcher who conducted in-depth interviews with local activists found that many of them maintained their activity not because they expected to be effective but rather because passivity would make them feel guilty (Christmann 1996). They typically stated thoughts such as this: in the future, when confronted with questions by our children about the disastrous state of the environment, we can at least tell them that we have done our share to prevent as much damage as possible.

This last aspect leads to a further complication in assessing the movement's impact: Should the success of the environmental movement be measured only in terms of the present state of the environment? And even if this state is horrifying, does it indicate only the failure of the environmental movement? Or doesn't it also represent the failure of other forces, including governments, which are formally responsible for the fate of the environment?

Instead of engaging in a normative discussion about whom to blame, I would like to stress the need for a more sophisticated treatment of environmental movement impact. First, unlike many other conflicts, environmental issues are often bound to long-term developments within states. The deterioration that can be seen at present is often the result of a series of decisions or nondecisions that were made far in the past. This insight was already voiced in Rachel Carson's *Silent Spring* (1962)—probably the first and most powerful book to contribute to the birth of the environmental movement. The long-term nature of consequences may also imply that environmentally sound measures have already been taken but their payoff can be seen only in the future. Second, stable or even deteriorating environmental conditions may "hide" positive impact by the environmental movement insofar as these conditions would have been worse without the movement's activities. In this context we have also to take into account that adequate environmental measures can be outflanked and thus made invisible by the negative impact of, say, population growth or an increase in living standards. Whenever environmental conditions deteriorate, it is certainly difficult to speak of the movement's success. But this is not to say that the movement has had no impact or even a negative one.

These few remarks on the possibility of hidden positive effects are not meant to gloss over the essentially skeptical assessment of the environmental movement's success, but it should be clear that we need more refined measures of the movement's impact. To achieve an assessment and, still more difficult, an explanation of this impact represents a fundamental theoretical and empirical challenge.

Assessing the State of the Environment in Western Nations

If we consider the state of the environment as the ultimate criterion for the success of environmental movements, it becomes crucial to measure this dependent variable empirically. In this respect, various restrictions have to be taken into account.

First, regarding the overall state of the environment at the global level, it is impossible to trace the effects of the entire plethora of actors that come into play. Who can claim to have an overall view of the activities and impact of all environmental movements around the globe, not to speak of other actors engaged in environmental policies? It may be more realistic to undertake a comparative analysis of the effects of environmental movements within national borders. In this case, however, the analysis must be restricted to those environmental problems which are exclusively, or at least mainly, caused and shaped by actors within the respective nations. Environmental problems that are beyond the control of a distinct nation—for instance, the ozone layer above Antarctica or the pollution of oceans—cannot be attributed to the policy of a single country and must therefore be excluded from the analysis.

Second, we cannot rely on a static measurement. The quality of the environment is the cumulative result of countless developments, decisions, and nondecisions in the past, heavily dependent on factors such as population density, economic structure, and degree of industrialization. If we simply measure the state of the environment at a given time, the result would not adequately reflect the efforts for and effects of environmental protection during recent years or decades. Thus, we have to identify *changes* in environmental quality between different times. These changes indicate the success or failure of environmental protection. Useful indicators include decreases or increases in toxic substances in the air, water, and soil; decreases or increases in the amount of protected land (nature reserves, wildlife parks); and changes in the effects of policies to reduce energy consumption.

Collecting comparative data on such measures is a science in its own right. For the most part, we have detailed data for only some countries. However, in recent years the Organization for Economic Cooperation and Development (OECD) (1985–95) has begun to gather standardized data on the state of the environment. Partly based on these statistics, a German research group headed by Martin Jänicke has collated data on the environmental performance of most of the OECD countries (Jänicke 1992, 1996; Jänicke and Weidner 1995). Combining various indicators, this group has positioned twenty-two countries according to the degree to which they managed (or failed) to improve domestic environmental quality between 1970 and 1985. According to the aggregate measurement, the countries can be ranked, from best to worst, in the following order: Japan, the Netherlands, Luxembourg, Sweden, Switzerland, Austria, Denmark, Norway, the United States, West Germany, Finland, Belgium, France, Great Britain, Canada, Italy, Portugal, Ireland, Yugoslavia, Spain, Greece, and Turkey (Jänicke 1992).

This list should be interpreted cautiously. It cannot be read as a rank order in terms of absolute environmental quality such that Japan is in the most and Turkey in the least favorable situation. We should also be careful in drawing firm conclusions about the impact of environmental movements in the listed countries, because the amounts and effects of both private and governmental measures are not necessarily a direct function of the pressure from the movements. As in other policy fields, environmental action may be initiated "from above." These reservations about a direct link between movement mobilization and tangible outcomes, which are supported by many studies about factors accounting for social movement mobilization, bring us to a discussion of how to develop an explanatory model.

Toward an Explanation of Environmental Movement Impact

In this section, I aim to develop and apply a model for explaining environmental movement impact. Available data are too scattered and too vague for a solid explanation to be offered. Thus, as a more modest attempt, this explanatory approach should be understood as a means to develop informed hypotheses that I will present and discuss in the final section of the chapter.

An Explanatory Model

In general, it can be assumed that social movement mobilization rarely translates directly into policy outcomes, for a variety of reasons. One reason is that social movements usually lack access to the decision-making process and therefore have to use indirect channels of influence. Another is that the effects of movement mobilization may be neutralized by counterstrategies on the part of the power holders or other societal forces. As for environmental politics, I have already discussed why, in many cases, we cannot expect a direct link between movement mobilization and the state of the environment. In consequence, our attention is directed toward a set of intervening factors. A consideration and conceptualization of these factors may shed some light on the process of environmental politics, which would otherwise be no more clear than a black box. These intervening factors may or may not transform environmental movement mobilization into state activities that, in turn, are crucial to ultimate changes in the state of environment.

Concentrating first on the factors that influence environmental policies, I assume that three key factors mediate the impact of mobilization: public opinion as represented in public statements; individual attitudes and behaviors; and green parties or their equivalent, that is, environmentally oriented tendencies within established parties. It is clear that environmental movements try to influence these factors because the movements are neither in power nor tend to have direct access to power holders. It is usually only through these intermediate links that the movements can make an impact on state policies.

Public Opinion

The fact that policy makers within the state administration cannot ignore public opinion is by no means specific to the domain of environmental politics. A great number of examples from different countries and fields of policy show that policy makers in liberal democracies not only tend to react to public opinion but, in some instances, directly depend on it. This, however, applies only to the extent that public opinion, which is usually represented by many and often contradictory voices, can be transformed into a consonant and determined chorus (Neidhardt 1994). Most obviously, this can be seen in the case of a political scandal, when public opinion manifests itself in an outcry of anger and indignation. Such a response is likely to result in procedural and/or personnel consequences, such as a quick legislative reform, strong governmental measures, the replacement of an officeholder, or even the demise of a government. Because of the potentially strong impact of a relatively unified public opinion, decision makers tend to watch and document public opinion attentively (e.g., by reading the daily editorials) and, in turn, try to influence public opinion using their own public relations instruments.

Individual Attitudes and Behaviors

This factor should be analytically and empirically separated from public opinion, because the two factors are not necessarily congruent.[4] The relevance of individual attitudes for policy makers in democracies becomes obvious when we consider that many state activities are dependent on the acceptance and even the cooperation of the citizens. This is particularly true when it comes to convincing people to play an active role in policy implementation, by participating in voluntary health checks, reducing energy consumption, or sorting waste to facilitate recycling, for example. Above all, political parties and governments have to take individual attitudes into account because, via general elections, the possibility of getting into and staying in power is dependent on the consent of the voters. No wonder that politicians more or less constantly seek to explore individual opinions through surveys, consultation hours, visits to their electorates, and the like. Particularly when delicate issues and decisions are at stake, politicians are eager to explore existing moods and potential reactions. The fact that politicians have to care about people's attitudes is further indicated by two phenomena: First, there is a growing tendency to initiate special surveys in order to learn what people really think about an issue, a political figure, or an envisaged measure. Second, politicians seek to garner acceptance via information campaigns when specific policies are to be implemented. For example, large but ultimately unsuccessful campaigns have been launched by public administrations to gain acceptance for nuclear power programs in Germany and Austria (Nowotny 1979; Flam 1994).

Green Parties

It is debatable whether or not green parties should be considered a vital part of the environmental movement or rather as an outgrowth that can be analytically separated from it. To the extent that green parties have more or less adopted the structure of the established parties and focus on electoral and parliamentary politics, they should be treated as a separate category. If this seems plausible, then we should acknowledge the relevance of the existence and strength of a party as a third intervening factor in our model. The influence of green parties that promote the demands of the environmental movement becomes apparent when we consider how sensitive parties and political decision makers react to direct competition on the electoral level. As soon as a political concern proves attractive and important enough to become the focus of a specialized party and, moreover, to render this party electorally relevant, most other parties feel a need to take this concern into account or at least to pay some lip service to it. Once such a specialized challenging party manages to win seats in a parliament or to occupy positions in an administration, it is likely that the concerns and demands of the movement close to this party will be transmitted into the decision-making process, though hardly without modifications and temperance. This pattern may be clearly observed with regard to the Greens in Germany, who not only hold seats on all levels, from local councils to the federal Parliament, but also are represented in a few state governments and, since the autumn of 1998, also in the national government.

These assumptions can be drawn together in a model of environmental movement impact (see figure 1). This model, however, needs to be complemented and refined. First, environmental problems have to be included in the model, for two reasons. On the one hand, it is obvious that environmental movements react to environmental burdens or threats, although we cannot assume that movement mobilization is a direct function of "objective" environmental problems. These problems are socially constructed.[5] Their potential risks, their causes, and their potential solutions are not immediately apparent but have to be brought to people's attention through a process of framing, interpreting, and arguing. Nevertheless, these problems can hardly be invented; they must somehow be grounded in reality. As far as environmental problems are concerned, the process of "problematizing" the state of the environment is strongly influenced by the natural sciences and medical research. But, to some extent, it is also dependent on the firsthand experience of the wider populace. On the other hand, state policies have to be introduced into the model, because they are the most crucial variable to substantially influence environmental quality. This is not to say that only state policy matters. Market powers, such as the increase in energy prices, as well as private action, ranging from individual behavior to the strategies of big business, may also have an impact on environmental quality. But these nonstate activities will be excluded from the model, because, for the most part, they are encouraged, facilitated, or even enforced by the state. Otherwise, there would be no need for a detailed and sophisticated state policy that, as it turns out, is most effective when it applies its ultimate means, namely coercion. Taken together, the elements discussed here represent what could be called the primary environmental policy cycle (marked with solid arrows in figure 1).

Furthermore, the model should be complemented by secondary flows of influence. We can assume that public opinions, individual attitudes, and green parties influence one another. Moreover, in some cases, environmental groups may directly influence policy makers through lobbying. Finally, state policies, besides having a direct influence on environmental movements through repression or facilitation, have an indirect influence on the mobilization of environmental movements through their impact on environmental problems. These effects, however, are hard to predict. In the case of deteriorating environmental conditions, the movement may become discouraged or, on the contrary, may feel a need to intensify its efforts. In a similar vein, improving environmental conditions may take the wind out of the movement's sails, but it could also inspire the movement to go further.

Figure 1. Impact of environmental movements

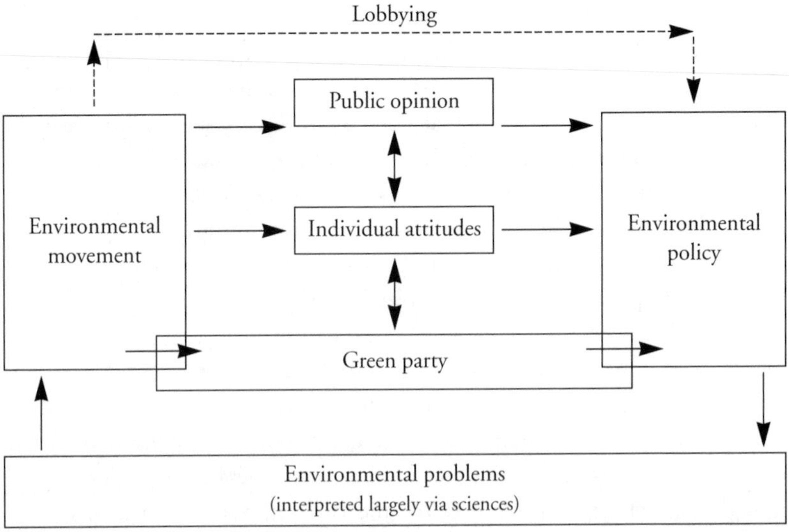

Notwithstanding these complications, we may assume a dominant flow of causality. Perceived environmental problems are taken up by the environmental movement, whose mobilization, mediated by three main factors, influences the environmental policy of the state, which in turn is the major factor in directly influencing environmental problems.[6] Because we have few reasons to assume a correspondence between the "objectively" given number of environmental problems and the amount of movement mobilization, it should suffice to begin a causal explanation with the latter factor. Hence, we can condense our expectations into the following hypothesis: *The stronger the pressure exerted by the environmental movement, the greater its impact on public opinion, individual attitudes, and green parties (or their equivalents), the more state policies take strong measures to protect the environment, which ultimately result in positive effects on environmental quality.*

This is a crude and somewhat mechanistic assumption that hardly applies to all situations. Consider a few examples: Public opinion does not necessarily react positively to powerful environmental movement mobilization. Even when environmental quality is perceived as highly valuable, strong and effective mobilization can be perceived as a threat to another and probably prioritized factor, such as full employment. In this case, the public mood may well turn against the movement's demand. This could explain why, according to Eurobarometer surveys, the strong environmental and antinuclear movements in Germany were confronted with relatively high levels of a negative attitude among the population during the 1980s (Fuchs and Rucht 1994). We may also assume that a powerful green party unintentionally weakens movement mobilization, because movement adherents may feel that the presence of such a party means that their commitment is no longer necessary. Finally, to give an example that is not in line with our central hypothesis, one may assume that in some cases the causal flow of influence works the opposite way. Consider that in the early 1970s, when the United Nations launched a campaign for environmental protection (see Caldwell 1984), awareness among political elites in some states was probably more developed than among the active parts of the citizenry. In this situation it was mainly the political elites who educated the public about the need for environmental protection. With such deviating cases in mind, our central hypothesis is less trivial than it may appear at first glance. It thus merits closer investigation.

Attempts at Operationalization

We can think about ways to operationalize the factors in the explanatory model and to look for data that would allow us to assess environmental movement impact. Among the twenty-two countries that were ranked according to their changes in environmental quality, four countries (Norway, Japan, Turkey, and Yugoslavia) have to be excluded from further analysis, because data on the other variables regarding these countries were not available. Thus we concentrate on the remaining eighteen countries.

Pressure from Environmental Movements

This factor can be conceived of as two variables: the size (number of mobilized people) and intensity (degree of radicalism) of mobilization as registered in protest-event analysis. Other measures—for instance, membership in environmental organizations—[7] are less indicative, insofar as membership per se does not represent political pressure. Therefore, membership data should be excluded or considered only when protest data are unavailable. Regarding environmental protests from a comparative perspective, we have data from only one major project, which covers four West European countries (Kriesi et al. 1992, 1995). In terms of the volume of environmental movement mobilization, when taking the different sizes of national populations into account, the following indices were found for the period from 1975 to 1989: Switzerland, 16; West Germany, 11; the Netherlands, 5; and France, 2 (Kriesi et al. 1995: 22).[8] This research was later complemented by data on Great Britain and Spain, though based on a smaller sample and a shorter time period (Koopmans 1996d). In the period from 1980 to 1989, environmental mobilization can be expressed in the following indices: Germany, 29; Switzerland, 27; the Netherlands, 13; Spain, 8; France, 5; and Great Britain, 5. If, in addition, we were to take the intensity of environmental protests into account, I assume that the rank order would change slightly, with Germany moving closer to, or even surpassing, Switzerland, and with France and Spain moving closer to the Netherlands, leaving Great Britain far behind.

Additional information can be drawn from Eurobarometer surveys, from which we are able to determine the number of environmental movement adherents in five countries. The mean values of the proportion of interviewed persons who identified themselves as activists or potential activists in four surveys between 1982 and 1989 are as follows: the Netherlands, 34.4%; West Germany, 30.8%; Great Britain, 22.1%; Italy, 21.7%; and France, 13.3% (Fuchs and Rucht 1994). Moreover, for a larger number of countries we have data on the appreciation of, or support for, environmental groups, based on the World Values Survey. Finally, I have rough estimates of pressure resulting from movement mobilization in several European Union (EU) member states, based on my own long-standing observation of environmental movements in various countries, as well as interviews with representatives from environmental groups on both national and EU levels (Rucht 1994, 1997). Again, these data and estimates are too sketchy to enable the determination of a distinct rank order. However, considering all these pieces of information, national environmental movements can be grouped, according to their differential pressure, into three broad categories, as shown in table 1.

Public Opinion

Rather than equating public opinion with the aggregate of individual attitudes as measured in survey research, I define it as statements by individuals or groups addressed to the public. Because the mass media are the most important (though not the only) forum to mirror or document public opinion, it would seem appropriate to measure public opinion using a content analysis of mass media. For instance, one could count the number and frequency of values expressed in statements on environmental matters and movements in the mass media. For comparative purposes, we would certainly have to weigh these statements released against the total of statements released on all political issues. Given the amount of resources needed for this task, it is no wonder that such data are not available. Therefore, this factor, in spite of its theoretical relevance, has to be excluded from the analysis.

Individual Attitudes

This factor, which should be distinguished from the category of public opinion, can be relatively easily measured by conventional survey research. Several cross-national surveys that measure attitudes toward environmental issues and movements are available. Most important among these are the following:

- various Eurobarometer surveys in the member states of the European Community (EC) and EU, respectively.
- further surveys covering twelve EU countries, conducted by Market and Opinion Research International (MORI) (1994)
- the two waves of the World Value Survey (around 1982 and 1991), focusing on forty-three and twenty-four countries, respectively
- the Health of the Planet Survey (1992), covering twenty-four countries

Depending on the questions in and timing of the surveys, the countries under investigation occupy different ranking positions in terms of support for the environmental cause. Various Eurobarometer surveys in the 1980s showed that environmental protection was highly valued in Denmark, Luxembourg, and West Germany. Medium support was found in Italy, Greece, the Netherlands, Spain, and Portugal, and relatively low support in France, Belgium, Great Britain, and Ireland.[9] According to the MORI survey, the high-support group is composed of Luxembourg, Germany, the Netherlands, and Denmark; the medium-support group includes Belgium, Ireland, and France; and the low-support group consists of Portugal, Italy, Great Britain, Spain, and Greece. The second wave of the World Values Survey revealed strong support for tax increases in order to improve environmental quality in Norway, Denmark, the Netherlands, Great Britain, and the United States; medium support in East Germany, Finland, Spain, Portugal, Italy, and France; and low support in West Germany, Ireland, and Japan. According to the Health of the Planet Survey, the percentage of interviewees who agreed to the statement that environmental problems were an "important and very serious problem in our country" was high in West Germany and Canada; medium in Portugal, the United States, Japan, and Norway; and low in Great Britain, Ireland, the Netherlands, Denmark, and Finland (Wissenschaftlicher Beirat der Bundesregierung 1996; see also Inglehart 1995). The fact that in the latter survey some countries that can usually be found in the top group now rank at the bottom is not necessarily inconsistent. Interviewees in those countries which have already taken major steps toward improving environmental quality may have less reason to consider environmental problems very serious when compared to countries with low environmental quality.

Taken together, these various surveys certainly do not allow a nonarbitrary rank order to be determined. Nevertheless, according to the degree to which the environmental cause is valued by individuals, the eighteen countries under consideration can at least be grouped into the three broad categories shown in table 1.

Green Parties

The most telling indicator for the strength of green parties is their share of the vote. This, however, may change considerably over time, so average values should be taken. Müller-Rommel offers data on the average electoral results of green parties in fifteen countries during the 1970s and 1980s (1993: 129). As for the functional equivalents of green parties, namely, ecologically oriented tendencies within other parties, it is very difficult to assess their strength. Hence, again, for some countries I have to rely on rough estimates.

Environmental State Policies

This is an extremely complex factor composed of dimensions such as the power of institutions (e.g., state secretaries of the environment, environmental protection agencies, and advisory boards; see Jörgens 1996), environmental laws and other regulations (e.g., thresholds for the amount of particular substances in drinking water), implementation capacities, monitoring systems and sanctions against violations of environmental regulations, procedural rules (e.g., access of environmental groups to courts, and freedom of information about environmental data), financial investments by the state to improve the quality of the environment, and efforts to educate the wider public.[10] Moreover, we would have to take these conditions and activities into account on all levels, from local to national. It would be completely unrealistic to measure all these factors in the eighteen countries under consideration. Thus, we have to limit ourselves to a relatively few simple indicators for assessing the volume and determination of environmental state policies. For instance, one could look for state expenses for environmental matters as a share of the total state budget; the rigidity of clean-air standards (Knoepfel and Weidner 1986); and the readiness to engage in and to implement domestically international treaties on the protection of the environment (Dietz and Kalof 1992). Based on such measures, experts on comparative environmental policies have identified some countries as leading and others as lagging behind, though we do not have a distinct rank order based on systematic data covering various dimensions. As far as EU member states are concerned, there is accumulated evidence of their eagerness to push environmental matters. In my interviews with various experts from EU administrations and nonstate environmental groups in Brussels, I got fairly consistent estimates, which may generally be illustrated by the image of a convoy. The environmental head of the convoy is formed by the Netherlands, Denmark, Sweden, Finland, Germany, Austria, and Luxembourg. Traveling in the middle of the convoy are France, Italy, Great Britain, Ireland, and Belgium. The rear guard consists of Spain, Portugal, and Greece. Considering these various pieces of information, again I have grouped the eighteen countries into three broad categories. Table 1 condenses and summarizes the available information, also grouping the eighteen countries according to their changes in environmental quality.

Discussion

Assuming that the countries are adequately grouped together according to the various factors discussed, we can assess whether or not these results are in

Table 1. Aspects of Environmental Politics in Eighteen Countries

Variable	Strong	Medium	Weak
Environmental movement pressure	Austria, Denmark, Finland, Germany, Luxembourg, the Netherlands, Switzerland, Sweden, United States	Belgium, Canada, Spain, France, Great Britain, Ireland, Italy	Greece, Portugal
Individual attitudes	Denmark, the Netherlands, Luxembourg	Austria, Canada, Spain, Finland, France, Germany, Italy, Switzerland, Sweden, United States	Belgium, Great Britain, Greece, Ireland, Portugal
Green parties	Austria, Belgium, France, Germany, Italy, Luxembourg, the Netherlands, Switzerland	Great Britain, Sweden	Canada, Denmark, Spain, Finland, Greece, Ireland, Portugal, United States
Policy efforts	Austria, Denmark, Finland, Germany, Luxembourg, the Netherlands, Switzerland, Sweden	Belgium, Canada, France, Great Britain, Ireland, Italy, United States	Spain, Greece, Portugal
Changes in environmental quality	Austria, Denmark, Luxembourg, the Netherlands, Switzerland, Sweden	Belgium, Canada, Finland, France, Germany, Great Britain, United States	Spain, Greece, Ireland, Italy, Portugal

line with our general hypothesis. Moreover, other hypotheses can be derived from this categorization.

When looking at the column categorizing the countries that exhibit strong values, we find the same countries with respect to most variables. This cluster effect is even more pronounced in the column listing countries with weak values. Overall, this tendency supports the general hypothesis that the higher the pressure exerted by environmental movements, the more state policies, in responding to intervening factors, tend to improve environmental quality, and vice versa.

Taking a closer look, however, we find exceptions to this rule. In a few cases, a country that has a weak value in one category has a strong value in another. This applies, for instance, to Italy when regarding changes in environmental quality and the strength of its green party, and it applies to Finland when regarding the pressure of environmental movements and the strength of its green party. Moreover, strong green parties exist in Belgium, Italy, and France—all countries that exhibit only a medium level of movement pressure. These patterns suggest that there is no correlation, or only a weak positive one, between the strength of green parties and movement pressure. The relationship between these two categories is shown more clearly in table 2. The explanation for this weak correlation may be found in other intervening factors that, in some countries, supposedly have a strong impact on the strength of green parties. Here one could point to the overall nature of the voting system (majoritarian or representative), to a "percent hurdle" that small parties face in some countries when they want to enter the parliament, and to fragmentation within a green party or even the existence of several green parties—all factors that may prevent potential sympathizers from voting "green." So it seems safe to conclude that strong movement pressure does not necessarily translate into strong green parties.

When relating environmental movement pressure to its ultimate goal, an improvement of environmental quality, we see a partly inconsistent pattern.

Table 2. Correlation Coefficients of Factors in Environmental Politics

Variable	Environmental movement pressure	Individual attitudes	Green parties	Policy efforts	Changes in environmental quality
Environmental movement pressure	1.0000	.6144**	.2820	.9031**	.6789**
Individual attitudes	.6144**	1.0000	.2670	.5702*	.6843**
Green parties	.2820	.2670	1.0000	.4421	.6045**
Policy efforts	.9031**	.5702*	.4421	1.0000	.7919**
Changes in environmental quality	.6789**	.6843**	.6045**	.7919**	1.0000

Note: Calculations based on values 1, 2, or 3 according to the categorizations weak, medium, and strong, respectively, in table 1.

*$p < .05$ **$p < .01$

For instance, the strong movement pressure in Germany, Finland, and the United States seems to have an impact on one or two intervening variables but ultimately results in only medium improvements in environmental quality. From this we can conclude that intervening variables do matter. In spite of strong movement pressure in Germany, Finland, and the United States, individual attitudes rank at only a medium level. In addition, there is only an extremely weak green party in the United States. Thus, the effect of movement mobilization seems to weaken on its way to the polity in these countries. A more specific explanation for this phenomenon may also lie in the relative strength of forces that oppose the environmental movements, such as the chemical industry and mining and lumber companies. These economic forces seem to be particularly strong in the United States and are thus likely to counterbalance even relatively strong movement mobilization.

Another striking feature becomes apparent when we consider a structural common denominator among the countries that are most prevalent in the columns with either strong or weak values. Countries in the first category tend to be most prosperous economically, whereas the opposite holds for countries with weak values. This suggests that economic performance might be a strong background variable, for two reasons: First, when trying to explain strong movement pressure, we may assume—in line with Maslow's hierarchy of needs—that in prosperous countries postmaterial values or new political issues such as environmental protection will find a greater resonance among the populace, because its elementary needs are largely satisfied.[11] In addition, we may assume that in these countries the education system is more developed and thus tends to provide more information on, and a better understanding of, environmental problems. Second, when considering state activities, it is also likely that prosperous countries have more economic resources to invest in environmental protection. In addition, industry can cope more easily with sudden financial burdens due to tight environmental standards without losing international competitiveness. In other words, unlike relatively poor countries, rich countries can afford environmental protection and, as can be seen in retrospect, may even attain a stronger position precisely because of their high environmental standards, making them more competitive in the long run.

Though the impact of economic performance on environmental policy has not yet been studied in much detail, this factor should be taken into account when it comes to explaining changes in environmental quality. As in the case of anti–nuclear power movements (Midttun and Rucht 1994), it seems that, beyond social and political factors, economic variables should also be included in the model presented here.

In conclusion, I admit that this essay has only scratched the surface of a complex web of interrelations in environmental politics. My aim is to shed some light on the difficulties in studying this topic; to develop an explanatory approach that, via intervening factors, links movement mobilization with ultimate changes in environmental quality; and to substantiate this approach using empirical data. In light of the scattered empirical data, this approach cannot be a "hard" test, but at least one can conclude that the available information does not contradict the assumptions presented here. Further compilation of data, which to a certain extent is already under way, may allow more systematic and empirically better informed analyses to be undertaken in this field.

Notes

This is an expanded and revised version of an article originally published in German in 1996 as "Wirkungen von Umweltbewegungen: Von den Schwierigkeiten einer Bilanz," in *Forschungsjournal Neue Soziale Bewegungen* 9 (4): 15–27. I am grateful to Marco Giugni for his comments on an earlier version of this chapter. Moreover, I thank Gabi Rosenstreich for her editorial assistance.

1. For cross-national comparisons of environmental movements, see Wörndl and Fréchet (1991), Heijden, Koopmans, and Giugni (1992), Dalton (1994), Rucht (1994), and Kriesi and Giugni (1996).

2. Writings about how to conceptualize the outcomes of social movements are rare (but see Rucht 1992; Giugni 1994; Burstein, Einwohner, and Hollander 1995). Typically, we find statements about the difficulties in assessing movement outcomes similar to that expressed in the title of one article, "Social Movements and Political Outcomes: Why Both Ends Fail to Meet" (Zimmermann 1990), but few empirical approaches. For exceptions, see Gamson (1975), Piven and Cloward (1977), Gurr (1980), Kitschelt (1986), Huberts (1989), Rüdig (1990), Midttun and Rucht (1994), and Giugni (1995).

3. According to press reports, a recent major report and projection on global environmental problems presented by the United Nations Environment Program in January 1997 seems to support the assumption that, on the whole, environmental conditions are worsening dramatically.

4. For example, in postwar Germany, anti-Semitism was stigmatized by the elites and therefore hardly manifested itself in public opinion. Nevertheless, and in spite of all attempts to "educate" people to give up prejudice, surveys found that a sizable part of the German population continued to have anti-Semitic attitudes (Stöss 1989).

5. In regard to Chernobyl, this argument has been demonstrated by Duyvendak and Koopmans (1995). For the general argument, see Douglas and Wildavsky (1982).

6. Besides the state, social factors also have an impact on deliberate changes in environmental quality (Jänicke 1992: 87).

7. Some comparative nonsurvey data on membership in environmental organizations are presented by Dalton (1994) and Kriesi (1996).

8. These indices represent the extent of participation in unconventional protest events initiated by environmental movements in one thousand per million inhabitants.

9. The bases for this rough categorization are the means of three surveys carried out in 1983, 1987, and 1989. Detailed results are documented by Hofrichter and Reif (1990: 130). Depending on the various questions that have been asked in similar surveys, the rank order of countries might change slightly.

10. Burstein, Einwohner, and Hollander (1995) have distinguished several dimensions of social movement impact upon the state.

11. Contrary to our expectation, Dunlap and Mertig (1996) found in their analysis of data from the 1992 Health of the Planet Survey that environmental consciousness in poor countries was surprisingly high. Most variables that measured environmental consciousness correlated negatively with the national GNP per capita. The authors assume that this has to do with the obtrusiveness of environmental deterioration that directly affects the living conditions in poor countries.

10

Ethnic and Civic Conceptions of Nationhood and the Differential Success of the Extreme Right in Germany and Italy

Ruud Koopmans and Paul Statham

Common Histories, Divergent Presents

Since the beginning of the 1980s, Western Europe has seen a resurgence of xenophobic and extreme-right mobilization, in the form of violent attacks on immigrant groups, neo-Nazi demonstrations, and the rise of extreme-right political parties. Though a lot of comparative work on these phenomena is available, much of it consists of edited volumes bringing together collections of single-country case studies (e.g., Baumgartl and Favell 1995; Merkl and Weinberg 1993; Hainsworth 1992). Truly comparative studies are few and far between, and so far there has been no systematic comparison of Italy and Germany.

This omission is surprising, if one considers that these are the two countries that, in the interbellum, witnessed the rise to totalitarian state power of fascist movements, which still function, implicitly or explicitly, as role models and ideological reference points for the present-day extreme right. In spite of the historical parallel, the recent histories of Germany and Italy could hardly be more divergent, if we consider the strength and electoral success of the contemporary extreme right. In Italy, the Alleanza Nazionale (AN), a direct heir of prewar fascism, gained 13.5% of the vote in the 1994 national elections. Another party based on a movement with strong ethnocentric—though not fascist—tendencies, the Lega Nord, achieved a further 8.4%. After the elections, both parties entered a coalition government with Silvio Berlusconi's Forza Italia. Although this governing coalition lasted only eight months, it constituted a historic landmark in the sense that it represented the first time in postwar Europe that the extreme right has attained governmental power. In the 1996 election, the significant presence of the AN (15.7%) and Lega Nord (10.1%) on the political landscape of the Second Republic was underlined, while a neofascist splinter group from the AN, MS-Fiamma, gained a further 0.9%.

In contrast, the German extreme right, despite a few limited successes in federal state and European elections, has not come close to entering the national Parliament. With 2.1% and 1.9% in the 1990 and 1994 elections, respectively, the German Republikaner—the most important of Germany's three extreme-right parties—is one of the weaker extreme-right political parties in Europe. This holds in comparison not only with its Italian counterparts but also with the French Front National (which numbered 15% in the 1995 presidential elections), the Flemish Vlaams Blok (which won 7.8% of the Belgian votes in 1995 and almost twice that percentage in Flanders), and the Austrian Freiheitliche Partei Österreichs (which totaled 22.1% in 1995). Moreover, while in Italy the extreme right has gained acceptance as a coalition partner and has moved from a position of "challenger" to one of "member" of the political system (Tilly 1978; Gamson 1990), in Germany it remains completely marginalized. None of the established political parties in Germany has been willing to enter coalitions or other forms of cooperation with the extreme right, even at the local or regional level. The three parties of the extreme right, the Republikaner, the Deutsche Volksunion, and the Nationaldemokratische Partei Deutschlands are officially branded "enemies of the constitution" and are routinely monitored by the internal security agencies, and their leaders and members have been subjected to various types of repression.

Thus, in terms of "acceptance" (one of the two fundamental types of social movement outcomes distinguished by Gamson [1990]), Italy and Germany are situated at opposite poles. As our discussion will show, however, this is not necessarily true for substantive policy outcomes ("new advantages," in Gamson's terminology). In fact, German foreign and immigration politics have been, at least until very recently, more restrictive and closer to the demands of the extreme right than has been the case in Italy.

In our view, the reasons for these differential outcomes can be related to the different configurations of ethnic and political foundations of citizenship and nationhood, and recent developments concerning the balance between the civic and ethnic components in the two countries. Many scholars (e.g., Gabriel 1996) have attributed the rise of the contemporary European extreme right to two main sources: the rise of xenophobic claims based on ethnic-nationalist conceptions of citizenship; and the crisis of legitimacy in established institutions for political representation (best captured by the German term *Politikverdrossenheit*). These two developments have tended to be treated independently. However, if one considers them from the perspective of the competitive tensions between ethnic and civic conceptions of citizenship and nationhood that have accompanied the nation-state—and Italy and Germany in particular—ever since its formation, they become two sides of the same coin. In this view, the rise of the extreme right is as much (or even more) a result of the crisis of the political community as a basis for national identities, as it is a result of the politicization of ethnic boundaries arising from increased immigration and cultural heterogeneity.

Opportunity and Discourse: A Theoretical Model

To analyze how the competition between ethnic and civic conceptions of citizenship and national identity influences the chances for the mobilization and success of the extreme right, we propose to combine two recent theoretical strands in social movement research. The first strand is centered on the concept of political opportunity structure (POS) and stresses the facilitating or constraining role played by institutional structures and power configurations (McAdam 1982; Tarrow 1994; Kriesi et al. 1995). Reacting to the earlier internal focus on social movement resources and strategies, the political opportunity model emphasizes the role played by the wider political context in which social movements operate. The model has been successfully applied both in longitudinal single-country studies (Tarrow 1989; Duyvendak 1995; Koopmans 1995) and in cross-national comparisons (Kitschelt 1986; Rucht 1994; Kriesi et al. 1995). However, it shares an important weakness with the resource mobilization model, namely, an inability to deal adequately with the discursive content of social movement mobilization. Thus, many aspects of political opportunity structure that have been proposed are "contentless" in the sense that they apply to social movements regardless of their goals, ideologies, and discourse. Factors such as the instability of political alignments, electoral volatility, and the institutional makeup of the political system may explain why opportunities for social movements in general are greater at some times than at others, and why social movements use more radical strategies in some polities than in others. However, the POS model has difficulty in dealing with the common finding that opportunity structures do not facilitate and constrain all movements to the same degree and in the same way. Of course, more elaborated versions of the political opportunity model have tried to deal with this finding by differentiating between movement types and policy arenas and by incorporating elements of political culture such as prevailing elite strategies and cleavage structures (Rucht 1994; Kriesi et al. 1995).

In extending itself so, however, the political opportunity model, to an important extent, has already exceeded its conceptual limits and moved into the domain of the framing perspective, a second strand of theory, which has concentrated on the discursive aspect of mobilization. In this view, the chances for the mobilization and success of social movements are determined by the ability of those movements to develop interpretive "frames" that can effectively link a movement and its cause to the interests, perceptions, and ideologies of potential constituencies (Snow et al. 1986). The framing model, however, has difficulty in explaining why some frames fail while others succeed in convincing the public, and why similar frames have differential impacts in different political contexts. Here as well, proposals have been made to overcome the problem, in this case by trying to link success to the degree of correspondence ("resonance," "commensurability," or "fidelity") of specific frames with external factors. To the extent that such an anchorage of frames is sought in objective problems and events, this effort allies the framing perspective with traditional grievance perspectives (for a critique, see Koopmans and Duyvendak 1995).[1] More fruitful in our view is the alternative focus on the fit between social movement frames and the wider political culture of a particular society (Snow and Benford 1992; Diani 1996).

This step involves introducing opportunity structures into the framing model. As such, there is nothing wrong with the broadening of perspectives that has taken place within the political opportunity and framing approaches. We think, however, that the convergence of the two perspectives needs to be conceptually acknowledged. Of course, the perspectives have not become identical. The political opportunity model still has its own domain, where it is concerned with institutional structures, power relations, or the strategic stance of potential alliance partners, about which the framing perspective has little to say. Conversely, the opportunity model is unable to account for the ways in which social movements mobilize symbolic resources to advance their cause—which is the particular strength of the framing perspective. Between the two domains, a common ground has developed where both perspectives refer to political-cultural or symbolic external constraints and facilitators of social movement mobilization. We propose to denote this set of variables by the term *discursive opportunity structure,* which may be seen as determining which ideas are considered "sensible," which constructions of reality are seen as "realistic," and which claims are held as "legitimate" within a certain polity at a specific time.

In the following sections, we analyze the effects of the structural level of opportunities on the chances for the mobilization and success of extreme-right political parties.[2] Regarding discursive opportunities, we focus on the strength of ethnic and civic conceptions of citizenship and national identity. Departing from a definition of the extreme right as a social movement that mobilizes an ethnic-cultural framing of national identity against the idea of the nation as a political or civic community, we derive the following hypotheses: the resonance of the extreme-right frame, and consequently its chances of mobilization and success, will be greater (1) the more the dominant discourse on national identity and citizenship corresponds to and legitimizes the ethnic-cultural ideal-type of national identity, and (2) the less the dominant conception of the nation is grounded in and legitimized by civic-political elements.[3]

This relatively simple model becomes more complicated once we introduce institutional opportunities. A first factor to be taken into account is the accessibility of the polity to extreme-right parties or, formulated in alternative conceptual terms, the balance between repression and facilitation. This leads us to the hypothesis that (3) the impact of the extreme right is likely to be greater, the more its access to the polity is facilitated and the less it is subject to repressive constraints. Second, we should acknowledge that challengers not only oppose the members of the polity but also compete with them. In addition to exerting repression, members of the polity may prevent a challenger's access to the polity by preemptively taking up some of its demands. Thus, (4) the mobilization opportunities of the extreme right will be more limited, the more ethnic-cultural conceptions of national identity are integrated into the programs and policies of the members of the polity. Paradoxically, this is most likely to be the case when hypothesis 1 applies, that is, when ethnic-cultural elements are an integral part of a nation's conception of nationhood and citizenship. In social movement literature, the degree of coherence and stability of the political elite has often been emphasized as a crucial factor influencing a challenger's opportunities to mobilize and to achieve success. This leads us to our final hypothesis: (5) the chances for the mobilization and success of the extreme right will be enhanced when the political elite is divided and political alignments are unstable, and in particular when the division and instability are related to questions of national identity, most clearly when they are caused by a legitimacy crisis of the civic-political basis of the polity. Before applying these hypotheses, we first discuss the distinction between ethnic and civic conceptions of nationhood and citizenship with respect to its relevance for explaining the mobilization and success of the extreme right.

National Identity as a Contested Discourse:
Competing Civic and Ethnic Variants for Nationhood

It has been well established by studies of nationalism that the institutional apparatus of the state is a vehicle used by the political elite for "nation building." In the realm of culture, the state exerted authority over traditional institutions. This involved the establishment of a state education system and a dominant religion and language that were designed to enforce the principle of national unity (Hobsbawm 1990; Gellner 1983; Anderson 1983).

Collective identities of nationhood that have been constructed in this nation-building process combine elements of two broadly defined ideal-types: ethnic nationalism, which asserts the unity of "the people" on the basis of cultural belonging to a presumed or real primordial identity, or ethnic group; and civic nationalism, which asserts the unity of "the people" on the universal ideal of a political community of equal citizens. National identities define a "contract" for membership within a community. In this sense, political culture is a "civil religion" that defines the duties of citizenship and the basis for inclusion and exclusion. As collective identity constructions, ethnic nationalism and civic nationalism imply two different basic ideal-types of relationships that bind a state and its citizens. Ethnic nationalism includes and excludes its "people" on the basis of a shared primordial belonging to an original *ethnie*. Civic nationalism includes and excludes its "people" on the basis of a shared belonging to a political community of universal political and legal rights.

In the postwar period, it has been common to equate nationalism with the civic variant, but, as the recent revival of nationalist movements has indicated, this association obscures the complex basis of national identities that by necessity retain elements of the ethnic variant. Particular historical variants of nationalism can be seen as collective identities that have been constructed by a symbiosis of ethnic and civic nationalism (Smith 1995).

Taking a cross-national comparative perspective within Europe, we see that ethnic nationalism has found its most prominent expression in German culture, whereas civic nationalism is most prominently expressed in the revolutionary tradition of French republicanism. However, it would be wrong simply to equate the outcomes of ethnic nationalism with an undemocratic, culturally exclusive, and expansionist state, and those of civic nationalism with a democratic, culturally inclusive, and nonexpansionist state. In recent times, the relatively peaceful ethnic nationalism of the Czech movement stands as a counterexample to that of the Serbs in the former Yugoslavia. Conversely, the historical example of French nationalism under Bonaparte demonstrates how the universalizing impulse of civic nationalism translates into an expansionist strategy. The different versions of nationalism that exist between countries and across time can be seen as combinations or "mixtures" of civic and ethnic codes. The civic and ethnic codes are the dimensions that actors use to construct specific variants of nationalism as collective identities. Hence, a dominant variant of nationalism, whether ethnic or civic, is an ideology of the ruling class or elite that is embedded in the agency of the state.

Historically different versions of nationalism have emerged within the nation-states of Europe, dependent upon the different class alignments, conflicts, and compromises that have "made nations" and have redefined the basis of citizenship. As a collective identity, the dominant variant of nationalism that is embodied within a nation-state remains open to cultural challenges from counterdiscourses that are carried by the mobilization of social movements. National identity is, thus, a contested field of political discourse (Gamson 1988, 1992) where a dominant discourse—which combines ethnic and civic elements—competes with other "challenger" variants that are carried by social movements. Social movements may draw upon resources of identity and countercodes to challenge the dominant conception of nationhood and the framework of citizenship obligations it entails. For example, at a time of the collapse of a political regime, by defeat in war or through internal crisis, there are opportunities for the "challenger" discourses of social movements to stimulate processes of "frame alignment" within the dominant discourse on nationalism.[4] However, opportunities for movements to introduce frame alignment are not necessarily reserved for such dramatic occurrences, nor do the frames of challengers necessarily translate into their intended outcomes. Another example of frame alignment within a dominant variant of civic nationalism is provided by the establishment of the social welfare state, which can be seen as an outcome of the challenge by the social democratic movement of the working class. The challenge of social reformism introduced a process of frame alignment into the dominant discourse on national citizenship by incorporating the "belonging" of the working classes into a new definition of the ideals of the political community. Within a civic nationalism based on more social rights in addition to political and legal rights, the working classes could be expected to identify more with the political culture of national citizenship than with the cultural bonds of class (Marshall 1950). The challenge of social democracy extended the basis of civic nationalism by redefining the contractual basis for citizenship within the political community and by establishing the social welfare state.

Even in the extreme example of social revolution and the overthrow of a political regime, it is not often the case that a dominant discourse on nationalism, whether relatively more ethnic- or more civic-defined, is replaced completely by a challenger variant. National traditions for political culture have proven to be resistant to the dynamics of social change. The establishment of the Weimar Republic in Germany after the Great War did not eradicate ethnic nationalism as the basis for national identity. On the contrary, the German variant of National Socialism was able to radicalize the ethnic nationalism of the Weimar Republic to its logical extreme by founding a fascist totalitarian state with an official policy for exterminating other *ethnies*. By comparison, Italian Fascism drew on a tradition of ethnic nationalism that was less strongly embedded and produced a more state-corporatist and less xenophobic variant of fascism.

A civic conception of the nation was forcibly imposed by the Western Allied forces on the defeated nations of ethnic nationalism, both in founding the Federal Republic of Germany and, to a lesser extent, the Italian First Republic. In postwar Western Europe, the dominance of civic nationalism has been institutionalized in the polity of the liberal democratic state and in the political discourses that provide it with legitimacy. Ethnic nationalism has become a challenger discourse that is carried by the ethnocentric and antisystemic critiques of extreme right movements.

The history of different variants of nationalism teaches us that as a cultural resource for identity, a model of national citizenship is deeply embedded in the structure of social relationships within a society, and that this gives it an enduring potentiality to resist transformation into its other variant. A state and its challengers disagree but share the same culture and political context for collective action. The collective action of challengers is constructed from the same set of cultural traditions and "tools" as its opponent (Swidler 1986), so that even on the rare occasions when a political regime is overthrown or collapses, its successors establish the national unity of the polity with reference to the same cultural framework as their predecessors. The cultural traditions that, as founding myths and collective identities, "make societies into nations" have an enduring quality that influences the potential of social movements to mobilize against a state. To explain the potential for successful outcomes by extreme-right mobilization, we argue that it is necessary to analyze the cultural opportunities provided by the discourse on nationalism, in addition to the institutional opportunities provided by the political system.

Scholars applying an international comparative approach to immigration policies and the legal status of ethnic minorities have identified different national traditions or models for citizenship rights (Brubaker 1992; Castles and Miller 1993; Kleger and D'Amato 1995; Rex 1996a; Bovenkerk, Miles, and Verbunt 1990). These differences show that despite the dominance of civic nationalism, traditions of ethnic nationalism are still an important variable in defining the political culture (and hence the discursive opportunity structure) of a nation-state. In West Germany the state definition of citizenship has retained a strong ethnic component. Membership in the political community and full citizenship rights are derived on the basis of ethnicity. German national identity is based not on the principle of territory or birthright, but on a foundation myth of the original ethnic community. This identity translates into a state policy that does not recognize the legitimacy of non-Germanic ties of cultural identity and is highly exclusive in the distribution of citizenship rights. In contrast, the French tradition of national identity has been strongly tied to the republican foundation myth, where citizenship is a territorial birthright that guarantees equality of membership in the political community regardless of ethnic origin. However, French civic culture is also "exclusive" in its refusal to accept the legitimacy of loyalties other than allegiance to the republic. French nationalism has traditionally denied political space to cultural difference. This was demonstrated by the famous refusal of a headmaster to allow a Muslim girl to wear a "head-scarf" in a state school (Husbands 1994).

In contrast to Germany and France, the cultural pluralism of Dutch and British nationalism has permitted the relative integration of ethnic communities to rights of citizenship. In the Dutch model for *verzuiling* (pillarization), the legitimacy of cultural difference based on religious, ethnic, or kinship ties is institutionally recognized by the division of the political community into different "pillars" of cultural groups. In contrast, the British tradition for cultural pluralism is based on a separation of the political community and the cultural realm into different spheres of action. Religion and kinship are relegated to private matters for individual conscience. However, even in this multicultural variant the authority of the state sponsors a preferred version of the civic culture, as British Muslims discovered when the state refused to act against Salman Rushdie on the basis of blasphemy laws (Rex 1996a).

Italy provides a southern European variant to these cases of national identities. Its geographical and political location has "made" a country that is the recipient of contrasting cultures and conflicting identities. The collective identity of the nation is best characterized as Catholic and Mediterranean (Ginsborg 1995). Primordial and familial identities have remained strong and divisive, as is expressed in the national divide between north and south and in communal rivalries between regions, localities, and even neighborhoods. Membership in the Catholic community and attachment to the family as the natural order of society have taken historical precedence over the establishment of a political community as a focus for Italian identity. Civic beliefs have remained subordinate to familial identities in the cultural sphere, and patron-client relationships have monopolized the state. The "ethnic" components of identity are strong in the sense that social relationships are based on communal and familial identities, but weak (except for the Fascist period) in defining the nation as the primary unit of collective identity.[5] This combination of a relatively weak national identity and a commitment to citizenship has produced a state that until recently has not addressed issues of cultural difference. Paradoxically, the Catholic dominance of the cultural realm provides a culture that is tolerant of ethnic difference in a paternalistic sense, but the strength of communal and familial bonding maintains a propensity toward intolerance for the culturally different.

Recent debates on citizenship have identified a crisis in the national identities of European states. This crisis has been attributed to the integration of Europe as supranational state (Rex 1996b) and the "individualization" processes of modernity that fragment identity. For example, Billig's "banal nationalism" thesis (1995) sees contemporary nationalism as an ideology that has fragmented into a cultural discourse, a politics of identity. Another example is Delantey (1996), who distinguishes "old nationalism," which defined itself in opposition to other nation-states as the "significant other," from a "new nationalism," which he claims is an ideology for exclusion rather than inclusion, which opposes welfare state "multiculturalism," and which defines itself in opposition to immigrants as the "significant other."

Instead of contrasting "new" with "old" nationalism, we argue for the analytic utility of the distinction between ethnic and civic nationalism as a means for defining the cultural opportunities for the extreme right that exist in a national context. This avoids the risk of inflating the recent wave of xenophobia into a new theory of nationalism and opens the way for empirical analysis. Within our framework, the extreme right is a challenger that mobilizes a set of ethnocentric claims against the concept of civic nationalism embodied in the liberal democratic state. Explaining the differential success of the extreme right in postwar Italy and Germany requires that we analyze the national cases of cultural discourses on national identity (as discursive opportunities) and their interplay with institutional opportunities for gaining access to the political system over time.

Germany: The Extreme Right as an Influential Outsider

In the postwar history of the German extreme right, three mobilization phases can be distinguished. Already during the period of Allied occupation, a number of ethnic nationalist parties were founded that were supported by a mixture of former National Socialists and Germans who had fled or had been expelled from the former German territories in Eastern Europe (the so-called *Vertriebenen*). In the first elections to the West German Parliament in 1949, these parties together received more than 10% of the vote. Their program included opposition to the Allies' reeducation and denazification policies, nonrecognition of the postwar German borders, and attention to the more material interests, such as employment and housing, of the *Vertriebenen*. After the lifting of the Allied party-licensing system in 1949, a more explicitly national socialist party emerged in the form of the Sozialistische Reichspartei. In 1951, it entered the state parliaments of Bremen and Lower Saxony, in the latter case with 11% of the vote and absolute majorities in thirty-five communities (Winkler 1994: 71). Its rise, however, abruptly ended in 1952 when the party was banned and dissolved by the Federal Constitutional Court, on the grounds that its program was "hostile to the constitution." Other nationalist parties continued to play a role, but they gradually lost support and did not survive into the 1960s. The reasons for this development were twofold. First, the entrance criteria for the national Parliament were twice made more restrictive during the 1950s, with the explicit aim of removing the smaller right-wing competitors from the political scene. While originally parties had to gain at least 5% of the vote in one of the federal states, since 1957 5% of the national vote has been required. Second, the Christian Democratic Parties (CDU and CSU) succeeded in integrating many of the demands and personnel of the national conservative parties and of the organizations of *Vertriebenen*.

Not least among the reasons for this integrative capacity was the *Wirtschaftswunder,* the remarkable economic recovery that was achieved under Christian Democratic rule. Although, as Almond and Verba's cross-national study of political culture (1963) showed, the Germans had not become convinced democrats and although many of them still longed for the authoritarian past, at least democracy and the social market economy had proved to "work." In addition, the ethnic nationalist conception of national identity, unlike many other features of prewar German politics, continued to be strongly anchored in citizenship legislation as well as in the discourse and programs of the major parties, including, in this period, the Social Democratic Party (SPD). Within the context of the cold war and a divided Germany, it was ideologically unthinkable to change the ethnic conception of citizenship that defined East Germans and "ethnic Germans" from other East European countries as part of the German nation represented by the West German state (Brubaker 1992: 168–71). Even "revanchist" sentiments could be integrated into mainstream politics, since, legitimated by anticommunism, Germany did not recognize the postwar borders until the reunification treaty of 1990 with the Allied powers.

The gradual containment of ethnic nationalist parties in the 1950s followed a pattern that, to an important extent, has remained typical since then: a strategy of preemption with regard to those actors and demands which can be integrated with the ethnic nationalist elements in mainstream political culture, combined with a strategy of repression with regard to those (more explicitly neo-Nazi or antidemocratic) demands and actors which go beyond these limits. Conversely, mobilization opportunities for the extreme right arose when the integrative capacities of mainstream politics declined. This became evident during the second extreme-right mobilization phase that is associated with the Nationaldemokratische Partei Deutschlands (NPD). Founded in 1964, the party succeeded between 1966 and 1968 in entering seven state parliaments, scoring up to 10% of the vote. This was the period of the so-called Grand Coalition between the CDU/CSU and the SPD, whose centrist policies, in the virtual absence of a parliamentary opposition, created room for new competitors on both the left and the right. As a result of the CDU/CSU's alliance with the SPD—which it had portrayed as a bedfellow of communism only a few years before—and the coalition's first cautious steps toward a normalization of relations with Eastern Europe and the German Democratic Republic (GDR), the Christian Democrats were no longer capable of containing the extreme-right challenge. In addition, the still-weak development of a civic basis for national identity became evident through the impact of the recession of 1966–1967, the limited objective extent of which bore no relation to the crisis it caused in the national consciousness. Again, however, the heyday of the extreme right did not last long. After the collapse of the Grand Coalition, the NPD failed to jump the 5% hurdle (reaching only 4.3%) and subsequently disappeared from all state parliaments. Now in the opposition, the CDU/CSU shifted back to the right and, alongside the organizations of *Vertriebenen,* stood at the forefront of massive demonstrations against the Brandt government's *Ostpolitik* of reconciliation with the East.

In the 1980s, dissatisfaction with the established conservatives' *Ostpolitik* significantly contributed to the emergence of the Republikaner as the main carrier of the third wave of extreme-right party mobilization. The party was founded in 1983 by a dissident group that split off from the CSU in protest at the substantial financial assistance that had been given by CSU leader and Bavarian prime minister Franz-Josef Strauß to the GDR regime. The first notable success of the Republikaner was in the Bavarian elections of 1986, in which it scored 3% of the vote. In 1989, it entered the Berlin state parliament (7.5%) and the European Parliament (7.1%). Another extreme-right party, the Deutsche Volksunion (DVU), which had split off from the NPD in the 1970s, achieved some success in the 1987 elections in Bremen (3.4%). However, these successes could not be repeated in the 1990 national elections just after reunification, when the extreme-right parties together scored a meager 2.4%. Again, it was the successful appropriation of the nationalist cause by the established right that was detrimental to the mobilization opportunities of the extreme right. Helmut Kohl's swift appropriation of the East German demonstrators' slogan *Wir sind ein Volk!* robbed the extreme right of one of its central themes, and most of its potential supporters rallied behind Kohl and his party as champions of the reunification of the nation.

In the late 1980s and early 1990s, the continuing relevance of ethnic elements for German national identity was demonstrated in the remarkably different ways in which the country's political elite dealt with two immigration waves. The breakdown of the Eastern European communist regimes set in motion the massive movement of people, driven mainly by economic motives, from these countries to Western Europe, and predominantly to Germany. Some of them came as asylum seekers; others came on the basis of the special provisions in the German constitution for ethnic German *Aussiedler* (resettlers), descendants of German-speaking people who, often centuries ago, migrated to Eastern Europe and the Balkans. These members of the German "imagined community," regardless of the fact that many of them did not even speak German, had an automatic right to German citizenship and received extensive financial and social support to help them integrate into German society. The influx of asylum seekers, on the contrary, was greeted with open hostility by leading Christian Democrats, who started a media campaign to restrict the constitutional right to political asylum. However, this demand met with fierce opposition from the liberal Free Democratic Party (FDP) and the SPD, as well as the Christian Democrat left wing. This conflict within the political elite brought the extreme right renewed opportunities for mobilization, this time not only in the form of electoral successes for the Republikaner and the DVU in several state elections, but also in the form of an unprecedented wave of violence against foreigners, and asylum seekers in particular.

This wave of mobilization had a remarkably strong impact on the further course of the asylum debate among the established parties and on successive restrictions of the rights of asylum seekers. Time series analyses have shown that increases in the level of extreme-right violence led to an intensification of the asylum debate, followed by the adoption of new restrictive legislation (see Koopmans 1996a, 1996c). A first wave of violence starting in September 1991 after large-scale antiforeigner riots in the Saxon town of Hoyerswerda was followed by a decision of the federal government and the *Länder* to tighten and speed up the procedures for asylum applications. One year later, similar riots in Rostock spurred a second wave of violence, which was followed in December 1992 by an agreement among the major parties to change the constitution much along the lines of the original demand of the Christian Democrats' right wing. These successes of the German extreme right thus show that violence can be a fruitful strategy for social movements, a conclusion that supports the findings of Piven and Cloward (1977) and Gamson (1990).

However, the closing of ranks among the political elite and the severe restriction of the constitutional right to asylum once more sealed the fate of the extreme right. After the new asylum legislation went into force in July 1993, the level of extreme-right violence strongly declined, although it remained at a higher level than in the 1980s. The extreme-right parties likewise lost ground, and in the national elections of 1994 they were again reduced to marginal proportions (1.9%). Apart from preemption (or substantive success), increased repression also played a role in explaining this decline (see Koopmans 1996b). Almost simultaneously with the restriction of the right to asylum, the most important extraparliamentary organizations of the extreme right were banned, and new legislation prohibiting the display of neo-Nazi symbols was adopted. In addition, the extreme-right parties were subjected to increased surveillance by the internal security services, and active members were threatened with exclusion from public service employment.

Again, from the point of view of movement outcomes, the picture is ambiguous. As a result of the strong ethnic component in the German discourse and institutional practice of citizenship and national identity, the ethnic-nationalist demands of the extreme right had a considerable impact on the content of immigration and foreign politics, through a mixture of preemption and responses to actual mobilization. At the same time, the political opportunity structure for the access of the extreme right to the polity was closed and repressive. To put it in Gamson's terms, while the German extreme right has been quite successful in gaining *new advantages*—and preventing the loss of existing advantages tied to Germany's ethnic conception of citizenship—it has not even come close to gaining *acceptance* as a legitimate actor within the political system.

There is one further element that contributes to the explanation of the relative weakness of the German extreme right that sheds a more positive light on the German political culture and that stands in contrast to the Italian situation. Over the course of West Germany's development, an important civic-political component of national identity has grown up next to—and in mostly latent opposition to—the ethnic-cultural tradition. If one compares recent public opinion data to those from the 1950s, Germany, or at least its western part, has experienced a shift in political culture that, in the light of the country's history, has a revolutionary quality. Levels of satisfaction with democracy and support for its institutions, as well as levels of political participation and interest now, can stand a comparison with those in the classical liberal democracies (see Klingemann and Fuchs 1995). While in the 1950s the large majority of respondents who were asked to name "the best period in German history" still mentioned the authoritarian empire or even the Third Reich, and the economic system and "national traits" *(Volkseigenschaften)* were mentioned as the main sources of "national pride," there is now wide support for the liberal democracy of the Federal Republic as the best system Germany has ever had (Greiffenhagen 1984). Thus, a new, civic form of national identification has developed, which has been labeled *Verfassungspatriotismus* (constitutional patriotism). Although more recently, as in most European countries, dissatisfaction with the political system and especially with the political parties has risen somewhat, *Politikverdrossenheit* in Germany is comparatively limited and not nearly as widespread as in countries such as Belgium, Austria, or—as we will see—Italy.

All this, however, is clearly more true for the former West Germany than for the eastern part of the country, whose inhabitants have hardly any experience with democracy and where dissatisfaction with the political system is more widespread as a result of the social and economic dislocations accompanying the process of unification. This is certainly one of the reasons for the greater virulence of extreme-right violence in the East. On the party-political level, however, the extreme right has not so far succeeded in making important inroads among the East German electorate. Rather, antisystemic critique is channeled by the Party of Democratic Socialism (PDS), the successor party to the East German Communist Party, which takes a clear pro-foreigner stance rooted in the traditions of socialist antifascism and internationalism. How stable this incorporation of antisystemic sentiments by the extreme left will be is an open question. It is not unthinkable that a prolongation of the economic crisis in the former East Germany will offer opportunities for the extreme right to capture part of this potential.

Nevertheless, for the moment we may conclude that while the ethnic-cultural components of national identity offer discursive opportunities to some of the ethnocentric ideas of the extreme right, the strong identification of the large majority of the German people *and* the political elite with the democratic political system has erected a strong barrier against that part of extreme-right discourse which is directed against liberal democracy. If there is room for an extreme right in Germany, it would be one that combines a strong identification with democracy inasfar as it applies to ethnic Germans, with an exclusive strategy with regard to people of foreign origin. The point, of course, is that, if one can still call this an extreme right, Germany has it already: the program described in the previous sentence is pretty much institutional practice and is part and parcel of the politics of the established conservatives.

Italy: The Surprising March of the Extreme Right through the Institutions

In 1994, the extreme right achieved a level of electoral success in Italy that was unprecedented in the European context. The Movimento Sociale Italiano–Destra Nazionale (MSI-DN) and the Lega Nord (Northern League) became the first parties of the extreme right to be democratically elected and to serve as junior partners in a coalition government. Rather than dismissing these events as Italian exceptionalism, we argue that the factors that produced such unusually successful outcomes—gaining "acceptance" for the extreme right—shed light on the general conditions that influence the potential for political mobilization by this type of collective actor. The following discussion refers to three historical phases of extreme-right mobilization in postwar Italy: the period of the First Republic; the collapse of the First Republic and the 1994 elections; and the period of the emergent Second Republic after the 1994 election.

The civic basis of the political culture of the First Republic has long been in disrepute with political scientists, comprehensively failing the tests of civic culture theorists, who have labeled it as moved by alienation or irrational beliefs or as oriented toward objects that at present do not exist (La Palombara 1965; Almond and Verba 1963). This one-sided view of Italian political culture fails to explain the enduring character of the political system of the First Republic and the reason why, despite a continuously unrivaled high level of dissatisfaction with democracy in Europe,[6] successive electorates continued to grant sufficient legitimacy to the practices of the political system. One structural factor accounting for the stability of the political system despite this "legitimacy gap" is economic success and a growing standard of living. After the economic crisis of 1974–75, Italy's gross domestic product (GDP) grew by more than 50 percent between 1976 and 1990, six percentage points above the average of the European member states (Ginsborg 1996: 21). Indeed, in longitudinal opinion data on the levels of overall life satisfaction, Italians register levels of satisfaction similar to the rest of Europe (Morlino and Tarchi 1996: 49).

The paradox of the survival of the political system despite a permanent legitimacy gap is partly explained by the relationship between the Christian-Democratic (DC)-dominated state and its citizens. The clientelistic structuring of relationships within a state monopolized by a center-party identity meant that people defined their interests in the parties and not the state. Even supporters of the ruling parties were able to blame the nation-state, on a civic basis, for its overall lack of provision, while remaining faithful to party allegiance. These factors relativize the claim of civic culture theorists that Italian political culture was "irrational," and enable us to identify a southern European or Mediterranean variant for civic values.

It is worth mentioning that, compared to Germany, the official morality expressed in the constitution of the First Republic was a legitimate expression of a tradition for resistance to fascism. Whereas German *Verfassungspatriotismus* was a later development, it was an ever-present though subordinate cultural code in the Italian First Republic that was kept alive by prominent intellectuals of the "resistance generation" (Ginsborg 1996).

The First Republic, dominated for forty-five years by the Christian Democrats, systematically excluded the ideological poles of left and right from the process of internal party bargaining that formed the many coalition governments. The power of the DC was consolidated by a series of ad hoc strategies for preemption against the excluded poles of left and right and an ideology that promoted national unity by shifting from antifascism to anti-communism. At the national level there were few institutional opportunities for the MSI, though there were limited chances at the local level of politics. The strict proportional basis of the Italian electoral system meant that the MSI retained a permanent presence in the Parliament and Senate and was able to exert influence at the debate and committee levels of policy making.[7] From 1953 to 1994, the MSI, drawing its membership, lineage, and heritage from the Fascist Salo Republic, gained between 4.5% and 8.7% of the vote at national elections. This achievement was on the basis of a set of policies that were explicitly neofascist: ethnic nationalism; the authority principle; law and order; demand for an extended role of the state as the organizing principle for society; capital punishment and military deployment to enforce public order; and a rejection of the pluralism of party politics in the liberal democratic state. The ideological opponents of the MSI were clearly defined on the basis of the historical cleavage between fascism and communism. The presence of a large Communist Party (PCI) made the internal "threat of communism" a galvanizing identity for the MSI during the cold-war period.

Whereas institutional opportunities for exerting power were highly restricted, the political demands of the MSI were preempted by the fervent
cold-war anticommunism of the Christian Democrats and the lack of legitimacy for a "failed" fascist model for society. The postwar success of the DC
was based on a strong law-and-order platform. Indeed, the inability of the
MSI to organize the mobilization of the *Fronte dell'Uomo Qualunque,* a
populist, antipolitical movement that enjoyed a brief success in the immediate postwar period, was due to the preemptive tactics of the DC (Tarchi
1996). The retention of political power at the ideological center by the DC
created a political space on the right that the MSI was able to fill only in
times of political crisis. It is not by chance that the peak of electoral support
for the MSI occurred in 1972, in the wake of protests and strikes by students
and trade unions. In the 1970s and early 1980s, intense spirals of extraparliamentary mobilization, violent clashes between youths, and organized
street violence were characteristic of the conflict between left and right radicals (della Porta 1992). While undoubtedly linked to the right-wing activists
in these waves of violent mobilization, and later to the terrorists pursuing a
"strategy of tension," the parliamentary wing of the MSI initiated an "entry-
ist" strategy from the 1970s onward. It adopted the veneer of a rhetoric of
liberal pluralism and attempted to work within the political framework,
while retaining explicit links to the cultural heritage of fascism committed to
the overthrow of liberal democracy (Griffin 1996). Nonetheless, the ruling
powers of the "partycratic" state remained unconvinced of the MSI's liberal
democratic credentials. If it is judged by the political bargaining power of its
organizational resources in the political system, the MSI was an irrelevance.
Throughout the First Republic, the MSI existed as a marginalized outpost
for ideologically motivated radicals who were committed to the ideals of
Italian fascism. The success of the preemptive strategies of Christian Democracy reduced the framing potential of the MSI's political ideology to a
ghetto of "nostalgia for fascism."[8]

Systematic exclusion and cultural alienation from the governing political framework limited opportunities for the MSI to develop the credentials
of a New Right, even when the integrative capacity of the centrist partycratic
state was challenged in the 1980s by waves of social protest (della Porta
1996). However, one protest actor that did emerge in this period, an antisystemic challenger to the state and an important carrier of ethnic codes of
identity, was the set of northern regionalist movements.

In the early stage of their development, the regional protest movements,
such as the Liga Veneta, expressed an "ethnolocal" collective identity against
the central economic power of the state. Their demand for economic au-

tonomy attributed an ethnic basis to the territorial idea of belonging (Diamanti 1993; D'Amato and Schieder 1995). They "imagined" a local community joined by primordial ties in opposition to the civic identity of the Italian state. Under Umberto Bossi's leadership, the Lega Lombarda contrasted the supposedly hardworking and productive qualities of the Lombardy people with the corrupt central state and southern Italians, who were stigmatized by the pejorative term *terrone* and branded as lazy and dependent. This ethnocentric basis for an antisystemic challenge fed off the tradition of racism and discrimination against southern Italians and also translated into intolerance against the cultural otherness of immigrants and homosexuals.[9] The thematization of the ethnic difference of immigrants by the Lega Lombarda coincided with the first wave of violence and intolerance against foreigners in Italy.[10]

In time, these relatively autonomous expressions of local belonging were extended to a more politically strategic formulation, where the region was defined as a "community of interests." The territorial boundaries for inclusion in the political community were extended to the whole of the north of Italy with the formation of the Northern League in 1990. This formula provided the basis for the electoral success of the League in 1992, when it gained 25.5% of the vote in the Veneto region and 23.6% of the vote in Lombardy. The League waged a campaign against the penetration of the central state into the local economy and society. It advocated federalism by threatening secession and attacked the corrupt and clientelist basis of the partycratic system.

It is beyond our scope to analyze the factors that caused the collapse of the First Republic. However, the collapse of the partycratic regime may be seen as the outcome of the inability of a state formed on the logic of patronage and internal division of resources to find a legitimate basis for regulating conflicts over social redistribution (Statham 1996a, 1996b). Domestic public spending was out of control, exacerbated by the corrupt and profligate excesses of the political elite during the economic boom of the 1980s, and in September 1992 the lira crashed. Italy's status in Europe seemed threatened by its almost certain exclusion from the European Monetary Union (Ginsborg 1996). The integrative capacities of the partycratic state, which had survived despite the long-standing legitimacy gap of a weak civic culture, finally gave way. The collapse of the First Republic became ritualized into a national spectacle by the televised *tangentopoli* trials of corrupt politicians, public servants, and businesspeople. By mid-1993, 447 members of Parliament were being investigated for bribes totaling L 620 billion, 90 percent of which was allegedly paid to the ruling Christian Democratic and Socialist (PSI) Parties (Statham 1996b).

In addition to the institutional opportunities that the collapse of the First Republic presented to the League and the MSI, the cleavage and uncertainty within a political culture that had been dominated for so long by Christian-Democratic hegemony offered discursive opportunities for challengers to introduce frame alignment processes into the dominant representations for political ideas. After the void in political culture caused by the collapse of the state, a rare period of competition emerged between the prospective challengers to fill the identity gap on the right of the political spectrum.

Paradoxically, the MSI had defined its interests within the survival of the political system that had excluded it in the postwar period. In 1993, the MSI unsuccessfully opposed the changes in the electoral system that were proposed by the referendum movement, fearing the ignominy of disappearance in a move away from strictly proportional representation. Changes in Italian political culture, in particular the collapse of communism and the reformation of the PCI into a democratic party, reduced the antisystemic neofascist challenge of the MSI to the anachronistic qualities of a cult. In contrast to the League, the challenger claims of the MSI had little relevance to the structural and institutional crisis. Even when the MSI stood in the 1994 election under the label Alleanza Nazionale, its policies were nothing new—they had a clear fascist heritage: a form of presidentialism based on direct referenda instead of Parliament; a tutelary role for the state in the national economy; and an internationally negotiated unification to bring Fiume, Istria, and Dalmatia back to Italy. The challenge of the League, in contrast, offered a more radical critique of the failings of the nation-state. The League's policies advocated a federalist and a neoliberal approach to society, the economy, and government by stressing local autonomy for fiscal measures and direct participation in democratic processes (Sznajder 1995).

The institutional opportunities for the League and the MSI to succeed in elections and to gain access to government were provided by Silvio Berlusconi's attempt to regroup a center-right from the debris of Christian Democracy. He achieved this by making electoral pacts with the two extreme-right challengers. Berlusconi's Forza Italia party was designed and marketed like a commercial product through his television network within a few weeks (Statham 1996a, 1996b). In the March 1994 election, Forza Italia gained 21% of the vote, the Alleanza Nazionale 13.5%, and the Northern League 8.4%, to form the first government of the Second Republic. By forming these two alliances, Berlusconi regrouped the center-right in a strategy designed to keep out the left and to promote market interests. A side effect of this strategy was to make the extreme-right "challengers" into "members" of the political system. In Gamson's terms, they gained "acceptance," and they would have the potential to exert real power.

Berlusconi's establishment of the "pole for good government" alliance with the MSI was a co-optative strategy for appropriating the political identity resources of national solidarity and a commitment to law and order and the family. By historical irony, the political exclusion of the MSI meant that it could claim to be the one party that had kept "clean hands" in the First Republic. Berlusconi's public recognition of the MSI as a legitimate coalition partner was the factor that enabled the organization to leave the ghetto of isolation within Italian political culture. Under the strong leadership of Gianfranco Fini, the MSI declared an era of "postfascism" at the Fiuggi Conference in 1995 and attempted to define a mainstream future role in the political system.[11]

Berlusconi's "Pole for Freedom" alliance with the League was co-optative with regard to the neoliberal economic critique of the state but preemptive with regard to the threat of secession or northern autonomy. The nationalism of the MSI, which achieved high electoral support in the south of Italy, is the ideological opponent of the northern separatism of the League. Berlusconi's attempt to consolidate the center-right by dealing with these two different and ideologically opposed extreme-right challengers, was successful at the election but proved unmanageable in office, when the League's defection brought down the government after eight months.

The electoral success of the MSI and the Lega in 1994, compared to other challengers for replacing the Christian Democracy on the right, can be attributed to the institutional opportunities provided by the coalition with Berlusconi.[12] Once the League and the MSI (under its new form, Alleanza Nazionale) had become members of the political system in the emergent Second Republic, the potential for them to exert influence over policy decisions increased. This has become an especially important factor with regard to political issues for which the two parties are able to mobilize the types of ethnocentric claims that were taboo in the political culture of the First Republic. In particular, the mobilization of the League and the MSI has contributed to making the presence of immigrants into a political issue concerning the citizenship rights of inclusion and exclusion for the culturally different. Previously, the Italian state tended to treat the presence of illegal immigrants in the labor market as a technical matter requiring better administrative regulation.

In 1995, the League blatantly politicized immigration as a social problem at the national level by refusing to pass the budget for Dini's technocratic government unless highly restrictive measures were brought in against immigrants.[13] Seeking to profit from a hostile climate toward immigrants, which was sparked by the high media profile of the rape of an Italian woman by two illegal immigrants, the League and the MSI were both active in mobilizing local communities in Milan, Florence, and Turin against immigrant quarters and settlements of nomads. At the national level, the League utilized the precarious balance of power at the time of the technocratic government to challenge the existing policy norms for immigrants. Under the Martelli Law of 1990, Italian immigration policy had followed a logic of social integration. These policy norms were contested by the League with claims that stigmatized the illegal immigrants present in Italy as "criminals."[14] The League's demands included that clandestine immigrants be expelled and immediately accompanied to the border; that those caught trying to reenter be given a prison sentence of up to three years; and that the state have the power to administer a prison sentence of up to six months for people who refused to show documentation. The Dini Decree (n. 489, November 18, 1995) did not accede to all of the League's demands, but it nonetheless introduced by far the most restrictive policy measures to date against immigrants.

This example shows that the relative shift from challenger to member status has given the extreme right a greater potential for thematizing issues of cultural difference into political conflicts over citizenship rights. It is on topics such as immigration that the League and the MSI have come closest to the ideal of receiving a "full response" to their political demands. The demands of the extreme right do not translate directly into policy outcomes, but its ability to mobilize the public through movement networks and to achieve media attention for these contentious topics sets a public agenda to which other political actors are forced to respond. In the Italian case, one likely outcome of the politicization of immigration is a greater social and cultural exclusion of immigrants and ethnic minorities. This occurs in a society that has previously exhibited a tolerance of foreigners relative to other European countries. It is worth noting that the framing that has been carried into Italian culture through the immigration debate distinguishes between Italians and *extracomunitari*. In the 1990s, "extracommunitarian" has become a pejorative category for those who are excluded from membership in the national community, whereas the weak civic culture of Italian citizenship is bolstered as an identity by reference to citizenship within the European Union. The demands of the League were an important supplier of the "cultural tools" for this frame alignment in the national conception of citizenship.

Conclusion

In our view, these two case studies confirm the usefulness of analytically dis-tinguishing between the realm of symbolic interaction and the strategic in-teraction between challengers and members of a polity. Political opportuni-ties, in the narrow institutional sense, are certainly important for explaining the mobilization success of the Italian extreme right, and its acceptance as a partner in government, within the context of the collapse of Italy's tradition-al party system. Likewise, the failure of the German extreme right to pene-trate the political system can be related to the restrictive hurdles in the elec-toral system and the repression that confronts its organizations and activists. Nonetheless, using only this approach, we would have missed an important part of the picture. The introduction of the notion of a discursive opportu-nity structure within the symbolic realm has enabled us to account for the reason why, despite its exclusion from the polity, the German extreme right has had a considerable impact on official politics. This influence occurred more often through the mechanism of preemption rather than as a result of the pressure of actual mobilization. Similarly, the less conducive discursive opportunities for ethnic nationalist challengers in Italy help explain why the impact of the participation of the Alleanza Nazionale, the heir of prewar fas-cism, in government has remained relatively limited in substantive terms. In the context of the recent immigration debate, it was the ethnic regionalist challenge of the Northern League that was able to gain the most impact from the combination of discursive and institutional opportunities. We may relate such different combinations of discursive and institutional opportuni-ties to the four types of outcomes distinguished by Gamson (1990: 29), as shown in figure 1.

If discursive and institutional opportunities are not available, the chal-lenger will find no support for its ideas and demands, nor will it be able to gain access to the polity. Though not necessarily leading to the challenger's collapse, as suggested by Gamson's label, the movement will at least be con-fined to an existence in the cultural and political margins. Where discursive opportunities are available but the political system is closed, the challenger will be able to exert some influence on the public discourse but cannot es-tablish itself as an active participant in the political game (as is the case in Germany). The most likely strategy followed by the political elite in this case will be preemption by taking up those demands and frames of the challenger which do not conflict with dominant interests and cultural codes, while simultaneously excluding or even repressing the challenger as a collective actor. In the opposite situation, with institutional opportunities available but

Figure1. Relation between discursive and institutional opportunities and movement outcomes

		Open	Closed
Institutional Opportunity Structure	Open	Full response	Co-optation
	Closed	Preemption	Collapse/ marginalization

Discursive Opportunity Structure

with unfavorable discursive opportunities, the most likely response will be co-optation. This elite strategy gives some access to the polity to those elements of the movement which are willing to adhere to the prevailing rules of the game, but this leads to few substantive concessions. Full response, in which the challenger gets both access and concessions, can be achieved only when opportunities are available in both the institutional and the discursive realms. In the 1990s, the situation of the Italian extreme right has at times come close to this ideal combination of opportunities—for example, in the case of the Northern League at the time of the political debate on immigration. However, the limited overall impact on official politics even when the Alleanza Nazionale and the League were members of the government shows that there were important co-optative elements, too.

To summarize, both discursive and institutional opportunities are necessary, but, on their own, they are insufficient preconditions for a truly successful challenge. An open discursive opportunity structure may give rise to a counterculture and may diffuse sentiments of dissatisfaction within the population, which may in turn have some effect on the strategies of the political elite, but this process will benefit a challenging social movement only when combined with opportunities on the institutional level. Conversely, an opening up of institutional opportunities, for instance, in the form of a political crisis, will increase the chances of success for those challengers which can build on available discursive opportunities. These opportunities are a necessary precondition for a challenger, so that its frames and collective actions may figure as a credible and legitimate alternative to the established political order.

Apart from these general theoretical points, a number of conclusions can be drawn from our discussion regarding the ways in which a further increase in the strength and influence of the extreme right in European politics might be prevented. In our view, the most adequate response does not lie in the strategic realm of repression or exclusion from the polity. As the German case shows, the extreme right can have a damaging impact on the relation between indigenous and immigrant communities without having direct access to the polity. A more important and effective strategy for European policy makers would be to strengthen the civic bases for national identity and citizenship and to withstand the temptation to revive ethnic cultural definitions of nationhood. Unfortunately, many European countries have recently been confronted with corruption scandals and evidence of governmental incompetence, Italy being perhaps the most notorious, but certainly not the only, example. Such developments, of course, are not suited to strengthening the idea of the nation as a political community, and it is therefore no coincidence that the extreme right has been most successful in those countries where the political system has been discredited most (e.g., Italy, Belgium, Austria, and France). In addition, the continuing breakdown of the welfare state threatens to lead to the development of an underclass with minimal social citizenship rights. Again, the probable outcome of such a process is a strengthening of ethnic-nationalist sources of collective identity that fill the void created by the erosion of civic-political mechanisms of inclusion.

Questions like these will most likely become more relevant for the construction of conceptions of European identity and citizenship, which currently lags far behind the process of European integration on the economic level. At present, the oligarchic decision-making structures within the EU, its closure to citizens' direct participation and influence, and the underdevelopment of a social component accompanying economic integration are hardly suited to stimulate the development of a civic-political sense of European identity. Instead, policies aimed at preventing immigration from outside the EU have heralded the advent of "Fortress Europe" and the differentiation, within each of the individual countries, between two classes of foreigners with different citizenship rights ("extracommunitarians," in contradistinction to those from other EU countries). In the long term, such developments threaten to promote an ethnic definition of the imagined community of "Union-Europeans" with the latent potential for translating into chauvinist sentiments and discrimination at the national and local levels.

Notes

1. The limitations of such attempts can easily be demonstrated for the case at hand. If the correspondence of the ethnonationalist frame of the extreme right with objective threats to the ethnic integrity of the nation were important, we would expect the

extreme right to be strong where the influx and size of the foreign population is large, that is, in Germany (with 7.6% foreigners in 1992) and not in Italy (with only 0.9% foreigners in 1992; Eurostat 1994: 8).

2. The detailed explanation of other forms of extreme-right mobilization, which often take the form of violence against ethnic minorities and immigrants, would require a separate study, in which the presence or absence of strong extreme-right parties would be one of the explanatory variables (see Koopmans 1996d).

3. These two hypotheses are formulated separately since, as we argue in the next section, conceptions of nationhood are usually a mixture of ethnic and civic elements that do not necessarily relate to each other in a zero-sum way. Note also that we use a broad conception of social movements, which may include conventional party activities as well as unorganized violence. In this view, the distinctive view of a social movement is its position as a challenging outsider vis-à-vis the political system—a position that is often, but not necessarily, linked to a reliance on extra-institutional forms of mobilization.

4. Here we take on the notion of "frame alignment" proposed by Diani (1996). The traditional notion of frame alignment (Snow et al. 1986; Tarrow 1994) defines the linking process from the values of a movement organization to the culture of potential constituents. Diani proposes instead that the concept of frame alignment be limited to "the integration of mobilizing messages with dominant representations of the political environment." This definition is preferable for our present purpose, as it locates the outcomes of framing processes within the context of political culture, which is defined as an interactive field rather than the property of one collective actor.

5. The observation 'We have made Italy; now we must make Italians' by the statesman Massimo d'Azeglio 135 years ago has been an often-repeated and resonant self-criticism within Italian political culture (Griffin 1997).

6. Between 1973 and 1993, the percentage of Italians who were rather dissatisfied or very dissatisfied with the working of democracy was always more than 24% higher than the percentage in other EC countries (Morlino and Tarchi 1996: 47). In the 1987 Eurobarometer poll 27, only 30.7% of Italians responded that they were very or fairly satisfied with the functioning of democracy in their country, which was the lowest percentage among the twelve member states. In contrast, West Germany ranked second only to Luxembourg, with 78% of West Germans expressing satisfaction with democracy (Flickinger and Studlar 1992: 9).

7. The presence in Parliament did provide a limited potential for disruptive influence. For example, Veugelers (1994: 42) notes that the MSI, acting with the PRI, tabled more than sixty amendments in Parliament in an initial attempt to disrupt the passage of the proposed law on immigration in 1989.

8. The position of the neofascist MSI in the First Republic is well characterized by the titles of two studies: *Il polo escluso,* "The excluded pole" (Ignazi 1989); and *Cinquant'anni di nostalgia,* "Fifty years of nostalgia" (Tarchi 1995).

9. According to official figures, levels of racist violence against immigrants has been low in Italy compared to other European countries. This fact has contributed to the official myth that, as a country with a tradition of emigration, Italians are tolerant of mi-

grants (Balbo and Manconi 1992). However, there has been a long history in the north of Italy of incidents of discrimination and xenophobic violence committed against southern Italian migrants, which somewhat discredits this myth. As recently as 1989, a southern immigrant was beaten to death by northerners (Ford 1991: 67).

10. The official figures of the Ministry of the Interior, based on police records for acts of violence and intolerance against foreigners, indicate a clear peak in 1990 (OECD 1995). The "late" appearance of waves of xenophobic mobilization against immigrants in Italy can be attributed to the relatively low numbers of foreign immigrants—1.4% of the population, compared to 8.2% in Germany, 6.4% in France, and 3.3% in the United Kingdom in 1990 (Organization for Economic Cooperation and Development 1992: 131)—and the relatively late influx of immigrants compared to northern European countries. Italy became a country of net immigration for the first time only in the 1980s.

11. Griffin's excellent analysis of the Fiuggi text (1996) identifies how a reference to fascist heritage is combined with a prognosis of the Italian crisis in the organization's ideological shift from the MSI to the AN. The transformation of the MSI has been at the level of political identity and not organizational structure and personnel, which have remained largely unchanged (Ignazi 1995). Also, the values of its members have been shown to differ considerably from those of its electoral supporters (Baldini and Vignati 1996; Tarchi 1996).

12. The failure of a party such as La Rete, which was formed on the civic basis of public morality against the corruption of the state and the Mafia, indicates that the demise of the First Republic was a case of regime collapse rather than the outcome of a challenge by a social movement. The *tangentopoli* crusade was carried by a small counter-elite of magistrates. The inability of La Rete to transform this challenge into a viable political movement bears testimony to the weak civic basis of Italian culture.

13. The League brought down Berlusconi's government and reverted to an anti-systemic critique after eight months in 1994. The Berlusconi government was replaced by a technocratic government that was supported effectively by the left alliance and the League. This gave the League considerable bargaining power to influence legislation.

14. The clandestine status of so many immigrants in Italy was due to the administrative and policy failings of a state that had accepted the benefits of migrant labor without defining the rights of migrants. In this sense the presence of illegal immigrants was officially accepted as normal in the First Republic and was considered a problem only insofar as it required better regulation.

Conclusion

From Interactions to Outcomes in Social Movements

Charles Tilly

Born in Turkey, Benali Kalkan entered France without regular papers in 1982. During the next few years he started his own business, worked in a legally declared enterprise, developed fluency in French, and married a Frenchwoman. But he did not acquire legal residence in France. Within a decade of arrival, as a consequence, he became a major player in a vivid political drama.

In 1989, the French government responded in a characteristic way to European Community (EC) agreements on immigration, to increased demands for asylum by immigrants from outside the EC, and to the right-wing National Front's exploitation of anti-immigrant sentiments: the government declared it would expedite its processing of asylum applications and rapidly expel clandestine immigrants who did not qualify. That move threatened unauthorized residents such as Benali Kalkan. Immediately, leaders of an established network of associations concerned with questions of immigration and asylum began consulting, mobilizing, and agitating in favor of countermeasures. Rejected applicants for asylum came to association headquarters asking for help. In response, the associations in question collectively created services for the Rejected *(déboutés)* and started to solicit public officials on their behalf.

Soon immigration activists and ethnic leaders were organizing a social movement in the French style: holding public meetings, drawing in trade unions, seeking media coverage, and above all addressing demands, public and otherwise, to agents of the national state. By 1991, their demands centered on wholesale acceptance of all the Rejected who had arrived in France before 1990 as well as full review of dossiers for all later comers. Simultaneously, leaders organized immigrant constituencies by occupation and by national origin, with Turks and Haitians prominent among the activists. Local organizations formed national federations aimed at the government in Paris.

And Benali Kalkan? Threatened with expulsion from the country by Bordeaux police, he began a hunger strike—a strategy already familiar to imprisoned militant Turks as a way of putting pressure on their jailers. Soon twenty-four other Turks joined him. The archbishop of Bordeaux provided the city's hunger strikers with a room, hence with symbolic and material support from the Catholic Church. Connected to the national federation of associations "in solidarity with immigrants" by a federation representative who was then vacationing in Bordeaux, the local strikers soon had counterparts in Alès, Audincourt, Val-de-Reuil, Saint-Dizier, Mulhouse, Strasbourg . . . and of course Paris.

As Johanna Siméant (from whose detailed study of the movement I have constructed my story) says, resort to hunger strikes

> seems to have been dictated by the meager resources and support to which the Rejected had access, and whose effectiveness they had to maximize. For the Rejected, with little money, rarely having cultural capital readily expendable in France, often living in marginal housing, their principal resources lay in support from associations devoted to solidarity with foreigners and refugees, which in general provided their chief contacts with members of the receiving society. (1993: 194)

Hunger strikes had multiple effects. They

- restored the then-faltering support of solidarity associations for the Rejected;
- provided imitable models for action elsewhere;
- defined a strategy whereby church officials could easily collaborate on humanitarian grounds rather than by making a declared political choice;
- drew sympathy and support from bystanders;
- attracted media attention; and thus
- publicized the cause on a national scale.

The choice of hunger strikes (as compared, say, with militant demonstrations, attacks on public buildings or officials, strikes at workplaces, or mass petition drives) also permitted tacit cooperation of public officials, both in day-to-day policing of the strikers and in a general redefinition of the problem as more humanitarian than legal.

When impatient Bordeaux city officials did try to break up the strike, the archbishop arrived in time to station himself inside as police broke down the door, strikers chained themselves together while refusing transfer to a hospital, and national television cameras filmed the whole episode. Soon the national government was agreeing to postpone all expulsions for three months and to improve screening procedures. On May 25, 1991, during the talks that produced the provisional agreement, about ten thousand demonstrators marched through Paris on behalf of—and including many of—the Rejected.

The focus on hunger strikes posed problems for negotiators at the national level. It involved association activists in monitoring and manipulating risky local events, gave exceptional leverage to a small number of strikers, and greatly limited national leaders' room to maneuver. Hunger strikers understandably insisted on their right to decide the risks they would run, while their national spokespersons understandably claimed superior knowledge of what would actually move the government. Representatives of solidarity associations, negotiating with governmental officials and scenting victory, but fearing the consequences of a death among the hunger strikers, pressed the martyrs to suspend their fasts pending the outcome of negotiations. Many strikers, however, held fiercely to the advantage and autonomy afforded them by sacrifice, at least for a few more days.

Finally national leaders prevailed; most local hunger strikes ended on May 28. But representatives of associations continued to bargain with the government. The result was a governmental decree on July 23, 1991. The decree fell far short of the associations' maximum demands, especially for the majority of asylum seekers who had arrived beginning in 1989. But by the time of the decree, the movement was already disintegrating. As rearguard actions, new rounds of hunger strikes occurred from September to December 1991, in early 1992, then again in September 1992. None of them significantly affected governmental policy. By the last round, indeed, the government had acquired sufficient confidence to break up hunger strikes by force.

Benali Kalkan, his Turkish fellow strikers, the archbishop of Bordeaux, a variety of public officials, television reporters, self-selected members of the French public, and a network of activists extending across France were engaging in a recognizable social movement, a campaign for changes in the state treatment of illegal immigrants. Although this book concerns not causes but outcomes of social movements, there is no way to trace outcomes of such complex social processes without having robust descriptions and explanations of their operations. I will try to show why this is true. I will also try to show what sort of explanation of a social movement makes sense in the present very incomplete state of knowledge about cause and effect in social movements.

In order to describe and explain what was happening in the French solidarity movement and in social movements at large, we must clear away two mistaken ideas. For reasons that will turn out to be crucial to an explanation of the social action involved, social movement activists themselves promulgate these mistaken ideas more or less deliberately. The first idea is that social movements are solidaristic, coherent groups, rather than clusters of performances. The second is that social movements have continuous, self-contained life histories in somewhat the same sense that individuals and organizations have life histories.

Both ideas are false, or at least very misleading. Although social movements often activate existing groups and create agreed-upon stories about their pasts, no analyst should imagine that the groups and the stories constitute the movement, any more than someone who watches a soccer match should imagine it as a single team's solo performance, for all the stories she can tell about that team's glorious past or previous iterations of a given cup final. A match becomes a match through the interaction of two teams, the referees, and the spectators, not to mention coaches, reporters, and league officials. Social movements similarly consist of bounded, contingent, interactive performances by multiple and changing actors.

Social movements have not always existed. If we identify them with the forms of interaction that were visible in the French solidarity mobilization of 1989–1992—the formation of associations and federations, public displays of determination and connectedness such as hunger strikes and demonstrations, encounters with public officials via mass media and closed negotiations, appeals to uninvolved citizens for support, and so on—then no social movements occurred anywhere before the nineteenth century. Even if we insist on parallels in such mobilizations as the Protestant Reformation or rebellions against successive Chinese dynasties, we must recognize that social movements happened rarely before 1800, then became standard political performances in Western Europe and North America before spreading to other parts of the globe. Yet they rapidly took their place among ways of making collective claims in the expanding world of parliamentary democracy.

Social movements took shape in close conjunction with two other clusters of performances that likewise deploy groups and histories but do not consist of groups and their histories: electoral campaigns and interest-group politics. Indeed, social movements gain some of their effectiveness as modes of claim-making from their potential bearing on electoral campaigns and interest-group politics. Although the three differ in timing, organization, co-ordination, and participants, they all qualify as campaigns in the sense that they are socially connected, clustered performances oriented to the same set of collective claims.

While electoral campaigns, interest-group politics, and social movements do not consist of continuous, self-contained life histories in the same sense that organisms do, they do lay down coherent histories within their boundaries. In that regard, they resemble wars, revolutions, soccer matches, street fairs, and jam sessions. None of them is a self-generating group and all of them involve complex encounters among changing actors, yet in all of them what happens early constrains what happens later. That chroniclers and theorists, then, sometimes cast their stories of wars, revolutions, and the rest as unfolding natural histories resembling the lives of violets, clams, or bacilli should not confuse us, the analysts of social movements.

How, then, will we recognize a social movement when we see one? It consists of *a sustained challenge to power holders in the name of a population living under the jurisdiction of those power holders by means of repeated public displays of that population's worthiness, unity, numbers, and commitment.* At a minimum, social movements involve continuous interaction between chal-lengers and power holders. The claim-making usually engages third parties such as other power holders, repressive forces, allies, competitors, and the citizenry as a whole. Such a definition excludes coups d'état, civil wars, in-surrections, feuds, and many other forms of contentious politics. It includes some interactions that overlap with industrial conflict, electoral campaigns, and interest-group politics, but by no means exhausts those domains; many an election, for example, proceeds without either sustained challenges to power holders or repeated public displays of worthiness, unity, numbers, and commitment.

No social movement is self-contained. None operates without involve-ment of at least three distinguishable populations: power holders who are the objects of claims, the minimum claim being to tolerate the movement's existence; participants, who range from minor contributors to leaders and are often connected by social movement organizations; and a subject popu-lation on whose behalf participants are making or supporting claims. The three can of course overlap, as when activists come exclusively from the sub-ject population or when a populist power holder deserts his fellows to ally with popular claimants. But they can also remain quite distinct, as when antiabortionist activists claim to speak on behalf of the unborn. Most social movements also involve additional parties: countermovement activists, competing power holders, police, sympathetic citizens. Sustained claim-making interaction among the three defining parties—power holders, participants, subject population—plus any other parties that involve themselves in the interaction constitutes the social movement.

By proposing such a definition, I am not claiming for a moment that its elements specify all aspects of social movements that one might find interesting or even crucial to their operation, including the sorts of public identities that people adopt, the place of social networks in recruitment, and the relationship of social movement programs to social change in general. I am instead making a strong analytic claim: that clusters of events that the definition identifies operate according to similar cause-and-effect relationships, differ significantly, with respect to causal processes, from adjacent phenomena that the definition excludes, and are empirically distinguishable from their neighbors. Definitions cannot be true or false, but they can be more or less useful. Useful definitions point to empirical means of grouping together phenomena that have common causal properties and of distinguishing phenomena that differ significantly in causal properties. I claim utility for my definition of social movements on just such principles.

Many social movement analysts will reject this claim on the grounds that the proposed definition is too broad, too narrow, or centered on the wrong features of social movements—in short, that it fails to coincide with what interests them. The very prestige of social movements as objects of analysis has generated two sorts of definitional struggles: proposed extensions of the term to analogous phenomena that another age would have called rebellions, intellectual currents, religious revivals, or something else; and shifts of emphasis toward phenomena that frequently overlap with social movements, such as ideological change and identity construction.

Consider a remarkable example of the shift to identity construction. Reporting on feminist activism in Columbus, Ohio, from the 1960s to the 1990s, Nancy Whittier declares:

> In order to tap the full range of women's movement activity and to recognize its continuity over time, I propose to define the women's movement in terms of the collective identity associated with it rather than in terms of its formal organizations. We see the movement, then, not just through the organizations it establishes, but also through its informal networks and communities and in the diaspora of feminist individuals who carry the concerns of the movement into other settings. What makes these organizations, networks, and individuals part of a social movement is their shared allegiance to a set of beliefs, practices, and ways

of identifying oneself that constitute feminist collective identity. . . . A focus on collective identity underscores the constantly changing nature of all social movements and recognizes that struggle occurs, not just in confrontations with the State, but in culture and daily life as well. (1995: 23–24)

Social movements, to Whittier's eye, do not merely rely on structures and processes that promote collective identity, they consist of those structures and processes, rather than of claims or collective actions that the relevant structures, processes, and collective identities support. With such a definition, we are not surprised to find Whittier arguing that feminist movements center on successive generations of participants who reshape their shared identities through struggle and daily practice.

Whittier's definition of social movements as identity-creating structures and processes, however, confronts four analytical objections:

- It implicitly claims that "shared allegiance to a set of beliefs, practices, and ways of identifying oneself" constitutes a distinct causal domain, a debatable proposition that, at a minimum, deserves explication and defense.

- It lacks a criterion separating (1) the sorts of interaction Whittier describes in the case of Columbus, Ohio, feminist activists from (2) other situations such as household membership, religious affiliation, employment by paternalistic firms, or citizenship, all of which also involve shared allegiance to a set of beliefs, practices, and ways of identifying oneself, but which most analysts would reject as social movements; most analysts would deny, furthermore, that these other situations share strong causal properties with social movements.

- It allows a social movement to exist in the absence of any public challenge whatsoever.

- It makes Whittier's main argument—that social movements persist and evolve through periods of public inactivity—true by definition rather than an object of empirical inquiry.

Although (as will soon be apparent) Whittier is addressing a crucial problem that social movement theorists in my own political-process tradition have mishandled, I regard the four objections to her definition as insuperable. But, in any case, to propose a competing definition—Whittier's or someone

else's—engages the analyst in claiming the existence of a coherent causal domain; in delineating and justifying the boundary between that domain and
adjacent domains; in demonstrating that the definition is empirically work-
able; in identifying causal regularities that occur within the selected domain;
and in showing that those causal regularities explain problematic features of
the phenomena within that domain. Since no social-scientific legislature
or Supreme Court adjudicates definitions, all I can do is show that my proposed definition usefully identifies distinctive causal properties of social
movements, then move on to examine implications of those causal properties for analysis of social movement outcomes.

Again, my definition of a social movement: a sustained challenge to
power holders in the name of a population living under the jurisdiction of
those power holders by means of repeated public displays of that population's worthiness, unity, numbers, and commitment. In recent versions, the
displays of social movements thus identified include public meetings, demonstrations, marches, the creation of special-purpose associations and coalitions of associations, mass media statements, pamphlets, petitions, the post-
ing or wearing of identifying symbols, and the adoption of distinctive
slogans. In Western countries, these elements have coexisted since the early
nineteenth century. Although demonstrations occur only intermittently (and
sometimes not at all) in the course of social movements, demonstrations
nicely encapsulate the distinctive features of social movement displays: occupation of public spaces; engagements with authorities or their representations; projection of collective identities; expressions of support for shared
demands; and performances validating worthiness, unity, numbers, and
commitment.

To be sure, social movement participants carry on all sorts of activities
that look very different from demonstrations. Police and authorities regularly participate in social movement interactions, but rarely as challengers or
demonstrators. Activists often spend their energies planning joint actions,
building alliances, struggling with competitors, mobilizing supporters, building collective identities, searching for resources, lobbying, and pursuing
other activities to sustain collective challenges. These activities, however, do
not distinguish social movement interaction from a wide variety of other
contentious politics, including wars, electoral campaigns, and revolutionary
conspiracies. The distinguishing features of social movements lie in sustained challenges to authorities and responses by those authorities, during
which at least one challenger publicly displays WUNC: worthiness, unity,
numbers, and commitment.

WUNC matters. Since the emergence and spread of social movements as distinctive forms of popular contention, participants in social movements (including authorities, repressive forces, allies, rivals, and spectators) have implicitly adopted a standard scorecard for challenges according to the following formula:

strength = worthiness × unity × numbers × commitment

If any of these values falls to zero, strength likewise falls to zero; the challenge loses credibility. High values on one element, however, make up for low values on another. As the French hunger strikes illustrate, a small number of activists who display their worthiness, unity, and commitment by means of simultaneous risk or sacrifice often have as large an impact as a large number of people who sign a petition, wear a badge, or march through the streets on a sunny afternoon. Relevant codes run something like this:

> *Worthiness:* sobriety, propriety of dress, incorporation of priests and other dignitaries, endorsement of moral authorities, evidence of previous undeserved suffering
>
> *Unity:* uniforms, marching or dancing in unison, chanting of slogans, singing, cheering, linking of arms, wearing or bearing of common symbols, direct affirmation of a common program or identity
>
> *Numbers:* filling of public space, presentation of petitions, representations of multiple units (e.g., neighborhood associations), direct claims of numerical support by means of polls, membership inscriptions, and financial contributions
>
> *Commitment:* persistence in costly or risky activity, declarations of readiness to persevere, resistance to attack

With variation in the precise means used to display these characteristics (e.g., the partial displacement of identifying banners by signs on sticks late in the nineteenth century), emphasis on WUNC has persisted from early in social movement history. The chief deviations from the code have occurred in pursuit of visibility and in deliberate assertions of difference, as when members of dissident factions have broken the façade of unity by resisting marching orders or when gay militants have violated conventional standards of worthiness by cross-dressing.

Why and how does WUNC matter? An initially puzzling feature of social movement activity provides crucial clues. As compared with attacking a tax collector, expelling a worker who accepts below-standard wages, or selling off a high-priced baker's bread for less than the asking price, social movement interactions exhibit a huge peculiarity: even in principle, hardly ever could a single claim-making session accomplish the challenger's professed ends. At best, social movement claim-making promotes its program cumulatively over many simultaneous and/or repeated meetings, demonstrations, marches, petitions, statements, and other interactions with objects of claims. Taken strictly as means-end action on behalf of stated demands, social movement activity is inefficient, even self-defeating.

So why has the social movement persisted as a prominent form of popular politics for almost two centuries? Theorists of identity such as Nancy Whittier have intuited the correct answer but have misstated its implications. They have recognized that social movements pour much of their energy into the construction of shared identities, but they have supposed that identity construction occupies so much attention because of its inherent satisfactions or its direct utility to individual participants in social movements. Construction of shared identities often does attract and commit individuals to social movements. Yet for all the satisfaction and utility that participants may receive from identity construction, the crucial process accounting for the persistence of social movements as forms of public claim-making is actually collective and political.

Social movements couple the making of public claims with the creation, assertion, and political deployment of collective identities. Far more than attacks on tax collectors, expulsions of nonconforming workers, and seizures of high-priced grain, social movements effectively establish the presence of an important entity—and identity—in national politics. They assert the existence of a worthy, unified, numerous, committed, and aggrieved claimant. Those characteristics increase the plausibility of the implied threat that the claimant will use its weight to enter, realign, or disrupt the existing polity. Whence the historical conjunction of social movements with electoral campaigns and interest-group politics. From the Chartist challenge of the 1830s and 1840s to feminist and environmentalist challenges of our own time, social movement politics has depended on the assertion of public collective identities.

Despite the tales that social movement activists and analysts tell, those identities almost never exist in advance, simply waiting to be activated. Examined from the viewpoint of challengers, social movement effectiveness depends in part on two varieties of mystification. First, worthiness, unity, numbers, and commitment, as they increase, almost necessarily contradict each other; to gain numbers, for example, generally requires compromise on worthiness, unity, and/or commitment. The actual work of organizers consists recurrently of patching together provisional coalitions, suppressing risky tactics, negotiating which of the multiple agendas that participants bring with them will find public voice in their collective action, and, above all, hiding backstage struggle from public view. Organizers almost always exaggerate their coalition's worthiness, unity, numbers, and commitment. Organizers of France's movement of solidarity with the Rejected faced just such difficulties in holding their coalition together.

Second, movement activists seek to present themselves and (if different) the objects of their solicitude as an integrated group, preferably a group with a long history and with coherent existence outside the world of public claim-making. Despite powerful evidence to the contrary, organizers of the French solidarity movement sought to represent the Rejected as a coherent category. In that regard, activists resemble state-seeking nationalists with their constructions of long, coherent, and distinctive cultural histories for their nations. Thus, feminists identify themselves with women's age-old struggles for rights in the streets and in everyday existence, civil rights leaders minimize class and religious differences within their racial category, and environmentalists present most of humanity as their eternal community.

The two varieties of mystification address several different audiences. They encourage activists and supporters to make high estimates of the probability that fellow adherents will take risks and incur costs for the cause, and thus that their own contributions will bear fruit. They also warn authorities, objects of claims, opponents, rivals, and bystanders to take the movement seriously as a force that can affect their fates.

Movements differ significantly in the relative attention they give to these various audiences, from carrying out self-absorbed tests of daring organized by small clusters of terrorists, to soliciting signatures on petitions from transient participants who wish some authority to know their opinion. These orientations frequently vary in the course of a given social movement, for example, in the transitions from internal building to ostentatious action to fighting off competitors and enemies. But the general effectiveness of social movement organizing as a way of making public claims depends on the constitution of credible collective actors that could disrupt existing political arrangements. Because the process of collective identity construction does often knit together existing networks and produce long-lasting organizations, many participants, observers, and analysts have drawn a mistaken conclusion: that social movements simply realize previously existing identities.

The distinctive relation of social movements to shared identities will become clearer if we examine the nature of political identities in general. An identity is principally an actor's experience of a shared social relation. A political identity is an actor's experience of a shared social relation in which at least one of the parties—including third parties—is a government or agent of government. Political identities usually double with shared public representations of both relation and experience. Thus, at various times the same people represent themselves as workers, local residents, ethnics, women, citizens, gays, partisans, and members of other categories that distinguish them from other parts of the population. In each case they engage in authenticating performances that establish worthiness, unity, numbers, and commitment, for example, by marching together, wearing badges, singing songs of solidarity, or shouting slogans.

Under specifiable social conditions, collective identities that people deploy in the course of contention correspond to embedded identities, those that inform their routine social lives—race, gender, class, ethnicity, locality, kinship, and so on. We know embedded identities not from any primordial content, inescapable character, or emotional depth but because they operate in everyday social exchange. Observers tend to label as either "spontaneous" or "traditional" the forms of collective vengeance, shaming, obstruction, and mutual manipulation that spring from embedded identities. Observers also commonly imagine the central causal mechanisms of embedded identities to be transformations of individual consciousness, when in fact selective fortification of certain social ties and divisions at the expense of others impels the mobilization. Although they usually operate on a small scale, when under attack by power holders and enemies embedded identities such as religious affiliation and ethnicity can become the basis of fierce, extensive contention. The Protestant Reformation and breakup of the Soviet Union featured just such activation of embedded identities.

Under other conditions, people turn to detached identities, ones that rarely or never govern everyday social relations. Detached collective identities often include associational memberships, asserted nationalities, and legal categories such as "minority," "tribe," or "handicapped persons." In these cases, participants invoke salient social ties much more selectively than with embedded identities. Political entrepreneurs, on the average, play much larger parts in the activation of detached identities. Beth Roy's analysis of how Bengali villagers came to redefine local conflicts as aligning "Hindus" against "Muslims" (1994) beautifully illustrates such entrepreneurially mediated mobilization: the farther intervening political entrepreneurs were situated from a particular village and the more heavily they were involved in national politics, the more they invoked generally recognizable categories.

The distinction between embedded and detached collective identities marks end points of a continuum. The collective identity "citizen," for example, falls somewhere in between, typically shaping relations between employers and workers and strongly affecting political involvements, but making little difference to a wide range of other social routines. The embedded/detached distinction denies, however, two common (and contradictory) ways of understanding the identities that prevail in contentious politics: either as simple activations of preexisting, even primordial, individual attributes, or as purely discursive constructions having little or no grounding in social organization. From embedded to detached, collective identities resemble linguistic genres in entailing coherent interpersonal collaboration but varying contingently in content, form, and applicability from setting to setting.

Reinforced by contention, internal organization, or acquisition of privileges, detached identities sometimes become salient in everyday social relations as well, but they begin elsewhere. Through its various policies from 1903 to 1981, the South African state reified and ratified racial categories that came to loom large in social routines. Eventually, the state and its diverse agents mapped such categories as Zulu, Xhosa, Afrikaner, and Coloured onto the entire population with such force that the categories governed significant shares of everyday social relations (Ashforth 1990; Marks and Trapido 1987). Thus, initially detached collective identities became embedded ones.

Through sharpening of categorical boundaries and promotion of shared activities, social movement participation has likewise partially embedded detached identities in routine social life among women, ethnic minorities, and military veterans. The process also runs in the other direction, generalizing and detaching embedded identities, as when carpenters in one shop, machinists in another, and pipe fitters in a third band together as generalized workers. Nevertheless, the distinction matters: the degree to which political identities are embedded or detached strongly affects the quantity of widely available knowledge they draw on, the density of underpinning social ties, the strength of conflicting commitments, the ease of emulation from one setting to another, and therefore the effectiveness of different organizing strategies.

The distinction between embedded and detached collective identities corresponds approximately to the difference between local contention and national social movement politics in early nineteenth-century Europe, when a major shift toward the national arena was transforming popular politics (Tarrow 1994; Traugott 1995). In such forms of claim-making interaction as shaming ceremonies (e.g., donkeying, Rough Music), grain seizures, and burning of effigies, people generally deployed collective identities corresponding closely to those that prevailed in routine social life: householder, carpenter, neighbor, and so on. We can designate these forms of interaction as *parochial* and *particularistic*, since they ordinarily occurred within localized webs of social relations, incorporating practices and understandings peculiar to those localized webs. They also often took a *patronized* form, relying on appeals to privileged intermediaries for intercession with more distant authorities.

In demonstrations, electoral campaigns, and public meetings, however, participants often presented themselves as party supporters, association members, citizens, and similar detached collective identities. The labels *national, modular,* and *autonomous* for these types of claim-making call attention to their frequent fixation on national issues and objects, their standardization from one setting or issue to another, and the frequency with which participants directly addressed power holders they did not see in everyday social contacts. The difference signified large contrasts in social relations among participants, mobilization patterns, and the organization of action itself. The shift from parochial, particularistic, often patronized forms of claim-making to autonomous, national, and modular forms was articulated in profound alterations in social structure.

To be sure, once national, autonomous, and modular forms of interaction were available as models, claim-makers could employ them on other scales: in the international arena (as with coordinated nineteenth-century campaigns against slavery), within particular regions or cities (as in many urban struggles from 1848 onward), and even within firms (as when workers have intermittently taken their strikes to the streets in bids for outside support). Modularity facilitated the transfer of claim-making routines from their proving grounds to distant social terrains.

These shifts in the predominant forms of claim-making in Europe took place in different versions and at different times and paces from one region to another. Altogether, they constituted a dramatic alteration of contentious repertoires. Repertoires of contention resemble conversational conventions linking particular sets of interlocutors to each other: far narrower than the technical capacities of the parties would allow or their interests alone prescribe, repertoires form and change through mutual claim-making. Like conversations, when operating well they feature incessant innovation that occurs closely enough to previously established patterns to achieve both drama and intelligibility; a completely stereotyped utterance or claim-making routine carries no conviction except as a joke, yet one that makes no use of existing cultural conventions fails to connect with its audience. Like economic institutions that evolve through interaction among organizations but significantly constrain the forms of economic relations at any particular time, repertoires limit possibilities for collective action and interaction (Nelson 1995).

Evolution of the demonstration as a means of claim-making, to take an obvious example, tilts activists, police, spectators, rivals, and political officials toward well-defined ways of organizing, anticipating, and responding to the claims made in this medium, in sharp distinctions to claims laid by bombing or bribing (Favre 1990). Strikes, sit-ins, mass meetings, and other forms of claim-making link well-defined identities to each other, involve incessant innovation, and change configuration over the long run, but they accumulate their own histories, memories, lore, laws, and standard practices. Repertoires, in short, are historically evolving and strongly constraining cultural products.

Social movements incorporate a special version of national, modular, and autonomous repertoires, one including association and coalition formation, public meetings, demonstrations, petitions, lobbying, media presentations, and related forms of interaction. Despite recurrent talk of direct action, social movement activists generally avoid direct action in the strong sense of attacks, seizures, occupations, and other immediate implementations of stated claims. Instead, they usually concentrate their public efforts on

- announcing the presence in the polity of a mobile bloc, characterized as a worthy, unified, numerous, committed, and aggrieved population;

- broadcasting the contingent commitment of that bloc to a program requiring public recognition and/or action;

- moving authorities to forward that program against the (implicit or explicit) threat of actions by the bloc that would disrupt existing political arrangements;

- persuading authorities to recognize the bloc as a legitimate political actor and themselves as its authorized interlocutors;

- producing or altering connections both among movement participants and between movement participants and other political actors; and

- transforming shared understandings of political possibilities, both among movement participants and outside.

These activities, in turn, often have significant effects on the subsequent lives of individual participants in social movements, as well as on the networks that connect them. Yet analysts of social movements, commonly drawn from participants and sympathizers, understandably follow movement leaders in preparing scorecards in terms of openly articulated claims. Marco Giugni's introduction to this volume and most of the chapters in it focus on just such questions: given a certain set of collective claims by activists, what determines the extent to which movement action produces results fulfilling those claims—or, for that matter, results impeding their fulfillment?

Although social movement leaders do generally organize their public accounting around their movements' announced programs, an enormous range of unanticipated effects qualify logically as outcomes of social movements. Even to participants, furthermore, effects other than collective increases in public power obviously matter. If William Gamson, a quarter century ago, rightly stressed acceptance and new advantages as the two most prominent goals publicly articulated by movement leaders (1975), we notice both that central claims concern the acceptance and welfare of others—fetuses, prisoners, victims of dread diseases, nonhuman animals—and that, at least in retrospect, leaders and activists often argue that the crucial movement victories took place not on the public, political front but in reorientations of their own lives. At times movements have their largest effects not through advancement of their programs but through these other outcomes—transformation of participants' lives, co-optation of leaders, or even renewed repression.

Movements also leave political by-products that lie outside their programs and sometimes even contradict them: new police personnel and practices; the generation of rival movements and organizations; alterations in laws of assembly, association, and publicity; co-optation of activists and their organizations by governments or political parties; transformation of social movement organizations into pressure groups; the creation of legal precedents for subsequent challenges by other social movements. We begin to see why the tracing of social movement outcomes causes such difficulty and controversy. This range of effects far surpasses the explicit demands made by activists in the course of social movements, and sometimes negates them. By any standard, "success" and "failure" hardly describe most of the effects.

Further complexities in the tracing of social movement outcomes arise. Independent actions of authorities, interventions of other interested parties, environmental changes, and the grinding on of nonmovement politics all produce consequences in the zone of a given social movement's activity and interest. Multiple causal chains lead to a plethora of possible effects in a situation where influences other than social movement activity necessarily contribute to the effects.

Figure 1 schematizes the logical situation as three overlapping circles representing, respectively, (1) all effects of movement actions; (2) all public claims made by movement activists; and (3) all effects of outside events and actions. Space A, the common ground of public claims and effects of movement actions, represents the commonsense meaning of social movement outcome: movement actions cause fulfillment of movement claims or fail to do so: we caused an expansion of protections for abortion, we lost our campaign for an Equal Rights Amendment, we suffered the assassination of our leaders.

The diagram, however, makes an analyst's logical problem immediately obvious: spaces B, C, and D also exist. No inductive methodology—no multivariate statistical analysis, no yes/no comparison checklist, no narrowing of the outcomes considered—can possibly solve the problem, nor can mere second-guessing of movement activists through the specification of tried-and-true strategies that would have given them more of whatever they

Figure 1. The problem of identifying social movement outcomes

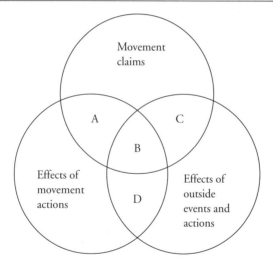

A = Effects of movement actions (but not of outside influences) that bear directly on movement claims

B = Joint effects of movement actions and outside influences that bear directly on movement claims

C = Effects of outside influences (but not of movement actions) that bear directly on movement claims

D = Joint effects of movement actions and outside influences that *don't* bear on movement claims were demanding. Both an inductive and an empathetic approach will founder in the complexity of the explanatory problem.

Only one response will work. That is (1) to formulate clear theories of the causal processes by which social movements produce their effects; (2) to limit investigations to the effects made plausible by those theories; (3) to work upstream by identifying instances of the effects, then seeing whether the hypothesized causal chain was actually operating; (4) to work downstream by identifying instances of the causal chain in operation, then seeing whether and how its hypothesized effects occurred; (5) to work midstream by examining whether the internal links of the causal chain operated as the theory requires; and (6) to rule out, to the extent possible, competing explanations of the effects.

This six-step approach breaks with conventional analyses of social movement outcomes, including William Gamson's classic analysis, which search for correspondences between attributes of social movements and alterations in their environments called for by their programs. It entertains the possibility that the major effects of social movements will have little or nothing to do with the public claims their leaders make. The critical causal theories, in any case, will turn out to concern not effects alone but also the very dynamics of social movement interactions.

Do we dispose of such sophisticated causal theories? We do not. The sketches of social movement dynamics I offered earlier suggest some likely elements of valid theories: the formation of detached identities for which potential niches exist in the polity, the production of WUNC and its consequences, feedback from collective interaction that reinforces WUNC instead of undermining it, credible threats that a WUNC-organized actor will disrupt established political arrangements, innovation within existing claim-making repertoires that combines drama with intelligibility, and so on. This is not the place to review the history and present condition of explanations for social movements. But it is very much the place to insist that only well-validated theories of social movement dynamics will give analysts a secure grip on social movement outcomes.

Notes

This chapter adapts a few paragraphs from my book *Durable Inequality* (Berkeley and Los Angeles: University of California Press, 1998) and paraphrases some arguments pursued at greater length and with more ample illustrations in my article "Social Movements as Historically Specific Clusters of Political Performances," *Berkeley Journal of Sociology* 38 (1993–94): 1–30. Marco Giugni, Francesca Polletta, and Viviana Zelizer gave me valuable critiques of previous drafts.

Bibliography

Abramowitz, Stephen I., and Alberta J. Nassi. 1981. "Keeping the Faith: Psychosocial Correlates of Activism Persistence into Middle Adulthood." *Journal of Youth and Adolescence* 10: 507–23.

Aldrich, John H. 1995. *Why Parties? The Origin and Transformation of Political Parties in America.* Chicago: University of Chicago Press.

Allison, Paul D. 1984. *Event History Analysis: Regression for Longitudinal Event Data.* Beverly Hills: Sage.

Almond, Gabriel A., and Sidney Verba. 1963. *The Civic Culture: Political Attitudes and Democracy in Five Nations.* Princeton: Princeton University Press.

Amenta, Edwin. 1991. "Making the Most of a Case Study: Theories of the Welfare State and the American Experience." *International Journal of Comparative Sociology* 32: 172–94.

Amenta, Edwin, Bruce G. Carruthers, and Yvonne Zylan. 1992. "A Hero for the Aged? The Townsend Movement, the Political Mediation Model, and U.S. Old-Age Policy, 1934–1950." *American Journal of Sociology* 98: 308–39.

Amenta, Edwin, and Jane D. Poulsen. 1994. "Where to Begin: A Survey of Five Approaches to Selecting Independent Measures for Qualitative Comparative Analysis." *Sociological Methods and Research* 23: 21–52.

Amenta, Edwin, Kathleen Dunleavy, and Mary Bernstein. 1994. "Stolen Thunder? Huey Long's Share Our Wealth, Political Mediation, and the Second New Deal." *American Sociological Review* 59: 678–702.

Anderson, Benedict. 1983. *Imagined Communities: Reflections on the Origin and Spread of Nationalism.* London: Verso.

Argersinger, Peter H. 1974. *Populism and Politics: William Alfred Peffer and the People's Party.* Lexington: University Press of Kentucky.

Arnold, R. Douglas. 1990. *The Logic of Congressional Action*. New Haven: Yale University Press.

Ash, Timothy Garton. 1991. "Germany at the Frontier." *New York Review of Books* (January 17): 21–22.

Ashforth, Adam. 1990. *The Politics of Official Discourse in Twentieth-Century South Africa*. Oxford: Clarendon.

Aubert, Jean-François. 1983. *Exposé des institutions politiques de la Suisse à partir de quelques affaires controversées*. 2d edition. Lausanne: Payot.

Auer, Andreas. 1989. *Le référendum et l'initiative populaires aux États-Unis*. Basel: Helbing und Lichtenhahn.

Avorn, Jerry L. 1969. *Up against the Ivy Wall: A History of the Columbia Crisis*. New York: Atheneum.

Bachrach, Peter, and Morton S. Baratz. 1970. *Power and Poverty*. New York: Oxford University Press.

Badie, Bertrand, and Pierre Birnbaum. 1982. *Sociologie de l'état*. Paris: Grasset.

Balbo, Laura, and Luigi Manconi. 1992. *I razzismi reali*. Milan: Feltrinelli.

Baldini, Gianfranco, and Rinaldo Vignati. 1996. "Dal MSI ad AN: Una nuova cultura politica?" *Polis* 10 (April 1): 81–101.

Banaszak, Lee Ann. 1996. *Why Movements Succeed or Fail: Opportunity, Culture, and the Struggle for Woman Suffrage*. Princeton: Princeton University Press.

Barber, Benjamin. 1984. *Strong Democracy: Participatory Politics for a New Age*. Berkeley and Los Angeles: University of California Press.

Barkan, Steven E. 1984. "Legal Control of the Civil Rights Movement." *American Sociological Review* 49: 552–65.

Bashevkin, Sylvia. 1994. "Facing a Renewed Right: American Feminism and the Reagan/Bush Challenge." *Canadian Journal of Political Science* 27: 669–98.

———. 1996. "Tough Times in Review: The British Women's Movement during the Thatcher Years." *Comparative Political Studies* 28: 525–52.

Bates, Tom. 1992. *The 1970 Bombing of the Army Math Research Center at the University of Wisconsin and Its Aftermath*. New York: HarperCollins.

Battelli, Maurice. 1932. *Les institutions de démocratie directe en droit Suisse et comparé moderne*. Paris: Librairie du Recueil Siren.

Baumgartl, Bernd, and Adrian Favell, eds. 1995. *New Xenophobia in Europe*. London: Kluwer Law International.

Baumgartner, Frank R., and Bryan D. Jones. 1993. *Agendas and Instability in American Politics*. Chicago: University of Chicago Press.

Bellush, Jewell, and Stephen M. David, eds. 1971. *Race and Politics in New York City*. New York: Praeger.

Berkowitz, William R. 1974. "Socioeconomic Indicator Changes in Ghetto Riot Tracts." *Urban Affairs Quarterly* 10: 69–94.

Betz, Michael. 1974. "Riots and Welfare: Are They Related?" *Social Problems* 21: 345–55.

Billig, Michael. 1995. *Banal Nationalism*. London: Sage.

Bindel, Julie, Kate Cook, and Liz Kelly. 1995. "Trials and tribulations—*Justice for*

Women: A Campaign for the 1990s." In *Feminist Activism in the 1990s,* edited by Gabriele Griffin, 65–76. London: Taylor and Francis.

Bloom, David E., and James Trussell. 1984. "What Are the Determinants of Delayed Childbearing and Permanent Childlessness in the United States?" *Demography* 21: 591–611.

Blum, Roger. 1977. *Die politische Beteiligung des Volkes im jungen Kanton Basellᵃⁿd (1832–1875).* Liestal, Switzerland: KDMZ.

Blumrosen, Alfred W. 1993. *Modern Law.* Madison: University of Wisconsin Press.

Bovenkerk, Frank, Robert Miles, and Gilles Verbunt. 1990. "Racism, Migration, and the State in Western Europe: A Case for Comparative Analysis." *International Sociology* 5: 475–90.

Brand, Karl-Werner. 1982. *Neue soziale Bewegungen: Entstehung, Funktion, und Perspektive neuer Protestpotentiale.* Opladen, Germany: Westdeutscher Verlag.

Breines, Wini. 1989. *Community and Organization in the New Left, 1962–1968: The Great Refusal.* New Brunswick, N.J.: Rutgers University Press.

Brenner, Johanna. 1996. "The Best of Times, the Worst of Times: Feminism in the United States." In *Mapping the Women's Movement,* edited by Monica Threlfall, 17–72. London: Verso.

Brill, Harry. 1971. *Why Organizers Fail: The Story of a Rent Strike.* Berkeley and Los Angeles: University of California Press.

Brubaker, Rogers. 1992. *Citizenship and Nationhood in France and Germany.* Cambridge: Harvard University Press.

Buchman, Marlis. 1989. *The Script of Life in Modern Society: Entry into Adulthood in a Changing World.* Chicago: University of Chicago Press.

Bundy, McGeorge. 1989. "The Emperor's Clothes." *New York Review of Books* (July 20): 5–8.

Burk, Martha, and Heidi Hartmann. 1996. "Beyond the Gender Gap." *Nation* (June 10): 18–21.

Burstein, Paul. 1979. "Public Opinion, Demonstrations, and the Passage of Antidiscrimination Legislation." *Public Opinion Quarterly* 43: 157–72.

———. 1985. *Discrimination, Jobs, and Politics.* Chicago: University of Chicago Press.

———. 1991. "Legal Mobilization as a Social Movement Tactic." *American Journal of Sociology* 96: 1201–25.

———. 1993. "Explaining State Action and the Expansion of Civil Rights: The Civil Rights Act of 1964." *Research in Political Sociology* 6: 117–37.

———. 1998a. "Bringing the Public Back In: Should Sociologists Consider the Impact of Public Opinion on Public Policy?" *Social Forces* 77: 27–62.

———. 1998b. "Interest Organizations, Political Parties, and the Study of Democratic Politics." In *Social Movements and American Political Institutions,* edited by Anne Costain and Andrew McFarland, 39–56. Boulder, Colo.: Rowman and Littlefield.

———. Forthcoming. "The Impact of EEO Law: A Social Movement Perspective." In *Controversies in Civil Rights,* edited by Bernard Grofman. Charlottesville: University Press of Virginia.

Burstein, Paul, Rachel L. Einwohner, and Jocelyn A. Hollander. 1995. "The Success of Political Movements: A Bargaining Perspective." In *The Politics of Protest*, edited by J. Craig Jenkins and Bert Klandermans, 275–95. Minneapolis: University of Minnesota Press.

Burstein, Paul, and William Freudenburg. 1978. "Changing Public Policy: The Impact of Public Opinion, Anti-War Demonstrations, and War Costs on Senate Voting on Vietnam War Motions." *American Journal of Sociology* 84: 99–122.

Button, James. 1978. *Black Violence: Political Impact of the 1960s Riots.* Princeton: Princeton University Press.

———. 1989. *Blacks and Social Change: Impact of the Civil Rights Movement in Southern Communities.* Princeton: Princeton University Press.

Byrne, Paul. 1996. "The Politics of the Women's Movement." In *Women in Politics*, edited by Joni Lovenduski and Pippa Norris, 55–70. Oxford: Oxford University Press.

Cahn, Anne Hessing. 1971. *Eggheads and Warheads.* Cambridge: MIT Press.

Caldwell, Lynton K. 1984. *International Environmental Policy: Emergence and Dimensions.* Durham, N.C.: Duke University Press.

Caldwell, Lynton K., Lynton R. Hayes, and Isabel M. MacWhirter. 1976. *Citizens and the Environment: Case Studies in Popular Action.* Bloomington: Indiana University Press.

Carmines, Edward G., and James A. Stimson. 1989. *Issue Evolution.* Princeton: Princeton University Press.

Carroll, Susan. 1985. *Women as Candidates in American Politics.* Bloomington: Indiana University Press.

———. 1995. "A Mixed Verdict: The Impact of Women on the Crime Bill." Paper presented at the annual meeting of the Midwest Political Science Association, Chicago, Ill., April 6–8.

Carson, Rachel. 1962. *Silent Spring.* Boston: Houghton Mifflin.

Castles, Stephen, and Mark Miller. 1993. *The Age of Migration: International Population Movements in the Modern World.* London: Macmillan.

Center for American Women and Politics. 1995. *News and Notes* 2. New Brunswick, N.J.

Charles, Nickie. 1995. "Feminist Politics, Domestic Violence, and the State." *Sociological Review* 43: 617–40.

Chong, Dennis. 1991. *Collective Action and the Civil Rights Movement.* Chicago: University of Chicago Press.

Christmann, Gabriela. 1996. "Zur kommunikativen Konstruktion und Rekonstruktion einer ökologischen Moral." Ph.D. diss., Sozialwissenschaftliche Fakultät der Universität Konstanz.

Clark, Robert Charles. 1977. "The Morphogenesis of Subchapter C: An Essay in Statutory Evolution and Reform." *Yale Law Journal* 47: 90–162.

Clemens, Elisabeth S. 1993. "Organizational Repertoires and Institutional Change: Women's Groups and the Transformation of U.S. Politics, 1890–1920." *American Journal of Sociology* 98: 755–98.

———. 1997. *The People's Lobby: Organizational Innovation and the Rise of Interest Group Politics.* Chicago: University of Chicago Press.

Clements, Kevin. 1988. *Back from the Brink: The Creation of a Nuclear-Free New Zealand.* Winchester, Mass.: Allen and Unwin.

Cloward, Richard A., and Frances Fox Piven. 1984. "Disruption and Organization: A Rejoinder." *Theory and Society* 13: 587–99.

Cockburn, Cynthia. 1977. *The Local State: Management of Cities and People.* London: Pluto.

Cohn, Samuel. 1993. *When Strikes Make Sense—and Why: Lessons from Third Republic French Coal Miners.* New York: Plenum.

Colby, David. 1982. "A Test of the Relative Efficacy of Political Tactics." *American Journal of Political Science* 26: 741–53.

Collins, Evelyn, and Elizabeth Meehan. 1994. "Women's Rights in Employment and Related Areas." In *Individual Rights and the Law in Britain,* edited by Christopher McCrudden and Gerald Chambers, 363–407. Oxford: Clarendon.

Commoner, Barry. 1958. "The Fallout Problem." *Science* 127: 1023–26.

Connelly, Marjorie. 1996. "Portrait of the Electorate: The Vote under a Microscope." <httpl//:search.nytimes.com/web/docsroot/library/politics/elect-port.html>. Available December 1996.

Cooney, Teresa M., and Dennis P. Hogan. 1991. "Marriage in an Institutionalized Life Course: First Marriage among American Men in the Twentieth Century." *Journal of Marriage and the Family* 53: 178–90.

Cooper, Alice. 1996. *Paradoxes of Peace: German Peace Movements since 1945.* Ann Arbor: University of Michigan Press.

Cortright, David. 1991. "Assessing Peace Movement Effectiveness in the 1980s." *Peace and Change* 16: 46–63.

———. 1993. *Peace Works.* Boulder, Colo.: Westview.

Costain, Anne N. 1992. *Inviting Women's Rebellion: A Political Process Interpretation of the Women's Movement.* Baltimore: Johns Hopkins University Press.

Costain, Anne N., and Steven Majstorovic. 1994. "Congress, Social Movements, and Public Opinion: Multiple Origins of Women's Rights Legislation." *Political Research Quarterly* 47: 111–35.

Craig, Gordon A. 1988. *Geld und Geist: Zürich im Zeitalter des Liberalismus, 1830–1869.* Munich: Beck.

Cronin, Thomas E. 1989. *Direct Democracy: The Politics of Initiative, Referendum, and Recall.* Cambridge: Harvard University Press.

Curti, Theodore. 1885. *Geschichte der Schweizerischen Volksgesetzgebung.* Zurich: Schröter.

Curtius, Julius. 1919. *Ueber die Einführung von Volksinitiativen und Volksreferendum in die neuen Verfassungen der deutschen Staaten.* Heidelberg.

Dahl, Robert. 1961. *Who Governs?* New Haven: Yale University Press.

———. 1967. *Pluralist Democracy in the United States: Conflict and Consent.* Chicago: Rand-McNally.

———. 1971. *Polyarchy: Participation and Opposition.* New Haven: Yale University Press.

Dalton, Russell J. 1994. *The Green Rainbow: Environmental Groups in Western Europe.* New Haven: Yale University Press.

D'Amato, Gianni, and Siegfried Schieder. 1995. "Die Lega Nord: Zwischen ethnischer Staatsbürgerschaft und föderalem Projekt." *PROKLA* 98: 53–68.

Daniels, Roger. 1971. *The Bonus March: An Episode of the Great Depression.* Westport, Conn.: Greenwood.

Darcy, Robert, Susan Welch, and Janet Clark. 1995. *Women, Elections, and Representation.* Lincoln: University of Nebraska Press.

DeBenedetti, Charles D. 1990. *An American Ordeal: The Antiwar Movement of the Vietnam Era.* Syracuse, N.Y.: Syracuse University Press.

Delantey, Gerard. 1996. "Beyond the Nation-State: National Identity and Citizenship in a Multicultural Society—A Response to Rex." *Sociological Research Online* 1, no. 3. <http://www.socresonline.org.uk/socresonline/1/3/1.html>.

della Porta, Donatella. 1992. "Spirals of Revenge: Biographical Accounts of Left-Wing and Right-Wing Radicals in Italy." *Politics and the Individual* 2: 87–98.

———. 1995. *Social Movements, Political Violence, and the State: A Comparative Analysis of Italy and Germany.* Cambridge: Cambridge University Press.

———. 1996. *Movimenti collettivi e sistema politico in Italia, 1960–1995.* Bari, Italy: Laterza.

———. 1998. "Police Knowledge and Protest Policing: Some Reflections on the Italian Case." In *Policing Protest: The Control of Mass Demonstration in Western Democracies,* edited by Donatella della Porta and Herbert Reiter, 228–52. Minneapolis: University of Minnesota Press.

della Porta, Donatella, and Dieter Rucht. 1995. "Left-Libertarian Movements in Context: A Comparison of Italy and West Germany, 1965–1990." In *The Politics of Social Protest: Comparative Perspectives on States and Social Movements,* edited by J. Craig Jenkins and Bert Klandermans, 229–72. Minneapolis: University of Minnesota Press.

della Porta, Donatella, and Herbert Reiter, eds. 1998. *Policing Protest: The Control of Mass Demonstration in Western Democracies.* Minneapolis: University of Minnesota Press.

Demerath, N. Jay, III, Gerald Marwell, and Michael T. Aiken. 1971. *The Dynamics of Idealism.* San Francisco: Jossey Bass.

Deploige, Simon. 1898. *The Referendum in Switzerland.* New York: Longmans, Green.

Diamanti, Ilvo. 1993. *La Lega: Geografia, storia e sociologia di un soggetto politico.* Rome: Donzelli Editore.

———. 1996. "The Northern League: From Regional Party to Party of Government." In *The New Italian Republic: From the Fall of the Berlin Wall to Berlusconi,* edited by Stephen Gundle and Simon Parker, 113–29. London: Routledge.

Diani, Mario. 1996. "Linking Mobilization Frames and Political Opportunities: Insights from Regional Populism in Italy." *American Sociological Review* 61: 1053–69.

Dibbern, John David. 1980. "Grass Roots Populism: Politics and Social Structure in a Frontier Community." Ph.D. diss., Stanford University.

Dietz, Thomas, and Linda Kalof. 1992. "Environmentalism among Nation-States." *Social Indicators Research* 26: 353–66.

Disney, Jennifer, and Joyce Gelb. Forthcoming. *Women and Politics.*

Dobash, R. Emerson, and Russell P. Dobash. 1992. *Women, Violence, and Social Change.* New York: Routledge.

Douglas, Mary, and Aaron Wildavsky. 1982. *Risk and Culture.* Berkeley and Los Angeles: University of California Press.

Downey, Gary L. 1988. "Reproducing Cultural Identity in Negotiating Nuclear Power: The Union of Concerned Scientists and Emergency Core Cooling." *Social Studies of Science* 18: 231–64.

Downs, Anthony. 1972. "Up and Down with Ecology: The 'Issue-Attention Cycle.'" *Public Interest* 28: 28–50.

Dunlap, Riley E., and Angela G. Mertig. 1996. "Weltweites Umweltbewußtsein: Eine Herausforderung für die sozialwissenschaftliche Theorie." In *Umweltsoziologie,* edited by Andreas Diekmann and Carlo C. Jaeger, 193–218. Kölner Zeitschrift für Soziologie und Sozialpysychologie, no. 36. Opladen, Germany: Westdeutscher Verlag.

Dunlap, Riley E., and Rik Scarce. 1991. "The Polls-Poll Trends: Environmental Problems and Protection." *Public Opinion Quarterly* 55: 651–72.

Duyvendak, Jan Willem. 1995. *The Power of Politics: New Social Movements in France.* Boulder, Colo.: Westview.

Duyvendak, Jan Willem, and Ruud Koopmans. 1995. "The Political Construction of the Nuclear Energy Issue." In *New Social Movements in Western Europe: A Comparative Analysis,* by Hanspeter Kriesi, Ruud Koopmans, Jan Willem Duyvendak, and Marco G. Giugni, 145–64. Minneapolis: University of Minnesota Press.

Easterlin, Richard. 1980. *Birth and Fortune.* New York: Basic Books.

Edelman, Murray. 1964. *The Symbolic Uses of Politics.* Urbana: University of Illinois Press.

———. 1977. *Political Language: Words That Succeed and Policies That Fail.* New York: Academic Press.

Ehrenreich, Barbara, and John Ehrenreich. 1969. *Long March, Short Spring: The Student Uprising at Home and Abroad.* New York: Monthly Review Press.

Elder, Glen H., Jr. 1974. *Children of the Great Depression: a Social Change in Life Experience.* Chicago: University of Chicago Press.

———. 1978. "Family History and the Life Course." In *Transitions: The Family and the Life Course in Historical Perspective,* edited by Tamara K. Hareven, 17–64. New York: Academic Press.

Elder, Glen H., Jr., and Avshalom Caspi. 1990. "Studying Lives in a Changing Society: Sociological and Personalogical Explorations." In *Studying Persons and Lives,* edited by A. I. Rabin, R. A. Zucker, R. Emmons, and S. Frank, 201–47. New York: Springer.

Elman, R. Amy, ed. 1996. *Sexual Politics and the European Union: The New Feminist Challenge.* Providence: Berghahn.

Elster, Jon. 1983. *Sour Grapes: Studies in the Subversion of Rationality.* Cambridge: Cambridge University Press.

———. 1988. "Arguments for Constitutional Choice: Reflections on the Transition to

Socialism." In *Constitutionalism and Democracy*, edited by Jon Elster and Rune Slagstad, 303–26. Cambridge: Cambridge University Press.

EMILY's List. 1996. "The Backlash Begins." *Notes from Emily* (March): 1–2.

Epple, Ruedi. 1979. "Die demokratische Bewegung im Baselbiet um 1860: Ein Beitrag zur Geschichte der direktdemokratischen Institutionen im politischen System der Schweiz." Master's thesis, Universität Konstanz.

———. 1997. "Der Paradigmenwechsel im Abstimmungsverhalten: Aspekte der politischen Kultur des Kantons Basel-Landschaft." *Swiss Review of Political Science* 3: 31–56.

Epstein, Steven. 1996. *Impure Science: AIDS, Activism, and the Politics of Knowledge*. Berkeley and Los Angeles: University of California Press.

Equal Opportunities Review. 1996. Nos. 67–70. Manchester, England: Equal Opportunities Commission.

Erie, Steven P., and Martin Rein. 1988. "Women and the Welfare State." In *The Politics of the Gender Gap*, edited by Carol McClurg Mueller, 173–91. Beverly Hills: Sage.

Eurostat. 1994. *Migration Statistics, 1994*. Luxembourg: Office for Official Publications of the European Communities.

Evangelista, Matthew. 1990. "Sources of Moderation in Soviet Security Policy." In *Behavior, Society, and Nuclear War*, edited by Robert Jervis, Philip Tetlock, et al. Vol. 2, 255–354. New York: Oxford University Press.

———. 1995. "The Paradox of State Strength: Transnational Relations and Security Policy in Russia and the Soviet Union." *International Organization* 49: 1–38.

Fascell, Dante. 1987. "Congress and Arms Control." *Foreign Affairs* 65: 730–49.

Favre, Pierre, ed. 1990. *La manifestation*. Paris: Presses de la Fondation Nationale des Sciences Politiques.

Fawcett Society. 1996a. "A Woman's Place." *Towards Equality* (autumn).

———. 1996b. *Working towards Equality: Annual Report, 1995/96*. London: Fawcett Society.

Feagin, Joe R., and Harlan Hahn. 1973. *Ghetto Revolts: The Politics of Violence in American Cities*. New York: Macmillan.

Fendrich, James M. 1974. "Activists Ten Years Later: A Test of Generational Unit Continuity." *Journal of Social Issues* 30: 95–118.

———. 1977. "Keeping Faith or Pursuing the Good Life: A Study of Participation in the Civil Rights Movement." *American Sociological Review* 42: 144–57.

———. 1993. *Ideal Citizens*. Albany: State University of New York Press.

Fendrich, James M., and Alison T. Tarleau. 1973. "Marching to a Different Drummer: Occupational and Political Correlates of Former Student Activists." *Social Forces* 52: 245–53.

Fendrich, James M., and Kenneth L. Lovoy. 1988. "Back to the Future: Adult Political Behavior of Former Student Activists." *American Sociological Review* 53: 780–84.

Fenno, Richard F., Jr. 1973. *Congressmen in Committees*. Boston: Little, Brown.

Ferejohn, John A., and James H. Kuklinski, eds. 1990. *Information and Democratic Processes*. Urbana: University of Illinois Press.

Ferree, Myra Marx, and Beth Hess. 1994. *Controversy and Coalition: The Feminist Movement across Three Decades of Change.* New York: Twayne.

Ferree, Myra Marx, and Patricia Yancey Martin, eds. 1995. *Feminist Organizations: Harvest of the New Women's Movement.* Philadelphia: Temple University Press.

Flam, Helena, ed. 1994. *States and Anti-nuclear Movements.* Edinburgh: Edinburgh University Press.

Flickinger, Richard S., and Donley T Studlar. 1992. "The Disappearing Voters? Exploring Declining Turnout in Western European Elections." *West European Politics* 15: 1–16.

Fligstein, Neil. 1992. "The Structural Transformation of American Industry: An Institutional Account of the Causes of Diversification in the Largest Firms, 1919–1979." In *The New Institutionalism in Organizational Analysis,* edited by Walter W. Powell and Paul J. DiMaggio, 311–36. New Haven: Yale University Press.

Foley, Marian. 1996. "Who Is in Control? Changing Responses to Women Who Have Been Raped and Sexually Abused." In *Women, Violence, and Male Power,* edited by M. Hester, Liz Kelly, and Jill Radford, 166–75. Buckingham, England: Open University Press.

Ford, Glyn, ed. 1991. *Committee of Inquiry on Racism and Xenophobia: Reports on the Findings of the Inquiry.* Luxembourg: European Parliament.

Forsberg, Randall. 1984. "The Freeze and Beyond: Confining the Military to Defense as a Route to Disarmament." *World Policy Journal* 1: 287–318.

Fox, Stephen. 1985. *The American Conservation Movement: John Muir and His Legacy.* Madison: University of Wisconsin Press.

Franzosi, Roberto. 1994. *The Puzzle of Strikes.* Cambridge: Cambridge University Press.

Freeman, Jo. 1993. "Feminism vs. Family Values: Women at the 1992 Republican and Democratic Conventions." *PS: Political Science and Politics* 26: 21–28.

Frei, Christoph. 1995. "Direkte Demokratie in Frankreich: Wegmarken einer schwierigen Tradition." *Kleine Schriften* 22. Liechtenstein: Liechtenstein-Institut.

Frey, R. Scott, Thomas Dietz, and Linda Kalof. 1992. "Characteristics of Successful American Protest Groups: Another Look at Gamson's *Strategy of Social Protest.*" *American Journal of Sociology* 98: 368–87.

Friedman, Debra, and Doug McAdam. 1992. "Collective Identity and Activism: Networks, Choices, and the Life of a Social Movement." In *Frontiers in Social Movement Theory,* edited by Aldon D. Morris and Carol McClurg Mueller, 156–73. New Haven: Yale University Press.

Fuchs, Dieter, and Dieter Rucht. 1994. "Support for New Social Movements in Five Western European Countries." In *A New Europe? Social Change and Political Transformation,* edited by Chris Rootes and Howard Davis, 86–111. London: UCL Press.

Fukuyama, Frank. 1989. "The End of History?" *National Interest* 16: 3–18.

Gabriel, Oscar W. 1996. "Rechtsextreme Einstellungen in Europa: Struktur, Entwicklung, und Verhaltensimplikationen." In *Rechtsextremismus: Ergebnisse und Perspektiven der Forschung,* edited by Jürgen W. Falter, Hans-Gerd Jaschke, and Jürgen R. Winkler, 344–60. Politische Vierteljahresschrift, no. 27. Opladen, Germany: Westdeutscher Verlag.

Gaddis, John Lewis. 1987. *The Long Peace.* New York: Oxford University Press.
———. 1989. "Hanging Tough Paid Off." *Bulletin of the Atomic Scientists* 45: 11–14.
Gale, Richard P. 1986. "Social Movements and the State: The Environmental Movement, Countermovement, and Governmental Agencies." *Sociological Perspectives* 29: 202–40.
Gamson, William A. 1975. *The Strategy of Social Protest.* Homewood, Ill.: Dorsey.
———. 1988. "Political Discourse and Collective Action." In *From Structure to Action: Social Movement Participation across Cultures,* edited by Bert Klandermans, Hanspeter Kriesi, and Sidney Tarrow, 219–44. Greenwich, Conn.: JAI.
———. 1990. *The Strategy of Social Protest.* 2d ed. Belmont, Calif.: Wadsworth.
———. 1992. "The Social Psychology of Collective Action." In *Frontiers in Social Movement Theory,* edited by Aldon D. Morris and Carol McClurg Mueller, 53–76. New Haven: Yale University Press.
Gamson, William A., and Andre Modigliani. 1987. "The Changing Culture of Affirmative Action." *Research in Political Sociology* 3: 137–77.
———. 1989. "Media Discourse and Public Opinion on Nuclear Power: A Constructionist Approach." *American Journal of Sociology* 95: 1–37.
Gamson, William A., and Emilie Schmeidler. 1984. "Organizing the Poor." *Theory and Society* 13: 567–85.
Garrow, David. 1978. *Protest at Selma: Martin Luther King and the Voting Rights Act of 1965.* New Haven: Yale University Press.
Gelb, Joyce. 1983. "The Politics of Wife Abuse." In *Families, Politics, and Public Policy,* edited by Irene Diamond, 250–62. New York: Longman.
———. 1987. "Social Movement 'Success': A Comparative Analysis of Feminism in the United States and United Kingdom." In *The Women's Movements of the United States and Western Europe,* edited by Mary Fainsod Katzenstein and Carol McClurg Mueller, 267–89. Philadelphia: Temple University Press.
———. 1989. *Feminism and Politics: A Comparative Perspective.* Berkeley and Los Angeles: University of California Press.
———. 1995. "Feminist Organization Success and the Politics of Engagement." In *Feminist Organizations: Harvest of the New Women's Movement,* edited by Myra Marx Ferree and Patricia Yancey Martin, 128–34. Philadelphia: Temple University Press.
Gelb, Joyce, and Marian Lief Palley. 1987. *Women and Public Policy.* Princeton: Princeton University Press.
———. 1996. *Women and Public Policies: Reassessing Gender Politics.* Charlottesville: University Press of Virginia.
Gellner, Ernest. 1983. *Nations and Nationalism.* Oxford: Blackwell.
Gerhards, Jürgen. 1993. *Neue Konfliktlinie in der Mobilisierung öffentlicher Meinung: Warum die IWF Tagung in Berlin 1988 zu einem öffentlichen Streitthema würde.* Berlin: Sigma.
Gilg, Peter. 1951. *Die Entstehung der demokratischen Bewegung und die soziale Frage: Die sozialen Ideen und Postulate der deuschschweizerischen Demokraten in den früheren 60er Jahren des 19. Jahrhunderts.* Affoltern am Albis: Weiss.

Ginsborg, Paul. 1995. "Italian Political Culture in Historical Perspective." *Modern Italy* 1: 3–17.

———. 1996. "Explaining Italy's Crisis." In *The New Italian Republic: From the Fall of the Berlin Wall to Berlusconi,* edited by Stephen Gundle and Simon Parker, 19–39. London: Routledge.

Gitlin, Todd. 1980. *The Whole World Is Watching: The Media in the Making and Unmaking of the New Left.* Berkeley and Los Angeles: University of California Press.

———. 1994. "From Universality to Difference: Notes on the Fragmentation of the Idea of the Left." In *Social Theory and the Politics of Identity,* edited by Craig Calhoun. Oxford: Blackwell.

Giugni, Marco G. 1994. "The Outcomes of Social Movements: A Review of the Literature." Working paper no. 197, Center for the Study of Social Change, New School for Social Research, New York, N.Y.

———. 1995. "Outcomes of New Social Movements." In *New Social Movements in Western Europe: A Comparative Analysis,* by Hanspeter Kriesi, Ruud Koopmans, Jan Willem Duyvendak, and Marco G. Giugni, 207–37. Minneapolis: University of Minnesota Press.

———. 1998. "Was It Worth the Effort? The Outcomes and Consequences of Social Movements." *Annual Review of Sociology* 24: 371–93.

Gmürr, Hans. 1948. "Die Entwicklung der Volksrechte in der Schweiz." *Die Volksrechte* 10: 15–30. Veröffentlichungen der Schweizerischen Verwaltungskurse an der Handels-Hochschule St. Gallen.

Goertz, Gary. 1994. *Contexts of International Politics.* Cambridge: Cambridge University Press.

Goffman, Erving. 1974. *Frame Analysis: An Essay on the Organization of Experience.* Cambridge: Harvard University Press.

Goldfield, Michael. 1989. "Worker Insurgency, Radical Organization, and New Deal Labor Legislation." *American Political Science Review* 83: 1257–82.

———. "Explaining New Deal Labor Policy" [reply to Skocpol and Finegold]. *American Political Science Review* 84: 1304–15.

Goldstein, Leslie F. 1988. *The Constitutional Rights of Women: Cases in Law and Social Change.* 2d ed. Madison: University of Wisconsin Press.

Goldstone, Jack A. 1980. "The Weakness of Organization: A New Look at Gamson's *The Strategy of Social Protest.*" *American Journal of Sociology* 85: 1017–42, 1426–32.

Goodwin, Jeff, and Theda Skocpol. 1989. "Explaining Revolutions in the Contemporary Third World." *Politics and Society* 17: 489–509.

Gould, Carol. 1988. *Rethinking Democracy: Freedom and Social Cooperation in Politics, Economy, and Society.* Cambridge: Cambridge University Press.

Gould, Roger. 1991. "Multiple Networks and Mobilization in the Paris Commune, 1871." *American Sociological Review* 56: 716–29.

———. 1995. *Insurgent Identities.* Chicago: University of Chicago Press.

Gould, Stephen Jay. 1995. *Dinosaur in a Haystack.* New York: Harmony.

Graham, Kennedy. 1989. *National Security Concepts of States: New Zealand.* New York: Taylor and Francis.

Greiffenhagen, Martin. 1984. "Vom Obrigkeitsstaat zur Demokratie: Die politische Kultur in der Bundesrepublik Deutschland." In *Politische Kultur in Westeuropa: Bürger und Staaten in der europäischen Gemeinschaft,* edited by Peter Reichel, 52–76. Frankfurt: Campus.

Griffin, Gabriele. 1995. *Feminist Activism in the 1990s.* London: Taylor and Francis.

Griffin, Roger. 1996. "The 'Postfascism' of the Alleanza Nazionale: A Case Study in Ideological Morphology." *Journal of Political Ideologies* 1: 123–45.

———. 1997. "Italy." In *European Political Culture: Conflict or Convergence?* edited by Roger Eatwell, 139–56. London: Routledge.

Grodzins, Morton, and Eugene Rabinowitch, eds. 1963. *The Atomic Age: Scientists and National and World Affairs: Articles from the* Bulletin of the Atomic Scientists, *1945–1962.* New York: Basic Books.

Gross, Andreas. 1983. "Die direkte Gesetzgebung durch das Volk: Die Utopie des Karl Buerkli (1823–1901): Ein Beitrag zur Entstehungsgeschichte der direktdemokratischen Institutionen im Kanton Zürich." Master's thesis, University of Lausanne.

Gross, Edward, and Amitai Etzioni. 1985. *Organizations in Society.* Englewood Cliffs, N.J.: Prentice Hall.

Gruner, Erich. 1968. *Die Arbeiter in der Schweiz im 19. Jahrhundert: Soziale Lage, Organisation, Verhaeltnis zu Arbeitgeber und Staat.* Bern: Francke Verlag.

Gurney, Joan N., and Kathleen T. Tierney. 1982. "Relative Deprivation and Social Movements: A Critical Look at Twenty Years of Theory and Research." *Sociological Quarterly* 23: 33–47.

Gurr, Ted R. 1980. "On the Outcomes of Violent Conflict." In *Handbook of Political Conflict,* edited by Ted R. Gurr, 238–94. New York: Free Press.

Gusfield, Joseph. 1980. "Social Movements and Social Change: Perspectives of Linearity and Fluidity." In *Research in Social Movements, Conflict, and Change,* edited by Louis Kriesberg, 317–39. Greenwich, Conn.: JAI.

Habermas, Jürgen. 1984. *Teoria dell'agire comunicativo.* Bologna: Il Mulino.

———. [1962] 1990. *Strukturwandel der Öffentlichkeit.* Frankfurt: Suhrkamp.

Hahn, Harlan. 1970. "Civic Responses to Riots: A Reappraisal of Kerner Commission Data." *Public Opinion Quarterly* 34: 101–7.

Haines, Herbert H. 1984. "Black Radicalization and the Funding of Civil Rights, 1957–1970." *Social Problems* 32: 31–43.

Hainsworth, Paul, ed. 1992. *The Extreme Right in Europe and the USA.* New York: St. Martin's.

Hall, Peter. 1993. "Policy Paradigms, Social Learning, and the State: The Case of Economic Policymaking in Britain." *Comparative Politics* 26: 275–96.

Hansen, John Mark. 1991. *Gaining Access: Congress and the Farm Lobby, 1919–1981.* Chicago: University of Chicago Press.

Hardin, Russell. 1982. *Collective Action.* Baltimore: Johns Hopkins University Press.

Harne, Lynne. 1988. "From 1971: Reinventing the Wheel." In '*68, '78, '88: From Women's Liberation to Feminism*, edited by Amanda Sebestyen, 63–71. Bridport, England: Prism.

Hart, Vivien. 1994. "Redesigning the Polity: Women, Workers, and European Constitutional Rights." Paper presented at the Conference on Redesigning the State, Australian National University, July.

Harwin, Nicola, and Thangam Debbonnaire. 1996. "WAFE." Paper presented at the International Conference on Violence, Abuse, and Women's Citizenship, Brighton, England, 11 November.

Havel, Václav. 1985. "The Power of the Powerless." In *The Power of the Powerless: Citizens against the State in Central-Eastern Europe*, edited by Václav Havel et al., 23–86. Armonk, N.Y.: Sharpe.

Heijden, Hein-Anton van der, Ruud Koopmans, and Marco G. Giugni. 1992. "The West European Environmental Movement." In *The Green Movement Worldwide*, edited by Matthias Finger, 1–40. Greenwich, Conn.: JAI.

Heineman, Kenneth J. 1993. *Campus Wars: The Peace Movement at American State Universities in the Vietnam Era*. New York: New York University Press.

Held, David. 1987. *Models of Democracy*. Cambridge, England: Polity.

Hernekamp, Karl. 1979. *Formen und Verfahren direkter Demokratie*. Frankfurt: Metzner Verlag.

Hester, Marianne, and Lorraine Radford. 1996. "Contradictions and Compromises: The Impact of the Children's Act on Women's and Children's Safety." In *Women, Violence, and Male Power*, edited by Marianne Hester, Liz Kelly, and Jill Radford, 81–98. Buckingham, England: Open University Press.

Heussner, Hermann K. 1994. "Volksgesetzgebung in den USA und in Deutschland." *Erlanger Juristische Abhandlungen* 43. Cologne: Carl Heymanns Verlag.

Hicks, Alexander, and Duane H. Swank. 1983. "Civil Disorder, Relief Mobilization, and AFDC Caseloads: A Reexamination of the Piven and Cloward Thesis." *American Journal of Political Science* 27: 695–716.

———. 1992. "Politics, Institutions, and Welfare Spending in Industrialized Democracies, 1960–82." *American Political Science Review* 86: 658–74.

Hilgartner, Stephen, and Charles Bosk. 1988. "The Rise and Fall of Social Problems." *American Journal of Sociology* 94: 53–78.

Hobsbawm, Eric. 1990. *Nations and Nationalism since 1780*. Cambridge: Cambridge University Press.

Hofrichter, Jürgen, and Karlheinz Reif. 1990. "Evolution of Environmental Attitudes in the European Community." *Scandinavian Political Studies* 13: 119–46.

Hogan, Dennis P. 1981. *Transitions and Social Change: The Early Lives of American Men*. New York: Academic Press.

Hollinger, David A. 1996. *Science, Jews, and Secular Culture: Studies in Mid-Twentieth Century American Intellectual History*. Princeton: Princeton University Press.

Holtzman, Abraham. 1963. *The Townsend Movement: A Political Study*. New York: Bookman.

Hopf, Ted. 1993. "Getting the End of the Cold War Wrong." *International Security* 18: 202–8.

Huber, Evelyn, Charles Ragin, and John D. Stephens. 1993. "Social Democracy, Christian Democracy, Constitutional Structure, and the Welfare State: Towards a Resolution of Quantitative Studies." *American Journal of Sociology* 99: 711–49.

Huberts, Leo. 1989. "The Influence of Social Movements on Government Policy." In *Organizing for Change: Social Movement Organizations in Europe and the United States,* edited by Bert Klandermans, 395–426. Greenwich, Conn.: JAI.

Hunt, Scott A., Robert D. Benford, and David A. Snow. 1994. "Identity Fields: The Social Construction of Movement Identity." In *New Social Movements: From Ideology to Identity,* edited by Enrique Larana, Joe Gusfield, and Hank Johnston, 185–208. Philadelphia: Temple University Press.

Husbands, Christopher T. 1994. "Crises of National Identity as the 'New Moral Panics': Political Agenda-Setting about Definitions of Nationhood." *New Community* 20 (2): 191–206.

Huygen, Maarten. 1986. "Dateline Holland: NATO's Pyrrhic Victory." *Foreign Policy* 62: 167–85.

Ignagni, Joseph, and James Meernik. 1994. "Explaining Congressional Attempts to Reverse Supreme Court Decisions." *Political Research Quarterly* 47: 353–71.

Ignazi, Piero. 1989. *Il polo escluso: Profilo del Movimento sociale italiano.* Bologna: Il Mulino.

———. 1995. "Alleanza Nazionale? È il MSI riverniciato." *Ideazione* 1: 64–68.

Inglehart, Ronald. 1990. *Culture Shift in Advanced Industrial Society.* Princeton: Princeton University Press.

———. 1995. "Public Support for Environmental Protection: Objective Problems and Subjective Values in Forty-Three Societies." *PS: Political Science and Politics* 28: 57–71.

Isaac, Larry, and William R. Kelly. 1981. "Racial Insurgency, the State, and Welfare Expansion: Local and National Evidence from the Postwar U.S." *American Journal of Sociology* 86: 1348–86.

Jackson, Keith, and Jim Lamare. 1988. "Politics, Public Opinion, and International Crisis: The ANZUS Issue in New Zealand Politics." In *ANZUS in Crisis: Alliance Management in International Affairs,* edited by Jacob Bercovitch, 160–90. London: Macmillan.

Jänicke, Martin. 1992. "Conditions for Environmental Policy Success: An International Comparison." In *Environmental Policy in Europe,* edited by Martin Jachtenfuchs and Michael Strübel, 71–97. Baden-Baden, Germany: Nomos.

———, ed. 1996. *Umweltpolitik der Industrieländer.* Berlin: Sigma.

Jänicke, Martin, and Helmut Weidner, eds. 1995. *Successful Environmental Policy.* Berlin: Sigma.

Jasper, James M. 1990. *Nuclear Politics: Energy and the State in the United States, Sweden, and France.* Princeton: Princeton University Press.

Jasper, James M., and Dorothy Nelkin. 1992. *The Animal Rights Crusade: The Growth of a Moral Protest.* New York: Free Press.

Jasper, James M., and Jane D. Poulsen. 1993. "Fighting Back: Vulnerabilities, Blunders, and Countermobilization by the Targets in Three Animal Rights Campaigns." *Sociological Forum* 8: 639–58.

Jenkins, J. Craig. 1981. "Sociopolitical Movements." In *The Handbook of Political Behavior,* edited by Samuel L. Long. Vol. 4, 81–153. New York: Plenum.

———. 1983. "Resource Mobilization Theory and the Study of Social Movements." *Annual Review of Sociology* 9: 527–53.

Jenkins, J. Craig, and Barbara Brents. 1989. "Social Protest, Hegemonic Competition, and Social Reform: A Political Struggle Interpretation of the Origins of the American Welfare State." *American Sociological Review* 54: 891–909.

Jenkins, J. Craig, and Charles Perrow. 1977. "The Insurgency of the Powerless: Farm Workers' Movements (1946–1972)." *American Sociological Review* 42: 249–68.

Jennings, Edward T. 1979. "Civil Turmoil and the Growth of Welfare Rolls: A Comparative State Policy Analysis." *Policy Studies Journal* 7: 739–45.

———. 1983. "Racial Insurgency, the State, and Welfare Expansion: A Critical Comment and Reanalysis." *American Journal of Sociology* 88: 1220–36.

———. 1987. "Residues of a Movement: The Aging of the American Protest Generation." *American Political Science Review* 81: 367–82.

Jennings, M. Kent, and Richard Niemi. 1981. *Generations and Politics.* Princeton: Princeton University Press.

Johnston, Hank, and Bert Klandermans, eds. 1995. *Social Movements and Culture.* Minneapolis: University of Minnesota Press.

Johnstone, Diana. 1984. *The Politics of the Euromissiles.* New York: Schocken.

Jones, Bryan D. 1994. *Reconceiving Decision-Making in Democratic Politics.* Chicago: University of Chicago Press.

Joppke, Christian. 1993. *Mobilizing against Nuclear Energy: A Comparison of Germany and the United States.* Berkeley and Los Angeles: University of California Press.

Jörgens, Helge. 1996. "Die Institutionalisierung von Umweltpolitik im internationalen Vergleich." In *Umweltpolitik der Industrieländer,* edited by Martin Jänicke, 59–11. Berlin: Sigma.

Joseph, Paul. 1993. *Peace Politics.* Philadelphia: Temple University Press.

Kaldor, Mary. 1983. "Beyond the Blocs: Defending Europe the Political Way." *World Policy Journal* (fall):1–21.

Kaldor, Mary, and Dan Smith, eds. 1982. *Disarming Europe.* London: Merlin.

Kasher, Steven. 1996. *The Civil Rights Movement: A Photographic History, 1954–68.* New York: Abbeville.

Katzenstein, Mary Fainsod. 1995. "Discursive Politics and Feminist Activism in the Catholic Church." In *Feminist Organizations: Harvest of the New Women's Movement,* edited by Myra Marx Ferree and Patricia Yancey Martin, 35–52. Philadelphia: Temple University Press.

Keller, Evelyn Fox. 1992. *Secrets of Life, Secrets of Death: Essays on Language, Gender, and Science.* London: Routledge.

Kelley, Stanley. 1983. *Interpreting Elections.* Princeton: Princeton University Press.

Kelly, William R., and David Snyder. 1980. "Racial Violence and Socioeconomic Changes among Blacks in the United States." *Social Forces* 58: 739–60.

Kerbo, Harold R., and Richard A. Shaffer. 1992. "Lower Class Insurgency and the Political Process: The Response of the U.S. Unemployed, 1890–1940." *Social Problems* 39: 139–54.

Kessler-Harris, Alice. 1994. "Feminism and Affirmative Action." In *Debating Affirmative Action: Race, Gender, Ethnicity, and the Politics of Inclusion,* edited by Nicolaus Mills, 68–79. New York: Delta.

Kevles, Daniel J. 1978. *The Physicists: The History of a Scientific Community in Modern America.* New York: Knopf.

Key, Vladimir Orlando, and Winston W. Crouch. 1939. "The Initiative and the Referendum in California." *Publications of the University of California at Los Angeles in Social Sciences.* Vol. 6, *1936–1939:* 323–592.

King, Gary, Robert Keohane, and Sidney Verba. 1994. *Designing Social Inquiry: Scientific Inference in Qualitative Research.* Princeton: Princeton University Press.

Kingdon, John. 1984. *Agendas, Alternatives, and Public Policies.* Boston: Little, Brown.

Kitschelt, Herbert. 1986. "Political Opportunity Structures and Political Protest: Anti-nuclear Movements in Four Democracies." *British Journal of Political Science* 16: 57–85.

———. 1990. "New Social Movements and the Decline of Party Organizations." In *Challenging the Political Order: New Social Movements in Western Democracies,* edited by Russell Dalton and Manfred Kuechler, 179–208. Cambridge, England: Polity.

———. 1993. "Social Movements, Political Parties, and Democratic Theory." *Annals of the American Academy of Political and Social Science* 528: 13–29.

———. 1994. *The Transformation of European Social Democracy.* Cambridge: Cambridge University Press.

Klandermans, Bert, and Dirk Oegema. 1987. "Potentials, Networks, Motivations, and Barriers: Steps toward Participation in Social Movements." *American Sociological Review* 52: 519–31.

Kleger, Heinz, and Gianni D'Amato. 1995. "Staatsbürgerschaft und Einbürgerung— oder: Wer ist ein Bürger? Ein Vergleich zwischen Deutschland, Frankreich und der Schweiz." *Journal für Sozialforschung,* 35 (3–4): 259–81.

Kleidman, Robert. 1993. *Organizing for Peace: Neutrality, the Test Ban, and the Nuclear Freeze.* Syracuse, N.Y.: Syracuse University Press.

Klingemann, Hans-Dieter, and Dieter Fuchs. 1995. *Citizens and the State.* Oxford: Oxford University Press.

Knoepfel, Peter, and Helmut Weidner. 1986. "Explaining Differences in the Perform-ance of Clean Air Policies: An International and Interregional Comparative Study." *Policy and Politics* 14: 71–91.

Knopf, Jeffrey W. 1993. "Beyond Two-Level Games: Domestic-International Interaction in the Intermediate-Range Nuclear Arms Negotiations." *International Organization* 47: 599–628.

Kölz, Alfred. 1992. *Neuere schweizerische Verfassungsgeschichte: Ihre Grundlinien vom Ende der Alten Eidgenossenschaft bis 1848.* Bern: Verlag Stämpfli.

Koopmans, Ruud. 1993. "The Dynamics of Protest Waves: West Germany, 1965 to 1989." *American Sociological Review* 58: 637–58.

———. 1995. *Democracy from Below: New Social Movements and the Political System in West Germany.* Boulder, Colo.: Westview.

Koopmans, Ruud. 1996a. "Asyl: Die Karriere eines politischen Konfliktes." In *Kommunikation und Entscheidung: Politische Funktionen öffentlicher Meinungsbildung und diskursiver Verfahren,* edited by Wolfgang van den Daele and Friedhelm Neidhardt, 167–92. Berlin: Sigma.

———. 1996b. "Dynamics of Repression and Mobilization: The German Extreme Right in the 1990s." Paper presented at the Conference on Conflict and Extremism in a Democratic Society, Ein Bokek, Israel, December 8–12.

———. 1996c. "Explaining the Rise of Racist and Extreme Right Violence in Western Europe: Grievances or Opportunities?" *European Journal of Political Research* 30: 185–216.

———. 1996d. "New Social Movements and Changes in Political Participation in Western Europe." *West European Politics* 19: 28–50.

Koopmans, Ruud, and Jan Willem Duyvendak. 1995. "The Political Construction of the Nuclear Energy Issue and Its Impact on the Mobilization of Anti-nuclear Movements in Western Europe." *Social Problems* 42: 201–18.

Kowalewski, David, and Paul Schumaker. 1981. "Protest Outcomes in the Soviet Union." *Sociological Quarterly* 22: 57–68.

Krauthammer, Charles. 1989. "Universal Dominion: Toward a Unipolar World." *National Interest* 18: 46–49.

Krehbiel, Kenneth. 1991. *Information and Legislative Organization.* Ann Arbor: University of Michigan Press.

Kriesi, Hanspeter. 1989. "The Political Opportunity Structure of the Dutch Peace Movement." *West European Politics* 12: 295–312.

———. 1995. "The Political Opportunity Structure of New Social Movements: Its Impact on Their Mobilization." In *The Politics of Social Protest: Comparative Perspectives on States and Social Movements,* edited by J. Craig Jenkins and Bert Klandermans, 167–98. Minneapolis: University of Minnesota Press.

———. 1996. "The Organizational Structure of New Social Movements in a Political Context." In *Comparative Perspectives on Social Movements: Political Opportunities, Mobilizing Structures, and Cultural Framings,* edited by Doug McAdam, John D. McCarthy, and Mayer N. Zald, 152–84. Cambridge: Cambridge University Press.

Kriesi, Hanspeter, and Marco G. Giugni. 1996. "Ökologische Bewegungen im internationalen Vergleich: Zwischen Konflikt und Kooperation." In *Umweltsoziologie,* edited by Andreas Diekmann and Carlo C. Jaeger, 324–49. Kölner Zeitschrift für Soziologie und Sozialpyschologie, no. 36. Opladen, Germany: Westdeutscher Verlag.

Kriesi, Hanspeter, Ruud Koopmans, Jan Willem Duyvendak, and Marco G. Giugni.

1992. "New Social Movements and Political Opportunities in Western Europe." *European Journal of Political Research* 22: 219–44.

———. 1995. *New Social Movements in Western Europe: A Comparative Analysis.* Minneapolis: University of Minnesota Press.

Kuhn, Thomas. 1962. *The Structure of Scientific Revolutions.* Chicago: University of Chicago Press.

Kuznick, Peter J. 1994. "The Ethical and Political Crisis of Science: The AAAS Confronts the War in Vietnam." Paper presented to the annual meeting of the History of Science Society.

Landais-Stamp, Paul, and Paul Rogers. 1989. *Rocking the Boat.* Oxford: Berg.

Langdon, Julia. 1997. "Hallo Boys." *Guardian* (January 6): 6–7.

Lange, David. 1985. "New Zealand's Security Policy." *Foreign Affairs* 63: 1000–1019.

La Palombara, Joseph G. 1965. "Italy: Isolation, Fragmentation, and Alienation." In *Political Culture and Political Development,* edited by Lucian W. Pye and Sidney Verba. Princeton: Princeton University Press.

Lapp, Ralph. 1965. *The New Priesthood: The Scientific Elite and the Uses of Power.* New York: Harper and Row.

Lasby, Clarence G. 1966. "Science and the Military." In *Scientists and Society in the United States,* edited by David D. Van Tassel and Michael G. Hall, 251–82. Homewood, Ill.: Dorsey.

Leslie, Stuart W. 1993. *The Cold War and American Science: The Military-Industrial-Academic Complex at MIT and Stanford.* New York: Columbia University Press.

Lester [Lord of Herne Hill]. 1996. "Discrimination Law in 1996." *Equal Opportunities Review* 65: 25–29.

Liang, Hsi-Huey. 1992. *The Rise of Modern Police and the European State System from Metternich to the Second World War.* Cambridge: Cambridge University Press.

Lieberson, Stanley. 1991. "Small N's and Big Conclusions: An Examination of the Reasoning in Comparative Studies Based on a Small Number of Cases." *Social Forces* 70: 307–20.

Liebeskind, Wolfgang-Amédée. 1952. "Un débat sur la démocratie genevoise." In *Mélanges Georges Sauser-Hall,* 99–107. Neuchâtel, Switzerland: Delachaux et Niestlé.

———. [1938] 1973. "La république des provinces-unies des Pays-Bas et le corps helvétique." In *Institutions politiques et traditions nationales,* edited by Wolfgang-Amédée Liebeskind, 286–309. Geneva: Georg.

Lipsky, Michael. 1968. "Protest as a Political Resource." *American Political Science Review* 62: 1144–58.

———. 1970. *Protest in City Politics: Rent Strikes, Housing, and the Power of the Poor.* Chicago: Rand McNally.

Lo, Clarence Y. H. 1990. *Small Property versus Big Government.* Berkeley and Los Angeles: University of California Press.

Lofland, John. 1993. *Polite Protesters: The American Peace Movement of the 1980s.* Syracuse, N.Y.: Syracuse University Press.

Lohmann, Susanne. 1993. "A Signaling Model of Informative and Manipulative Political Action." *American Political Science Review* 87: 319–33.

———. 1994. "The Dynamics of Informational Cascades: The Monday Demonstrations in Leipzig, East Germany, 1989–91." *World Politics* 47: 42–101.

———. 1995. "A Signaling Model of Competitive Political Pressures." *Economics and Politics* 7: 181–206.

Lovenduski, Joni. 1986. *Women and European Politics: Contemporary Feminism and Public Policy.* Amherst: University of Massachusetts Press.

———. 1996. "Sex, Gender, and British Politics." In *Women in Politics,* edited by Joni Lovenduski and Pippa Norris, 1–16. Oxford: Oxford University Press.

Lovenduski, Joni, Helen Margetts, and Stefania Abrar. 1996. "Sexing London: The Gender Mix of Policy Actors." Paper presented at the annual meeting of the American Political Science Association, San Francisco, Calif., August 29–September 1.

Lovenduski, Joni, and Vicky Randall. 1993. *Contemporary Feminist Politics: Women and Power in Britain.* Oxford: Oxford University Press.

Lowi, Theodore J. 1969. *The End of Liberalism.* New York: Norton.

———. 1971. *The Politics of Disorder.* New York: Basic Books.

———. 1979. *The End of Liberalism.* 2d ed. New York: Norton.

Lukes, Steven. 1974. *Power: A Radical View.* London: Macmillan.

Luthardt, Wolfgang. 1994. *Direkte Demokratie: Ein Vergleich in Westeuropa.* Baden-Baden, Germany: Nomos.

Lyttle, Bradford. 1988. *The Chicago Anti–Vietnam War Movement.* Chicago: Midwest Pacifist Center.

Mackay, Fiona. 1996. "The Zero Tolerance Campaign: Setting the Agenda." In *Women in Politics,* edited by Joni Lovenduski and Pippa Norris, 208–22. Oxford: Oxford University Press.

Macmillan, Stuart. 1987. *Neither Confirm nor Deny: The Nuclear Ships Dispute between New Zealand and the United States.* New York: Praeger.

Magraw, Katherine. 1989. "The Nuclear Weapons Policy Debate in the 1980s: A Reevaluation of the Role of Congress." Paper presented at the annual meeting of the American Political Science Association, Atlanta, Georgia, September 2.

Mansbridge, Jane J. 1992. "A Deliberative Theory of Interest Representation." In *The Politics of Interests,* edited by Mark P. Petracca, 32–57. Boulder, Colo.: Westview.

Marini, Margaret Mooney. 1984a. "Age and Sequencing Norms in the Transition to Adulthood." *Social Forces* 63: 229–44.

———. 1984b. "Women's Educational Attainment and the Timing of Entry into Parenthood." *American Sociological Review* 49: 491–511.

Markovits, Andrei. 1983. "Reflections and Observations on the Elections in West Germany." *New German Critique* 58: 2–51.

Marks, Shula, and Stanley Trapido, eds. 1987. *The Politics of Race, Class, and Nationalism in Twentieth-Century South Africa.* London: Longman.

Marshall, Susan. 1995. "Confrontation and Co-optation in Antifeminist Organizations." In *Feminist Organizations: Harvest of the New Women's Movement,* edited by Myra

Marx Ferree and Patricia Yancey Martin, 323–35. Philadelphia: Temple University Press.

Marshall, Thomas H. 1950. *Citizenship and Social Class and Other Essays.* Cambridge: Cambridge University Press.

Marullo, Sam. 1994. *Ending the Cold War at Home.* Lexington, Mass.: Lexington Press.

Marwell, Gerald, Michael T. Aiken, and N. Jay Demerath III. 1987. "The Persistence of Political Attitudes among 1960s Civil Rights Activists." *Public Opinion Quarterly* 51: 359–75.

Marwell, Gerald, and Pamela Oliver. 1993. *The Critical Mass in Collective Action: A Micro-social Theory.* Cambridge: Cambridge University Press.

Marwell, Gerald, Pamela Oliver, and Ralph Prahl. 1988. "Social Networks and Collective Action: A Theory of the Critical Mass III." *American Journal of Sociology* 94: 502–34.

Mayhew, David. 1974. *Congress: The Electoral Connection.* New Haven: Yale University Press.

McAdam, Doug. 1982. *Political Process and the Development of Black Insurgency, 1930–1970.* Chicago: University of Chicago Press.

———. 1983. "Tactical Innovation and the Pace of Insurgency." *American Sociological Review* 48: 735–54.

———. 1988. *Freedom Summer: The Idealists Revisited.* Oxford: Oxford University Press.

———. 1989. "The Biographical Consequences of Activism." *American Sociological Review* 54: 744–60.

———. 1992. "Gender as a Mediator of the Activist Experience: The Case of Freedom Summer." *American Journal of Sociology* 97: 453–76.

———. 1994. "Culture and Social Movements." In *New Social Movements: From Ideology to Identity,* edited by Enrique Laraña, Hank Johnston, and Joseph R. Gusfield, 36–57. Philadelphia: Temple University Press.

———. 1995. "'Initiator' and 'Derivative' Movements: Diffusion Processes in Protest Cycles." In *Repertoires and Cycles of Collective Action,* edited by Mark Traugott, 217–39. Durham, N.C.: Duke University Press.

McAdam, Doug, John D. McCarthy, and Mayer N. Zald. 1988. "Social Movements." In *Handbook of Sociology,* edited by Neil J. Smelser, 695–737. Beverly Hills: Sage.

———, eds. 1996. *Comparative Perspectives on Social Movements: Political Opportunities, Mobilizing Structures, and Cultural Framings.* Cambridge: Cambridge University Press.

McAdam, Doug, Kelly Moore, and James W. Shockey. 1992. "Life-Course Constraints on Activism." Paper presented at the annual meeting of the American Sociological Association, Cincinnati, Ohio.

McAdam, Doug, and Ronnelle Paulsen. 1993. "Specifying the Relationship between Social Ties and Activism." *American Journal of Sociology* 98: 735–54.

McCaffery, Peter. 1993. *When Bosses Ruled Philadelphia: The Emergence of the Republican Machine, 1867–1933.* University Park: Pennsylvania State University Press.

———. 1977. "Resource Mobilization and Social Movements." *American Journal of Sociology* 82: 1212–41.

McCrea, Frances B., and Gerald E. Markle. 1989. *Minutes to Midnight: Nuclear Weapons Protest in America.* Newbury Park, Calif.: Sage.

McPhail, Clark. 1971. "Civil Disorder Participation: A Critical Examination of Recent Research." *American Sociological Review* 36: 1058–73.

Meehan, Elizabeth, and Evelyn Collins. 1996. "Women, the European Union and Britain." In *Women in Politics,* edited by Joni Lovenduski and Pippa Norris, 223–36. Oxford: Oxford University Press.

Melucci, Alberto. 1982. *L'invenzione del presente.* Bologna: Il Mulino.

———. 1985. "The Symbolic Challenge of Contemporary Movements." *Social Research* 52: 789–816.

———. 1988. "Getting Involved: Identity and Mobilization in Social Movements." In *From Structure to Action: Comparing Social Movement Research across Cultures,* edited by Bert Klandermans, Hanspeter Kriesi, and Sidney Tarrow, 329–48. Greenwich, Conn.: JAI.

———. 1989. *Nomads of the Present: Social Movements and Individual Needs in Contemporary Society.* London: Hutchinson; Philadelphia: Temple University Press.

———. 1996. *Challenging Codes: Collective Action in the Information Age.* Cambridge: Cambridge University Press.

Merkl, Peter H., and Leonard Weinberg, eds. 1993. *Encounters with the Contemporary Radical Right.* Boulder, Colo.: Westview.

Messinger, Sheldon L. 1955. "Organizational Transformation: A Case Study of a Declining Social Movement." *American Sociological Review* 20: 3–10.

Meyer, David S. 1990. *A Winter of Discontent: The Nuclear Freeze and American Politics.* New York: Praeger.

———. 1990–91. "How We Helped End the Cold War (and Let Someone Else Take All the Credit)." *Nuclear Times* (winter): 9–14.

———. 1991. "Peace Movements and National Security Policy: A Research Agenda." *Peace and Change* 16: 131–61.

———. 1993. "Political Process and Protest Movement Cycles: American Peace Movements in the Nuclear Age." *Political Research Quarterly* 46: 451–79.

———. 1994. "Political Opportunity and Nested Institutions: Protest and Policy in New Zealand's Nuclear-Free Zone." Paper presented at the annual meeting of the Midwest Political Science Association, Chicago, Ill., April 14.

———. 1995. "Framing National Security: Elite Public Discourse on Nuclear Weapons during the Cold War." *Political Communication* 12: 173–92.

Meyer, David S., and Nancy Whittier. 1994. "Social Movement Spillover." *Social Problems* 41: 277–98.

Meyer, David S., and Sam Marullo. 1992. "Grassroots Mobilization and International

Politics: Peace Protest and the End of the Cold War." *Research in Social Movements, Conflict, and Change* 14: 99–140.

Meyer, David S., and Suzanne Staggenborg. 1996. "Movements, Countermovements, and the Structure of Political Opportunity." *American Journal of Sociology* 101: 1628–60.

Michnik, Adam. 1982. "We Are All Hostages." *Telos* 51: 173–81.

Midttun, Atle, and Dieter Rucht. 1994. "Comparing Policy Outcomes of Conflicts over Nuclear Power: Description and Explanation." In *States and Anti-nuclear Movements,* edited by Helena Flam, 371–403. Edinburgh: Edinburgh University Press.

Mirowsky, John, and Catherine Ross. 1981. "Protest Group Success: The Impact of Group Characteristics, Social Control, and Context." *Sociological Focus* 14: 177–92.

Mishler, William, and Reginald S. Sheehan. 1994. "Popular Influence on Supreme Court Decisions: Response." *American Political Science Review* 88: 716–24.

Möckli, Silvano. 1994. *Direkte Demokratie: Ein internationaler Vergleich.* Bern: Haupt.

Modell, John F. 1989. *Into One's Own: From Youth to Adulthood in the United States, 1920–1975.* Berkeley and Los Angeles: University of California Press.

Moore, Kelly. 1996. "Organizing Integrity: American Science and the Creation of Public Interest Science Organizations, 1955–1975." *American Journal of Sociology* 101: 1592–1627.

Morlino, Leonardo, and Marco Tarchi. 1996. "The Dissatisfied Society: The Roots of Political Change in Italy." *European Journal of Political Research* 30: 41–63.

Morris, Aldon D., and Carol McClurg Mueller, eds. 1992. *Frontiers in Social Movement Theory.* New Haven: Yale University Press.

Moss, Frances. 1995. "Making the Invisible Visible: The Rise of a Professional Women's Network in the 1990s." In *Feminist Activism in the 1990s,* edited by Gabriele Griffin, 171–81. London: Taylor and Francis.

Mueller, Carol McClurg. 1978. "Riot Violence and Protest Outcomes." *Journal of Political and Military Sociology* 6: 49–63.

———, ed. 1988. *The Politics of the Gender Gap.* Beverly Hills: Sage.

Mukerji, Chandra. 1989. *A Fragile Power.* Princeton: Princeton University Press.

Müller-Rommel, Ferdinand. 1993. *Grüne Parteien in Westeuropa.* Opladen, Germany: Westdeutscher Verlag.

Myrdal, Alva. 1982. *The Game of Disarmament.* New York: Pantheon.

Nagel, Joane. 1995. "Politics and the Resurgence of American Indian Ethnic Identity." *American Sociological Review* 60: 947–65.

Nassi, Alberta J., and Stephen I. Abramowitz. 1979. "Transition of Transformation: Personal and Political Development of Former Berkeley Free Speech Movement Activists." *Journal of Youth and Adolescence* 8: 21–35.

National Alliance of Women's Organisations (NAWO). 1996. *1995 Annual Report.* London: NAWO.

National Research Council. 1945–1993. *Survey of Earned Doctorates.*

National Science Foundation. 1977. *National Patterns of R and D Resources: Funds and Manpower in the United States.* Washington, D.C.: USGPO.

Neidhardt, Friedhelm. 1994. "Öffentlichkeit, öffentliche Meinung, soziale Bewegungen." In *Öffentlichkeit, öffentliche Meinung, soziale Bewegungen,* edited by Friedhelm Neidhardt, 7–41. Kölner Zeitschrift für Soziologie und Sozialpysychologie, no. 34. Opladen, Germany: Westdeutscher Verlag.

Nelson, Barbara J., and Kathryn A. Carver. 1994. "Many Voices but Few Vehicles: The Consequences for Women of Weak Political Infrastructure in the United States." In *Women and Politics Worldwide,* edited by Barbara J. Nelson and Nazma Chowdhury, 738–57. New Haven: Yale University Press.

Nelson, Richard R. 1995. "Recent Evolutionary Theorizing about Economic Change." *Journal of Economic Literature* 33: 48–90.

Neustadtl, Alan. 1990. "Interest-Group PACsmanship: An Analysis of Campaign Contributions, Issue Visibility, and Legislative Impact." *Social Forces* 69: 549–64.

Nichols, Elizabeth. 1987. "U.S. Nuclear Power and the Success of the American Antinuclear Movement." *Berkeley Journal of Sociology* 32: 167–92.

Norpoth, Helmut, and Jeffrey A. Segal. 1994. "Popular Influence on Supreme Court Decisions: Comment." *American Political Science Review* 88: 711–16.

Norris, Pippa. 1996. "Mobilizing the 'Women's Vote': The Gender-Generation Gap in Voting Behaviour." *Parliamentary Affairs* 49: 333–42.

Nowotny, Helga. 1979. *Kernenergie: Gefahr oder Notwendigkeit: Anatomie eines Konflikts.* Frankfurt: Suhrkamp.

Oberholzer, Ellis Paxson. 1912. *The Referendum in America.* New York: Scribner's.

O'Connor, Robert E., and Michael E. Berkman. 1995. "Religious Determinants of State Abortion Policy." *Social Science Quarterly* 76: 447–59.

Offe, Claus. 1985. "New Social Movements: Changing Boundaries of the Political." *Social Research* 52: 817–68.

O'Neill, William L. 1971. *Coming Apart: An Informal History of America in the 1960's.* Chicago: Quadrangle.

Organization for Economic Cooperation and Development (OECD). 1985–1995. *Environmental Data: Compendium 1985, 1987, 1989, 1991, 1993, 1995.* Paris: OECD.

———. 1995. *Immigrazione straniera in Italia: Rapporto annuale del Censis al Sistema di Osservazione Permanente sull'Immigrazione dell'OCSE.* Rome: Censis.

Ostrom, Elinor. 1990. *Governing the Commons: The Evolution of Institutions for Collective Action.* Cambridge: Cambridge University Press.

Page, Benjamin I., and Robert Y. Shapiro. 1983. "Effects of Public Opinion on Policy." *American Political Science Review* 77: 175–90.

———. 1992. *The Rational Public.* Chicago: University of Chicago Press.

Parenti, Michael. 1970. "Power and Pluralism: A View from the Bottom." *Journal of Politics* 32: 501–30.

Pearce, Diana. 1990. "Welfare Is Not *for* Women: Why the War on Poverty Cannot

Conquer the Feminization of Poverty." In *Women, the State, and Welfare,* edited by Linda Gordon, 265–79. Madison: University of Wisconsin Press.

Pegg, Chris. 1990. "A 'Pretended Family.'" In *Surviving the Blues: Growing Up in the Thatcher Decade,* edited by Joan Scanlon, 156–71. London: Virago.

Perrigo, Sarah. 1996. "Women and Change in the Labour Party, 1979–1995." In *Women in Politics,* edited by Joni Lovenduski and Pippa Norris, 118–31. Oxford: Oxford University Press.

Piven, Frances Fox, and Richard A. Cloward. 1971. *Regulating the Poor: The Functions of Public Welfare.* New York: Vintage.

———. 1977. *Poor People's Movements: Why They Succeed, How They Fail.* New York: Pantheon.

———. 1978. "Social Movements and Societal Conditions: A Reply to Roach and Roach." *Social Problems* 26 (2).

———. 1979. *Poor People's Movements: Why They Succeed, How They Fail.* New York: Vintage.

———. 1980. "Doctrine in Command of Politics: A Reply to Roach and Roach." *Sociological Quarterly* 21.

———. 1992. "Normalizing Collective Protest." In *Frontiers in Social Movement Theory,* edited by Aldon D. Morris and Carol McClurg Mueller, 301–25. New Haven: Yale University Press.

———. 1993. *Regulating the Poor: The Functions of Public Welfare.* 2d ed. New York: Vintage.

Plotke, David. 1996. *Building a Democratic Political Order: Reshaping American Liberalism in the 1930s and 1940s.* Cambridge: Cambridge University Press.

Pond, Elizabeth. 1990. "A Wall Destroyed: The Dynamics of German Unification in the GDR." *International Security* 15: 35–66.

Porter, Gareth, and Janet Welsh Brown. 1991. *Global Environmental Politics.* Boulder, Colo.: Westview.

Porter, Jack Nusan. 1973. *Student Protest and the Technocratic Society: The Case of ROTC.* Chicago: Adams.

Price, Charles M. 1975. "The Initiative: A Comparative State Analysis and Reassessment of a Western Phenomenon." *Western Political Quarterly* (June): 243–62.

Price, Don K. 1965. *The Scientific Estate.* Cambridge: Harvard University Press.

Princen, Thomas, and Matthias Finger, eds. 1994. *Environmental NGOs in World Politics: Linking the Local and the Global.* London: Routledge.

Pugh, Michael C. 1989. *The ANZUS Crisis, Nuclear Visiting, and Deterrence.* Cambridge: Cambridge University Press.

Putnam, Jackson K. 1970. *Old-Age Politics in California: From Richardson to Reagan.* Stanford: Stanford University Press.

Radford, Jill, and Elizabeth A. Stanko. 1996. "Violence against Women and Children: The Contradictions of Crime Control under Patriarchy." In *Women, Violence, and*

Male Power, edited by Marianne Hester, Liz Kelly, and Jill Radford, 65–80. Buckingham, England: Open University Press.

Ragin, Charles C. 1987. *The Comparative Method.* Berkeley and Los Angeles: University of California Press.

———. 1989. "The Logic of the Comparative Method and the Algebra of Logic." *Journal of Quantitative Anthropology* 1: 373–98.

Ragin, Charles C., and Howard Becker. 1992. *What Is a Case? Exploring the Foundations of Social Inquiry.* Cambridge: Cambridge University Press.

Rappard, William E. 1912. "The Initiative, Referendum, and Recall in Switzerland." *Annals of the American Academy of Political and Social Science* 110.

Rein, Martin, and D. A. Schoen. 1977. "Problem Setting in Policy Research." In *Using Social Research for Public Policy Making,* edited by C. Weiss, 235–51. Lexington, Mass.: Lexington Books.

Reinelt, Claire. 1995. "Moving onto the Terrain of the State: The Battered Women's Movement and the Politics of Engagement." In *Feminist Organizations: Harvest of the New Women's Movement,* edited by Myra Marx Ferree and Patricia Yancey Martin, 84–104. Philadelphia: Temple University Press.

Rex, John. 1996a. *Ethnic Minorities in the Modern Nation State: Working Papers in the Theory of Multiculturalism and Political Integration.* Basingstoke, England: Macmillan.

———. 1996b. "National Identity in the Democratic Multi-cultural State." *Sociological Research Online* 1, no. 2. <http://www.socresonline.org.uk/socresonline/1/2/1.html>.

Riger, Stephanie. 1994. "Challenges of Success: Stages of Growth in Feminist Organizations." *Feminist Studies* 20: 275–300.

Riker, William. 1982. *Liberalism against Populism.* Prospect Heights, Ill.: Waveland.

Rindfuss, Ronald R., C. Gray Swicegood, and Rachel A. Rosenfeld. 1987. "Disorder in the Life Course: How Common and Does It Matter?" *American Sociological Review* 52: 785–801.

Rindfuss, Ronald R., and Craig St. John. 1983. "Social Determinants of Age at First Birth." *Journal of Marriage and the Family* 45: 553–65.

Rindfuss, Ronald R., Larry L. Bumpass, and Craig St. John. 1980. "Education and Fertility: Implications for the Roles Women Occupy." *American Sociological Review* 45: 431–47.

Risse-Kappen, Thomas. 1988. *The Zero Option: INF, West Germany, and Arms Control.* Boulder, Colo.: Westview.

———. 1991a. "Did 'Peace through Strength' End the Cold War?" *International Security* 16: 162–88.

———. 1991b. "Public Opinion, Domestic Structure, and Foreign Policy in Liberal Democracies." *World Politics* 43: 479–512.

Roach, Jack L., and Janet K. Roach. 1978. "Organizing the Poor: Road to a Dead End." *Social Problems* 26 (2).

———. 1980. "Turmoil in Command of Politics: Organizing the Poor." *Sociological Quarterly* 21.

Rochon, Thomas R. 1988. *Mobilizing for Peace: The Antinuclear Movements in Western Europe.* Princeton: Princeton University Press.

———. 1997. *Ideas in Movement: Critical Communities, Movements, and Cultural Change.* Princeton: Princeton University Press.

Rochon, Thomas R., and Daniel A. Mazmanian. 1993. "Social Movements and the Policy Process." *Annals of the American Academy of Political and Social Science* 528: 75–87.

Rochon, Thomas R., and David S. Meyer, eds. 1997. *Coalitions and Political Movements: The Lessons of the Nuclear Freeze.* Boulder, Colo.: Rienner.

Rosenfeld, Rachel, and Kathryn Ward. 1991. "The Contemporary Women's Movement." *Sociological Forum* 6: 471–500.

Roth, Roland. 1994. *Demokratie von unten: Neue soziale Bewegungen auf dem Wege zur politischen Institution.* Cologne: Bund Verlag.

Rothstein, Bo. 1990. "Marxism, Institutional Analysis, and Working Class Power: The Swedish Case." *Politics and Society* 18: 317–46.

———. 1992. "Labor-Market Institutions and Working-Class Strength." In *Structuring Politics: Historical Institutionalism in Comparative Analysis,* edited by Sven Steinmo, Kathleen Thelen, and Frank Longstreth, 33–56. Cambridge: Cambridge University Press.

Rowbotham, Sheila. 1996. Introduction to *Mapping the Women's Movement,* edited by Monica Threlfall, 1–16. London: Verso.

Roy, Beth. 1994. *Some Trouble with Cows: Making Sense of Social Conflict.* Berkeley and Los Angeles: University of California Press.

Rucht, Dieter. 1992. "Studying the Effects of Social Movements: Conceptualization and Problems." Paper presented at the European Consortium for Political Research Joint Sessions, Limerick, Ireland, March 30–April 4.

———. 1993. "'Think Globally, Act Locally'? Needs, Forms, and Problems of Environmental Groups' Internationalization." In *European Integration and Environmental Policy,* edited by Duncan Liefferink, Philip Lowe, and Arthur Mol, 75–95. London: Belhaven.

———. 1994. *Modernisierung und neue soziale Bewegungen: Deutschland, Frankreich und USA im Vergleich.* Frankfurt: Campus.

———. 1995. "The Impact of the Anti-nuclear Power Movement in International Comparison." In *Resistance to New Technology,* edited by Martin Bauer, 277–92. Cambridge: Cambridge University Press.

———. 1997. "Limits to Mobilization: Environmental Policy for the European Union." In *Transnational Social Movements and Global Politics: Solidarity beyond the State,* edited by Jackie Smith, Charles Chatfield, and Ron Pagnucco, 195–213. Syracuse, N.Y.: Syracuse University Press.

Rüdig, Wolfgang. 1990. *Anti-nuclear Movements: A World Survey of Opposition to Nuclear Energy.* Harlow, England: Longman.

Russell, Lynne, Duncan Scott, and Paul Wilding. 1996. "The Funding of Local Voluntary Organisations." *Policy and Politics* 24: 395–412.

SAS Institute. 1996. *SAS/STAT Software: Changes and Enhancements through Release 6.11.* Cary, N.C.: SAS Institute.

Schaffner, Martin. 1982. *Die demokratische Bewegung der 1860er Jahre.* Basel: Helbing und Lichtenhahn.

Schattschneider, Elmer E. 1960. *The Semi-sovereign People.* New York: Holt, Rinehart and Winston.

Scheer, Robert. 1982. *With Enough Shovels: Reagan, Bush, and Nuclear War.* New York: Random House.

Scheff, Thomas. 1994. *Bloody Revenge: Emotions, Nationalism, War.* Boulder, Colo.: Westview.

Schramm, Sanford F., and J. Patrick Turbett. 1983. "Civil Disorder and the Welfare Explosion: A Two Step Process." *American Sociological Review* 48: 408–14.

Schumaker, Paul D. 1975. "Policy Responsiveness to Protest-Group Demands." *Journal of Politics* 37: 488–521.

———. 1978. "The Scope of Political Conflict and the Effectiveness of Constraints in Contemporary Urban Protest." *Sociological Quarterly* 19: 168–84.

Scott, W. Richard. 1994. "Institutions and Organizations: Toward a Theoretical Synthesis." In *Institutional Environments and Organizations,* edited by W. Richard Scott and John W. Meyer, 55–80. Thousand Oaks, Calif.: Sage.

Seaborg, Glenn T., with Benjamin S. Loeb. 1981. *Kennedy, Khrushchev, and the Test Ban.* Berkeley and Los Angeles: University of California Press.

Shefter, Martin. 1994. *Political Parties and the State: The American Historical Experience.* Princeton: Princeton University Press.

Shorter, Edward, and Charles Tilly. 1971. "Le déclin de la grève violente en France de 1890 à 1935." *Le Mouvement Social* 79: 95–118.

———. 1974. *Strikes in France, 1830–1968.* Cambridge: Cambridge University Press.

Siegenthaler, Hansjörg. 1993. *Regelvertrauen, Prosperität, und Krisen.* Tübingen: Mohr.

Siméant, Johanna. 1993. "Le mouvement des déboutés du droit d'asile, 1990–1992." In *Sociologie de la protestation: Les formes de l'action collective dans la France contemporaine,* edited by Olivier Fillieule, 181–208. Paris: L'Harmattan.

Skocpol, Theda. 1985. "Bringing the State Back In: Strategies of Analysis in Current Research." In *Bringing the State Back In,* edited by Peter B. Evans, Dietrich Rueschmeyer, and Theda Skocpol, 3–37. Cambridge: Cambridge University Press.

———. 1995. "Response" [to Sparks and Walniuk]. *American Political Science Review* 89: 720–30.

Skocpol, Theda, and Edwin Amenta. 1986. "States and Social Policies." *Annual Review of Sociology* 12: 131–57.

Skocpol, Theda, and Kenneth Finegold. 1990. "Explaining New Deal Labor Policy" [reply to Goldfield]. *American Political Science Review* 84: 1297–1304, 1313–15.

Skocpol, Theda, Marjorie Abend-Wein, Christopher Howard, and Susan Goodrich Lehmann. 1993. "Women's Associations and the Enactment of Mothers' Pensions in the United States." *American Political Science Review* 87: 686–701.

Small, Melvin. 1988. *Johnson, Nixon, and the Doves.* New Brunswick, N.J.: Rutgers University Press.

Smelser, Neil J. 1963. *Theory of Collective Behavior.* New York: Free Press.

Smith, Alice Kimball. 1965. *A Peril and Hope: The Scientists' Movement in America, 1945–1947.* Chicago: University of Chicago Press.

Smith, Anthony D. 1995. *Nations and Nationalism in a Global Era.* Cambridge, England: Polity.

Snow, David A., E. Burke Rochford Jr., Steven K. Worden, and Robert D. Benford. 1986. "Frame Alignment Processes, Micromobilization, and Movement Participation." *American Sociological Review* 51: 464–81.

Snow, David A., and Pamela E. Oliver. 1995. "Social Movements and Collective Behavior: Social Psychological Dimensions and Considerations." In *Sociological Perspectives on Social Psychology,* edited by Karen Cook, Gary Fine, and James House, 571–99. Boston: Allyn and Bacon.

Snow, David A., and Robert D. Benford. 1988. "Ideology, Frame Resonance, and Participant Mobilization." In *From Structure to Action: Comparing Social Movement Research across Cultures,* edited by Bert Klandermans, Hanspeter Kriesi, and Sidney Tarrow, 197–218. Greenwich, Conn.: JAI.

———. 1992. "Master Frames and Cycles of Protest." In *Frontiers in Social Movement Theory,* edited by Aldon D. Morris and Carol McClurg Mueller, 133–55. New Haven: Yale University Press.

Snyder, David, and William R. Kelly. 1976. "Industrial Violence in Italy, 1878–1903." *American Journal of Sociology* 82: 131–62.

———. 1979. "Strategies for Investigating Violence and Social Change: Illustrations from Analyses of Racial Disorders and Implications for Mobilization Research." In *The Dynamics of Social Movements: Resource Mobilization, Tactics, and Social Control,* edited by Mayer N. Zald and John D. McCarthy, 212–37. Cambridge, Mass.: Winthrop.

Solo, Pam. 1988. *From Protest to Policy: Beyond the Freeze to Common Security.* Cambridge, Mass.: Ballinger.

Sørenson, Annemette. 1983. "Women's Employment Patterns after Marriage." *Journal of Marriage and the Family* 45: 311–21.

Southall Black Sisters (SBS). 1996. *Annual Report, 1994–1995.* London: SBS.

Spalter-Roth, Roberta, and Ronnee Schreiber. 1995. "Outsider Issues and Insider Tactics: Strategic Tensions in the Women's Policy Network during the 1980s." In *Feminist Organizations: Harvest of the New Women's Movement,* edited by Myra Marx Ferree and Patricia Yancey Martin, 105–27. Philadelphia: Temple University Press.

Sparks, Cheryl Logan, and Peter R. Walniuk. 1995. "The Enactment of Mothers' Pensions: Civic Mobilization and Agenda Setting or Benefits of the Ballot?" [reply to Skocpol et al.]. *American Political Science Review* 89: 710–20, 728–29.

Squires, Judith. 1996. "Quotas for Women: Fair Representation?" In *Women in Politics,* edited by Joni Lovenduski and Pippa Norris, 71–88. Oxford: Oxford University Press.

Staggenborg, Suzanne. 1988. "The Consequences of Professionalization and Formaliza-
tion in the Pro-Choice Movement." *American Sociological Review* 53: 585–605.

———. 1991. *The Pro-choice Movement: Organization and Activism in the Abortion
Conflict.* Oxford: Oxford University Press.

Starr, Paul. 1982. *The Social Transformation of American Medicine.* New York: Basic Books.

Statham, Paul. 1996a. "Berlusconi, the Media, and the New Right in Italy." *Harvard
International Journal of Press/Politics* 1: 87–105.

———. 1996b. "Television News and the Public Sphere in Italy: Conflicts at the
Media/Politics Interface." *European Journal of Communication* 11: 511–56.

Steedly, Homer R., and John W. Foley. 1979. "The Success of Protest Groups:
Multivariate Analyses." *Social Science Research* 8: 1–15.

Stimson, James A., Michael B. MacKuen, and Robert S. Erikson. 1995. "Dynamic
Representation." *American Political Science Review* 89: 543–65.

Stone, Deborah A. 1988. *Policy Process and Political Reason.* Boston: Little, Brown.

Stöss, Richard. 1989. *Die extreme Rechte in der Bundesrepublik: Entwicklung-Ursachen-
Gegenmaßnahmen.* Opladen, Germany: Westdeutscher Verlag.

Sunstein, Cass R. 1988. "Constitutions and Democracies: An Epilogue." In
Constitutionalism and Democracy, edited by Jon Elster and Rune Slagstad, 327–53.
Cambridge: Cambridge University Press.

Swidler, Ann. 1986. "Culture in Action: Symbols and Strategies." *American Sociological
Review* 51: 273–86.

Sznajder, Mario. 1995. "Heirs of Fascism? Italy's Right-Wing Government: Legitimacy
and Criticism." *International Affairs* 71: 83–102.

Taft, Philip, and Philip Ross. 1969. "American Labor Violence: Its Causes, Character,
and Outcome." In *Violence in America: Historical and Comparative Perspectives,*
edited by Hugh D. Graham and Ted R. Gurr, 281–395. New York: Bantam.

Talbott, Strobe. 1984. *Deadly Gambits: The Reagan Administration and the Stalemate in
Arms Control.* New York: Knopf.

Tarchi, Marco. 1995. *Cinquant'anni di nostalgia.* Milan: Rizzoli.

———. 1996. "After the Breakdown of the 'First Republic': A Turning Point for the
Italian Extreme Right?" *Res Publica* 38: 385–96.

Tarrow, Sidney. 1989. *Democracy and Disorder: Protest and Politics in Italy, 1965–1975.*
Oxford: Oxford University Press.

———. 1992. "Mentalities, Political Cultures, and Collective Action Frames." In
Frontiers in Social Movement Theory, edited by Aldon D. Morris and Carol McClurg
Mueller, 174–202. New Haven: Yale University Press.

———. 1993. "Social Protest and Policy Reform: May 1968 and the *Loi d'Orientation*
in France." *Comparative Political Studies* 25: 579–607.

———. 1994. *Power in Movement: Social Movements, Collective Action, and Politics.*
Cambridge: Cambridge University Press.

———. 1998. *Power in Movement: Social Movements and Contentious Politics.* 2d ed.
Cambridge: Cambridge University Press.

Taylor, Verta, and Nancy Whittier. 1992. "Collective Identity in Social Movement

Communities: Lesbian Feminist Mobilization." In *Frontiers in Social Movement Theory,* edited by Aldon D. Morris and Carol McClurg Mueller, 104–29. New Haven: Yale University Press.

———. 1995. "Analytical Approaches to Social Movement Culture: The Culture of the Women's Movement." In *Social Movements and Culture,* edited by Hank Johnston and Bert Klandermans, 163–87. Minneapolis: University of Minnesota Press.

Thompson, E. P. 1982. *Beyond the Cold War.* New York: Pantheon.

———. 1990. "History Turns on a New Hinge." *Nation* (January 29): 117–18.

Thompson, E. P., and Dan Smith, eds. 1981. *Protest and Survive.* New York: Monthly Review Press.

"Through a Glass Darkly." 1996. *Economist* (August 10): 51.

Tilly, Charles. 1978. *From Mobilization to Revolution.* Reading, Mass.: Addison-Wesley.

———. 1984. "Social Movements and National Politics." In *Statemaking and Social Movements,* edited by Charles Bright and Susan Harding, 297–317. Ann Arbor: University of Michigan Press.

———. 1995. "To Explain Political Processes." *American Journal of Sociology* 100: 1594–1610.

———. 1996. "Invisible Elbow." *Sociological Forum* 11: 589–601.

Tilly, Charles, Louise Tilly, and Richard Tilly. 1975. *The Rebellious Century, 1830–1930.* Cambridge: Harvard University Press.

Tismaneanu, Vladimir. 1989. "Nascent Civil Society in the German Democratic Republic." *Problems of Communism* 38: 91–111.

Trattner, Walter I., ed. 1983. *Social Welfare or Social Control? Some Historical Reflections on "Regulating the Poor."* Knoxville: University of Tennessee Press.

Traugott, Mark, ed. 1995. *Repertoires and Cycles of Collective Action.* Durham, N.C.: Duke University Press.

Tuma, Nancy Brandon, and Michael T. Hannan. 1984. *Social Dynamics.* New York: Academic Press.

Union of Concerned Scientists (UCS). 1970. "UCS Committee on Environmental Pollution: An Overview." UCS Papers, Massachusetts Institute of Technology, Cambridge, Massachusetts.

———. 1984. "Fifteen Years of UCS." *Nucleus: A Quarterly Report* 6(1): 2–9.

United Kingdom. Cabinet Office. Women's National Commission. 1990. *Women's Organisations in Great Britain, 1989–1990.*

U.S. Bureau of the Census. 1990. *Statistical Abstract of the United States.* Washington, D.C.: USGPO.

U.S. Department of Labor. Bureau of Labor Statistics. 1973. *Employment of Scientists and Engineers, 1950–1970.* Washington, D.C.: USGPO.

Valocchi, Steve. 1990. "The Unemployed Workers Movement: A Reexamination of the Piven and Cloward Thesis." *Social Problems* 37: 191–205.

Veugelers, John W. P. 1994. "Recent Immigration Politics in Italy: A Short Story." *Western European Politics* 17: 33–49.

Walker, Jack L., Jr. 1991. *Mobilizing Interest Groups in America*. Ann Arbor: University of Michigan Press.

Waller, Doug. 1987. *Congress and the Nuclear Freeze: An Inside Look at the Politics of a Mass Movement*. Amherst: University of Massachusetts Press.

Wapner, Paul. 1996. *Environmental Activism and World Civic Politics*. Albany: State University of New York Press.

"The War between the Sexes." 1994. *Economist* (March 5): 80–81.

Webb, Keith, Ekkart Zimmermann, Michael Marsh, Anne-Marie Aish, Christina Mironesco, Christopher Mitchell, Leonardo Morlino, and James Walston. 1983. "Etiology and Outcomes of Protest: New European Perspectives." *American Behavioral Scientist* 26: 311–31.

Weinberger, Caspar W. 1990. *Fighting for Peace: Seven Critical Years in the Pentagon*. New York: Warner.

Welch, Susan. 1975. "The Impact of Urban Riots on Urban Expenditures." *American Journal of Political Science* 29: 741–60.

Whalen, Jack, and Richard Flacks. 1980. "The Isla Vista 'Bank Burners' Ten Years Later: Notes on the Fate of Student Activists." *Sociology* 12: 61–78.

———. 1984. "Echoes of Rebellion: The Liberated Generation Grows Up." *Journal of Political and Military Sociology* 12: 61–78.

———. 1989. *Beyond the Barricades: The Sixties Generation Grows Up*. Philadelphia: Temple University Press.

Whittier, Nancy. 1995. *Feminist Generations: The Persistence of the Radical Women's Movement*. Philadelphia: Temple University Press.

Wicker, A. 1969. "Attitudes and Action: The Relationship of Verbal and Overt Behavioral Responses to Attitude Objects." *Journal of Social Issues* 25: 41–78.

Willelms, H., M. Wolf, and R. Eckert. 1993. *Unruhen und Politikberatung: Funktion, Arbeitweise, Ergebnisse, und Auswirkung von Untersuchungskommissionen in der USA, Grossbritannien, und der Bundesrepublik Deutschland*. Opladen, Germany: Westdeutscher Verlag.

Wilson, James Q. 1961. "The Strategy of Protest: Problems of Negro Civic Action." *Journal of Conflict Resolution* 5: 291–303.

Winkler, Jürgen R. 1994. "Die Wählerschaft der rechtsextremen Parteien in der Bundesrepublik Deutschland 1949 bis 1993." In *Rechtsextremismus: Einführung und Forschungsbilanz*, edited by Wolfgang Kowalsky and Wolfgang Schroeder, 69–88. Opladen, Germany: Westdeutscher Verlag.

Wissenschaftlicher Beirat der Bundesregierung. 1996. *Globale Umweltveränderung: Welt im Wandel*. Berlin: Springer.

Wolfe, Leslie, and Jennifer Tucker. 1995. "Feminism Lives: Building a Multicultural Women's Movement in the US." In *The Challenge of Local Feminisms*, edited by Amrita Basu, 435–64. Boulder, Colo.: Westview.

Wolfle, Dael. 1989. *Renewing a Scientific Society: The AAAS from World War II to 1970*. Washington, D.C.: American Association for the Advancement of Science.

Worldwatch Institute, ed. 1992. *Worldwatch Institute Report: Zur Lage der Welt—1992. Daten für das Überleben unseres Planeten.* Frankfurt: Fischer.

Wörndl, Barbara, and Guy Fréchet. 1991. "Institutionalization Tendencies in Ecological Movements." In *Convergence or Divergence? Comparing Recent Trends in Industrial Societies,* edited by Simon Langlois, with Thedore Caplow, Henri Mendras, and Wolfgang Glatzer, 247–68. Frankfurt: Campus; Montreal: McGill-Queens's University Press.

Wright, John R. 1985. "PACs, Contributions, and Roll Calls." *American Political Science Review* 79: 400–414.

Yamaguchi, K. 1991. *Event History Analysis.* Newbury Park, Calif.: Sage.

Zald, Mayer. 1988. "The Trajectory of Social Movements in America." *Research in Social Movements, Conflict, and Change* 10: 19–41.

Zelditch, Morris. 1978. "Review Essay: Outsiders' Politics." *American Journal of Sociology* 83: 1514–20.

Zemans, Frances Kahn. 1983. "Legal Mobilization: The Neglected Role of the Law in the Political System." *American Political Science Review* 77: 690–703.

Zimmermann, Ekkart. 1990. "Social Movements and Political Outcomes: Why Both Ends Fail to Meet." Paper presented at the Twelfth World Congress of Sociology, Madrid, Spain, July 9–13.

Contributors

EDWIN AMENTA is associate professor of sociology at New York University. He is the author of *Bold Relief: Institutional Politics and the Origins of Modern American Social Policy*, as well as many articles concerning political sociology, social movements, and social policy. He is currently writing a book about the impact of the Townsend movement and American money radicals.

PAUL BURSTEIN is professor of sociology and adjunct professor of political science at the University of Washington at Seattle. He has studied the influence of the civil rights and women's movements on congressional and judicial actions relating to equal employment opportunity, and he is interested in the role of social movement organizations in democratic political systems. He is currently synthesizing work on social movement organizations, interest groups, and political parties.

DONATELLA DELLA PORTA is professor of political science at the University of Florence. She has carried out research in Italy, France, Spain, the Federal Republic of Germany, and the United States. Her main fields of study include social movements, political violence, terrorism, political corruption, maladministration, public order, and the police. Among her recent books are *Policing Protest: The Control of Mass Demonstrations in Western Democracies* (coedited with Herbert Reiter; Minnesota, 1998) and *Social Movements, Political Violence, and the State*.

JOYCE GELB is professor of political science at City College and at the Graduate Center of the City University of New York, and is codirector of the Activist Women's Oral History Project at the Graduate Center. She is the author of *Feminism and Politics: A Comparative Perspective* and coauthor of *Women of Japan and Korea* and *Women and Public Policies.* Her research interests relate to women and women's movements, politics, and policy in the United States, Britain, and Japan.

MARCO GIUGNI is a researcher at the Department of Political Science at the University of Geneva. He has authored or coauthored several books and articles on social movements. He is author of *Entre stratégie et opportunité,* coauthor of *New Social Movements in Western Europe: A Comparative Analysis* (Minnesota, 1995) and *Histoires de mobilisation politique en Suisse,* and coeditor of *From Contention to Democracy.* His current research focuses on mobilization over ethnic relations, citizenship, and immigration in a crossnational comparative project (MERCI); he specializes in the French and Swiss cases.

VIVIEN HART is professor of American studies at the University of Sussex in Brighton, England, and visiting professor of history at The Ohio State University. She has written widely on the comparative politics of Britain and the United States. Her most recent book is *Bound by Our Constitution: Women, Workers, and the Minimum Wage.* She is currently working on an international study of constitutions and gender.

RUUD KOOPMANS is senior researcher in the Department of the Public Sphere and Social Movements at the Wissenschaftszentrum Berlin für Sozialforschung. He has authored or coauthored several books on social movements, including *Democracy from Below: New Social Movements and the Political System in West Germany, New Social Movements in Western Europe: A Comparative Analysis* (Minnesota, 1995), and *Acts of Dissent.* His current research focuses on mobilization over ethnic relations, citizenship, and immigration in a cross-national comparative project (MERCI); he specializes in the German case.

HANSPETER KRIESI is full professor of political science at the University of Geneva. His fields of interest include social movements, comparative politics, Swiss politics, and direct democracy. He is a coauthor of *New Social Movements in Western Europe: A Comparative Analysis* (Minnesota, 1995).

DOUG MCADAM is professor of sociology at Stanford University and the author of *Political Process and the Development of Black Insurgency, 1930–1970*. He also wrote *Freedom Summer*, which won the C. Wright Mills Award in 1990, among other prizes. He is the coeditor (with John McCarthy and Mayer Zald) of *Comparative Perspectives on Social Movements*.

DAVID S. MEYER is associate professor of political science at the City College of New York and the City University Graduate Center. He is the author of *A Winter of Discontent: The Nuclear Freeze and American Politics*. He has coedited (with Sidney Tarrow) *The Social Movement Society* and (with Thomas Rochon) *Coalitions and Political Movements*. He has written many articles on social-protest politics and is currently engaged, with Suzanne Staggenborg, in research on movement/countermovement interaction in the American abortion conflict.

KELLY MOORE is assistant professor of sociology at Barnard College, Columbia University. Her main research interests concern social movements, formal organizations, and the sociology of science. She is currently writing a book on the effects on American science of protest against the Vietnam War.

DIETER RUCHT is professor of sociology at the University of Kent at Canterbury (England). His research interests include modernization processes in a comparative perspective, social movements, and political protest. He has edited *Research on Social Movements: The State of the Art in Western Europe and the USA* and authored *Modernisierung und neue soziale Bewegungen: Deutschland, Frankreich, und USA im Vergleich*.

PAUL STATHAM is senior researcher in the Department of the Public Sphere and Social Movements at the Wissenschaftszentrum Berlin für Sozialforschung. He completed his doctoral research on environmental movements and the media at the European University Institute in Florence, Italy. He has published articles on environmental movements in Europe and on media and politics in Italy. His current research focuses on mobilization over ethnic relations, citizenship, and immigration in a cross-national comparative project (MERCI); he specializes in the British and Italian cases.

SIDNEY TARROW is Maxwell Upson Professor of Government at Cornell. He is the author of *Power in Movement* (1998) and an associate editor of the University of Minnesota Press series Social Movement, Protest, and Contention. He is currently collaborating with Doug McAdam and Charles Tilly in a study on the dynamics of contention.

CHARLES TILLY, who teaches sociology, history, and political science at Columbia University, has been studying contentious politics, chiefly European, since 1954.

DOMINIQUE WISLER is assistant professor of political science at the University of Geneva. He has contributed to several journals on subjects such as political violence, social movements, and police and mass demonstrations.

MICHAEL P. YOUNG is finishing his Ph.D. in sociology at New York University. His research interests include the sociology of culture and religion, social movements, and historical sociology. His dissertation examines the relationship between forms of collective action and fields of conflict in the emergence of single-issue social movements in antebellum America.

Index

AAAS. *See* American Association for the Advancement of Science
Abortion, 174, 178, 179; antifeminist political regimes and, 176; women's movement and, 150, 162–64
Abramowitz, Stephen, 120
ACLU. *See* American Civil Liberties Union
Activist/nonactivist colleges, attendance at, 141
Activists/activism: biographical consequences for, 118–22; co-optation of, 268; self-presentation by, 263
Adaptive preferences, 42
Adarand v. Pena (1995), 166
Advocacy groups, women's, 157
Affirmative action, 18, 165, 174
Age/birth of first child, effects of variables on, 140–41 (table)
Age/marriage, 145n1; effects of variables on, 139–40 (table)
AIDS, 104, 105
Aiken, Michael, 119, 120, 121
AL. *See* Alternative List
Albright, Madeleine, 160–61
Alleanza Nazionale (AN), 226, 244, 245,

247, 251n11; support for, 225; Liga Nord and, 248
Alternative goods, locating, 27–30
Alternative List (AL), 78, 80, 81, 84, 85, 87; violent groups and, 89
Alternative patterns, 136, 137, 138
Amendments, direct-democratic, 44–45
Amenta, Edwin, xx, xxii, 22–41
American Association for Social Responsibility in Science, 110
American Association for the Advancement of Science (AAAS), 106, 115n9; Committee on Science for Human Welfare, 108
American Civil Liberties Union (ACLU), 163; Reproductive Freedom Project and, 162
American Federation of Labor, direct democracy in, 53
American Medical Association, 106
American Physical Society, 115nn7, 9
American Political Science Review, 16
American Society for Microbiology, 115n9
American Sociological Review, 120
AN. *See* Alleanza Nazionale
Animal rights movement, 33, 34, 103